The Nature of Causation

THE NATURE
OF CAUSATION

Edited and with an Introduction by
MYLES BRAND

UNIVERSITY OF ILLINOIS PRESS
Urbana Chicago London

Library of Congress Cataloging in Publication Data

Main entry under title:

The Nature of causation.

Bibliography: p.
CONTENTS: The regularity theory: Hume, D. Of
the idea of necessary connection. Ducasse, C. J.
Causality. Nagel, E. The logical character of
scientific laws. Chisholm, R. M. Law statements
and counterfactual inference. Goodman, N. The
problem of counterfactual conditionals. Stalnaker, R.
A theory of conditionals. — The activity theory:
Collingwood, R. G. Causation. Gasking, D.
Causation and recipes. — The logical entailment
theory: Blanshard, B. Necessity in causation. — The
necessary connection theory: The nonlogical
entailment version: Burks, A. [etc.]
    1. Causation — Addresses, essays, lectures.
2. Conditionals (Logic) — Addresses, essays,
lectures. I. Brand, Myles.
BD591.N37   122   76-110
ISBN 0-252-00407-8

Contents

Preface

Questions about the nature of causation have troubled philosophers since Aristotle — and Aristotle notes that these issues were suggested by the pre-Socratic philosophers. Contemporary discussion about causation finds its impetus in Hume, who concentrated on causal relations among events (Aristotle's efficient causality). There is good reason for this historical and continuing interest in the nature of causation. Causal phenomena are a constant factor in our lives; they are part of the ordinary furnishings of the universe. Understanding the nature of causation, moreover, is a prerequisite for understanding free will, human action, time, laws of nature, empirical knowledge — indeed, almost every area of philosophical inquiry. Contemporary philosophers are paying increasing attention to the analysis of causation as they recognize its centrality in the philosophical enterprise. It would not be an exaggeration to say that the analysis of causation is now, as it has been in the past, one of the most pressing philosophical issues.

This volume is intended to introduce the reader to the problems involved in analyzing causation. It contains statements of the classical theories that attempt to assimilate causation to recurrent change, to human activity, and to logical relatedness. Recently, philosophers have challenged the claim that causation can be assimilated to some other sorts of phenomena. Several attempts to clarify the nature of causation internally, so to speak, are also included. The introduction to the volume first gives a methodological framework in which to classify and examine analyses of causation and then investigates the success of these attempted analyses. It may be best to read the introduction after reading some or all of the reprinted material. A careful reading of this volume will put one in a position to understand and evaluate the contemporary debate about causation.

I want to thank my many colleagues and students who listened to my lectures on causation and have helped with searching criticisms and suggestions. I especially want to thank Paul Teller for critically reading the final draft of the introduction. My thinking about causation began with, and was influenced by, Richard Taylor. The Method of Locution Sets presented in the introduction was suggested to me by several of Taylor's remarks, especially in his "Thought and Purpose" (in *The Nature of Human Action*, ed. Brand). He would no doubt disagree with the manner in which I have developed his insights. I should also like to express my gratitude to Doug Johnston, who prepared the contemporary sections of the bibliography.

MYLES BRAND
*University of Illinois
at Chicago Circle
January, 1974*

The Nature of Causation

Introduction: Defining "Causes"

THE NATURE OF CAUSATION

There are at least two good reasons to be concerned with the nature of causation. The first is that the concept of causation is one of the central operating notions in our ordinary life, and part of the function of philosophy is to clarify these central notions. Causal chains are an evident and constant feature of our practical life. They play roles in the performance of actions, from simple ones such as my raising my arm (now) to complex ones such as the assassination of Kennedy. They are involved in the occurrences of natural phenomena, from the movement of a leaf to the eruption of a volcano. The descriptive metaphysician is charged with mapping segments of our ordinary conceptual framework, and the notion of causation is a central part of that framework.

The second reason for clarifying the notion of causation concerns its implications for other philosophical issues. The mark of a significant philosophical issue is that it is essentially connected with other philosophical issues. Clarity about causation is vital for the solution of problems in the areas of metaphysics, epistemology, the philosophy of science, the philosophy of language, the philosophy of logic, and others.

Consider the free will problem. This problem can be divided into two components: universal causal determinism and free action. Clarification of causation is necessary to assess both universal causal determinism, the doctrine that every event is caused, and the nature of free action, particularly with respect to whether free action is compatible with universal causal determinism. Another metaphysical issue tied to causation is the nature of human action. Recently, philosophers have been concerned with whether causal explanation is appropriate for human action. Those defending the appropriateness of causal explanation have argued that every human action is caused by the agent's having reasons to act, while those arguing for the inappropriateness of causal explanation have sometimes claimed that human action essentially involves noncausal, goal-directed activity. To take another example, the solution to the problem concerning the relationship between mental events and physical events — the mind-body problem

— depends on an understanding of causation, for it has been argued that mental and physical events causally interact.

The understanding of causation is relevant to epistemological issues — for example, whether an adequate analysis of empirical knowledge must make reference to the causal source of the knowledge claim. In the philosophy of language it has been argued that causal notions are needed in order to understand the referential function of linguistic expressions. In the philosophy of science an inquiry into the nature of causation has repercussions for issues concerned with lawfulness and the nature of time. Some philosophers have argued, for example, that the asymmetry of time can only be established by appealing to causal processes. Indeed, it is difficult to locate any traditional philosophical area of inquiry or major philosophical problem for which it would not be beneficial to have a clear understanding of causation.

In the next section I shall specify a framework in which to clarify the nature of causation; namely, the Method of Locution Sets. After discussing this methodological approach, I shall turn to the substantive issues.

THE METHOD OF LOCUTION SETS

In linguistic terms, we are concerned to find an adequate definition of the key locution "*e* caused *f*," where *e* and *f* range over events.

Locutions such as "*e* caused *f*" fall naturally into families. The family pertaining to causation includes, in addition to "*e* caused *f*," "*e* is causally sufficient for *f*," "*e* produced *f*," "it is causally necessary that if *e* occur, *f* occur," "*e* brought about *f*," and so on. Similarly, there are families of epistemic terms, the key one being "*S* knows that *p*"; of ethical terms, the key one being "*x* is a right action"; of human action terms, the key one being "*S* performed *a*"; and so on.

There are two types of philosophical definitions of these key locutions. The first type is one in which the definiens contains no locutions belonging to the same family to which the definiendum — the key locution — belongs; the second type is one in which the definiens contains some locutions belonging to the same family to which the definiendum belongs. The first type of definition can be labeled "reductive" since it reduces, or translates, talk from one family of locutions to another. The second type of definition can be labeled "nonreductive," for no attempt is made to translate or reduce talk involving the key locution. I prefer the pair of terms "extrasystemic — systemic" to the pair "reductive — nonreductive"; the latter pair unfortunately connates a hierarchical ordering of families of locutions.

A more careful differentiation of these types of definitions is in order. We need, first, some working terminology. A *locution* is an open sentence such as "*e* caused *f*" and "*S* knows that *p*"; it is symbolized by *l*. In this discussion we take as primitive the predicate ". . . is definable using only - - -," where ". . ." is replaced by a locution and "- - -" is replaced by one or more locutions or other expressions, possibly complex. This predicate is to be taken as veridical in the sense that if ϕ is definable using only ψ, then there exists some definition of ϕ in terms of ψ that admits of no counterexamples from the preanalytic data. (The preanalytic data are, here, the set of clear cases in which the locution in question can be said to apply or not to apply.)

For talk about families of locutions, let us substitute talk about *locution sets*. A *preanalytic locution set*, symbolized by *A*, is a locution set that contains all and only those locutions that are categorically bound, as it were. An example is the preanalytic locution set pertaining to causation. Two other examples are the preanalytic locution sets pertaining to empirical knowledge and to human action:

{*S* knows that *p*, *S* has evidence for *p*, *S* is justified in believing that *p*, *S* has adequate grounds for believing that *p*, . . .}

{*S* performed *a*, *S* brought about *e*, *S* brought about *e* intentionally, *S* tried to perform *a*, *S* wanted to perform *a*, *S* has the ability to perform *a*, . . .}

The final primitive notion required is that of *the base locution set of l*, written $B(l)$. It is the set of locutions formed by the union of those preanalytic locution sets, excluding the one to which *l* belongs, that is required for every reasonable attempt to define *l*. In current discussions of the nature of empirical knowledge, for example, there is a great deal of disagreement about what conditions must be added to true belief in order to obtain a case of knowledge. But all concerned accept the claim that a person knows that *p* only if *p* is true and *S* believes that *p;* any reasonable attempt to define "*S* knows that *p*" must include these two conditions. In our terminology, then, the base locution set of "*S* knows that *p*" includes the preanalytic locution sets pertaining to truth {*p* is true, *p* is false, . . .} and to belief {*S* believes that *p*, *S* disbelieves that *p*, it is not the case that *S* believes that *p*, . . .}. Similarly, the base locution set of the key human action locution

"*S* performed *a*" includes the members of the preanalytic locution sets pertaining to causation, to events, and so on.

Locution sets are governed by principles of admission and completeness. An obvious principle of admission for preanalytic locution sets is that for any A, if l_i is deducible from l_j by syntactical considerations alone or conversely, then at most one of l_i and l_j is a member of A. A similar requirement of independence obtains for base locution sets: each base locution set is such that its contained preanalytic locution sets are distinct; that is, for any B, A^i, A^j, where $A^i \subseteq B$ and $A^j \subseteq B$, $\sim (A^i \subseteq A^j)$.

The significant factors determining admission and completeness of locution sets are nonsyntactical. We are not concerned here with finding a general procedure for isolating or discovering locution sets. Rather, the concern is for distinguishing between types of definitions once a preanalytic locution set is located. The device of organizing the data into locution sets serves clarifying and heuristic purposes, but this device, by itself, does not yield a method for discovering the data. The Method of Locution Sets yields a standard procedure by which to compare and contrast philosophical analyses. But this method does not solve philosophical problems. Questions of definitional adequacy are substantive and must be answered by examining the particular proposals. We will use the Method of Locution Sets to organize and clarify the various proposals about the analysis of causation, but each proposal must be examined for adequacy; the Method of Locution Sets will not by itself produce these substantive results.

Let us assume that we have isolated the preanalytic and base locution sets for some key locution, l. Several kinds of philosophical definitions might then be proposed.

(D1) l is systemically definiable with respect to A *iff:* (i) $l \in A$ and (ii) there is a $B(l)$ such that l is definable using only the locutions contained in A, $B(l)$, and the laws of logic.

(D2) l is extrasystemically definable with respect to A *iff:* (i) $l \in A$ and (ii) there is a $B(l)$ and an A^* such that $A \cap A^* = \Lambda$ and l is definable using only the locutions contained in A^*, $B(l)$, and the laws of logic.

That is, a locution is systemically defined when it is defined solely in terms of other locutions belonging to the same family (and the base locution set). If locutions from a different preanalytic set are used in the definition of the key locution, then that locution is defined extrasystemically. For example, if it argued that causal locutions are needed in the definition of "*S* knows that *p,*" and if it is granted that the preanalytic locution set pertaining to empirical knowledge is wholly distinct from the preanalytic locution set pertaining to causation, then an extrasystemic definition of "*S* knows that *p*" is being suggested.

Notice that according to (D1) and (D2) a locution *l* can be defined both systemically and extrasystemically. Even if it is granted that *l* can be defined in terms of a locution set other than the one to which it belongs, it might nevertheless prove helpful to observe the interconnections between *l* and other members of its preanalytic locution set. In some cases, however, it might be argued that some locution is systemically definable but not extrasystemically definable, or the converse. These types of philosophical definitions are:

(D3) *l* is purely systemically definable with respect to *A iff:* (i) *l* is systemically definable with respect to *A* and (ii) there is no *A** such that *l* is extrasystemically definable with respect to *A**.

(D4) *l* is purely extrasystemically definable with respect to *A iff:* (i) *l* is extrasystemically definable with respect to *A* and (ii) it is not the case that there is a *B(l)* such that *l* is definable using only the locutions contained in *A, B(l),* and the laws of logic.

It may be that it is controversial whether a locution belongs to a particular preanalytic locution set. In the case of human action, for example, it is controversial whether "*S* has the opportunity to perform *a*" belongs to the locution set whose key member is "*S* performed *a,*" for, it might be argued, "*S* has the opportunity to perform *a*" is definable solely in physicalistic terms.[1] If a situation of this type arises, two preanalytic locution sets should be formulated, one containing the locution in question and the other excluding it. The manner in which the key locution is definable with respect to each resulting locution set should then be determined. It may result that "*S* performed *a*" is extrasystemically definable with respect to one of these preanalytic locution sets but not the other. It must be emphasized that (D1) through (D4) provide a method for classifying and comparing philo-

---

[1] Cf. Myles Brand, "On Having the Opportunity," *Theory and Decision,* 2 (1972), 307–313.

See Myles Brand, "On Philosophical Definitions," forthcoming *Philosophy and Phenomenological Research* for additional comments on systemic and extra-systemic definitions.

sophical analyses; they do not provide an algorithm for determining the preanalytic data, nor do they provide a method for settling substantive disagreements.

Let us suppose that some locution, *l,* is purely systemically definable. It is compatible with this assumption that there are alternative systemic proposals. The Method of Locution Sets does not supply a normative criterion for evaluating these alternative proposals. A normative criterion of this sort could be consistently added to the Method of Locution Sets, but the method by itself serves only the descriptive function of organizing data and making substantive proposals easily comparable. It is not clear, moreover, whether such a normative criterion can produce a unique ordering of alternative proposals. Once a systemic proposal meets the obvious conditions of including all the locutions of the preanalytic set and of being formally consistent, it is unclear what additional conditions must be met in order for it to be a *good* systemic proposal. One definition is to be preferred to another if it is more informative than the other. But the issue remains: it is unclear what constitutes informativeness of a definition. Similar remarks apply to a locution, *l,* which is purely extrasystemically definable. Beyond the obvious conditions, it is difficult to determine conditions that would enable us to prefer one extrasystemic proposal to another. In the case of a locution being purely extrasystemically definable, it may be relevant to consider a particular proposal in the context of definitions of other key locutions, that is, in the context of an entire philosophical theory.

The debate about the nature of causation can be viewed as a debate about whether an extrasystemic definition of "*e* caused *f*" is available. Hume and Mill thought that such a definition is available; so did Collingwood and Blanshard, though for different reasons. In the next sections I shall argue that no adequate extrasystemic definition is available; that is, I shall argue that "*e* caused *f*" is purely systemically definable. The alternative to accepting the pure systemic nature of causation is to abandon the intelligibility of causal talk. But this alternative is clearly unacceptable: causal talk is intelligible. To accept the intelligibility of causal talk and to conclude that "*e* caused *f*" is purely systemically definable is, however, only half the battle. An adequate systemic account must be provided. In the latter sections I shall briefly discuss the systemic proposals of Burks, Taylor, and Mackie. These attempts have not been wholly successful.

HUME'S DEFINITION

The first step in applying the Method of Locution Sets to the problem of causation is to specify the preanalytic locution set pertaining to "*e* caused *f.*" As might be expected, the history of the discussion provides clues concerning the membership of this locution set. In his *Treatise of Human Nature*, Hume indicates its membership when he says, ". . . the terms of *efficacy, agency, power, force, energy, necessity, connexion,* and *productive quality,* are all nearly synonymous" (Bk. I., Part III, sec. XIV). The preanalytic locution set would be, translated into contemporary terminology, the following:

$A^c = \{$ *e* caused *f, f* is *the* effect of *e, f* is *an* effect of *e,* it is causally necessary that if *e* occurs, *f* occurs, *e* is causally sufficient for *f, e* is causally necessary for *f, e* made *f* happen, *L* is a causal law, . . .$\}$.

Hume can be interpreted as arguing that "*e* caused *f*" is extrasystemically definable with respect to A^c. (A reasonable case might be made for understanding Hume as holding a stronger view, namely, that "*e* caused *f*" is *purely* extrasystemically definable with respect to A^c.) Basically, Hume proposed to define "*e* caused *f*" solely in terms of locution sets pertaining to event occurrence and recurrence, temporal order, and geographic proximity. In the *Treatise,* he says, "We may define a CAUSE to be 'an object precedent and contiguous to another, and where all the objects resembling the former are placed in like relations of precedency and contiguity to those objects, that resemble the latter' " (Bk. I, Part III, sec. XIV), and in his *Inquiry Concerning Human Understanding* he says, ". . . we may define a cause to be *an object followed by another, and where all the objects, similar to the first, are followed by objects similar to the second*" (Part VII).[2] We can reformulate Hume's *Treatise* proposal in the following way:

(DA) For every event *e* and every event *f, e* caused *f iff:*

  (i) the occurrence of *e* began before the occurrence of *f* began;

  (ii) *e* occurred in the immediate geographic area of *f;* and

---

[2] It is sometimes claimed that Hume offers two definitions of "cause." Several sentences after this passage quoted from the *Treatise,* he says "A CAUSE is an object precedent and contiguous to another, and so united with it, that the idea of the one determines the mind to form the idea of the other, and the impression

(iii) for every event similar to *e* that occurred, there is
some event similar to *f* that occurred in the immediate
geographic area and after it.

There is some difficulty with the contiguity condition (ii). We recognize cases of causation in which the causally related events are not geographically proximate; for example, the war in Indochina caused the disorders on American college campuses in the late 1960s, or the hijacking to Cuba of the plane carrying the heart surgeon caused the death of Smith in New York. One way out of this difficulty is simply to eliminate condition (ii) — which Hume does, perhaps for independent reasons, in the *Inquiry*. Another possibility is to reconstrue the definiendum of (DA) as "*e* proximately caused *f*" and define "*e* remotely caused *f*" in terms of it. Perhaps: *e* remotely caused *f* *iff* there is a nonempty ordered *n*-tuple of events $<g_1, g_2, \ldots, g_n>$ such that *e* proximately caused g_1 and g_1 proximately caused g_2 and ... and g_n proximately caused *f*. I prefer the simpler procedure, that of eliminating condition (ii), but in any case the success or failure of (DA) does not depend on condition (ii).

A more important criticism concerns condition (i). Although we might agree that no effect precedes its cause, there are cases of simultaneous cause and effect. For example, Jack's descent on the seesaw causes Jill to go up. Here, the event of Jack's going down endures for exactly the same period of time as the event of Jill's going up. It might be objected that the seesaw bends slightly before Jill starts to rise and also after Jack stops going down, and hence the events are not exactly

---

of the one to form a more lively idea of the other." These two definitions are not cointensional, since the former but not the latter is consistent with:

(i) $(\exists e)(\exists f)$ (*e* and *f* are events that occurred in a way that is not observable by persons, and *e* caused *f*).

Moreover, these two definitions are not coextensional, since it is reasonable to believe that (i) is true. It is reasonable to believe, for example, that there were causally related events before men evolved and that there will be causally related events when men cease to exist. A sympathetic reading of Hume is that the definiendum of each definition is distinct. In the former definition, the definiendum is "*e* caused *f*," and in the latter the definiendum is "(person) *S* takes *e* to have caused *f*," or some similar epistemic locution (cf. Thomas Richards, "Hume's Two Definitions of 'Cause,' " *Philosophical Quarterly*, 15 (1965), 247–253).

An interesting further point is that in the *Inquiry* when Hume again proposes these two definitions, he adds immediately after the one corresponding to the definition quoted in the text: "Or, in other words, where, if the first object had not been, the second [would] never [have]...existed" (sec. VII). Here we seem to have a second distinct rendering of "*e* caused *f*" and one more in line with a systemic, necessary connection view of causation. (Cf. David Lewis, "Causation," *Journal of Philosophy*, 70 (1973), 556–567.)

simultaneous. One might reply that we obtain a genuine case of simultaneous causation if we think of the seesaw as inelastic. However, this reply is not wholly satisfactory, since there are no perfectly inelastic seesaws in neighborhood playgrounds. A slight change of example is required in order to meet the objection. The cause in this case is again Jack's going down, but the effect is the seesaw's descent. Since the objects that are moving in this case, unlike the case involving Jill, are contiguous, there is no temporal lag.

A final, somewhat desperate objection might be proposed. We do not have a case of causation here at all, it might be said, since the situation described involves not two events but rather a single event. This objection rests primarily on the truth of the claim:

(1) Jack's going down on the seesaw $=$ the seesaw's going down.

But (1) is false. The following principle concerning event identity is exceedingly plausible: $e = f$ only if the spatial volume in which e occurs is identical with the spatial volume in which f occurs. Since the spatial volume in which the seesaw goes down does not include Jack, while clearly the spatial volume in which Jack goes down includes Jack, (1) is false.

Definition (DA) has to be amended in order to accommodate cases of simultaneous causation. Leaving out the contiguity condition, the revised definition is:

(DA′)   For every event e and every event f, e caused f *iff:*
  (i)   the occurrence of f did not begin before the occurrence of e began; and
  (ii) for every event similar to e that occurred there is some event similar to f that occurred simultaneously or after it.

However, this revised definition is inadequate. One problem for (DA′) is that in general it fails to make the distinction between cause and effect. If we let $e = f$, then the definiens is satisfied, since every event is simultaneous with itself, and condition (ii) is trivially satisfied. But no event causes itself, at least if "cause" is taken in its ordinary sense. It might be replied that this objection can be met simply by adding to the definiens an additional condition,

  (iii) $e \neq f$.

The objection, however, cuts deeper than that. In cases of simultaneous cause and effect, counterinstances to (DA′) can be generated when we substitute for *e* a description of the effect and for *f* a description of the cause. That is, in cases of simultaneous causation, cause and effect cannot be distinguished by an appeal to the temporal condition, nor can they be distinguished by an appeal to the primary condition of the definiens, since, for example, seesaws' goings down also regularly accompany going down on the seesaw.

Another problem for this definition, one that was noted in the eighteenth century by Thomas Reid, is how to distinguish genuine cases of causation from accidental correlation. Reid's well-known example is that although the coming of this day was not caused by the coming of last night, the definiens is satisfied since the coming of night regularly precedes the coming of day and this day began later than last night. The coming of this day and the coming of last night have some common causal ancestor, namely, the movements of the sun and planets, but they themselves are not related as cause to effect. C. J. Ducasse has a version of this objection in which the events in question are not even ancestrally related: although Jones's normal birth did not cause the tenth return of the moon since his mother conceived, normal births regularly precede the tenth return of the moon since conception.[3]

A third problem is that (DA′) is not adequate to deal with cases of unique events. Suppose that *e* and *f* are such that no events that in fact occurred are similar to *e* and *f* in the relevant respects. Suppose also that *e* and *f* are causally independent and that *e* occurred before *f*. This set of circumstances is clearly logically possible. But, contrary to hypothesis, (DA′) yields the result that *e* caused *f;* for condition (ii) is trivially satisfied.

A related difficulty concerns the notion of similarity.[4] "Similar" in (DA′) does not mean "exactly similar." There is one and only one event exactly similar to *e* and one and only one event exactly similar to *f*, namely, *e* and *f*, respectively. Hence, if "similar" means "exactly similar," (DA′) yields the untoward result that any two events that are simultaneous or such that one occurs prior to the other are causally related. Further, "similar" does not mean "similar in most respects." Let *e* be the event of Jones wielding a knife and let *f* be the event of Smith dying from a stab wound. Assume, however, that Jones failed

---

[3] C. J. Ducasse, "Causality: Critique of Hume's Analysis," p. 70 below.
[4] Cf. Arthur Pap, "Philosophical Analysis, Translation Schemas, and the Regularity Theory of Causation," *Journal of Philosophy,* 49 (1952), esp. 657–663; and Richard Taylor, "Causation," pp. 285 ff. below.

to stab Smith and that Smith was stabbed instead by a second assassin, Robinson. Thus, it is false that *e* caused *f*. Nevertheless, the definiens is satisfied. There are events similar in most (but not all) respects to Jones's action that are followed by the victim's death by stabbing. What went wrong in this case is that the events adduced to satisfy (ii) are not similar in the appropriate respects to *e;* in particular, they are not similar in the *causally relevant* respects. However, when "similar" in (ii) is interpreted to mean "similar in the causally relevant respects," definition (DA′) no longer has extrasystemic status.

Revision of (DA′) appears hopeless. At best, the definiens supplies an epistemic criterion for determining whether *e* caused *f*. We have good evidence, good reason to believe, that *e* caused *f* if, to the best of our knowledge, *f* did not occur before *e* and each time an event similar to *e* occurred, an event similar to *f* occurred. But the definiens does not state a logically sufficient condition for the truth of a sentence of the form "*e* caused *f*."

Some philosophers have reacted to these criticisms of Hume's proposal by formulating the definiens in terms of laws of nature. Hume is almost right, they reason, and then attempt to give a "neo-Humean" definition. An analysis in terms of natural laws, provided that it remains extrasystemic, would be in the spirit of Hume's proposal and, perhaps, a natural extension of it, but it would not follow Hume himself, since his own proposal was not in terms of laws.

THE LAW OF NATURE VIEW

The most interesting recent attempt to explicate "*e* caused *f*" extrasystemically has been in terms of natural laws. A singular causal statement is to be understood, basically, as an instance of a natural law. Natural laws are, in turn, to be distinguished from mere accidental correlations.

More exactly, this theory can be specified as follows. Let L be a conjunction of sentences $L_1, L_2, \ldots, L_n$, where each L_i is a *law of nature* that obtains in the world and where for any L^*, if L^* is a law of nature obtaining in the world, then $L^* \equiv L_1 \text{ v } L^* \equiv L_2 \text{ v} \ldots \text{v} L^* \equiv L_n$. Similarly, let I be the conjunction of $I_1, I_2, \ldots, I_n$, where each I_i is a sentence describing an initial condition that obtains in the world and where the conjunctive sentence I is exhaustive. (Assume for simplicity that the law sentences and initial-condition sentences are each finite.) Also, let us introduce the predicate "O . . . ," where ". . ." is replaced by the name of an event or a variable ranging over events and which is read ". . . occurs (occurred, will occur)." The nontemporal, primary condition in the definiens is then: $\vdash (L \& I) \supset (Oe \supset Of)$ but not $\vdash L \supset (Oe \supset Of)$ or $\vdash I \supset (Oe \supset Of)$. Stated in a way parallel to the reformulation of Hume's proposal:

(DB)   For every event e and every event f, e caused f *iff:*

(i)   the occurrence of f did not begin before the occurrence of e began; and

(ii)   that f occurred follows from (1) a statement of the laws of nature, (2) a statement of the initial conditions, and (3) a statement that e occurred, but not from any two or one of these statements.

There are, however, problems for this proposal. One set of problems concerns specification of the initial conditions. For example, is a Carnapian state description — that is, an exhaustive listing for every individual whether or not it has each property — adequate for this purpose? However, I shall deal only with issues concerning laws of nature, in part because these present overwhelming difficulties for the natural law view interpreted as an extrasystemic proposal.[5]

To begin, it is clear that definition (DB) must be amended so that L is a conjunctive statement of a specified subset of the set of natural laws. Statement L cannot be the conjunction of all nomic universals, where a nomic universal is any nonlogical law used by the scientific community in its scientific work, for some nomic universals do not express a universal causal relation, and, hence, instances of them would not be true singular causal statements. Some nomic universals, for example, state a functional interdependence between magnitudes. The ideal gas law, $PV = nRT$, does not say that a change in pressure, volume, or absolute temperature *brings about* a change in the others; rather, it asserts that a change in volume (or pressure) accompanies a change in temperature. That the laws of functional interdependence do not express a universal causal relation is evident from the fact that these statements are symmetrical, whereas statements of causal dependency are asymmetrical. Biological developmental laws constitute an-

[5] Hempel and others draw a distinction between law statements and lawlike statements, which are exactly like the former except that they might be false. See, for example, Hempel and Oppenheim's "Studies in the Logic of Explanation," reprinted in *Aspects of Scientific Explanation* (New York, 1965), pp. 256 ff. Having noted this distinction, I shall for simplicity ignore it.

other kind of noncausal nomic universal. "The formation of lungs in human embryos never precedes the formation of the circulatory system" does not assert that the formation of the circulatory system causes the formation of the lungs. Although the formation of the circulatory system and the formation of the lungs are the (remote) effects of a single cause, they merely accompany each other in a regular temporal pattern and are not related as cause to effect. Still another kind of noncausal nomic universal is the statistical, or probabilistic, law. These laws, which play fundamental roles in the social and behavioral sciences as well as in the physical sciences, say that, in the long run and without interfering conditions, the occurrences of events of one sort are accompanied with a relative frequency by occurrences of events of another sort. But events are causally related only if one sort *invariably* accompanies another sort, provided that there are no interfering conditions.[6] The revision of (DB) required, in short, is that L is the exhaustive conjunction of the *causal* laws of nature.

In order to sustain the Natural Laws view as an extrasystemic proposal, then, "L_i is a causal law" must be explicated without appealing to any causal locution. One such extrasystemic explication has a high degree of initial plausibility. This defense of (DB) — call it the "primary defense" — is that the causal laws are interstate laws. The primary defense is widely held by philosophers of science; Philipp Frank, for example, says, "We shall call every law a *causal law* which allows us to infer from information about one region of space and time some information about another region of space and time."[7] On this view the dynamic laws of Newtonian mechanics comprise the core of causal laws, the primary one being:[8]

$$(2) \qquad \bar{F} = m \ d\bar{v}/dt.$$

For it is these laws that enable us to determine the state of the system at one time, given its state at some other time. The laws of statics are not causal laws on the primary defense, since they are intrastate laws. The characterization of other kinds of laws, such as laws pertaining to fluid continua, fields and so on, as causal depends on the tenability of the special case of the Newtonian dynamic laws.

The primary defense, however, is not adequate. Since all causal laws

---

[6] See Nagel, "The Logical Character of Scientific Laws," pp. 88 ff. below.

[7] *Philosophy of Science* (Englewood Cliffs, 1957), p. 264. A similar view is held by Hempel, "Aspects of Scientific Explanation," in *Aspects*, 347 ff.

[8] We ignore the controversy of whether (2) is definitional instead of lawful. See Ernest Nagel, *The Structure of Science* (New York, 1961), pp. 185 ff.

are interstate laws, it follows that there are no causal laws concerning simultaneous causation and, hence, no true singular statements of simultaneous causation. But there are cases of simultaneous causation: if Jack is sitting on the seesaw, his going down causes the seesaw's going down.

Statement (2) and similar statements are formulated in terms of state variables. In (2) the velocities and locations of the mass points are determined for an instantaneous time, where an instantaneous time is a state of the system. In the commonsense view, causal laws are formulated in terms of variables ranging over events. Events endure; they take time to occur; they are not instantaneous. Some philosophers, for example Ducasse and von Wright,[9] hold that some events do not involve change. They are, as it were, unchanges. Jack's remaining perfectly stationary on the seesaw is an event, but not one involving change. However, both sorts of events, changes and unchanges, take time.

Causal laws, conceived on the model of Newtonian dynamics, are laws for closed systems. The systems are closed in that the only variables taken into consideration are the variables of state. External factors, that is, the boundary conditions, are assumed to have no influence on the system. Laws such as (2) are to be thought of as being qualified by a *ceteris paribus* clause saying that external factors are irrelevant. Since the system is closed, there is a positive and exhaustive formulation of this *ceteris paribus* clause. It says that the initial conditions and only the initial conditions, which can be exhaustively given by assigning a value to every state variable, are to be the conditions used in determining the state of the system at any time. (It is true that in the Newtonian case certain other assumptions are made. For example, it is assumed that the bodies are negligibly small in relation to their distances. The additional assumptions, however, are not to be included in the *ceteris paribus* clause. Rather, they pertain to the meanings of the terms in which the laws and initial conditions are stated. The assumption about the size of a body, for example, is included in the meaning of the term "mass point.")

The situation is different for ordinary causal laws. Examples of ordinary causal laws are:

(3)　Throwing bricks at windows produces the windows' breaking.

[9] C. J. Ducasse, *Nature, Mind, and Death* (La Salle, Ill., 1951), pp. 108 ff.; Georg Henrik von Wright, *Norm and Action* (New York, 1963), chap. 2.

(4) Heart stoppage in normal persons produces death.

(5) Conductors make orchestras begin playing by lowering their batons.

These generalizations pertain to open systems. There is no explicit set of boundary conditions for an ordinary causal law. Statement (3), for example, must also be qualified by a *ceteris paribus* clause. But the factors that have to be taken into consideration in the clause are not definitely enumerable. Statement (3), as stated, is false. Some bricks are thrown against "unbreakable" windows, sometimes a brick's flight is interrupted, and so on. In order for (3) to be made true, a *ceteris paribus* clause must be added that excludes these and other interfering conditions. There is, however, no informative and systematic way to do this. The best that can be done is to specify some vague clause saying that there are no extraordinary circumstances or that background conditions are standard as compared with other situations or some such. The *ceteris paribus* clause of an ordinary causal law is not even a promissory note; there is no expectation that the class of relevant factors can be informatively and exhaustively isolated.

It should be emphasized that a terminological issue is not in question. I am not disputing the right to label nomic universals such as the laws of motion "causal laws." Rather, I am arguing for the substantive claim that the laws of motion and similar statements are significantly different from what we ordinarily and from the commonsense point of view take to be causal laws. If one were to persist in calling the laws of motion and similar statements "causal laws," then the claim is, stated somewhat paradoxically, that ordinary causal laws are not causal laws. No matter how valuable the laws of motion and similar statements are — and there is no doubt of their value — they are excluded from the class of genuine causal laws.

That the range of the variables and the content of the *ceteris paribus* clause are not the same for ordinary causal laws as for causal laws on the primary defense is symptomatic of an even greater difference between these two kinds of laws. Statement (2) occurs within a developed theory. The terms of this theory do not refer to the objects or phenomena of our ordinary experience. What we ordinarily understand by "force," for example, bears an intimate relationship to $\bar{F}$ in the equations of motion; but whatever this relationship is exactly, it is not one of identity. There are, presumably, metalinguistic statements that correlate or "bridge the gap" between "force" and $\bar{F}$. These bridge statements are needed precisely because "force" and *F* are not identical in meaning. We all know the advantages of refining and redefining our ordinary notions. But the fact remains that after this refining process the resulting notion is distinct from the one with which we began. "Mass point" just does not refer to the sort of object we encounter in our daily lives.

In short, the attempt to explicate "L_i is a causal law" extrasystemically in terms of interstate laws, primarily Newtonian dynamic laws, fails. The laws required for the adequacy of definition (DB) are ordinary causal laws, not laws forming part of a developed science.[10] However, distinguishing between ordinary causal laws and the laws of a developed science, such as mechanics, is not sufficient for our purposes. Ordinary causal laws are a subset of generalizations about the world that appears to us. Some of these generalizations are not lawful; they describe accidental concomitances between sorts of events. We require a procedure for isolating ordinary causal laws.

ORDINARY LAWS

Consider the following nonlaw generalizations:

(6)   All the persons in this room are philosophers.
(7)   All the eggs in Mary's basket are broken.
(8)   All the objects in my pocket conduct electricity.

We must distinguish between (6) through (8) and ordinary law statements, examples of which are the ordinary causal laws (3) through (5) above. Clearly, it will not suffice to say that (3) through (5) are true universal statements using the causal terms "produces" or "makes," whereas (6) through (8) do not use those terms. For ordinary causal laws might be written in the standard "All *S*'s are *P*'s" form, which conceals the fact that they are causal laws. For example, (3) and (4) might have been written:

(3′)   All cases in which bricks are thrown at windows are cases in which the windows break.
(4′)   All cases in which heart stoppage in normal persons occurs are cases in which death of the person follows.

---

[10] Some caution is needed here, since ordinary causal laws might be incorporated into some social sciences. In *Social Causation* (Boston, 1942), for example, R. M. MacIver proposes that the foundations of sociology should consist of ordinary causal laws.

These statements are ordinary law statements and do not use the causal predicates "produces" or "makes" or so on.

One proposal for differentiating ordinary laws from nonlaw generalizations is to distinguish between the semantic properties of the predicates of each type of universal statement. Two such distinctions might be cited:

(Pa) The predicates of law statements, unlike the predicates of nonlaw generalizations, are unlimited in scope.

(Pb) The predicates of law statements, unlike the predicates of nowlaw generalizations, do not require reference to, individuals or spatiotemporal locations in order to explicate their meanings.

Feature (Pa) is not adequate to differentiate between law and nonlaw statements. The predicates of the genuine law (4′) are not unlimited in scope. The total number of cases in which persons have heart stoppages and death follows is large, but as all the evidence indicates, it is finite. Persons have been on earth only a limited time and will, in all likelihood, evolve out of existence, destroy themselves, or be destroyed by the course of natural events.

It might be objected that the intent of (Pa) has been misinterpreted. It is to be understood as an epistemic condition, in that the extension of the class of things of which the predicate is true is unknown. However, this version of (Pa) is also inadequate. In the nonlaw generalization (6), the predicate "is a philosopher" meets the epistemic condition of having an unknown extension. Moreover, the proposal cannot be saved by arguing that both predicates must meet this epistemic condition. For imagine that the room in question is the grand ballroom in which the annual smoker of the American Philosophical Association is held. The extension of the second predicate of (6), "is a person in this room," is then also unknown, since no one may have counted the many philosophers in the room.

Turning to (Pb), Hempel calls predicates whose sense is explicable without reference to any individual or spatiotemporal location "purely qualitative."[11] Presumably the predicates "is an egg in Mary's basket" and "is a person in this room" are not purely qualitative, and thus (6) and (7) do not qualify as law statements. However, this proposal is also problematical. The ordinary counterpart of Kepler's first law,

[11] Hempel and Oppenheim, "Studies in the Logic of Explanation."

which states that the planets revolve in elliptical orbits with the sun as one focus of each ellipse, would be legislated to nonlaw status since the predicates are not purely qualitative.

Taking our cue from Hempel again, we might try to salvage (Pb) by limiting its domain to *fundamental laws,* where a law is fundamental if it is a universal statement containing no individual constants and all of whose predicates are purely qualitative. Any other universal statement qualifies as a law just in case it is deducible from some set of fundamental laws. Universal statements so deducible are called *derivative laws.*

But this salvage attempt also fails. For one reason, some derivative laws do not satisfy the condition of being deducible from fundamental laws alone. Nagel argues that Kepler's first law is not deducible from Newtonian theory alone, but rather requires premises stating the relative masses and velocities of the planets and the sun.[12] Moreover, the ordinary counterpart to the law stating that the velocity of light is (approximately) 186,000 miles per second would be legislated to nonlaw status, since the units of length and time are defined by reference to the size and periodicity of the rotation of the earth. If nonlaw premises were permitted in the deduction of derivative laws from fundamental ones, then obvious nonlaw statements would qualify as law statements. For example, the nonlaw universal (8) is deducible from the ordinary law statement "All pieces of copper conduct electricity" and a statement containing a predicate that is not purely qualitative, namely, "All the objects in my pocket are made of copper." Another reason for the failure of Hempel's salvage attempt is that it permits seemingly nonlaw universal conditionals to qualify as derivative law statements. From the ordinary law statement

(9) $(x)(t)$ if x is a piece of copper during t and x is heated during t, then x expands during t,

the following nonlaw statement is deducible:

(10) (t) if this penny is a piece of copper during t and this penny is heated during t, then the penny expands during t.

Some restrictions on the sorts of inferences permitted in deducing derivative laws is required. But it is not clear what these restrictions are.

Nagel mentions other proposals for distinguishing between laws and nonlaw generalizations.[13] The most promising of these proposals is that

[12] "The Logical Character of Scientific Laws," p. 89 below.
[13] *Ibid.,* pp. 96 ff. below.

ordinary law statements, unlike nonlaw generalizations, support or warrant their corresponding counterfactual conditionals. This proposal raises the issue of truth conditions for counterfactuals, an issue of interest independent of the question of lawfulness.

It should be noted that a direct appeal to counterfactuals might be made in the definition of "*e* caused *f*," sidestepping (on the surface, at least) the relationship between causation and lawfulness. That is, the following definition might be proposed:[14]

(DC)   For every event *e* and every event *f*, *e* caused *f* iff:
     (i)   the occurrence of *f* did not begin before the occurrence of *e* began; and
     (ii) *f* would not have occurred if *e* had not occurred.

We shall not deal with definition (DC) directly. Difficulties for this definition are apparent from the discussion of lawfulness and counterfactuals.

COUNTERFACTUALS

We can say that a *conditional,* being partly stipulative, is any sentence of the form "If . . . , then - - -," or some syntactical equivalent to it, where it is not required that ". . ." and "- - -" be replaced by sentences. A *subjunctive conditional* is a conditional whose truth value does not depend solely on the truth values of the antecedent and consequent clauses or on satisfaction of the clauses if they are nonsentential. A *counterfactual conditional* is a subjunctive conditional that by itself or in virtue of the context in which it occurs presupposes that the antecedent is false (or unsatisfied if it is nonsentential). Clearly, some subjunctive conditionals are not counterfactuals. For example, the following subjunctive conditional presupposes the truth, not the falsity, of its antecedent:

(11)   If Jones had taken arsenic, then he would have shown exactly those symptoms that he now shows.[15]

These distinctions apply to both singular and universal statements. The primary logical forms for subjunctives and counterfactuals are:

(12)   If *a* which is not *F* were *F,* then *a* would be *G;*

[14] Definition (DC) has recently been defended by David Lewis; see his "Causation."

[15] See Alan R. Anderson, "A Note on Counterfactuals," *Analysis,* 12 (1952), p. 36.

and

(13)   For every *x*, if *x* were *F*, then *x* would be *G*.

It will sometimes be necessary, however, to consider counterfactuals as having forms different from (12) and (13).

Subjunctives and counterfactuals are not analyzable by means of material conditionals and universal generalizations of them. For singular material conditional statements are true if the antecedent is false. Suppose that

(14)   If this egg were dropped, then it would bounce

is taken as equivalent to

(15)   If this egg is dropped, then it bounces,

where the "If . . . then - - -" of (15) is the material conditional. Suppose also that, as a matter of fact, the egg is not dropped. Thus, (15) is true. And on the supposition that (14) is equivalent to (15), it follows that (14) is true. However, (14) is surely false: eggs break, not bounce, when dropped. Hence, the equivalence between (14) and (15) does not obtain. A similar situation occurs when we consider universal counterfactuals and make the assumption that the antecedent is vacuously satisfied. That the antecedent of a material conditional is in fact false tells us nothing about whether the consequent would be true if the antecedent were true.

One major attempt to find a criterion for the truth conditions of a counterfactual can be called the Deduction Theory.[16] There are certain counterfactuals that are obviously true. For example,

(16)   If Harry were captain of the team and its best shot, then he would be the best shot on the team.

In this example, the indicative of the consequent is deducible from the indicative of the antecedent. The Deduction Theory attempts to generalize from this type of case and claims that there is a deducibility relationship between the indicative form of the consequent and the indicative form of the antecedent. Clearly, however, most true counterfactuals do not have the structure of (16). Hence, the deduction theorist adds that the indicative form of the consequent follows from the indicative of the antecedent *plus other statements*.

The Deduction Theory becomes interesting — and problematical —

---

[16] Sometimes this theory is called the Metalinguistic Theory. See David Lewis, *Counterfactuals* (Cambridge, Mass., 1973), pp. 65 ff., and J. L. Mackie, *Truth, Probability and Paradox* (Oxford, 1973), pp. 84 ff.

when attempts are made to specify these additional statements. If the additional statements consist only of laws, then the Deduction Theory yields the untoward result that some apparently true counterfactuals are false. Suppose that

(17)   If Jones had stayed home last night, he would have shot his wife

is true. It is difficult, to say the least, to find laws that warrant the deduction of "Jones shot his wife" from "Jones stayed home last night." At best, we might be able to say that when we have an adequate psychology and sociology, we would then be able to carry out the deduction. The situation is more problematical when there do not in principle appear to be laws warranting the deduction. Consider the counterfactuals "If Stevenson had been elected President, there would have been peace in Southeast Asia" or, worse, "If wishes were horses, beggars would ride."

For some counterfactuals, the deduction from the indicative of the antecedent to the indicative of the consequent can be accomplished only if statements of the background conditions, in addition to universal statements, are added. Consider

(18)   If that match had been scratched, it would have lighted.

Unless a statement of the background conditions, say,

(19)   The match is dry; oxygen is present; . . .

is included, "The match lighted" cannot be deduced from the laws and the indicative of the antecedent. For the law in question says that struck matches light, provided that conditions are standard, and that the conditions are in fact standard must be indicated.

Specification of the background conditions, however, is not straightforward. In "Counterfactual Conditionals" Goodman discusses the problems involved in specifying these conditions.[17] One obvious problem is that the indicative of the antecedent is assumed to be false for a counterfactual. If the statement of the background conditions specifies the actually obtaining conditions, then it will include a statement contradicting the indicative of the antecedent. Hence, the indicative of the consequent will follow, since any statement follows from a contradiction. Since this situation obtains for every counterfactual, it therefore follows that every counterfactual is true. But surely this is not the case. Goodman solves this problem, and related ones, by placing restrictions on the statement of the background conditions.

[17] See pp. 117 ff. below.

Goodman's arguments for the restrictions he suggests are admirably clear and need not be repeated here. The central restrictions can be summarized as follows, where *A* is the indicative of the antecedent and *C* the indicative of the consequent of a counterfactual,

(G) *S* is an adequate statement of the background conditions *iff S* is a conjunction of true statements such that:
(i) *S* is compatible with *C* and not $-C$;
(ii) *A & S* is self-compatible and leads by law to *C*;
(iii) there is no *S'* compatible with *C* and not $-C$ such that *A & S'* is self-compatible and leads by law to not $-C$;
(iv) neither *S* nor *S'* follows by law from not $-A$.

(Condition (ii) rules out the situation in which a counterfactual is true simply because the indicative of the antecedent is false.)

However, as Goodman himself notes, (G) is not adequate. Consider again

(18) If that match had been scratched, it would have lighted,

and compare it to

(20) If that match had been scratched, it would not have been dry.

The familiar case is that (18) is true and (20) false. But suppose that the statement of the background conditions is

(21) The match is scratched; it does not light; oxygen is present. . . .

From (21) and the natural laws, we can deduce

(22) The match was not dry.

Hence, contrary to expectation, (20) is asserted to be true. The problem results from including in the statement of the background conditions a conjunct, though compatible with the indicative of the antecedent of (20), that *would not be true if the indicative of the antecedent were true*. That is, as Goodman states the case,

(23) The match does not light,

which is included in (21), is not *cotenable* with the indicative of the antecedent of (20), where *A* is cotenable with *S* if it is false that if *A* were true, *S* would not be true. In order to make (G) adequate to account for this situation, we are required to add the following condition:

(v) *A & S* is self-cotenable.

However, Goodman suggests that (G) is now viciously circular. Cotenability is explicated by means of counterfactuals, and an account of the truth of a counterfactual requires cotenability.

But is Goodman correct in his analysis of the situation? Consider (18) and (20) again. Is (18) true and is (20) false, as they seem at first glance? The law relevant to (18) is

(24) (x) if x is a match and x is dry and x is scratched, then x lights,

where time reference is suppressed. But (24), it seems, is equivalent to

(25) (x) if x is a match and x does not light and x is scratched, then x is not dry.

The conditions obtaining and (25) yield the truth of (20). Hence, it appears that both (18) and (20) are true, and it is not necessary to add condition (v) to (G).

Nevertheless, we intuitively feel that (18) is true and (20) false. Wilfrid Sellars traces the problem to a misinterpretation of (20).[18] The surface grammar of (20) is the same as (18) in that both statements appear to indicate the result of performing certain actions. Statement (18) says that, in ordinary circumstances, striking dry matches causes them to ignite. Understood in this way, (20) is false. Striking matches which do not ignite at that time does not cause them to become (or be) wet. The reason why (20) appears true is that there is an interpretation of it different from the interpretation of (18), namely,

(26) Since that match did not light, if it had also been the case that it was scratched, it would have been the case that it was not dry.

Statement (26) *describes* a situation: it indicates what is taking place, not reporting some causal connection. Hence, if we accept Sellars's reading of (20) as (26), the question of the cotenability of the background conditions with (20) does not arise. Statement (18) explains — that is, indicates in causal language — the relationship between striking matches and their igniting, given standard background conditions; statement (20) describes what happens when we find that a struck match does not ignite, namely, we *also* find that it is not dry.

Recently, some philosophers have taken a different approach to the semantics of counterfactuals. The key idea, originated by Leibniz and recently used by Kripke,[19] is that situations alternative to the actual

[18] See his "Counterfactuals, Dispositions, and the Causal Modalities," in *Minnesota Studies in the Philosophy of Science*, 2 (Minneapolis, 1958), 227–248.

[19] See Saul Kripke, "Semantical Analysis of Modal Logics," *Zeitschrift für mathematische Logik und Grundlagen der Mathematik*, 9 (1963), 67–96.

one can be thought of as possible worlds.[20] Truth is defined in terms of obtainment in possible worlds. This procedure is especially apt for modal statements. Simplifying somewhat, the statement form "It is (logically) possible that p" is true if there is some possible world (including the actual one) in which p is true; similarly, "It is (logically) necessary that p" is true if p is true in every possible world. In "A Theory of Conditionals," Stalnaker develops this apparatus in order to specify truth conditions for counterfactuals.[21]

More carefully, Stalnaker's theory contains three elements. The first is the accessibility relation R, which delineates the possible worlds to be considered. The second element, introduced for formal considerations, is that a world is designated as the *absurd world*, λ, the world in which every statement, including every contradiction, is true. The third element is a *selection function, f;* it is a function such that given a statement and a possible world, it will yield a possible world. Given the indicative of the antecedent of a counterfactual, this function selects a unique world in which the antecedent obtains. We determine whether the entire conditional is true by determining whether the consequent obtains in the selected world. The selected world is the absurd world if there is no accessible world in which the antecedent is true.

Letting $A > B$ represent the counterfactual conditional and a the actual world, we can summarize the truth conditions as follows:[22]

(27) $A > B$ is true in a *iff* B is true in $f(A, a)$.

Let β be the world selected by $f(A, a)$. Then β is such that A is true in β; β is λ, the absurd world, if there is no world accessible to a, and β differs minimally from a. Thus, Stalnaker adds the conditions that if A is true in a, $\beta = a$, and for any two antecedents A' and A'', if A'' is true in $f(A', a)$ and A' is true in $f(A'', a)$, then $f(A', a) = f(A'', a)$. From these semantic considerations Stalnaker produces an axiomatization of this logic. I shall not deal with these formal issues here, but rather make several comments on the philosophical import of Stalnaker's theory.

[20] There is controversy concerning the nature of possible worlds, whether they are merely a conceptual device represented by sets of statements or they exist in much the same way as the actual world. I shall not comment on this issue except to restate a compelling, though odd, argument by David Lewis (*Counterfactuals,* p. 86). If possible worlds are sets of statements, then the actual world is a set of statements, since the actual world is a possible world. But surely we do not live in a set of statements. Hence, possible worlds are not sets of statements.

[21] See pp. 142 ff. below.

[22] See pp. 156 ff. below.

The selection function f yields a unique closest world, differing minimally from the actual one. But do our ordinary intuitions about the truth of counterfactuals agree with this restriction? Consider

(28)   If I were not six feet tall, I would have been six feet, one inch tall,

and

(29)   If I were not six feet tall, I would not have been six feet, one inch tall.

Presumably it is not the case that both (28) and (29) are true. Stalnaker requires that we be able to judge that one but not the other of these statements is true. He suggests that we use some *pragmatic* criteria. However, our ordinary intuition is that, given only these statements, there is no way to determine which one is true — no way to determine, in Stalnaker's way of talking, the closest possible world. In general, Stalnaker's theory makes valid the law of Conditional Excluded Middle: $(A > B) \text{ v } (A > -B)$.[23]

Stalnaker's account must be supplemented by a well-developed pragmatic theory. Even if we agree that there is a unique world selected in each case, we need guidance, in terms of a pragmatic theory, that will indicate *which* world it is. If Stalnaker's analysis is to yield a distinction between laws and accidental generalizations, then the causal laws must obtain in the selected world. For if the selected world contained a different set of laws, then support by a corresponding counterfactual would not guarantee that the universal statement is a law. However, if the pragmatic theory selects only those worlds in which the laws of nature obtain, then the pragmatic theory implicitly makes the distinction between laws and nonlaws. But how is the pragmatic theory to make this distinction? The issue has only been pushed back a step, not resolved. Again, put in summary form, the objection is that the pragmatic theory accompanying Stalnaker's formal account must contain a manner of distinguishing laws from accidental generalizations if corresponding counterfactuals are to support, and only support, laws. But if the accompanying pragmatic theory contains this distinction, then the account cannot be used to make the distinction. That procedure would be viciously circular.

This last objection to Stalnaker suggests a more general objection

[23] Cf. Lewis, *Counterfactuals*, esp. chap. 1, for a system of conditionals that uses possible world semantics but does not make valid the law of Conditional Excluded Middle.

against drawing the distinction between laws and nonlaw generalizations by appeal to counterfactuals. This objection does not depend on a particular theory of the truth conditions for counterfactuals. Ordinary law statements *support* or *warrant* their corresponding counterfactuals.[24] What does this mean exactly? The word "support" occurs naturally in epistemic contexts in which questions of evidence are relevant. One might, for instance, support his claim that Ted Kennedy will win in 1976 by quoting current polls, by citing Kennedy's proficiency at conducting campaigns, and so on. Similarly, "warrant" has a natural epistemic occurrence in which it also concerns evidence. If you claim that Smith is the murderer, but do so without having evidence for your claim, then I could reply that your accusation is unwarranted. The suggestion, then, is that a law statement is evidence for — indeed, let us say, *good* evidence for — its corresponding counterfactual conditional, whereas a nonlaw generalization is not.

Consider, however, the corresponding counterfactual conditional for the nonlaw generalization "All the eggs in Mary's basket are broken":

(30)   If this egg (or object) were an egg in Mary's basket, then it would be broken.

Contrary to the above suggestion, the nonlaw generalization *is* good evidence for (30). A natural understanding of the situation is that Mary started with unbroken eggs in her basket. If all the eggs in the basket are broken, then it is likely that some violent act occurred, such as the basket's having been dropped. If the act was sufficiently violent to break all the eggs in the basket, then it is likely that if another egg were also in the basket, it, too, would be broken. Thus, while the nonlaw generalization is not conclusive evidence for (30), it is quite good evidence.

There is another sense of "support" (though it is unclear whether there is a corresponding sense of "warrant") that means "entails." For example, the premises of a valid argument are often said to support the conclusion. The suggestion is, then, that law statements entail their corresponding counterfactual conditionals, whereas nonlaw generalizations do not. Thus, "Heart stoppage in normal persons produces death" would entail

[24] Cf. Roderick M. Chisholm, "Law Statements and Counterfactual Inference," pp. 113 ff. below.

(31)   (x) if x were a case in which heart stoppage in a normal person occurred, then x would be a case in which death of the person followed.

Two sorts of entailment among statements have to be distinguished. The first sort concerns syntactical considerations alone: statement S_1 entails S_2 if S_2 is deducible from S_1 using some logistic system. However, on this view of entailment, although (30) is not entailed by its corresponding universal, (31) is also not entailed by its corresponding universal. One major problem concerning counterfactual conditionals is determining their logical form. But no matter how they are to be stated, the purely syntactical relationship between (30) and its corresponding universal is identical to that between (31) and its corresponding universal.

The second sort of entailment is one in which S_1 entails S_2 if S_2 is deducible from S_1 using some logistic system and a set of meaning relations, M. The success of this suggestion, clearly, depends on the criterion for inclusion in M. Commonly, the members of M are taken to be statements about relationships among predicates. Since, however, the predicates of the universals and their corresponding conditionals are the same in all cases, meaning relations of this sort are of no help. Rather, statements of meaning relationship between *entire* statements are required. That (31) is entailed by its corresponding universal is to be excluded. But in that case, determining the extension of M is simply determining which universals entail their corresponding counterfactual conditionals.

THE ACTIVITY THEORY

The result of the discussion concerning the natural law analysis of causation is that it does not yield an extrasystemic definition of "*e* caused *f*" since there is no known noncircular manner of distinguishing laws from accidental generalizations. A closer look at ordinary causal laws shows that attempts to delineate them extrasystemically should be unsuccessful. The general form of an ordinary causal law is

(32) $(x)[Fx \supset (y)(Gy \supset xRy)]$,

where x and y are replaced by descriptions of *sorts* or *kinds* of events. Ordinary causal laws have the property of *expressing productivity*. Statements of the form (32) have this property only if: (i) R is asymmetrical; and (ii) the statement entails, though not necessarily in virtue of syntactical considerations alone, that x is the producer and that y is produced. This second condition can be labeled *the condition of producer isolation*. Thus, for example, the ordinary causal law indicated above,

(33)   Throwing bricks at windows produces the windows' breaking,

meets both necessary conditions for having the property of expressing productivity. The relation ". . . produces - - -" is asymmetrical, and (33) entails that the throwing of the bricks is the producer and that the breaking of the windows is produced. The Newtonian laws of motion, to give another example, satisfy neither condition. Written in standard form, the primary law is

(34) $(x)[x = \bar{F} \supset (y)(y = m \ d\bar{v}/dt \supset x = y)]$.

In this case R is "$=$," which is symmetrical. This statement, moreover, does not satisfy the condition of producer isolation; it fails to indicate which of several kinds of processes is taking place. It does not distinguish, for example, processes in which, for a constant mass, an increased force is producing an increased acceleration and processes in which, again for a constant mass, an increased acceleration is producing an increased force. But now, if it is correct to characterize ordinary causal laws as having the property of expressing productivity, then no extrasystemic definition "*e* causes *f*" in terms of "*L* is a causal law" is to be expected, for the locution "(statement) *S* expresses productivity" is a member of the preanalytic locution set pertaining to causation. Put another way, statements having the property of expressing productivity are perspicuously written when R is "produces," as in (33). The locution "(event sort) *x* produces (event sort) *y*" is clearly a member of the preanalytic locution set pertaining to causation.

Recognizing this difficulty with the natural laws analyses of causation, a number of philosophers have attempted an alternative extrasystemic definition. They urge that the preanalytic locution set in which "*e* causes *f*" is to be explicated is the one pertaining to human activity. Causal talk, it is said, is anthropomorphic, in that our notion of causal relations among events results from our intervening in the normal proceedings of the world by performing actions. As Collingwood has argued, this view is supported by the philological evidence that historical uses of causal talk pertained to human activity and intervention.[25]

25 See pp. 169 ff. below.

Analyses building on this intuition have been proposed by Douglas Gasking and Georg Henrick von Wright.[26] Let us consider Gasking's defense of this view.

Gasking's idea is that we assert that events are causally related when we have a manipulative technique for bringing about one event by making the other happen. For example, we claim that striking matches causes them to ignite because we have techniques for striking matches so that the match ignites as a result of applying this technique. Reformulating somewhat, Gasking suggests:

(DD)   For every event e and every event f, e caused f *iff*:
    (i)   the occurrence of f did not begin before the occurrence of e began; and
    (ii)   there is a person S such that S used a manipulative technique for making e occur and f occurred.

This definition, however, is subject to counterexamples from the pre-analytic data. The pull of the moon causes particular tide formations on earth, and the coming of the ice age caused the extinction of dinosaurs, although no person can bring about the manipulations needed to make the moon exert a gravitational force or to make an ice age occur. Foreseeing this difficulty, Gasking argues that sometimes the manipulative techniques in question concern not individual events but rather sorts of events. Although we cannot bring about the extinction of a species by producing an ice age, we can bring about an event of the same sort — for example, lowering the temperature in a spatial volume for a period of time so that a group of animals freezes to death. This revision can be incorporated in the definition by replacing (ii) with

(ii')   there is a person S such that S used a manipulative technique for making e occur and f occurred,
    or
there is a person S such that S used a manipulative technique for making something relevantly similar to e occur and something relevantly similar to f occurred.

But this revised definition shares difficulties with the Humean pro-

[26] Gasking, "Causation and Recipes," pp. 215–223 below; von Wright, *Explanation and Understanding* (Ithaca, N.Y., 1971), chap. 2. Michael Scriven, in "The Logic of Cause," *Theory and Decision,* 2 (1971), 49–66, seems also to suggest this view.

posal (DA′). In the first place, it fails to distinguish between cases of correlation and those of causation. For example, there may be, by sheer coincidence, some intricate and esoteric dance, each performance of which has been followed by rain. In that case, the revised definiens of (DD) is satisfied, despite causal independence. Secondly, the second disjunct of condition (ii′) is problematical. If "relevantly similar" means "exactly similar," then since only *e* is exactly similar to *e* and only *f* is exactly similar to *f,* (ii′) collapses to (ii); hence, the problem confronting Gasking's original definition remains. Further, "relevantly similar" does not mean "similar in many (or, in most) respects," for if it did, counterinstances could be generated: events *e* and *f* might be causally independent even though events similar in many respects to them are causally related. In order to avoid the counterinstances, "relevantly similar" in (ii′) has to be interpreted to mean "similar in the causally relevant respects." But in that case, the cost of avoiding the counterinstances is the failure to sustain (DD) as an extrasystemic definition.

Consider one further attempt to defend (DD). Condition (ii), it might be suggested, should be replaced by

> (ii″)   there is a person *S* such that if *S* had a manipulative technique for making *e* occur, *f* would occur.

This revision appears not to incorporate locutions pertaining to causal efficacy and appears not to be subject to the counterexamples facing the original definition. If one did have a technique for bringing about the ice age, then the extinction of the dinosaurs would have followed.

However, this definition, like the previous two versions of the activity theory, is not able to distinguish between cases of correlation and causation. Condition (ii″) is satisfied in cases of mere correlation, such as the performance of an esoteric dance being followed, coincidentally, by rain. It might be objected that (ii″) is not satisfied in cases of mere correlation. There is, it should be admitted, a reading of (ii″) in which this objection is true. But that reading says that if *S* has a manipulative technique for making *e* occur, *f would result,* where "would result" means "would causally result." Though this interpretation of (ii″) disqualifies counterexamples relying on cases of coincidence, it does so at the expense of the activity theory's status as an extrasystemic proposal. As a general rule, reformulation in terms of counterfactuals does not preserve extrasystemic status.

The Entailment Theory

Another traditional extrasystemic attempt to define "*e* caused *f*" is in terms of locutions pertaining to logical entailment. One of the most able recent defenders of this view is Brand Blanshard.[27] Blanshard argues that a person's way of thinking in moving from premises to conclusion in a valid deductive argument is exactly similar to his way of thinking when he reasons from cause to effect. Since his way of thinking in deductive argumentation depends solely on the logically necessary connection between the premises and the conclusion, and since the way of thinking in causal reasoning is the same, there is a logically necessary connection between cause and effect. These claims are intended to justify the following (reformulated) definition:

(DE)   For every X and every Y, X caused Y *iff:*
   (i) X is not later than Y; and
   (ii) X is the set of conditions each member of which is logically necessary for Y and which jointly are logically sufficient for Y.

Blanshard's justification for (DE) has strong overtones of idealism. It presupposes that we can determine what is the case by determining our way of thinking about what is the case. However, even if the idealism-realism issue is left aside, this justification for (DE) is problematical. The way of thinking involved in causal reasoning is similar to, but not exactly like, that involved in logical reasoning. In causal reasoning, if an appeal is made to laws, it is made to contingent, that is, factual, laws. But such laws are not an indispensable part of logical reasoning. I can make successful armchair discoveries about logical matters, but I cannot make discoveries about causal connections without some experience of the factual conditions.

In any case, the resulting definition (DE) is defective. The range of X and Y in (DE) is ambiguous. According to condition (ii), X and Y are sets of statements, for it is statements that are the arguments of "... is logically necessary for - - -" and "... is logically sufficient for - - -." But according to condition (i), X and Y range over events or complexes of events, for it is events that are temporally ordered. More importantly, the definiendum of (DE) requires that X

---

[27] See pp. 226–253 below. Sellars, in "Counterfactuals, Dispositions, and the Causal Modalities," argues for a modified version of the Entailment Theory.

and Y range over events, or at least that they not range over statements, since the causal relation is a relation between events. Even ignoring this ambiguity, definition (DE) is problematical. It fails to account for the asymmetry between cause and effect. The predicate ". . . is later than - - -" is not asymmetrical, and the predicate ". . . is the set of conditions logically necessary and sufficient for - - -" is symmetrical. This objection to (DE) can also be made by pointing out that counter-examples arise in cases of simultaneous causation in which a description of the effect is substituted for X and a description of the cause is substituted for Y.

A Systemic Approach: The Logic of Causal Necessity

We have investigated the primary extrasystemic attempts to define "e caused f," each of which has failed. The failures provide good evidence for the claim that "e caused f" is purely systemically definable. It is important to emphasize that no proof has been given for this claim. There would be conclusive evidence that "e caused f" is purely systemically definable if it were shown that *all* plausible extrasystemic definitions are untenable. The possibility remains that some extrasystemic proposal, now unknown, will be adequate. The discussion about causation is, then, at the stage of attempting to supply a systemic definition. It should not be thought, however, that this task is easily accomplished.

One important systemic suggestion has been made by Arthur Burks in his influential paper "The Logic of Causal Propositions."[28] Burks's strategy can be interpreted as defining "causes" in terms of causal necessity and then explicating causal necessity by specifying its logic. In detail, Burks proposes the following definition,

$$(\text{DF}) \qquad A \, c \, B = \text{df.} \; \boxed{c} \, (A \supset B),$$

where Burks reads c as ". . . causes - - -" and $\boxed{c}$ as "It is causally necessary that - - -."[29] There are initial, but not defeating, difficulties for this definition. The definiens does not include a temporal condition. If we agree that effects do not precede their causes, then we should add a temporal condition saying that the occurrence of the effect did not begin before the occurrence of the cause. A more important difficulty is that the relation c (". . . causes - - -") takes

---

[28] See pp. 257–276 below.
[29] See pp. 368, 377 below.

singular terms as arguments, but if the definiens is to make sense, A and B must be replaced by sentences. One way to proceed is to specify a function, $g(A) = A'$, that takes event-describing sentences into their gerundives (A') and to replace A and B in the definiendum of (DF) with the result of applying this function. If, for example, A is "Jones raises his arm," g (Jones raises his arm) is "Jones's raising of his arm." Although this procedure has the advantage of retaining continuity with the previous definitions considered, we shall, for the sake of simplicity of exposition, reinterpret Burks's proposal by saying that c is to be read as "It being the case that . . . causes it to be the case that - - -," where ". . ." and "- - -" are now replaced by sentences.[30]

The focus of Burks's systemic definition is the explication of causal necessity. He proceeds by giving the syntactical development of an interpreted modal logic in which $\boxed{c}$ is introduced as being weaker than $\square$ (where $\square$ is read "it is logically necessary that . . ."). One motivation for this suggestion is the long-known — but not well understood — view that causal necessity is weaker than logical necessity but stronger than the relationship that the consequent bears to the antecedent in a material implicative statement. Burks's system consists of a standard system of truth-functional and quantificational logic supplemented by the following axioms and rule governing $\square$:

A1	$\square A \supset \boxed{c} A$
A2	$\boxed{c} A \supset A$
A3	$\square (A \supset B) \supset (\square A \supset \square B)$
A4	$\boxed{c} (A \supset B) \supset (\boxed{c} A \supset \boxed{c} B)$
A5	$(x) \square A \supset \square (x) A$
A6	$(x) \boxed{c} A \supset \boxed{c} (x) A$
N	If $\vdash A$, then $\vdash \square A$.

(The alethic fragment is Feys's system T plus the Barcan formula.)

The single most important feature of Burks's system is axiom A1. It is by means of A1 that a nonalethic modal logic of causal necessity is embedded in an alethic modal logic. Axiom A1, it should be said, reflects a widely accepted and widely used philosophical claim, one that might be supported by the following plausibility argument. To say that A is logically necessary is to say that A is true in all possible worlds. To say that A is causally necessary is to say that A is true in all worlds

---

[30] For problems in construing the causal relation as a relation between facts or propositions, rather than between events, see Donald Davidson, "Causal Relations," pp. 355–367 below.

similar to ours in the relevant respects, whatever those respects are. Hence, A1 is true, since every world relevantly similar to ours is a possible world.

But A1 is highly problematical. Since the range of A is unrestricted in axiom A1, logical truths are causally necessary. Substituting $q \supset q$ for A in A1, for example, yields, by the rules of necessitation and detachment,

(35) $\qquad\qquad$ $\boxed{c}\,(q \supset q).$

But (35) is absurd. Only sentences about events are causally necessary. A sentence expressing causal necessity is true just in case it says that some event or events occurred (are occurring or will occur), when the events named in fact had to (or have to) occur. Logical truths are not sentences about what event or events have to (or had to) occur; they are not sentences about events at all. To put the matter in an almost metaphorical way, (35) is a category mistake. The set of sentences for which it makes sense to prefix $\square$ is exclusive of the set of sentences for which it makes sense to prefix $\boxed{c}$.[31]

Again, let O be a one-place predicate which is read "the event of . . . occurred (is occurring, will occur)," where ". . ." is replaced by a name of an event or a variable ranging over events. The sentence

(36) $\qquad\qquad$ $\square\,(Oe \supset Oe)$

is true: it is an instance of the logical truth $\square\,(p \supset p)$.
But

(37) $\qquad\qquad$ $\boxed{c}\,(Oe \supset Oe)$

is not true. A sentence is about the occurrence of an event only if it entails

(38) $\qquad\qquad$ $(\exists e)\,Oe;$

and clearly, (37) does not entail (38).

---

[31] An attempt might be made to defend Burks by citing text in which he interprets $\boxed{c}$ as a disjunctive functor which is read "it is logically or causally necessary that . . ." (see pp. 273–274 below). On this reading of $\boxed{c}$, (35) is true, not absurd. However, Burks is not unambiguous here. He says "*c* means 'causally sufficient'" and claims that universal statements whose main connective is *c* are *causal laws* (pp. 261–264 below). These remarks about $\boxed{c}$ joined with his definition (DF) preclude the disjunctive reading of $\boxed{c}$. In any case, no matter what Burks's official position is, $\boxed{c}$ will not be given a disjunctive reading. If $\boxed{c}$ is to be used in understanding locutions such as "*e* causes *f*" and "*e* is causally sufficient for *f*," $\boxed{c}$ has to be read "it is causally necessary that. . . ." Note, moreover, that there is no advantage to giving $\boxed{c}$ the disjunctive reading and defining a new functor in terms of it: namely, $\boxed{c}*A$ = df. $\boxed{c}\,A\,\&\,-\,\square\,A$. The reason is that the logical structure of $\boxed{c}*A$ remains to be made explicit.

Events occur in bounded space-time regions. The event of Jones's raising his arm, for example, occurs in the area including Jones and endures for a limited time. But tautologies, such as $Oe \supset Oe$, do not name spatiotemporally bounded occurrences. If logical truths name anything, they name nonspatiotemporal propositions.

It is important to emphasize that (35) and (37) are absurd or senseless and not merely false, for if (37) were false (and if it is assumed that the denial of a false sentence is a true one), then

(39) $\qquad\qquad \langle\!\!\diamond\!\!\!\!_\mathrm{c}\rangle\ (Oe\ \&\ -Oe),$

which says that a contradiction is causally possible, would be true. But (39) is also absurd. It is absurd for the same sort of reason that $\boxed{\mathrm{c}}\ (Oe \supset Oe)$ is: sentences naming occurrences of events, not contradictions, are causally possible. Intuitively, to say that A is causally possible is to say that A names what can happen. But $p\ \&\ \sim p$ fails to describe an event and hence does not name what can happen.

The reply to the plausibility argument for A1 is now clear. The argument is simply unsound. In the premise saying that A is true in all possible worlds, A ranges over logically necessary truths. However, if A ranges over logically necessary truths in the premise concerning causal necessity, then that premise is senseless. Alternatively, if we make the premise concerning causal necessity true by restricting the range of A to sentences naming event occurrences, then the premise saying that A is true in all possible worlds is false.

To continue the criticism, the rule of causal necessitation,

(CN)　If $\vdash A$, then $\vdash \boxed{\mathrm{c}}A$,

is provable in Burks's system. (The proof is straightforward.)[32] From (CN) it follows that, for example $\boxed{\mathrm{c}}\ (p \supset p)$ is a theorem of the system. But tautologies are logically necessary, not *causally* necessary. This consequence of Burks's system is traceable to axiom A1, since (CN) is derivable in the system because of A1. In general, a system that adequately reflects the logic of causal necessity will not contain the causal analogue to the rule of necessitation.[33]

---

[32] Cf. Burks, p. 276 below.

[33] Suppose that we adopt definition (DC), which defines "causes" directly in terms of counterfactuals. If we then also adopt Stalnaker's logic for counterfactuals, difficulties similar to those facing Burks's logic arise. From Stalnaker's axiom (a3), $\Box\ (A \supset B) \supset (A > B)$, the Godel rule of necessitation, and substitution, we obtain $A > A$ (pp. 159 ff. below). From definition (DC) we then obtain the result that every event caused itself, which is absurd. The problem seems to result, as it does in Burks's case, from having a modal logic that is too strong.

The difficulties noted for Burks's construal of causal necessity discredit definition (DF). Since the ranges of A and B in (DF) are unrestricted, $p \supset p$ and $q \supset (q \supset q)$ can be substituted for A and B, respectively. It follows, then, from A1 and detachment that $\boxed{c}\{(p \supset p) \supset [q \supset (q \supset q)]\}$. And hence, by (DF),

(40) $\qquad\qquad\qquad (p \supset p)\, c\, [q \supset (q \supset q)]$.

That is, one logical truth causes another. But this result is untoward: sentences naming events, not logical truths, are the arguments of c. Further, if (37) is granted,

(41) $\qquad\qquad\qquad\qquad Oe\, c\, Oe$

follows from (DF). However, no event causes itself, at least according to the ordinary notion of causation.

Some of these difficulties for Burks's construal of causal necessity disappear when the proper restrictions are placed on A and B. Let an O-sentence be an atomic O-sentence or a molecular O-sentence, where an atomic O-sentence is a sentence of a form Oe and a molecular O-sentence is a truth-functional compound of atomic O-sentences. Any O-sentence that is not true or false in virtue of its syntactical form alone is a *nonlogical* O-sentence. Substitutions in (DF), in sentences prefixed by $\boxed{c}$, and so on, are then to be restricted to nonlogical O-sentences. It is thus apparent that an adequate account of causal necessity (and also of causation and causal laws) is to be grounded on a theory of events. A major failing of Burks's discussion is his not seeing this dependence of causal necessity on events.

Some other difficulties disappear when Burks's system is not taken as the underlying logic of causal necessity. Burks attempted to capture the insight that causal necessity is weaker than logical necessity by using axiom A1 to embed the logic of causal necessity in an alethic modal logic. The result was that the nonalethic fragment of Burks's system structurally mirrors the alethic fragment: for every axiom or theorem containing $\square$, there is an axiom or theorem exactly like it, except that $\boxed{c}$ replaces $\square$. This result proved unhappy. It is not clear which alethic modal logic (or logics) adequately reflects the structure of logical necessity.[34] But this much is clear: the appropriate logic contains the rule of necessitation. Hence, the logic of causal necessity does

---

[34] Perhaps Fey's T or Lewis's S4 or S5 or Anderson's and Belnap's E (see, for example, Anderson and Belnap, "Pure Calculus of Entailment," *Journal of Symbolic Logic*, 27 [1962], 19–52).

not structurally mirror the logic of logical necessity, for the logic of causal necessity does not contain the analogue to the rule of necessitation. Causal necessity is weaker than logical necessity in that the logic of logical necessity contains axioms or theorems for which there are no analogues in the logic of causal necessity. The structure of the logic of causal necessity, however, is not clear.[35]

A Second Systemic Approach: Causally Necessary and Sufficient Conditions

In the recent literature, a number of attempts have been made to define "*e* caused *f*" systemically in terms of the notion of causal sufficiency. This attempt can be directly related to Burks's definition (DF) by the following principle:

(P1) e is causally sufficient for f iff $\boxed{c}$ $(Oe \supset Of)$.

The acceptability of (P1) depends in part on the existence of the function g, which maps event-describing sentences onto their gerundives, and the existence of its inverse, $g^{-1}(A') = A$. With respect to g^{-1}, if A' is a nominalized sentence, then we obtain A by substituting A' for "..." in "The event of ... occurred" and deleting those portions of A' that become redundant by virtue of this operation. Events, however, may be named by singular terms such as "The Battle of Waterloo," "the first event that occurred yesterday," or perhaps even "Henry." If we followed the treatment for nominalized sentences in these cases, we would obtain, for example, "The event of the Battle of Waterloo occurred" and "The event of Henry occurred." The latter, at least, is awkward. We might specify g^{-1} as complex, resulting in the sentence "The event named 'Henry' occurred" or something similar in these cases. It would appear that nothing relevant is lost, however, if we treat g^{-1} as a simple function and accept the awkwardness in these special cases.

Accepting principle (P1) and excluding the temporal condition for simplicity, Burks's definition (DF) becomes:

[35] An interesting alternative to Burks's logic is E. J. Lemmon's "E-systems." See Lemmon, "New Foundations for Lewis' Modal Systems," *Journal of Symbolic Logic,* 22 (1957), 176–186, and "Algebraic Semantics for Modal Logics" parts 1 and 2, *Journal of Symbolic Logic,* 31 (1966), 46–65, 191–218. Lemmon's views are further developed in the appendix of Brand and Marshall Swain, "Causation and Causal Necessity," *Philosophical Studies,* in press.

(DF′) For every event *e* and every event *f*, *e* caused *f* *iff* *e* is causally sufficient for *f*.[36]

Putting Burks's definition in this form points to another deficiency in the proposal. The definiens is not sufficiently complex to account for all the preanalytic cases of causation. More is required than getting clear about the logic of causal necessity in order to supply an adequate systemic definition. Definition (DF′) cannot account for cases of over-determination. Suppose that our man Jones is placed before a firing squad and that as a result of his situation he has a heart attack. Before the heart attack can kill him, however, he dies of bullet wounds. In this case, we would say that his having the heart attack is causally sufficient for his death but did not cause his death. There are, further, straightforward cases that do not fall within the scope of (DF′). To use J. L. Mackie's case, the short circuit in the electrical system of a house caused the house's burning but was not causally sufficient for the burning, since the presence of oxygen and combustible materials are also needed.[37]

Mackie attempts to account for these difficulties. The essential features of his proposal can be given by the following definitions. Let *A*, *P*, *X*, and *Y* be singular terms which may be complex and which refer to empirical conditions or factors (that is, *events*).[38] In particular, let *X* be the conjunction of conditions such that *AX* is a causally minimally sufficient condition for the result *P*, and let *Y* be the disjunction of all other causally minimally sufficient conditions for *P*. (*AX* is a minimally sufficient condition for *P* just in case *AX* is a causally sufficient condition for *P*, but neither *A* alone nor *X* alone is a causally sufficient condition for *P*.) Now,

(DG1) For every *A* and *P*, *A* is an INUS condition of *P* *iff* there is an *X* and *Y* such that (*AX* or *Y*) is a causally necessary and sufficient condition for *P*.

[36] Under one reading of the counterfactual definition (DC), p. 19 above, it is equivalent to (DF′). In which case, the problems for (DF′) are problems for (this interpretation of) (DC).

[37] See "Causes and Conditions" pp. 308 ff. below.

[38] Mackie assumes, without argument, that there are operations on singular terms exactly analogous to the operations on sentences — operations such as negation and conjunction. This view has come under attack by Kim. (See Jaegwon Kim, "Causes and Events: Mackie on Causation," *The Journal of Philosophy*, 68 (1971), 426–441.) For the present, let us adopt Mackie's proposal rather than attempt to reformulate it into one in which only standard operations, such as those on sentences or sets, are used.

(The relation "... is causally necessary for - - -" is defined in terms of causal sufficiency, namely, A is causally necessary for B *iff* B is causally sufficient for A.) An INUS condition, as described earlier, is an *in*sufficient but *n*ecessary part of a condition that is itself *un*necessary but *s*ufficient for a result P. For example, the short circuit in the electrical system of a house is an INUS condition of the house's burning; the short circuit is not causally sufficient for the house's burning, since the presence of oxygen and other conditions are also needed, and it is not causally necessary since the fire could have started in some other way. Rather, "the short circuit ... is ... an indispensable part of a complex sufficient (but not necessary) condition of the fire."[39]

    (DG2)   For every A, P, X, and Y, A is *at least* an INUS condition of P *iff* there is a set of conditions causally necessary and sufficient for P that has one of the following forms: $(AX$ or $Y)$, $(A$ or $Y)$, AX, or A.

And finally,

    (DG3)   For every A, P, X, and Y, A caused P *iff:*
        (i) A is at least an INUS condition of P;
        (ii) A occurred;
        (iii) if X is nonvacuous, X occurred; and
        (iv) every disjunct in "Y" not containing "A" as a conjunct did not occur.

One minor difficulty for (DG3) is that it contains no temporal condition. This condition can be easily added. The relation "... is causally sufficient for - - -," which forms the primitive base for these definitions, does not specify any temporal ordering.

A more serious difficulty results from the claim that the set of conditions, be it A, AX, $(A$ or $Y)$, or $(AX$ or $Y)$, is causally necessary and sufficient for P, for this claim, in conjunction with several acceptable principles, yields a contradiction. Mackie, moreover, is not alone in facing this difficulty; any proposal that entails that A causes B only if A is the set or, better, *group* of conditions individually necessary and jointly sufficient for the occurrence of the set or group of conditions B results in a contradiction. For example, Richard Taylor is also subject to this criticism, since he holds that "A true interpreted statement of the form 'A was the cause of B' means that both A and B are conditions or sets of conditions that occurred; that each was, given all the

[39] See p. 309 below.

other conditions that occurred, but only those *both necessary and sufficient for* the occurrence of the other. . . ."[40]

The argument that this view yields a contradiction is detailed in Brand and Swain's "On the Analysis of Causation."[41] In summary, the argument says that the relation ". . . is causally necessary and sufficient for - - -" is transitive and symmetrical. In these respects, it resembles the relation ". . . is logically necessary and sufficient for - - -," though of course it differs from the latter relation with respect to the range of arguments that yield meaningful sentences. From these properties of the relation, it follows that A is causally necessary and sufficient for A. Hence, according to the view held by Mackie and Taylor, an event (or set or group of conditions) can be the cause of itself. However, in the usage that has been in question throughout this essay, A causes B only if A and B are distinct events. Therefore, any definition that entails that A caused B only if B is causally necessary and sufficient for B is to be revised to exclude this entailment or rejected if such revision is not possible.

Objection to this argument might be made because it presupposed that A is the total and, hence, *unique* set of conditions for B. That is, it presupposes that if A is the group of conditions each member of which is individually necessary and jointly sufficient for the occurrence of the members of B, then A is the only such set. Therefore, the objection continues, the possibility that there are two distinct sets of conditions, say A' and A'', each of which is causally necessary and sufficient for B, is mistakenly precluded. For example, it precludes the possibility that A is causally necessary and sufficient for the windows' breaking, the windows' breaking is causally necessary and sufficient for the pro-

[40] *Action and Purpose* (Englewood Cliffs, 1966), p. 39. Taylor makes equivalent claims in "Causation," see below pp. 288–303, and in "Causation" in *The Encyclopedia of Philosophy*, 2 (New York, 1967), 56–66. Later, in *Action and Purpose*, however, he modifies this proposal.

A. J. Ayer is also subject to this criticism. In *Problem of Knowledge* (Baltimore, 1956), p. 17, he claims that ". . . to say that *a* is the cause of *b*, when *a* and *b* are separate events, is, in the usage which is here in question, to imply either that *a* is a [causally] sufficient condition of *b*, or that it is a necessary condition of *b*, *or that it is both a sufficient and a necessary condition . . .*" (italics added).

[41] See pp. 346–351 below. Also cf. Risto Hilpinen, "On the Conditions of Causality," *Philosophical Studies*, 24 (1973), 386–391; Brand and Swain, "Causation and Necessary and Sufficient Conditions: Reply to Hilpinen," *Philosophical Studies*, 25 (1974), 357–364; John A. Barker, "Brand and Swain on Causation," *Synthese*, 26 (1974), 396–400; David H. Sanford, "Causal Necessity and Logical Necessity," *Philosophical Studies*, 28 (1975), 103–112; and Brand and Swain, "Causation and Causal Necessity: Reply to Sanford," forthcoming *Philosophical Studies*.

duction of a certain noise, and A does not include the production of the noise.[42]

In reply, it should be pointed out that it appears correct to preclude the possibility of there being two distinct sets of conditions, each of which is causally necessary and sufficient for a set, B. If there are two sets of distinct conditions, each necessary for B, then neither set alone is sufficient for B, for if only one of these sets occurs, then B will not occur, since there will be conditions required for B's occurrence that did not take place. Similarly, if there are two sets of distinct conditions, each sufficient for B, then neither set is necessary for B, for it is enough for one of these two sets of conditions to occur in order for B to occur; neither set is such that it is required that it occur in order for B to occur. With respect to the noise example, if A is in fact causally necessary and sufficient for the windows' breaking, then A does include the production of the noise.

Some uneasiness may remain. How can the set of conditions necessary and sufficient for the windows' breaking include the production of the noise? The uneasiness might result from the fact that the occurrence of the noise comes after that which caused the window to break. But this result is acceptable. The relation ". . . is causally necessary and sufficient for - - -" does not indicate a temporal ordering. Moreover, this relation does not indicate a direction of production. "A is causally necessary and sufficient for B" is compatible with both the claims that A caused B and that B caused A. This last comment indicates that this relation is poorly suited as the primary condition in the definiens of a definition of causation. Counterexamples to the definition can be produced in cases of simultaneous causation by substituting the description of the cause for the effect and the converse.

It might be thought that the relation of causal necessity and sufficiency does indicate the direction of production. If one has these intuitions, then one will not accept the principles stating that the relation is symmetrical and transitive, for these principles entail that A can be causally necessary and sufficient for itself and hence precluding production. It may be claimed that these principles are appropriate for specifying the relation of *logical* necessity and sufficiency, not causal necessity and sufficiency. It is then incumbent upon the person holding these intuitions to specify this new relationship and to show how it

---

[42] Cf. Barker, "Brand and Swain on Causation." The uniqueness of A is made explicit in principle (P4) of Brand and Swain's argument, p. 349 below.

can be used in the analysis of causation without resulting in the problems indicated by Brand and Swain's argument.

DIRECTIONS FOR FURTHER DISCUSSION

Further discussion about causation should best proceed in three directions: continuation of the necessity-and-sufficiency proposal, clarification of the base locution set pertaining to causation, and exploration of related issues. First, the definition of causation in terms of causally necessary and sufficient conditions must be studied in light of the criticism brought by Brand and Swain. In particular, the meaning of the key locution "*e* is causally sufficient for *f*" must be explored further. What is the relationship between this locution and "*L* is a causal law"? Can we offer an extrasystemic account of this locution, as Mackie suggests?[43] Do we need to introduce a different locution into our causal talk that is like "*e* is causally sufficient for *f*" except that it carries the implication that *e* produced *f*? Getting clear about "*e* is causally sufficient for *f*" would put us in a better position to map intrarelations of the entire locution set pertaining to causation.

The second group of issues concerns clarification of the base locution set pertaining to causation. The primary locution sets contained in the base locution set are those pertaining to temporal ordering and to events. Issues about temporal ordering can be raised in an interesting way by attempting to answer the question "Can an effect precede its cause?" There is significant literature on this subject.[44] An adequate answer to this question will take one into the philosophy of time.

Issues about the nature of events are the most interesting subsidiary issues connected with causation. One reason is that the locution set pertaining to events forms part of the base locution sets pertaining to

---

[43] See "Causes and Conditions," pp. 324 ff.

[44] The primary literature on this topic is the following: Max Black, "Why Cannot an Effect Precede Its Cause?" *Analysis,* 16 (1956), 49–58; Roderick Chisholm and Richard Taylor, "Making Things to Have Happened," *Analysis,* 20 (1960), 73–78; A. E. Dummett, "Can an Effect Precede Its Cause?" *Proceedings of the Aristotelian Society,* 28 (1954), 27–44; Michael Dummett, "Bringing About the Past," *Philosophical Review,* 73 (1964), 338–359; Anthony Flew, "Can an Effect Precede Its Cause?" *Proceedings of the Aristotelian Society,* 28 (1954), 45–62; Richard Gale, "Why a Cause Cannot Be Later Than Its Effect," *Review of Metaphysics,* 19 (1965–66), 209–234; Samuel Gorowitz, "Leaving the Past Alone," *Philosophical Review,* 73 (1964), 360–372; Michael Scriven, "Randomness and the Causal Order," *Analysis,* 17 (1956), 5–9; Richard Taylor, "Can a Cause Precede Its Effect?" *Monist,* 48 (1964), 136–142; and J. S. Wilkie, "The Problem of the Temporal Relation of Cause and Effect," *British Journal for the Philosophy Science,* 1 (1950), 211–229.

human action, to mind, and to explanation, three topics of special interest to contemporary philosophers. Another reason is that, despite its centrality to the key issues in metaphysics, a great deal of work remains to be done on the theory of events.

In "Causal Relations," Davidson argues that the set of locutions pertaining to events should be included in the base locution set pertaining to causation.[45] In this article, but primarily in other places, he also argues that events are, in essential respects, like physical objects. Events are, according to Davidson, nonrepeatable particulars. This view should be mirrored in our canonical way of talking about events, namely, that first-order quantificational logic is adequate for these purposes.

Davidson's view has intuitive appeal. It does seem that events are particular, concrete things in the world, that they are part of the ordinary furnishings of the world. But despite its intuitive appeal, Davidson's view is problematical. There are difficulties in establishing identity conditions for events. A statement of the form $o_1 = o_2$, where o_1 and o_2 name physical objects, is true, it is plausible to hold, just in case o_1 and o_2 occupy the exact same spatiotemporal regions. However, $e_1 = e_2$ can be false when e_1 and e_2 name events occupying the same spatiotemporal regions. The swimming of the English Channel and the catching of a cold take place for exactly the same time and in the same spatial regions, but yet each is a distinct event. Another problem for Davidson's theory is the problem of recurrence. How are we to make sense of statements such as "It happened again" and "Jones and Smith did the same thing" if events are nonrepeatable particulars? I am not suggesting that these (and other problems) are defeating objections to Davidson's view. But they are difficult and must be answered adequately if one is to hold that Davidson's view is correct.[46]

Logicians sometimes divide linguistic expressions into three groups: singular terms, predicates, and statements. If each kind of expression names, then they name particulars, properties, and propositions, respectively. Davidson has argued for events having the ontological status of particulars. Some philosophers have argued for events having the status of properties, and some philosophers have argued for events

---

[45] See pp. 355–367 below.

[46] See Brand, "Particulars, Events and Actions," in Brand and Douglas Walton, eds., *Action Theory: Proceedings of the Winnipeg Action Theory Conference* (Synthese Library, forthcoming), for a particularist theory of events that attempts to meet objections about identity conditions and recurrence.

having the status of propositions.[47] There are difficulties for these com-
peting views, too. For example, identity conditions for properties and
propositions are far from clear. Moreover, nominalistically inclined
philosophers have argued against the view that, in addition to particulars, there are properties and propositions. In any case, an investigation into the nature of events is a fruitful enterprise.

The third group of issues for further discussion consists of related
and miscellaneous topics. One issue is the formulation of an adequate
logic of causal necessity. The answer may lie in the direction suggested
by Lemmon, but that is a conjecture. Another issue is the semantics
for ordinary causal statements in natural languages. For example, are
causal contexts referentially transparent?[48] Another issue is distinguishing between being *the* cause and being a causal factor.[49] The short
circuit in the electrical circuit was *the* cause of the house fire, while the
presense of oxygen was a mere causal factor. There is something non-
standard about the short circuit, while the presence of oxygen is a
standard or normal condition. But how do we specify this sort of nor-
mality? The most far-reaching issue in this group concerns ordinary
causal explanation. Does causal explanation have the same structure
as scientific explanation? Does it, for example, fit the Deductive-
Nominological model? Does causal explanation differ from explanations in terms of reasons for actions? From explanations in terms of
goals and purposes? From explanations in terms of biological functions?[50] As in the case of any significant philosophical problem, investigation into the nature of causation raises issues in almost every area
of inquiry.

[47] In addition to "Causal Relations," see the following articles by Davidson:
"Events as Particulars," *Nous,* 4 (1970), 25–32; "Eternal *vs.* Ephemeral Events,"
Nous, 5 (1971), 335–348; "The Individuation of Events," in Nicholas Rescher,
et al., eds., *Essays in Honor of Carl G. Hempel* (Dordrecht, 1969); "On Events
and Event-Descriptions," in Joseph Margoles, ed., *Fact and Existence* (Oxford,
1969); and "The Logical Form of Action Sentences," in Nicholas Rescher, ed.,
The Logic of Decision and Action (Pittsburgh, 1967). The view that events have
the ontological status of properties is defended by Alvin Goldman, *A Theory of
Human Action,* pp. 1–19, and by Jaegwon Kim in, for example, "Events as Property Exemplifications: Considerations and Reconsiderations," in Brand and Walton,
eds., *Action Theory.* The third view is that event talk can be assimilated to propositional talk. This view has been defended by Roderick Chisholm in, for example,
"Events and Propositions," *Nous,* 4 (1970), 15–24, and "States of Affairs Again,"
Nous, 5 (1971), 171–189.
[48] Cf. Lawrence Davis, "Extensionality and Singular Causal Sentences," *Philosophical Studies,* forthcoming.
[49] See Samuel Gorowitz, "Causal Judgments and Causal Explanations," *Journal
of Philosophy,* 62 (1965), 695–711.
[50] See von Wright, *Explanation and Understanding.*

I. The Regularity Theory

Of the Idea
of Necessary Connection

David Hume

Reprinted from David Hume, *An Inquiry Concerning Human Understanding,* ed. Charles
W. Hendell. Copyright © 1955 by The Liberal Arts Press; reprinted by permission
of The Bobbs-Merrill Co., Inc. Text follows the version published in 1777; first edition,
1741.

OF THE IDEA OF NECESSARY CONNECTION [1]

PART I

THE GREAT ADVANTAGE of the mathematical sciences above the moral consists in this, that the ideas of the former, being sensible, are always clear and determinate, the smallest distinction between them is immediately perceptible, and the same terms are still expressive of the same ideas without ambiguity or variation. An oval is never mistaken for a circle, nor a hyperbola for an ellipsis. The isosceles and scalenum are distinguished by boundaries more exact than vice and virtue, right and wrong. If any term be defined in geometry, the mind readily, of itself, substitutes on all occasions the definition for the term defined, or, even when no definition is employed, the object itself may be presented to the senses and by that means be steadily and clearly apprehended. But the finer sentiments of the mind, the operations of the understanding, the various agitations of the passions, though really in themselves distinct, easily escape us when surveyed by reflection, nor is it in our power to recall the original object as often as we have occasion to contemplate it. Ambiguity, by this means, is gradually introduced into our reasonings: similar objects are readily taken to be the same, and the conclusion becomes at last very wide of the premises.

One may safely, however, affirm that if we consider these sciences in a proper light, their advantages and disadvantages nearly compensate each other and reduce both of them to a state of equality. If the mind, with greater facility, retains the ideas of geometry clear and determinate, it must carry on a much longer and more intricate chain of reasoning and com-

1 [Entitled in Editions K and L: "Of the Idea of Power, or Necessary Connexion."]

pare ideas much wider of each other in order to reach the abstruser truths of that science. And if moral ideas are apt, without extreme care, to fall into obscurity and confusion, the inferences are always much shorter in these disquisitions, and the intermediate steps which lead to the conclusion much fewer than in the sciences which treat of quantity and number. In reality, there is scarcely a proposition in Euclid so simple as not to consist of more parts than are to be found in any moral reasoning which runs not into chimera and conceit. Where we trace the principles of the human mind through a few steps, we may be very well satisfied with our progress, considering how soon nature throws a bar to all our inquiries concerning causes and reduces us to an acknowledgment of our ignorance. The chief obstacle, therefore, to our improvement in the moral or metaphysical sciences is the obscurity of the ideas and ambiguity of the terms. The principal difficulty in the mathematics is the length of inferences and compass of thought requisite to the forming of any conclusion. And, perhaps, our progress in natural philosophy is chiefly retarded by the want of proper experiments and phenomena, which are often discovered by chance and cannot always be found when requisite, even by the most diligent and prudent inquiry. As moral philosophy seems hitherto to have received less improvement than either geometry or physics, we may conclude that if there be any difference in this respect among these sciences, the difficulties which obstruct the progress of the former require superior care and capacity to be surmounted.

There are no ideas which occur in metaphysics more obscure and uncertain than those of "power," "force," "energy," or "necessary connection," of which it is every moment necessary for us to treat in all our disquisitions. We shall, therefore, endeavor in this Section to fix, if possible, the precise meaning of these terms and thereby remove some part of that obscurity which is so much complained of in this species of philosophy.

It seems a proposition which will not admit of much dispute that all our ideas are nothing but copies of our impressions, or, in other words, that it is impossible for us to *think* of anything which we have not antecedently *felt,* either by our external or internal senses. I have endeavored [2] to explain and prove this proposition, and have expressed my hopes that by a proper application of it men may reach a greater clearness and precision in philosophical reasonings than what they have hitherto been able to attain. Complex ideas may, perhaps, be well known by definition, which is nothing but an enumeration of those parts or simple ideas that compose them. But when we have pushed up definitions to the most simple ideas and find still some ambiguity and obscurity, what resources are we then possessed of? By what invention can we throw light upon these ideas and render them altogether precise and determinate to our intellectual view? Produce the impressions or original sentiments from which the ideas are copied. These impressions are all strong and sensible. They admit not of ambiguity. They are not only placed in a full light themselves, but may throw light on their correspondent ideas, which lie in obscurity. And by this means we may perhaps obtain a new microscope or species of optics by which, in the moral sciences, the most minute and most simple ideas may be so enlarged as to fall readily under our apprehension and be equally known with the grossest and most sensible ideas that can be the object of our inquiry.

To be fully acquainted, therefore, with the idea of power or necessary connection, let us examine its impression and, in order to find the impression with greater certainty, let us search for it in all the sources from which it may possibly be derived.

When we look about us toward external objects and consider the operation of causes, we are never able, in a single instance, to discover any power or necessary connection, any quality which binds the effect to the cause and renders the one an infallible consequence of the other. We only find that the one does actually in fact follow the other. The impulse of

2 Section II.

one billiard ball is attended with motion in the second. This is the whole that appears to the *outward* senses. The mind feels no sentiment or *inward* impression from this succession of objects; consequently, there is not, in any single particular instance of cause and effect, anything which can suggest the idea of power or necessary connection.

From the first appearance of an object we never can conjecture what effect will result from it. But were the power or energy of any cause discoverable by the mind, we could foresee the effect, even without experience, and might, at first, pronounce with certainty concerning it by the mere dint of thought and reasoning.

In reality, there is no part of matter that does ever, by its sensible qualities, discover any power or energy, or give us ground to imagine that it could produce anything, or be followed by any other object, which we could denominate its effect. Solidity, extension, motion—these qualities are all complete in themselves and never point out any other event which may result from them. The scenes of the universe are continually shifting, and one object follows another in an uninterrupted succession; but the power or force which actuates the whole machine is entirely concealed from us and never discovers itself in any of the sensible qualities of body. We know that, in fact, heat is a constant attendant of flame; but what is the connection between them we have no room so much as to conjecture or imagine. It is impossible, therefore, that the idea of power can be derived from the contemplation of bodies in single instances of their operation, because no bodies ever discover any power which can be the original of this idea.[3]

Since, therefore, external objects as they appear to the senses give us no idea of power or necessary connection by

[3] Mr. Locke, in his chapter of Power, says that, finding from experience that there are several new productions in matter, and concluding that there must somewhere be a power capable of producing them, we arrive at last by this reasoning at the idea of power. But no reasoning can ever give us a new, original, simple idea, as this philosopher himself confesses. This, therefore, can never be the origin of that idea.

their operation in particular instances, let us see whether this idea be derived from reflection on the operations of our own minds and be copied from any internal impression. It may be said that we are every moment conscious of internal power while we feel that, by the simple command of our will, we can move the organs of our body or direct the faculties of our mind. An act of volition produces motion in our limbs or raises a new idea in our imagination. This influence of the will we know by consciousness. Hence we acquire the idea of power or energy, and are certain that we ourselves and all other intelligent beings are possessed of power.[4] This idea, then, is an idea of reflection since it arises from reflecting on the operations of our own mind and on the command which is exercised by will both over the organs of the body and faculties of the soul.[5]

We shall proceed to examine this pretension [6] and, first, with regard to the influence of volition over the organs of the body. This influence, we may observe, is a fact which, like all other natural events, can be known only by experience, and can never be foreseen from any apparent energy or power in the cause which connects it with the effect and renders the one an infallible consequence of the other. The motion of our body follows upon the command of our will. Of this we are every moment conscious. But the means by which this is effected, the energy by which the will performs so extraordinary an operation—of this we are so far from being immediately conscious that it must forever escape our most diligent inquiry.

For, *first,* is there any principle in all nature more mysterious than the union of soul with body, by which a supposed

---

4 [Editions K and L add: "The operations and mutual influence of bodies are perhaps sufficient to prove that they also are possessed of it."]

5 [Editions K to N: "of the mind."]

6 [Editions K and L read: "We shall proceed to examine this pretension, and shall endeavor to avoid, as far as we are able, all jargon and confusion in treating of such subtile and such profound subjects.

"I assert then, in the first place, that the influence of volition over the organs of the body is a fact, etc."]

spiritual substance acquires such an influence over a material one that the most refined thought is able to actuate the grossest matter? Were we empowered by a secret wish to remove mountains or control the planets in their orbit, this extensive authority would not be more extraordinary, nor more beyond our comprehension. But if, by consciousness, we perceived any power or energy in the will, we must know this power; we must know its connection with the effect; we must know the secret union of soul and body, and the nature of both these substances by which the one is able to operate in so many instances upon the other.

Secondly, we are not able to move all the organs of the body with a like authority, though we cannot assign any reason, besides experience, for so remarkable a difference between one and the other. Why has the will an influence over the tongue and fingers, not over the heart or liver? This question would never embarrass us were we conscious of a power in the former case, not in the latter. We should then perceive, independent of experience, why the authority of the will over the organs of the body is circumscribed within such particular limits. Being in that case fully acquainted with the power or force by which it operates, we should also know why its influence reaches precisely to such boundaries, and no further.

A man suddenly struck with a palsy in the leg or arm, or who had newly lost those members, frequently endeavors, at first, to move them and employ them in their usual offices. Here he is as much conscious of power to command such limbs as a man in perfect health is conscious of power to actuate any member which remains in its natural state and condition. But consciousness never deceives. Consequently, neither in the one case nor in the other are we ever conscious of any power. We learn the influence of our will from experience alone. And experience only teaches us how one event constantly follows another, without instructing us in the secret connection which binds them together and renders them inseparable.

Thirdly, we learn from anatomy that the immediate object of power in voluntary motion is not the member itself which is moved, but certain muscles and nerves and animal spirits, and, perhaps, something still more minute and more unknown, through which the motion is successively propagated ere it reach the member itself whose motion is the immediate object of volition. Can there be a more certain proof that the power by which this whole operation is performed, so far from being directly and fully known by an inward sentiment or consciousness, is to the last degree mysterious and unintelligible? Here the mind wills a certain event; immediately another event, unknown to ourselves and totally different from the one intended, is produced. This event produces another, equally unknown, till, at last, through a long succession the desired event is produced. But if the original power were felt, it must be known; were it known, its effect must also be known, since all power is relative to its effect. And, *vice versa,* if the effect be not known, the power cannot be known nor felt. How indeed can we be conscious of a power to move our limbs when we have no such power, but only that to move certain animal spirits which, though they produce at last the motion of our limbs, yet operate in such a manner as is wholly beyond our comprehension?

We may therefore conclude from the whole, I hope, without any temerity, though with assurance, that our idea of power is not copied from any sentiment or consciousness of power within ourselves when we give rise to animal motion or apply our limbs to their proper use and office. That their motion follows the command of the will is a matter of common experience, like other natural events; but the power or energy by which this is effected, like that in other natural events, is unknown and inconceivable.[7]

---

[7] It may be pretended, that the resistance which we meet with in bodies, obliging us frequently to exert our force and call up all our power, this gives us the idea of force and power. It is this *nisus* or strong endeavor of which we are conscious, that is the original impression from which this idea is copied. But, *first,* we attribute power to a vast number of objects where we never can suppose this resistance or exertion of force to take place: to the Supreme Being, who never meets with any

OF THE IDEA OF NECESSARY CONNECTION   79

Shall we then assert that we are conscious of a power or energy in our own minds when, by an act or command of our will, we raise up a new idea, fix the mind to the contemplation of it, turn it on all sides, and at last dismiss it for some other idea when we think that we have surveyed it with sufficient accuracy? I believe the same arguments will prove that even this command of the will gives us no real idea of force or energy.

First, it must be allowed that when we know a power, we know that very circumstance in the cause by which it is enabled to produce the effect, for these are supposed to be synonymous. We must, therefore, know both the cause and effect and the relation between them. But do we pretend to be acquainted with the nature of the human soul and the nature of an idea, or the aptitude of the one to produce the other? This is a real creation, a production of something out of nothing, which implies a power so great that it may seem, at first sight, beyond the reach of any being less than infinite. At least it must be owned that such a power is not felt, nor known, nor even conceivable by the mind. We only feel the event, namely, the existence of an idea consequent to a command of the will; but the manner in which this operation is performed, the power by which it is produced, is entirely beyond our comprehension.

Secondly, the command of the mind over itself is limited, as well as its command over the body; and these limits are not known by reason or any acquaintance with the nature of cause and effect, but only by experience and observation, as in all other natural events and in the operation of external

---

resistance; to the mind in its command over its ideas and limbs, in common thinking and motion, where the effect follows immediately upon the will, without any exertion or summoning up of force; to inanimate matter, which is not capable of this sentiment. *Secondly,* this sentiment of an endeavor to overcome resistance has no known connection with any event: What follows it we know by experience, but could not know it *a priori.* It must, however, be confessed that the animal *nisus* which we experience, though it can afford no accurate precise idea of power, enters very much into that vulgar, inaccurate idea which is formed of it.*

* The last sentence is not in Editions K and L.

objects. Our authority over our sentiments and passions is much weaker than that over our ideas; and even the latter authority is circumscribed within very narrow boundaries. Will anyone pretend to assign the ultimate reason of these boundaries, or show why the power is deficient in one case, not in another?

Thirdly, this self-command is very different at different times. A man in health possesses more of it than one languishing with sickness. We are more master of our thoughts in the morning than in the evening; fasting, than after a full meal. Can we give any reason for these variations except experience? Where then is the power of which we pretend to be conscious? Is there not here, either in a spiritual or material substance, or both, some secret mechanism or structure of parts upon which the effect depends, and which, being entirely unknown to us, renders the power or energy of the will equally unknown and incomprehensible?

Volition is surely an act of the mind with which we are sufficiently acquainted. Reflect upon it. Consider it on all sides. Do you find anything in it like this creative power by which it raises from nothing a new idea and, with a kind of *fiat,* imitates the omnipotence of its Maker, if I may be allowed so to speak, who called forth into existence all the various scenes of nature? So far from being conscious of this energy in the will, it requires as certain experience as that of which we are possessed to convince us that such extraordinary effects do ever result from a simple act of volition.

The generality of mankind never find any difficulty in accounting for the more common and familiar operations of nature, such as the descent of heavy bodies, the growth of plants, the generation of animals, or the nourishment of bodies by food; but suppose that in all these cases they perceive the very force or energy of the cause by which it is connected with its effect, and is forever infallible in its operation. They acquire, by long habit, such a turn of mind that upon the appearance of the cause they immediately expect, with assurance, its usual attendant, and hardly conceive it possible that any other event could result from it. It is only

OF THE IDEA OF NECESSARY CONNECTION   81

on the discovery of extraordinary phenomena, such as earth-
quakes, pestilence, and prodigies of any kind, that they find
themselves at a loss to assign a proper cause and to explain
the manner in which the effect is produced by it. It is usual
for men, in such difficulties, to have recourse to some invisible
intelligent principle [8] as the immediate cause of that event
which surprises them, and which they think cannot be accounted for from the common powers of nature. But philosophers, who carry their scrutiny a little further, immediately
perceive that, even in the most familiar events, the energy of
the cause is as unintelligible as in the most unusual, and that
we only learn by experience the frequent conjunction of objects, without being ever able to comprehend anything like
connection between them. Here, then, many philosophers
think themselves obliged by reason to have recourse, on all
occasions, to the same principle which the vulgar never appeal
to but in cases that appear miraculous and supernatural. They
acknowledge mind and intelligence to be, not only the ultimate and original cause of all things, but the immediate and
sole cause of every event which appears in nature. They pretend that those objects which are commonly denominated
"causes" are in reality nothing but "occasions," and that the
true and direct principle of every effect is not any power or
force in nature, but a volition of the Supreme Being, who
wills that such particular objects should forever be conjoined
with each other. Instead of saying that one billiard ball moves
another by a force which it has derived from the author of
nature, it is the Deity himself, they say, who, by a particular
volition, moves the second ball, being determined to this
operation by the impulse of the first ball, in consequence of
those general laws which he has laid down to himself in the
government of the universe. But philosophers, advancing still
in their inquiries, discover that as we are totally ignorant of
the power on which depends the mutual operation of bodies,
we are no less ignorant of that power on which depends the

---

[8] Θεὸς ἀπὸ μηχανῆς. [Edition K reads: "*Quasi deus ex machina.*"
Edition L adds the reference: "Cicero *de Natura deorum.*"]

operation of mind on body, or of body on mind; nor are we able, either from our senses or consciousness, to assign the ultimate principle in the one case more than in the other. The same ignorance, therefore, reduces them to the same conclusion. They assert that the Deity is the immediate cause of the union between soul and body, and that they are not the organs of sense which, being agitated by external objects, produce sensations in the mind; but that it is a particular volition of our omnipotent Maker which excites such a sensation in consequence of such a motion in the organ. In like manner, it is not any energy in the will that produces local motion in our members: It is God himself, who is pleased to second our will, in itself impotent, and to command that motion which we erroneously attribute to our own power and efficacy. Nor do philosophers stop at this conclusion. They sometimes extend the same inference to the mind itself in its internal operations. Our mental vision or conception of ideas is nothing but a revelation made to us by our Maker. When we voluntarily turn our thoughts to any object and raise up its image in the fancy, it is not the will which creates that idea, it is the universal Creator who discovers it to the mind and renders it present to us.[9]

Thus, according to these philosophers, everything is full of God. Not content with the principle that nothing exists but by his will, that nothing possesses any power but by his concession, they rob nature and all created beings of every power in order to render their dependence on the Deity still more sensible and immediate. They consider not that by this theory they diminish, instead of magnifying, the grandeur of those attributes which they affect so much to celebrate. It argues, surely, more power in the Deity to delegate a certain degree of power to inferior creatures than to produce everything by his own immediate volition. It argues more wisdom to contrive at first the fabric of the world with such perfect foresight that of itself, and by its proper operation, it may

[9] [Hume refers here to the French philosopher, Nicolas de Malebranche (1638-1715), and his major work, *De la Recherche de la vérité* (1674).— Ed.]

serve all the purposes of Providence than if the great Creator were obliged every moment to adjust its parts and animate by his breath all the wheels of that stupendous machine.

But if we would have a more philosophical confutation of this theory, perhaps the two following reflections may suffice:

First, it seems to me that this theory of the universal energy and operation of the Supreme Being is too bold ever to carry conviction with it to a man sufficiently apprised of the weakness of human reason and the narrow limits to which it is confined in all its operations. Though the chain of arguments which conduct to it were ever so logical, there must arise a strong suspicion, if not an absolute assurance, that it has carried us quite beyond the reach of our faculties when it leads to conclusions so extraordinary and so remote from common life and experience. We are got into fairyland long ere we have reached the last steps of our theory; and *there* we have no reason to trust our common methods of argument or to think that our usual analogies and probabilities have any authority. Our line is too short to fathom such immense abysses. And however we may flatter ourselves that we are guided, in every step which we take, by a kind of verisimilitude and experience, we may be assured that this fancied experience has no authority when we thus apply it to subjects that lie entirely out of the sphere of experience. But on this we shall have occasion to touch afterwards.[10]

Secondly, I cannot perceive any force in the arguments on which this theory is founded. We are ignorant, it is true, of the manner in which bodies operate on each other. Their force or energy is entirely incomprehensible. But are we not equally ignorant of the manner or force by which a mind, even the Supreme Mind, operates, either on itself or on body? Whence, I beseech you, do we acquire any idea of it? We have no sentiment or consciousness of this power in ourselves. We have no idea of the Supreme Being but what we learn from reflection on our own faculties. Were our ignorance, therefore, a good reason for rejecting anything, we should be

[10] Section XII.

led into that principle of denying all energy in the Supreme Being, as much as in the grossest matter. We surely comprehend as little the operations of the one as of the other. Is it more difficult to conceive that motion may arise from impulse than that it may arise from volition? All we know is our profound ignorance in both cases.[11]

PART II

But to hasten to a conclusion of this argument, which is already drawn out to too great a length: We have sought in vain for an idea of power or necessary connection in all the sources from which we would suppose it to be derived. It appears that in single instances of the operation of bodies we never can, by our utmost scrutiny, discover anything but one event following another, without being able to comprehend

11 I need not examine at length the *vis inertiae* which is so much talked of in the new philosophy, and which is ascribed to matter. We find by experience that a body at rest or in motion continues forever in its present state, till put from it by some new cause; and that a body impelled takes as much motion from the impelling body as it acquires itself. These are facts. When we call this a *vis inertiae,* we only mark these facts, without pretending to have any idea of the inert power, in the same manner as, when we talk of gravity, we mean certain effects without comprehending that active power.* It was never the meaning of Sir Isaac Newton to rob second causes of all force or energy, though some of his followers have endeavored to establish that theory upon his authority. On the contrary, that great philosopher had recourse to an ethereal active fluid to explain his universal attraction, though he was so cautious and modest as to allow that it was a mere hypothesis not to be insisted on without more experiments. I must confess that there is something in the fate of opinions a little extraordinary. Descartes insinuated that doctrine of the universal and sole efficacy of the Deity, without insisting on it. Malebranche and other Cartesians made it the foundation of all their philosophy. It had, however, no authority in England. Locke, Clarke, and Cudworth never so much as take notice of it, but suppose all along that matter has a real, though subordinate and derived, power. By what means has it become so prevalent among our modern metaphysicians?

* Editions K and L: "matter."

any force or power by which the cause operates or any connection between it and its supposed effect. The same difficulty occurs in contemplating the operations of mind on body, where we observe the motion of the latter to follow upon the volition of the former, but are not able to observe or conceive the tie which binds together the motion and volition, or the energy, by which the mind produces this effect. The authority of the will over its own faculties and ideas is not a whit more comprehensible, so that, upon the whole, there appears not, throughout all nature, any one instance of connection which is conceivable by us. All events seem entirely loose and separate. One event follows another, but we never can observe any tie between them. They seem *conjoined,* but never *connected.* But as we can have no idea of anything which never appeared to our outward sense or inward sentiment, the necessary conclusion *seems* to be that we have no idea of connection or power at all, and that these words are absolutely without any meaning when employed either in philosophical reasonings or common life.

But there still remains one method of avoiding this conclusion, and one source which we have not yet examined. When any natural object or event is presented, it is impossible for us, by any sagacity or penetration, to discover, or even conjecture, without experience, what event will result from it, or to carry our foresight beyond that object which is immediately present to the memory and senses. Even after one instance or experiment where we have observed a particular event to follow upon another, we are not entitled to form a general rule or foretell what will happen in like cases, it being justly esteemed an unpardonable temerity to judge of the whole course of nature from one single experiment, however accurate or certain. But when one particular species of events has always, in all instances, been conjoined with another, we make no longer any scruple of foretelling one upon the appearance of the other, and of employing that reasoning which can alone assure us of any matter of fact or existence. We then call the one object "cause," the other "effect." We suppose that there is some connection between them, some power in the one by which it infallibly produces the other and operates with the greatest certainty and strongest necessity.

It appears, then, that this idea of a necessary connection among events arises from a number of similar instances which occur, of the constant conjunction of these events; nor can that idea ever be suggested by any one of these instances surveyed in all possible lights and positions. But there is nothing in a number of instances, different from every single instance, which is supposed to be exactly similar, except only that after a repetition of similar instances the mind is carried by habit, upon the appearance of one event, to expect its usual attendant and to believe that it will exist. This connection, therefore, which we *feel* in the mind, this customary transition of the imagination from one object to its usual attendant, is the sentiment or impression from which we form the idea of power or necessary connection. Nothing further is in the case. Contemplate the subjects on all sides, you will never find any other origin of that idea. This is the sole difference between one instance, from which we can never receive the idea of connection, and a number of similar instances by which it is suggested. The first time a man saw the communication of motion by impulse, as by the shock of two billiard balls, he could not pronounce that the one event was *connected,* but only that it was *conjoined* with the other. After he has observed several instances of this nature, he then pronounces them to be *connected.* What alteration has happened to give rise to this new idea of *connection?* Nothing but that he now *feels* these events to be *connected* in his imagination, and can readily foretell the existence of one from the appearance of the other. When we say, therefore, that one object is connected with another, we mean only that they have acquired a connection in our thought and gave rise to this inference by which they become proofs of each other's existence—a conclusion which is somewhat extraordinary, but which seems founded on sufficient evidence. Nor will its evidence be weakened by any general diffidence of the understanding or skeptical suspicion concerning every conclusion which is new and extraordinary. No conclusions can be more agreeable to skepticism than such as make discoveries concerning the weakness and narrow limits of human reason and capacity.

And what stronger instance can be produced of the surprising ignorance and weakness of the understanding than the present? For surely, if there be any relation among objects which it imports us to know perfectly, it is that of cause and effect. On this are founded all our reasonings concerning matter of fact or existence. By means of it alone we attain any assurance concerning objects which are removed from the present testimony of our memory and senses. The only immediate utility of all sciences is to teach us how to control and regulate future events by their causes. Our thoughts and inquiries are, therefore, every moment employed about this relation; yet so imperfect are the ideas which we form concerning it that it is impossible to give any just definition of cause, except what is drawn from something extraneous and foreign to it. Similar objects are always conjoined with similar. Of this we have experience. Suitably to this experience, therefore, we may define a cause to be *an object followed by another, and where all the objects, similar to the first, are followed by objects similar to the second.* Or, in other words, *where, if the first object had not been, the second never had existed.* The appearance of a cause always conveys the mind, by a customary transition, to the idea of the effect. Of this also we have experience. We may, therefore, suitably to this experience, form another definition of cause and call it *an object followed by another, and whose appearance always conveys the thought to that other.* But though both these definitions be drawn from circumstances foreign to the cause, we cannot remedy this inconvenience or attain any more perfect definition which may point out that circumstance in the cause which gives it a connection with its effect. We have no idea of this connection, nor even any distinct notion what it is we desire to know when we endeavor at a conception of it. We say, for instance, that the vibration of this string is the cause of this particular sound. But what do we mean by that affirmation? We either mean *that this vibration is followed*

*by this sound, and that all similar vibrations have been
followed by similar sounds; or, that this vibration is followed
by this sound, and that, upon the appearance of one, the mind
anticipates the senses and forms immediately an idea of the
other.* We may consider the relation of cause and effect in
either of these two lights; but beyond these we have no idea
of it.[1]

To recapitulate, therefore, the reasonings of this Section:

[1] According to these explications and definitions, the idea of *power*
is relative as much as that of *cause*; and both have a reference to an effect, or some other event constantly conjoined with the former. When
we consider the *unknown* circumstance of an object by which the degree
or quantity of its effect is fixed and determined, we call that its power.
And accordingly, it is allowed by all philosophers that the effect is the
measure of the power. But if they had any idea of power as it is in itself, why could they not measure it in itself? The dispute, whether the
force of a body in motion be as its velocity, or the square of its velocity;
this dispute, I say, needed not be decided by comparing its effects in
equal or unequal times, but by a direct mensuration and comparison.*

As to the frequent use of the words "force," "power," "energy," etc.,
which everywhere occur in common conversation as well as in philosophy, that is no proof that we are acquainted, in any instance, with the
connecting principle between cause and effect, or can account ultimately
for the production of one thing by another. These words, as commonly
used, have very loose meanings annexed to them, and their ideas are very
uncertain and confused. No animal can put external bodies in motion
without the sentiment of a *nisus* or endeavor; and every animal has a
sentiment or feeling from the stroke or blow of an external object that is
in motion. These sensations, which are merely animal, and from which
we can *a priori* draw no inference, we are apt to transfer to inanimate
objects, and to suppose that they have some such feelings whenever they
transfer or receive motion. With regard to energies, which are exerted
without our annexing to them any idea of communicated motion, we
consider only the constant experienced conjunction of the events; and
as we *feel* a customary connection between the ideas, we transfer that
feeling to the objects, as nothing is more usual than to apply to external
bodies every internal sensation which they occasion.†

* This note was first introduced in Edition L.
† Instead of this concluding passage there stood in Edition L: "A
cause is different from a *sign*, as it implies precedence and contiguity in
time and place, as well as constant conjunction. A *sign* is nothing but
a correlative effect from the same cause."

Every idea is copied from some preceding impression or sentiment; and where we cannot find any impression, we may be certain that there is no idea. In all single instances of the operation of bodies or minds there is nothing that produces any impression, nor consequently can suggest any idea, of power or necessary connection. But when many uniform instances appear, and the same object is always followed by the same event, we then begin to entertain the notion of cause and connection. We then *feel* a new sentiment or impression, to wit, a customary connection in the thought or imagination between one object and its usual attendant; and this sentiment is the original of that idea which we seek for. For as this idea arises from a number of similar instances, and not from any single instance, it must arise from that circumstance in which the number of instances differ from every individual instance. But this customary connection or transition of the imagination is the only circumstance in which they differ. In every other particular they are alike. The first instance which we saw of motion, communicated by the shock of two billiard balls (to return to this obvious illustration), is exactly similar to any instance that may at present occur to us, except only that we could not at first *infer* one event from the other, which we are enabled to do at present, after so long a course of uniform experience. I know not whether the reader will readily apprehend this reasoning. I am afraid that, should I multiply words about it or throw it into a greater variety of lights, it would only become more obscure and intricate. In all abstract reasonings there is one point of view which, if we can happily hit, we shall go further toward illustrating the subject than by all the eloquence and copious expression in the world. This point of view we should endeavor to reach, and reserve the flowers of rhetoric for subjects which are more adapted to them.

Causality:
Critique of Hume's Analysis

C. J. Ducasse

Reprinted with permission of the publisher from C. J. Ducasse, *Nature, Mind and Death* (La Salle, Ill.: Open Court Publishing Co., 1951), chap. 7, pp. 91–100.

Chapter 7

CAUSALITY: CRITIQUE OF HUME'S ANALYSIS

The notion of causality will play an essential part at many places in the remaining chapters of this book; but a variety of opinions are current today as to the nature and the role of the causal relation. One finds accounts of what science now means by causal connection, but also statements that the notion of cause is not employed in science at its maturity, but only appears at the crude, early stages of its development. Again, many philosophers are dissatisfied with Hume's analysis of causality, upon which Mill's failed to improve. Yet, in default of some definite and more acceptable positive analysis, Hume's probably remains still the most influential. Inasmuch as the analysis of causality I shall offer in the next chapter diverges sharply from Hume's, I shall now first set forth the reasons I see for rejecting his account.

1. Hume's Skepticism

Hume's famous skepticism is not, like that of some of the ancients, a doctrine he propounds, but rather the acknowledgment by him of "a malady, which can never be radically cur'd, but must return upon us every moment, however we may chace it away, and sometimes may seem entirely free from it."[1] This malady, as Hume observes it in himself, consists in the fact that although reflection shows certain ones and certain others of our beliefs to be mutually incompatible, yet we cannot give up either the ones or

---

[1] Hume, *A Treatise of Human Nature,* Selby-Bigge ed., p. 218.

the others.   The self-stultification which is noticeable at so many points in Hume's writings, and which so baffles the reader who would extract from them a consistent doctrine, is rooted in that malady.   Again and again, especially in the *Treatise,* Hume disregards at one place conclusions he had reached earlier, and he could not without doing so proceed to say what he next wants to say.   The *Treatise,* I believe, is thus to be regarded not as an attempt to set forth one consistent doctrine, but much rather only as an account of the philosophical sights to be seen from the road one travels under the guidance of certain principles which Hume accepts from the outset—one of the chief of these being that nothing exists or is known to us except "perceptions."   Hume simply follows these principles remorselessly wherever they seem to him to lead; and when the conclusions to which they bring him are mutually incompatible or incompatible with firm natural beliefs, he just admits the fact as he would admit having gout or a cold in the head and similarly calls it a malady.   His great service to philosophy thus is not that he solved, but much rather that he raised, important philosophical problems.   There is perhaps no philosophical book more intellectually irritating—nor therefore more thought-provoking—than his *Treatise.*   This is true in particular of what he has to say in it concerning causation.

2. Hume's Analysis of Causality

Hume's "official" view on this subject may perhaps be summarized as follows: To be is to be perceived. No connection is ever perceived between a cause and its effect. Therefore there is none. An "object" of kind A is called the cause of one of kind B if, in our experience, objects of kind A have always been followed each by an object of kind B. But such following of one object upon a certain other is not "necessary." In logic and mathematics, that is necessary the contradictory of which is self-contradictory. But no self-contradiction is ever involved in supposing an object we

CAUSALITY: HUME'S ANALYSIS   93

call a cause to exist without its effect following, or one we call an effect to exist without having been preceded by one such as we call its cause. Where objects are concerned, "necessity" is the name not of a relation among them, but only of the felt "propensity, which custom produces, to pass from an object to the idea of its usual attendant." Necessity, then, is "but an internal impression of the mind"; it is a relation between certain ideas, something "that exists in the mind, not in objects." Hume accordingly offers two definitions of cause. According to one, formulated in purely objective terms, "we may define a cause to be *an object, followed by another, and where all the objects similar to the first are followed by objects similar to the second."* According to the other we may say, in subjective terms, that a cause is *"an object followed by another, and whose appearance always conveys the thought to that other."*[2] The first of these is the basic one, since unless we had experience of causation as there described, the "conveying of the thought," in terms of which the second definition is worded, would not occur.

3. Hume's Analysis Fails To Fit Some of the Facts

As stated at the outset, I believe that this account of the nature of causation—simply as succession *de facto* regular—represents an incorrect analysis of the ordinary notion of cause—of the notion, that is to say, in the light of which our ordinary judgments of causation actually are made. To make evident the incorrectness of that analysis it will be sufficient to show, on the one hand, that there are cases which conform to Hume's definition but where we judge the events concerned not to be related as cause to effect; and on the other hand, that there are cases which do not conform to Hume's definition but which we nevertheless judge to be cases of causation.

As to the first, if a man were so situated as always to have heard

---

[2] Hume, *An Enquiry Concerning Human Understanding.* Open Court ed., p. 79.

two clocks striking the hours, one of which always struck immediately before the other, he would according to Hume's definition
of cause have to say that the strokes of the first cause the strokes
of the second; whereas in fact they do not. Of course, the relation he observes between the strokes of the two clocks is the effect
of a common remote cause of the strokes of the two clocks. But
although this is true, it is irrelevant; for to say that *B* is caused by
A is one thing, and to say that both *B* and *A* are caused by *C* is
quite another thing. The example thus shows that Hume's definition of the relation of cause and effect fits some cases where the
relation between the two events concerned is in fact not that of
cause to effect but a different one.

Other examples of sequences which are regular, and yet the
terms of which are not related as cause to effect, are not hard to
find. Thomas Reid mentioned the succession of day and night;
and we may add to the list the fact, for instance, that in infants
the growth of hair is regularly followed by the growth of teeth;
or that in human beings birth regularly follows the tenth return
of the moon since conception.[3]

In connection with such cases, it should be noted that what observation of *de facto* regular succession or correlation of two
events does is not to *answer* the question whether one of the two
events causes the other, but much rather to *raise* the question as to
whether one causes the other, or whether some antecedent third
causes both, or whether the conjunction of the two is simply accidental. For although causation of *B* by *A* entails constancy of
their conjunction (*i.e.,* recurrence of *B* as often as *A* recurs), the
converse does not hold: constancy of conjunction, far from itself

---

[3] A striking instance, in the case of which the relation between the events concerned is patently neither that of cause to effect nor that of joint effects of a common cause, is quoted by Morris Cohen (*Reason and Nature,* p. 92) from an
unpublished study by George Marshall at the Brookings Institute. It is that, for a
number of years, the membership in the International Association of Machinists
shows a very high correlation (86%) with the death rate in the Indian state of
Hyderabad.

being the relation of cause to effect, is not sure evidence even of indirect or of as yet hidden causal connection between the events concerned.

To show now, on the other hand, that there are cases which do not conform to Hume's definition, but which we nevertheless judge to be cases of causation, I shall mention a simple experiment I have sometimes performed with students. I bring into the room and place on the desk a paper-covered parcel tied with string in the ordinary way, and ask the students to observe closely what occurs. Then, proceeding slowly so that observation may be easy, I put my hand on the parcel. The end of the parcel the students face then at once glows. I then ask them what caused it to glow at that moment, and they naturally answer that the glowing was caused by what I did to the parcel immediately before.

In this case it is clear that what the spectators observed, and what they based their judgment of causation upon, was not repetition of a certain act of mine followed each time by the glow, but *one single case* of sequence of the latter upon the former. The case, that is to say, does not conform to Hume's definition of causation as constant conjunction but is nevertheless judged by unprejudiced observers to be a case of causation.

If I then further ask: What makes you think that my having done what I did caused the parcel to glow? they answer: Because nothing else happened to the parcel at the time. Thus, by the *cause* of the observed glowing they do not mean some event having repeatedly preceded it. They mean *the only change introduced into the situation immediately before the glowing occurred.*

It may be said truly, of course, that the change they observed was perhaps not the only change which actually occurred in that situation, and that their judgment as to the cause of the observed glowing was thus perhaps mistaken. To urge this, however, is to question not their conception of the meaning of "causation," but their claim that what they observed was a true case of what they meant and still mean by that word. For what indicates what they meant when they called what I did the cause of the observed glowing is not whether what I did *really* was the only change that occurred in the situation immediately before, but whether they *believed* it to have been the only change. So long as they do believe it to have been the only change, they continue to describe it as having been the cause of that glowing—even if a glowing should never again occur on repetition of my act.

4. Hume on Ascertainment of Causation by a Single Experiment

In this connection, it is interesting to note that Hume himself asserts that "we may attain the knowledge of a particular cause merely by one experiment, provided it be made with judgment, and after a careful removal of all foreign and superfluous circumstances." But how a *single* experiment, in which a case of B was observed to have followed a case of A, can assure us that *every* case of A is followed by a case of B is anything but obvious. One would expect, rather, that, once causation has been defined merely as *de facto* constant conjunction, the only way to observe its presence or absence would be to observe *many* cases of A and note whether or not a case of B follows constantly, *i.e.*, each time.

Hume perceives this difficulty, or rather the difficulty corresponding to it when his second definition of causation is the one considered—the difficulty, namely, how the customary expectation of B upon the occurrence of A, which he has stated before is the result of having *repeatedly* observed B following after A, can be present when the sequence, A,B has been observed not repeatedly but only once. He attempts to meet this difficulty by saying that even then we have had millions of experiments "to convince us of this principle, *that like objects placed in like circumstances, will always produce like effects*," and that this principle then "bestows an evidence and firmness on any opinion, to which it can be applied."[4]

By itself, however, this principle would support equally the generalizing of *any* sequence observed—of one which is accidental as well as of one which turns out to be causal. The possibility of its being useful therefore rests on the stipulated preliminary "careful removal of all foreign and superfluous circumstances." But the principle does not tell us how to discover by one experiment which these are; for obviously the "foreign and superfluous circumstances" are those which are not the cause, *i.e.,* on his view, those which are not *constantly* followed by *B*. Preliminary removal of the circumstances which are "foreign and superfluous" therefore amounts to preliminary discovery of the circumstance which *is* the cause! Thus, the principle is good not for discovering the cause in a single experiment, but *only for generalizing it* if we have already managed somehow to discover it by a single experiment. If, however, causation can be ascertained by a single experiment, then causation does not consist in constancy of conjunction even if it entails such constancy.

5. Hume's "Rules by Which To Judge of Causes and Effects"

Hume appears to have been obscurely conscious of this. For one thing, he introduces the two definitions of cause quoted above by the remark: "So imperfect are the ideas which we form concerning [the relation of cause and effect] that it is impossible to give any just definition of cause, except what is drawn from something extraneous and foreign to it." And, after the second definition, he repeats that both definitions are "drawn from circumstances foreign to the cause." Again, in his "Rules by which to judge of causes and effects," which are rules for discovering a cause by a single experiment and therefore, as pointed out above, really concern causation in a sense other than that of empirically

---

[4] Hume, *Treatise*, pp. 104–5.

98   FUNDAMENTAL CATEGORIES

constant conjunction, Hume at first refers to causation as "that
constant conjunction, on which the relation of cause and effect
totally depends"; but in the third rule, he no longer says "totally"
but instead "chiefly"; and in the fourth rule he describes "constant repetition" only as that "from which the *first* idea of [the
causal relation] is derived."[5]

Of the rules given by Hume for discovering a cause by a single
experiment, the fifth, sixth, and seventh are the clearest statements not only up to Hume's time, but until the appearance of
Herschel's *Discourse* nearly a hundred years later, of what Mill
afterwards called the experimental methods of Agreement, Difference, and Concomitant Variations. Hume's fourth, fifth, and
sixth rules, which are the most important theoretically, are as follows:

4. The same cause always produces the same effect, and
the same effect never arises but from the same cause. This
principle we derive from experience, and is the source of
most of our philosophical reasonings. For when by any clear
experiment we have discovered the causes or effects of any
phenomenon, we immediately extend our observation to every
phenomenon of the same kind, without waiting for that constant repetition, from which the first idea of this relation is
derived.

5. There is another principle, which hangs upon this, *viz.*
that where several different objects produce the same effect,
it must be by means of some quality, which we discover to be
common amongst them. For as like effects imply like causes,
we must always ascribe the causation to the circumstance,
wherein we discover the resemblance.

6. . . . The difference in the effects of two resembling
objects must proceed from that particular, in which they
differ. For as like causes always produce like effects, when
in any instance we find our expectation to be disappointed,
we must conclude that this irregularity proceeds from some
difference in the causes.

---
[5] Hume, *Treatise,* pp. 173 ff. (Italics mine.)

CAUSALITY: HUME'S ANALYSIS   99

It will be noticed that in the fourth rule the principle mentioned earlier (same cause, same effect) is supplemented by its converse (same effect, same cause), but is now presented explicitly as a principle not for discovering causal relations but only for generalizing them once we have managed to discover them somehow in a single case by a "clear experiment." But the fifth and sixth rules might be thought to give us just what we need for such discovery, *viz.*, the criteria by which to decide which circumstances are "foreign and superfluous" to the cause.

Scrutiny of them, however, reveals that they do not do this, for they are presented by Hume as corollaries of the principle mentioned in the fourth rule (*viz.*, same cause, same effect; same effect, same cause), and this principle is not as he there asserts derived from experience, nor is it derivable from it. As he himself has shown earlier with admirable clearness,[6] neither reason nor experience gives us anything which would warrant us in assuming (as the principle in his fourth rule does assume and has to assume if the fifth and sixth rules are to be corollaries of it) that those instances, of which we have had as yet no experience, resemble those of which we have had experience. A principle, which experience might conceivably have yielded, would be that like antecedents placed in like circumstances *have always been observed to have had* like sequents, and that like sequents have always been observed to have had like antecedents. But this principle not only does not yield his fifth and sixth rules as corollaries, but indeed is itself *invalidated by every situation to which Hume would apply these two rules.* For (to quote from rule 5) "where several different objects produce the same effect" what obviously follows is that, as a strict matter of experience, an *exception* to the principle "same effect, same cause" is then confronting us and the principle is thereby invalidated. Just this is what follows, and not, as Hume asserts, that these different objects must have some hidden

---

[6] Hume, *Treatise,* pp. 87 ff.

100   Fundamental Categories

common quality; for either such a common quality is itself observed, and then the objects are experienced as alike rather than,
as supposed, different; or else a common quality is not observed,
and then, to know that it exists nonetheless we should need to
know that the same effect has the same cause in all cases, future
as well as past; and, as recalled above, Hume himself has shown
that neither experience nor reason can give us this knowledge.

The Logical Character
of Scientific Laws

Ernest Nagel

Reprinted with permission of the publishers from Ernest Nagel, *The Structure of Science*, pp. 49–78. © 1961 by Harcourt Brace Jovanovich, Inc.; published in Great Britain by Routledge & Kegan Paul Ltd.

The Logical Character
of Scientific Laws

4 The requirements for adequate explanations considered thus far have been discussed with only incidental reference to the nature of the relations asserted by scientific laws or theories. It has been tacitly assumed that laws have the form of generalized conditionals, in the simplest case represented by the schema 'For any *x*, if *x* is A then *x* is B' (or alternatively by 'All A is B').[1] However, it is by no means the case that any true

[1] The assumption that this simple schema is an adequate representation of the logical form of scientific laws has been repeatedly made in previous chapters, and will frequently be made throughout the volume. However, this assumption is adopted in the main for the sake of avoiding complexities that would arise were less simple but more realistic schema recognized—complexities that are largely irrelevant to the chief points under discussion. There undoubtedly are many scientific laws which do exhibit the simple formal structure mentioned above. Nevertheless, there are also many laws whose logical form is more complicated—a fact of considerable importance in analyzing the rationale of inductive and verificatory procedures in science, though only of subsidiary interest in the present context of discussion.

One type of complexity in the formal structure of laws is illustrated by the following two examples. The content of the law that copper expands if heated is made more explicit by restating it as: 'For any *x*, if *x* is copper and *x* is heated at time *y*, then *x* expands at time *y*.' As in other conditionals (or "if-then" formulations), the clause introduced by 'if' is known as the "antecedent," and the clause introduced by 'then' as the "consequent." The present example also contains as "prefixes" the two expressions 'for every *x*' and 'for every *y*' (technically known as "universal quantifiers"), unlike the simple schema in the text, which contains only one universal quantifier. Again, the so-called "law of biogenesis" that all life comes from pre-existing life can be rendered by: 'For any *x*, there is a *y*, such that if *x* is a living organism then *y* is a parent of *x*.' In this case, the statement contains not only the universal quantifier 'for every *x*,' but also the expression 'there is a *y*' (called

statement having this form is invariably counted among the laws of nature. In any event, despite the fact that proposed explanations may conform to the requirements already mentioned, they are frequently rejected as unsatisfactory on at least two grounds: although the universal premises of an explanation may be acknowledged to be true, they are said for one reason or another not to be genuine "laws"; and, although the universal premises may be admitted to the status of scientific law, they allegedly fail to meet some further conditions, such as that of being "causal" laws.

Suppose, for example, that, in answer to the question why a certain screw s is rusty, one is told that all the screws in Smith's current car are rusty and that s is a screw in Smith's car. Such an explanation is likely to be rejected as quite unsatisfactory, on the ground that the universal premise is not even a law of nature, to say nothing of its not being a causal law. A *prima facie* distinction between "lawlike" universal statements (i.e., statements which, if true, qualify for the designation "law of nature") and universal statements that are not lawlike thus underlies the objection to the proposed explanation.

On the other hand, a proposed explanation of the fact that a given bird b is black, because all crows are black and b is a crow, is sometimes put aside as inadequate on the ground that even if the universal premise is assumed to be a law of nature it does not "really" explain why b is black. Now on one interpretation of this objection it undoubtedly confounds two different things: an explanation of the fact that b is black, as distinct from an explanation of the assumed law that all crows are black. Accordingly, a decisive rejoinder to the objection might very well be that, while the explanation does not explain why all crows are black, it does explain why b is black: for the explanation shows at the very least that the color of b's plumage is not an idiosyncrasy of b but is a trait b shares with every other bird which, like itself, is a crow. Nevertheless, the objection can also be understood as an expression of dissatisfaction with the proposed explanation of b's black plumage, on the ground that the assumed law does not give a causal account of the bird's coloring.

These examples, which illustrate a widespread if tacit acceptance of conditions for satisfactory explanations additional to those already discussed, thus invite a consideration of some of the features that sup-

---

an "existential quantifier"). This statement thus contains more than one quantifier, and these moreover of an unlike (or "mixed") kind. A large fraction of quantitative laws, especially in theoretical physics, contain several quantifiers, often of a mixed kind. However, it seems unlikely that any statement would normally be counted as a law if it did not contain at least one universal quantifier, usually as the initial prefix. It is for this reason that the simplifying assumption adopted in the text does not appear to be a fatal oversimplification.

posedly distinguish natural laws from other universal conditionals, and causal laws from noncausal ones. We must examine several far-flung issues generated by these distinctions.

I. *Accidental and Nomic Universality*

The label 'law of nature' (or similar labels such as 'scientific law,' 'natural law,' or simply 'law') is not a technical term defined in any empirical science; and it is often used, especially in common discourse, with a strong honorific intent but without a precise import. There undoubtedly are many statements that are unhesitatingly characterized as 'laws' by most members of the scientific community, just as there is an even larger class of statements to which the label is rarely if ever applied. On the other hand, scientists disagree about the eligibility of many statements for the title of 'law of nature,' and the opinion of even one individual will often fluctuate on whether a given statement is to count as a law. This is patently the case for various theoretical statements, to which reference was made in the previous chapter, which are sometimes construed to be at bottom only procedural rules and therefore neither true nor false, although viewed by others as examples par excellence of laws of nature. Divergent opinions also exist as to whether statements of regularities containing any reference to particular individuals (or groups of such individuals) deserve the label of 'law.' For example, some writers have disputed the propriety of the designation for the statement that the planets move on elliptic orbits around the sun, since the statement mentions a particular body. Similar disagreements occur over the use of the label for statements of statistical regularities; and doubts have been expressed whether any formulation of uniformities in human social behavior (e.g., those studied in economics or linguistics) can properly be called 'laws.' The term 'law of nature' is undoubtedly vague. In consequence, any explication of its meaning which proposes a sharp demarcation between lawlike and non-lawlike statements is bound to be arbitrary.

There is therefore more than an appearance of futility in the recurring attempts to define with great logical precision what is a law of nature—attempts often based on the tacit premise that a statement is a law in virtue of its possessing an inherent "essence" which the definition must articulate. For not only is the term 'law' vague in its current usage, but its historical meaning has undergone many changes. We are certainly free to designate as a law of nature any statement we please. There is often little consistency in the way we apply the label, and whether or not a statement is *called* a law makes little difference in the way in which the statement may be used in scientific inquiry. Nevertheless, members of the scientific community agree fairly well on the applicability of the term for a considerable though vaguely delimited class of universal statements. Accordingly, there is some basis for the conjecture that the predication of the label, at least in those cases where the consensus is unmistakable, is controlled by a felt difference in the "objective" status and function of that class of statements. It would indeed be futile to attempt an ironclad and rigorously exclusive definition of 'natural law.' It is not unreasonable to indicate some of the more prominent grounds upon which a numerous class of statements is commonly assigned a special status.

The *prima facie* difference between lawlike and non-lawlike universal conditionals can be brought out in several ways. One effective way depends on first recalling in what manner modern formal logic construes statements that have the form of universal conditionals. Two points must be noted in this connection. Such statements are interpreted in modern logic to assert merely this: any individual fulfilling the conditions described in the antecedent clause of the conditional also fulfills, *as a matter of contingent fact,* the conditions described in the consequent clause. For example, in this interpretation the statement 'All crows are black' (which is usually transcribed to read 'For any x, if x is a crow then x is black') merely says that any individual thing which happens to exist whether in the past, present, or future and which satisfies the conditions for being a crow is in point of fact also black. Accordingly, the sense assigned to the statement by this interpretation is also conveyed by the equivalent assertions that there never was a crow that was not black, there is no such crow at present, and there never will be such a crow. Universal conditionals construed in this way, so that they assert only matter-of-fact connections, are sometimes said to formulate only a "constant conjunction" of traits and to express "accidental" or *de facto* universality.

The second point to be noted in this interpretation is an immediate consequence of the first. On this interpretation a universal conditional is true, provided that there are no things (in the omnitemporal sense of 'are') which satisfy the conditions stated in the antecedent clause. Thus, if there are no unicorns, then all unicorns are black; but also, if there are no unicorns, then all unicorns are red.[2] Accordingly, on the construc-

---

[2] This will be evident from the following: If there is no x such that x is a unicorn, then clearly there is no x such that x is a unicorn that is not black. But on the standard interpretation of the universal conditional, this latter statement immediately yields the conclusion that for any x, if x is a unicorn then x is black. Accordingly, if there are no unicorns then all unicorns are black.

It can also be shown that a universal conditional is true no matter what its antecedent clause may be, provided that everything of which the consequent clause can be significantly predicated satisfies the consequent clause. But we shall ignore any difficulties generated by this feature of universal conditionals.

tion placed upon it in formal logic, a *de facto* universal conditional is true, irrespective of the content of its consequent clause, if in point of fact there happens to be nothing which satisfies its antecedent clause. Such a universal conditional is said to be "vacuously" true (or "vacuously satisfied").

Does a law of nature assert no more than accidental universality? The answer commonly given is in the negative. For a law is often held to express a "stronger" connection between antecedent and consequent conditions than just a matter-of-fact concomitance. Indeed, the connection is frequently said to involve some element of "necessity," though this alleged necessity is variously conceived and is described by such qualifying adjectives as 'logical,' 'causal,' 'physical,' or 'real.'[3] The contention is that to say that 'Copper always expands on heating' is a law of nature is to claim more than that there never has been and never will be a piece of heated copper that does not expand. To claim for that statement the status of a law is to assert, for example, not merely that there does not happen to exist such a piece of copper, but that it is "physically impossible" for such a piece of copper to exist. When the statement is assumed to be a law of nature, it is thus construed to assert that heating any piece of copper "physically necessitates" its expansion. Universal conditionals understood in this way are frequently described as "universals of law" or "nomological universals," and as expressing a "nomic" universality.

The distinction between accidental and nomic universality can be brought out in another way. Suppose that a piece of copper *c* which has never been heated is called to our attention, and is then destroyed so that it will never be heated. Suppose, further, that after the work of destruction is over we are asked whether *c* would have expanded had it been heated, and that we reply in the affirmative. And suppose, finally, that we are pressed for a reason for this answer. What reason can be advanced? A reason that would generally be accepted as cogent is that the natural law 'All copper when heated expands' warrants the contrary-to-fact conditional 'If *c* had been heated, it would have expanded.' Indeed, most people are likely to go further, and maintain that the nomological universal warrants the subjunctive conditional 'For any *x*, if *x* were copper and were heated, then *x* would expand.'

Laws of nature are in fact commonly used to justify subjunctive and contrary-to-fact conditionals, and such use is characteristic of all nomological universals. Moreover, this function of universals of law also suggests that the mere fact that nothing happens to exist (in the omnitem-

[3] Cf. A. C. Ewing, *Idealism*, London, 1934, p. 167; C. I. Lewis, *An Analysis of Knowledge and Valuation*, La Salle, Ill., 1946, p. 228; Arthur W. Burks, "The Logic of Causal Propositions," *Mind*, Vol. 60 (1951), pp. 363-82.

poral sense) which satisfies the antecedent clause of a nomological conditional is not sufficient to establish its truth. Thus, the assumption that the universe contains no bodies which are under the action of no external forces suffices to establish neither the subjunctive conditional that if there were such bodies their velocities would remain constant, nor the nomological universal that every body which is under the action of no external forces does not maintain a constant velocity.

On the other hand, the patently accidental universal 'All the screws in Smith's current car are rusty' does not justify the subjunctive conditional 'For any x, if x were a screw in Smith's current car x would be rusty.' [4] Certainly no one is likely to maintain on the strength of this *de facto* universal that, if a particular brass screw now resting on a dealer's shelf were inserted into Smith's car, that screw would be rusty. This *prima facie* difference between accidental and nomic universality can be briefly summarized by the formula: A universal of law "supports" a subjunctive conditional, while an accidental universal does not.

II.   *Are Laws Logically Necessary?*

No one seriously disputes the claim that a distinction something like the one baptized by the labels 'accidental' and 'nomic' universality is recognized in common speech and in practical action. The question in dispute is whether the *prima facie* differences that have been noted require the acceptance of the "necessity" associated with universals of law as something "ultimate" or whether nomic universality can be explicated in terms of notions that are less opaque. If this necessity is interpreted, as it has been, as a form of *logical* necessity, the meaning of 'necessary' in this sense is quite transparent; and indeed a systematic and generally accepted analysis of such necessity is provided by logical theory. Accordingly, though the view that nomological universals are logically necessary faces grave difficulties, as will be noted in a moment, the view has at least the merit of clarity. On the other hand, those who maintain that the necessity of universals of law is *sui generis* and at bottom not further analyzable postulate a property whose nature is essentially obscure. This obscurity is only named and not lightened by such labels as 'physical necessity' or 'real necessity.' Moreover, since it is generally supposed that this allegedly special type of necessity can be recognized only by some "intuitive apprehension," predicating such necessity

---

[4] This subjunctive conditional is not to be construed as saying that if any screw were *identical with* one of the screws in Smith's car it would be rusty. The latter subjunctive conditional is clearly true if indeed all the screws in Smith's current car are rusty. The subjunctive conditional in the text is to be understood as saying that for any object x—whether or not it is identical with one of the screws now in Smith's car—if x were a screw in that car it would be rusty.

The Logical Character of Scientific Laws 53

(whether of statements or of relations between events) is subject to all the vagaries of intuitive judgments. To be sure, the necessity that ostensibly characterizes universals of law may indeed be unique and not analyzable, but for the reasons noted it seems advisable to accept this conclusion only as a last resort.

The view that universals of law in general and causal laws in particular state a logical necessity has been frequently advanced. However, those who adopt this position usually do not claim that the logical necessity of nomological universals can in fact be established in every case. They contend only that genuine nomologicals are logically necessary, and could "in principle" be shown to be such, even though for the most part a demonstration of the necessity is lacking. For example, in discussing the nature of causality a contemporary writer maintains that "The cause logically entails the effect in such a way that it would be in principle possible, with sufficient insight, to see what kind of effect must follow from examination of the cause alone without having learnt by previous experience what were the effects of similar causes." [5] In some cases such a view is based on an allegedly direct perception of the logical necessity of at least a few nomological universals, and on the assumption that all other nomologicals must therefore also share this characteristic; in other cases, the view is adopted because the validity of scientific induction is held to depend on it; [6] and at least one proponent of the position has frankly admitted that the most impressive arguments for it are the objections to any alternative view. [7]

The difficulties confronting the position are nevertheless formidable. In the first place, none of the statements generally labeled as laws in the various positive sciences are in point of fact logically necessary, since their formal denials are demonstrably not self-contradictory. Accordingly, proponents of the view under discussion must either reject all these statements as not cases of "genuine" laws (and so maintain that no laws have yet been discovered in any empirical science), or reject the proofs that these statements are not logically necessary (and so challenge the validity of established techniques of logical proof). Neither horn of the dilemma is inviting. In the second place, if laws of nature are logically necessary, the positive sciences are engaged in an incongruous performance whenever they seek experimental and observational evidence for a

[5] A. C. Ewing, "Mechanical and Teleological Causation," *Aristotelian Society,* Suppl. Vol. 14 (1935), p. 66. Cf. also G. F. Stout: "If we had a sufficiently comprehensive and accurate knowledge of what really takes place, we should see how and why the effect follows from the cause with logical necessity."—*Aristotelian Society,* Suppl. Vol. 14 (1935), p. 46.

[6] A. C. Ewing, "Mechanical and Teleological Causation," *Aristotelian Society,* Suppl. Vol. 14 (1935), p. 77.

[7] C. D. Broad, *Aristotelian Society,* Suppl. Vol. 14 (1935), p. 94.

supposed law. The procedure appropriate for establishing a statement as logically necessary is that of constructing a demonstrative proof in the manner of mathematics, and not that of experimentation. No one today knows whether Goldbach's conjecture (that every even number is the sum of two primes) is logically necessary; but also no one who understands the problem will try to establish the conjecture as logically necessary by performing physical experiments. It is, however, fantastic to suggest that when the truth of an alleged physical law, for example about light, is in doubt the physicist ought to proceed as a mathematician does. And finally, despite the fact that the statements believed to be laws of nature are not known to be logically necessary, those statements successfully play the roles in science that are assigned to them. It is therefore gratuitous to maintain that, unless those statements were logically necessary, they could not do the tasks which they manifestly do perform. The statement known as Archimedes' law of buoyancy, for example, enables us to explain and predict a large class of phenomena, even though there are excellent reasons for believing that the law is not logically necessary. However, the assumption that the law really must be necessary does not follow from the fact that it is successfully used to explain and predict. Accordingly, the assumption postulates a characteristic that plays no identifiable part in the actual use made of the law.

It is, nevertheless, not difficult to understand why laws of nature sometimes appear to be logically necessary. For a given *sentence* may be associated with quite different meanings, so that while it is used in one context to express a logically contingent truth, in another context the *same sentence* may state something that is logically necessary. There was a time, for example, when copper was identified on the basis of properties that included none of the electrical properties of the substance. After electricity was discovered, the sentence 'Copper is a good electrical conductor' was asserted on experimental grounds as a law of nature. Eventually, however, high conductivity was absorbed into the defining properties of copper, so that the sentence 'Copper is a good electrical conductor' acquired a new use and meaning. In its new use, the sentence no longer expressed merely a logically contingent truth, as it did before, but served to convey a logically necessary truth. There is undoubtedly no sharp line separating those contexts in which copper is identified without reference to properties of conductivity from those contexts in which high conductivity is taken to belong to the "nature" of copper. In consequence, the status of what is being asserted by the sentence 'Copper is a good electrical conductor' is not always clear, so that the logical character of the assertion it is used to make in one context can be easily confounded with the character of the assertion made by it in some other context.[8] Such varying usage for the same sentence helps to explain why the view that laws of nature are logically necessary seems so plausible to many thinkers. It suggests a source for the conviction, apparent in declarations such as the following, that any alternative to this view is absurd: "I can attach no meaning to a causation in which the effect is not necessarily determined, and I can attach no meaning to a necessary determination which would leave it perfectly possible for the necessarily determined event to be different without contradicting either its own nature or the nature of that which determines it."[9] But in any event, the shifts in meaning to which sentences are subject as a consequence of advances in knowledge are an important feature in the development of comprehensive systems of explanation. It is a feature that will receive further attention in subsequent chapters.

The issue as to the nature of the ostensible necessity of nomological universals has occupied many thinkers since Hume proposed an analysis of causal statements in terms of constant conjunctions and *de facto* uniformities. Ignoring important details in Hume's account of the spatio-temporal relations of events which are said to be causally connected, the substance of the Humean position is briefly as follows. The objective content of the statement that a given event c is the cause of another event e, is simply that c is an instance of a property C, e is an instance of a property E (these properties may be quite complex), and any C is

[8] Another example may help to make the point more clearly. Consider the law of the lever in the form that if equal weights are placed at the extremities of a homogeneous rigid bar suspended at its midpoint, the lever is in equilibrium; and suppose that none of the expressions used in the statement of the law are defined in ways which involve assumptions about the behavior of levers. On this supposition, the statement is clearly an empirical law, and is not a logically necessary statement. On the other hand, suppose that two bodies are defined to be equal in weight if, when they are placed at the extremities of the equal arms of levers, the levers are in equilibrium. In contexts in which such a definition of "equality in weight" is employed, the above sentence about levers cannot be denied without self-contradiction, so that it does not express an empirical law for which experimental evidence is relevant but states a logically necessary truth. Sentences which appear to state laws but which are in fact employed as definitions, are commonly called "conventions"; and the role of such conventions and their articulation with laws will be discussed at greater length later on.

[9] A. C. Ewing, reference cited in footnote 5. It is only by an ellipsis that effects are said to be inferred from causes, since from the statement that an alleged cause has occurred the statement about the occurrence of a corresponding effect does not in fact follow logically. To infer the statement about the effect, the statement about the cause must be supplemented with a general law. Thus, the statement that a given billiard ball collides with a second ball does not logically entail any statement about the subsequent behavior of the second ball. Such a further statement can be derived only if some law (e.g., concerning the conservation of momentum) is added to the initial statement. The thesis that statements about causes logically imply statements about effects thus confounds the relation of logical necessity that holds between a set of explanatory premises and the explanandum, with the contingent relation affirmed by laws contained in these premises.

as a matter of fact also *E*. On this analysis, the "necessity" allegedly characterizing the relation of *c* to *e* does not reside in the objective relations of the events themselves. The necessity has its locus elsewhere—according to Hume, in certain habits of expectation that have been developed as a consequence of the uniform but *de facto* conjunctions of *C* and *E*.

The Humean account of causal necessity has been repeatedly criticized, partly on the ground that it rests on a dubious psychology; and the merits of criticisms of this sort are now generally acknowledged. However, Hume's psychological preconceptions are not essential to his central thesis—namely, that universals of law can be explicated without employing irreducible modal notions like "physical necessity" or "physical possibility." Accordingly, the burden of much of the current criticism of the Humean analysis is that the use of such modal categories is unavoidable in any adequate analysis of nomic universality. The issue remains unsettled and continues to be debated; and some of the problems connected with it have come to be discussed on a highly technical level. It will not be profitable to examine most of these technical details,[10] and only the outlines of an essentially Humean interpretation of nomic universality will be developed.

III.   *The Nature of Nomic Universality*

With this end in view, let us consider whether, if by imposing a number of logical and epistemic requirements upon universal conditionals (interpreted in the manner of modern formal logic, as explained above), conditionals satisfying them can plausibly be regarded as lawlike statements. It will be helpful to begin by comparing a patently accidental universal ('All the screws in Smith's current car are rusty,' or in more expanded form 'For every *x*, if *x* is a screw in Smith's car during the time period *a*, then *x* is rusty during *a*,' where *a* designates some definite time period), with a commonly acknowledged example of a universal of law ('All copper expands on heating' or, more explicitly, 'For any *x* and for any *t*, if *x* is copper and *x* is heated at time *t*, then *x* expands at time *t*').

---

[10] Some of these technical details are relevant only on an assumption that does not appear to be reasonable. The implicit assumption is that, short of adopting some modal notions as ultimate, if an adequate explication of nomic universality is to be obtained each universal law must be treated as a unit and shown to be translatable into a properly constructed *de facto* universal also treated as a complete unit. But there surely is an alternative to this assumption: namely, the explication of nomological universals by indicating some of the logical and epistemic conditions under which *de facto* universals are accepted as universals of law. Moreover, some of the technical details are generated by the aim to exclude every possible "queer" case that could theoretically arise, even though they rarely if ever arise in scientific practice.

The Logical Character of Scientific Laws   57

1. Perhaps the first thing that will strike us is that the accidental universal contains designations for a particular individual object and for a definite date or temporal period, while the nomological universal does not. Is this difference the decisive one? Not if we wish to count among the laws of nature a number of statements frequently so classified—for example, the Keplerian laws of planetary motion, or even the statement that the velocity of light in vacuum is 300,000 kilometers per second. For the Keplerian laws mention the sun (the first of the three laws, for instance, asserts that the planets move on elliptic orbits with the sun at one focus of each ellipse); and the law about the velocity of light tacitly mentions the earth, since the units of length and time used are defined by reference to the size of the earth and the periodicity of its rotation. But although we can exclude such statements from the class of laws, it would be highly arbitrary to do so. Moreover, the refusal to count such statements as laws would lead to the conclusion that there are few if any laws, should there be merit in the suggestion (discussed more fully in Chapter 11) that the relations of dependence codified as laws undergo evolutionary changes. According to the suggestion, different cosmic epochs are characterized by different regularities in nature, so that every statement properly formulating a regularity must contain a designation for some specific temporal period. However, no statement containing such a designation could be counted as a law by those who find the occurrence of a proper name in a statement to be incompatible with the statement's being a nomological universal.

A way of outflanking this difficulty has been proposed in several recent discussions of lawlike statements. In the first place, a distinction is drawn between predicates which are "purely qualitative" and those which are not, where a predicate is said to be purely qualitative if "a statement of its meaning does not require reference to any *particular* object or spatiotemporal location." [11] Thus, 'copper' and 'greater current strength' are examples of purely qualitative predicates, while 'lunar' and 'larger than the sun' are not. In the second place, a distinction is introduced between "fundamental" and "derivative" lawlike statements. Ignoring fine points, a universal conditional is said to be fundamental if it contains no individual names (or "individual constants") and all its predicates are purely qualitative; a universal conditional is said to be derivative if it is a logical consequence of some set of fundamental lawlike statements; and finally, a universal conditional is said to be lawlike if it is either fundamental or derivative. Accordingly, the Keplerian statements can be counted among the laws of nature if they are the logical

[11] Carl G. Hempel and Paul Oppenheim, "Studies in the Logic of Explanation," *Philosophy of Science,* Vol. 15 (1948), p. 156.

consequences of presumably true fundamental laws, such as Newtonian theory.

On the face of it, this proposed explication is most attractive, and reflects an undoubted tendency in current theoretical physics to formulate its basic assumptions exclusively in terms of qualitative predicates. The proposal nevertheless runs into two unresolved difficulties. In the first place, it just happens that universal conditionals containing predicates that are not purely qualitative are sometimes called laws, even if they are not known to follow logically from some set of fundamental laws. This was the case, for example, for the Keplerian laws before the time of Newton; and if we label as "law" (as some do) the statement that the planets all revolve around the sun in the same direction, this is the case today for this law. But in the second place, it is far from certain that such statements as Kepler's are in fact logically derivable even today from fundamental laws *alone* (as is required by the proposal under discussion, if those statements are to be classified as laws). There appears to be no way of deducing the Keplerian laws from Newtonian mechanics and gravitational theory, *merely* by substituting constant terms for variables occurring in the latter and *without* using additional premises whose predicates are not purely qualitative. And if this is so, the proposed explication would rule out from the class of lawlike statements an indefinite number of statements that are commonly said to be laws.[12] In effect, therefore, the proposed explication is far too restrictive, and fails to do justice to some of the important reasons for characterizing a statement as a law of nature.

Let us therefore compare that paradigm of accidental universality, 'For any x, if x is a screw in Smith's car during the time period a, then x is rusty during a,' with the first Keplerian law 'All planets move on elliptic orbits with the sun at one focus of each ellipse' (or, in comparable logical form, 'For any x and for any sufficiently long time interval t, if x is a planet, then x moves on an elliptic orbit during t and the sun is at one focus of this ellipse'). Both statements contain names of individuals and

---

[12] On the other hand, if one relaxes the requirement that all the premises from which a derivative law is to be deduced must be fundamental, such patently unlawlike statements as the one about the screws in Smith's car will have to be counted as laws. Thus this statement follows from the presumably fundamental law that all iron screws exposed to oxygen rust, conjoined with the additional premises that all the screws in Smith's current car are iron and have been exposed to oxygen.

It is indeed possible to deduce from Newtonian theory that a body which is under the action of an inverse-square law will move on an orbit that is a conic section with its focus as the origin of the central force. But in order to derive the further conclusion that the conic is an ellipse, additional premises appear to be unavoidable—premises which state the relative masses and the relative velocities of the planets and the sun. This circumstance is one reason for doubting that Kepler's laws are deducible from premises containing only fundamental laws.

predicates that are not purely qualitative. Nevertheless, there is a difference between them. In the accidental universal, the objects of which the predicate 'rusty during the time period a' is affirmed (let us call the class of such objects the "scope of predication" of the universal) are severely restricted to things that fall into a specific spatiotemporal region. In the lawlike statement, the scope of predication of the somewhat complex predicate 'moving on an elliptic orbit during the time interval t and the sun is at one focus of this ellipse' is not restricted in this way: the planets and their orbits are not required to be located in a fixed volume of space or a given interval of time. For convenience, let us call a universal whose scope of predication is not restricted to objects falling into a fixed spatial region or a particular period of time an "unrestricted universal." It is plausible to require lawlike statements to be unrestricted universals.

It must be noted, however, that whether or not a universal conditional is unrestricted cannot invariably be decided on the basis of the purely grammatical (or syntactical) structure of the sentence used to state the conditional, even if grammatical structure is often a reasonably safe guide. For example, one might coin the word 'scarscrew' to replace the expression 'screw in Smith's car during the period a,' and then render the accidental universal by 'All scarscrews are rusty.' But the syntactical structure of this new sentence does not reveal that its scope of predication is restricted to objects satisfying a given condition during only a limited period. Accordingly, familiarity must be assumed with the use or meaning of the expressions occurring in a sentence, in deciding whether the statement conveyed by the sentence is unrestrictedly universal. It must also be noted that, though a universal conditional is unrestricted, its scope of predication may actually be finite. On the other hand, though the scope is finite, the fact that it is finite must not be inferrible from the term in the universal conditional which formulates the scope of predication, and must therefore be established on the basis of independent empirical evidence. For example, though the number of known planets is finite, and though we have some evidence for believing that the number of times the planets revolve around the sun (whether in the past or distant future) is also finite, these are facts which cannot be deduced from Kepler's first law.

2. But though unrestricted universality is often taken as a necessary condition for a statement to be a law, it is not a sufficient one. An unrestricted universal conditional may be true, simply because it is vacuously true (i.e., nothing whatever satisfies its antecedent clause). But if such a conditional is accepted for this reason alone, it is unlikely that anyone will number it among the laws of nature. For example, if we

assume (as we have good reason to) that there are no unicorns, the rules of logic require us also to accept as true that all unicorns are fleet of foot. Despite this, however, even those familiar with formal logic will hesitate to classify this latter statement as a law of nature—especially since logic also requires us to accept as true, on the basis of the very same initial assumption, that all unicorns are slow runners. Most people would in fact regard it as at best a mild joke were a universal conditional labeled a law because it is vacuously true. The reason for this lies in good part in the uses which are normally made of laws: to explain phenomena and other laws, to predict events, and in general to serve as instruments for making inferences in inquiry. But if a universal conditional is accepted on the ground that it is vacuously true, there is nothing to which it can be applied, so that it cannot perform the inferential functions which laws are expected to perform.

It may therefore seem plausible that a universal conditional is not to be called a law unless we know that there is at least one object which satisfies its antecedent. However, this requirement is too restrictive, for we are not always in the position to know this much, even though we are prepared to call a statement a law. For example, we may not know whether there are in fact any pieces of copper wire at minus 270° C temperature, and yet be willing to classify as a law the statement that all copper wire at minus 270° C temperature is a good conductor of electricity. But if we do accept the statement as a law, on what evidence do we accept it? By hypothesis, we have no direct evidence for it, since we have assumed that we do not know whether there is any copper wire at near absolute zero temperatures, and have therefore not performed any experiments on such wire. The evidence must accordingly be indirect: the statement is accepted as a law, presumably because it is a consequence of some *other* assumed laws for which there is evidence of some kind. For example, the statement is a consequence of the ostensible law that all copper is a good electric conductor, for which there is considerable evidence. Accordingly, we can formulate as follows an additional requirement implicit in classifying an unrestricted universal as a law of nature: the vacuous truth of an unrestricted universal is not sufficient for counting it a law; it counts as a law only if there is a set of other assumed laws from which the universal is logically derivable.

Unrestricted universals whose antecedent clauses are believed to be satisfied by nothing in the universe thus acquire their status as laws, because they are part of a system of deductively related laws and are supported by the empirical evidence—often comprehensive and of a wide variety—which supports the system. It is pertinent to ask, nevertheless, why, even though a universal statement has such support, it should be

The Logical Character of Scientific Laws   61

classified as a law if it is also alleged to be vacuously true. Now there are two possible reasons for such an allegation. One is that no instances satisfying the antecedent clause of the law have been found, despite persistent search for such instances. Although such negative evidence may sometimes be impressive, it is frequently not very conclusive, since such instances may after all occur in overlooked places or under special circumstances. The law may then be employed for calculating the logical consequences of the supposition that there are in fact positive instances in some unexplored regions or under imagined conditions. The calculation may thus suggest how the area of further search for positive instances can be narrowed, or what experimental manipulations should be undertaken for generating such instances. The second and usually more decisive reason for believing a law to be vacuously true is a proof to the effect that the assumed existence of any positive instances for the law is logically incompatible with other laws belonging to the system. The vacuously true law may then indeed be otiose, and may represent so much dead lumber, because it serves no inferential function. On the other hand, if the laws used to establish this vacuous truth are themselves suspect, the ostensibly vacuously true law may be used as a basis for obtaining further critical evidence for these laws. There are doubtless other imagined uses for vacuously true laws. The point is that unless they do have some use, they are not likely to be included in codified bodies of knowledge.

One further question requires brief notice in this connection. It is frequently maintained that some of the laws in physics (and in other disciplines as well, for example in economics), accepted as at least temporarily ultimate, are known to be vacuously true. In consequence, the present account seems not to be adequate, since unrestricted universals are called "laws" despite the fact that they are not derived from other laws. A familiar example of such an ultimate vacuously true law is Newton's first law of motion, according to which a body under the action of no external forces maintains a constant velocity; and the familiar claim is that there are in fact no such bodies, since the assumption that there are is incompatible with Newtonian gravitation theory. Little will be said at this place about the example, since it will receive considerable attention in a later chapter. But two points can be made quickly. Even if the claim is granted that the Newtonian law is vacuously true, it is not for this reason that it is accepted as a law. Why then is it accepted? Waiving the question as to how the Newtonian statement is to be interpreted (e.g., whether or not it is in effect a definitional statement of what it is to be a body under the action of no external forces), and waiving also the question whether or not it is deducible from some other assumed law (e.g., Newton's second law of motion), an examination of its use shows that when the motions of bodies are analyzed in terms of the vectorial components of the motions, the velocities of bodies are constant in directions along which there are no effective forces acting on the bodies. In short, it is a gross oversimplification to claim that the law is vacuously true; for the law is an element in a system of laws for which there are certainly confirmatory instances. More generally, if an "ultimate" law were vacuously satisfied, it would be difficult to understand what use it would have in the system of which it is a part.

3. It is plausible to assume that candidates for the title of "law of nature" must satisfy another condition, one suggested by the considerations just mentioned. Quite apart from the fact that the paradigm accidental universal about the rusty screws in Smith's current car is not unrestrictedly universal, it exhibits a further feature. That universal conditional (let us refer to it as S) can be construed as a compendious way of asserting a finite conjunction of statements, each conjunct being a statement about a particular screw in a finite class of screws. Thus, S is equivalent to the conjunction: 'If s_1 is a screw in Smith's car during period a then s_1 is rusty during a, and if s_2 is a screw in Smith's car during period a then s_2 is rusty during a, and . . . , and if s_n is a screw in Smith's car during period a then s_n is rusty during period a,' where n is some finite number. S can therefore be established by establishing the truth of a finite number of statements of the form: 's_i is a screw in Smith's car during period a and s_i is rusty during period a.'

Accordingly, if we accept S, we do so because we have examined some fixed number of screws which we have reason to believe exhaust the scope of predication of S. If we had grounds for suspecting that the examined screws did not exhaust the lot in Smith's car, but that there are an indefinite number of further screws in the car which have not been examined, we would not be in the position to assert S as true. For in asserting S we are in effect saying that each of the examined screws is rusty, and that the examined screws are all the screws there are in Smith's car. It is important, however, not to misunderstand what is the point being stressed. In the first place, S might be accepted as true, not because each screw in Smith's car has been found to be rusty, but because S is deduced from some other assumptions. For example, we might deduce S from the premises that all the screws in Smith's current car are iron, that they have been exposed to free oxygen, and that iron always rusts in the presence of oxygen. But even in this case the acceptance of S depends on our having established a fixed number of statements having the form 's_i is an iron screw in Smith's car and it has been exposed to oxygen,' where the examined screws exhaust the scope of application of S. In the second place, S might be accepted on the ground that we have examined only a presumably "fair sample" of screws in Smith's car, and have inferred the character of the unexamined screws from the observed character of the screws in the sample. But here too the presumption of the inference is that the screws in the sample come from a class of screws that is complete and will not be augmented. For example, we assume that no one will remove a screw from the car and replace it by another, or that no one will drill a fresh hole in the car in order to insert a new screw. If we accept S as true on the basis of what we find in the sample, we do so in part because we assume that the sample has been obtained from a population of screws that will neither increase nor be altered during the period mentioned in S.

On the other hand, no analogous assumption appears to be made concerning the evidence on which statements called laws are accepted. Thus, although the law that iron rusts in the presence of free oxygen was at one time based exclusively on evidence drawn from an examination of a finite number of iron objects which had been exposed to oxygen, that evidence was not assumed to exhaust the scope of predication of the law. However, if there had been reason to suppose that this finite number of objects exhausted the class of iron objects exposed to oxygen which have ever existed or will ever exist in the future, it is doubtful whether the universal conditional would be called a law. On the contrary, if the observed cases were believed to exhaust the scope of application of the conditional, it is more likely that the statement would be classified simply as a historical report. In calling a statement a law, we are apparently asserting at least tacitly that as far as we know the examined instances of the statement do not form the exhaustive class of its instances. Accordingly, for an unrestricted universal to be called a law it is a plausible requirement that the evidence for it is not known to coincide with its scope of predication and that, moreover, its scope is not known to be closed to any further augmentation.

The rationale for this requirement is again to be found in the inferential uses to which statements called laws are normally put. The primary function of such statements is to explain and to predict. But if a statement asserts in effect no more than what is asserted by the evidence for it, we are being slightly absurd when we employ the statement for explaining or predicting anything included in this evidence, and we are being inconsistent when we use it for explaining or predicting anything not included in that evidence. To call a statement a law is therefore to say more than that it is a presumably true unrestricted universal. To call a statement a law is to assign a certain function to it, and thereby to say in effect that the evidence on which it is based is assumed not to constitute the total scope of its predication.

This requirement appears to be sufficient for denying the title of "law" to a certain class of manufactured statements that would normally not be so classified but which ostensibly satisfy the requirements previously discussed. Consider the statement 'All men who are the first to see a living human retina contribute to the establishment of the principle of conservation of energy.' Let us assume that the statement is not vacuously true and that it is an unrestricted universal, so that it can be transcribed as 'For any x and any t, if x is the man who sees a living human retina at time t and no man sees a living human retina at any time before t, then x contributes to the establishment of the principle of conservation of energy.' [13] Everyone who recalls the history of science will recognize the reference to Helmholtz, who was both the first to see a living human retina and also a founder of the conservation principle. Accordingly, the above statement is true, and by hypothesis satisfies the requirement of unrestricted universality. Nevertheless, it is plausible to assume that most people would be loath to call it a law. The reason for this conjectured reluctance becomes clear when we examine what evidence is needed to establish the statement. To establish it as true it is sufficient to show that Helmholtz was indeed the first human being to see a living human retina, and that he did contribute to founding the conservation principle. However, if Helmholtz was such a person, then, in the nature of the case, *logically* there cannot be another human being who satisfies the conditions described in the antecedent clause of the above statement. In brief, we *know* in this case that the evidence upon which the statement is accepted coincides with the scope of its predication. The statement is useless for explaining or predicting anything not included in the evidence, and is therefore not given the status of a law of nature.

4. One further point concerning statements commonly designated as laws requires to be noted, though it is difficult in this connection to formulate anything like a "requirement" that lawlike statements must invariably satisfy. The point bears on the standing which laws have in the corpus of our knowledge, and on the cognitive attitude we often manifest toward them.

The evidence on the strength of which a statement L is called a law can be distinguished as either "direct" or "indirect." (a) It may be "direct" evidence, in the familiar sense that it consists of instances falling into the scope of predication of L, where all the examined instances possess the property predicated by L. For example, direct evidence for the law that copper expands on heating is provided by lengths of copper wire which expand on heating. (b) The evidence for L may be "indirect" in two senses. It may happen that L is jointly derivable with other laws

[13] Hans Reichenbach, *Nomological Statements and Admissible Operations,* Amsterdam, 1954, p. 35.

L_1, L_2, etc., from some more general law (or laws) M, so that the direct evidence for these other laws counts as (indirect) evidence for L. For example, the law that the period of a simple pendulum is proportional to the square root of its length, and the law that the distance traversed by a freely falling body is proportional to the square of the time of fall, are jointly derivable from the assumptions of Newtonian mechanics. It is customary to count the direct confirming evidence for the first of these laws as confirmatory evidence, although only as "indirectly" confirmatory evidence, for the second law. However, the evidence for L may be "indirect" in the somewhat different sense that L can be combined with a variety of special assumptions to yield other laws each possessing a distinctive scope of predication, so that the direct evidence for these derivative laws counts as "indirect" evidence for L. For example, when the Newtonian laws of motion are conjoined with various special assumptions, the Keplerian laws, the law for the period of a pendulum, the law for freely falling bodies, and the laws concerning the shapes of rotating masses can all be deduced. Accordingly, the direct evidence for these derived laws serves as indirect evidence for the Newtonian laws.

Suppose now that, while some of the evidence for L is direct, there is also considerable indirect evidence for L (in either sense of "indirect"). But suppose also that some apparent exceptions to L are encountered. We may nevertheless be most reluctant to abandon L despite these exceptions, and for at least two reasons. In the first place, the combined direct and indirect confirmatory evidence for L may outweigh the apparently negative evidence. In the second place, in virtue of its relations to other laws and to the evidence for these latter, L does not stand alone, but its fate affects the fate of the system of laws to which L belongs. In consequence, the rejection of L would require a serious reorganization of certain parts of our knowledge. However, such a reorganization may not be feasible because no suitable replacement is momentarily available for the hitherto adequate system; and a reorganization may perhaps be avoided by reinterpreting the apparent exceptions to L, so that these latter are construed as not "genuine" exceptions after all. In that event, both L and the system to which it belongs can be "saved," despite the ostensible negative evidence for the law. This point is illustrated when an apparent failure of a law is construed as the result of careless observation or of inexpertness in conducting an experiment. But it can be illustrated by more impressive examples. Thus, the law (or principle) of the conservation of energy was seriously challenged by experiments on beta-ray decay whose outcome could not be denied. Nevertheless, the law was not abandoned, and the existence of a new kind of entity (called a "neutrino") was assumed in order to bring the law into concordance with experimental data. The rationale for this assumption is that the rejection of the conservation law would deprive a large part of our physical knowledge of its systematic coherence. On the other hand, the law (or principle) of the conservation of parity in quantum mechanics (which asserts that, for example, in certain types of interactions atomic nuclei oriented in one direction emit beta-particles with the same intensity as do nuclei oriented in the opposite direction) has recently been rejected, even though at first only relatively few experiments indicated that the law did not hold in general. This marked difference in the fates of the energy and parity laws is an index of the different positions these assumptions occupy at a given time in the system of physical knowledge, and of the greater intellectual havoc that would ensue at that stage from abandoning the former assumption than is involved in rejecting the latter.

More generally, we are usually quite prepared to abandon an assumed law for which the evidence is exclusively direct evidence as soon as *prima facie* exceptions to it are discovered. Indeed, there is often a strong disinclination to call a universal conditional *L* a "law of nature," despite the fact that it satisfies the various conditions already discussed, if the only available evidence for *L* is direct evidence. The refusal to call such an *L* a "law" is the more likely if, on the assumption that *L* has the form 'All *A* is *B*,' there is a class of things *C* that are not *A* which resemble things that are *A* in some respects deemed "important," such that while some members of *C* have the property *B*, nevertheless *B* does not invariably characterize the members of *C*. For example, although all the available evidence confirms the universal statement that all ravens are black, there appears to be no indirect evidence for it. However, even if the statement is accepted as a "law," those who do so will probably not hesitate to reject it as false and so to withdraw the label should a bird be found that is ostensibly a raven but has white plumage. Moreover, the color of plumage is known to be a variable characteristic of birds in general; and in fact species of birds similar to ravens in biologically significant respects, but lacking a completely black plumage, have been discovered. Accordingly, in the absence of known laws in terms of which the black color of ravens can be explained, with the consequent absence of a comprehensive variety of indirect evidence for the statement that all ravens are black, our attitude to this statement is less firmly settled than it is toward statements called laws for which such indirect evidence is available.

Such differences in our readiness to abandon a universal conditional in the face of apparently contradictory evidence is sometimes reflected in the ways we employ laws in scientific inference. Up to this point we have assumed that laws are used as premises *from which* consequences are derived in accordance with the rules of formal logic. But when a law is regarded as well-established and as occupying a firm position in the body of our knowledge, the law may itself come to be used as an empirical principle *in accordance with which* inferences are drawn. This difference between premises and rules of inference can be illustrated from elementary syllogistic reasoning. The conclusion that a given piece of wire *a* is a good electric conductor can be derived from the two premises that *a* is copper and all copper is a good electrical conductor, in accordance with the rule of formal logic known as the *dictum de omni*. However, that same conclusion can also be obtained from the single premise that *a* is copper, if we accept as a principle of inference the rule that a statement of the form '*x* is a good electrical conductor' is derivable from a statement of the form '*x* is copper.'

On the face of it, this difference is only a technical one; and from a purely formal standpoint it is always possible to eliminate a universal premise without invalidating a deductive argument, provided we adopt a suitable rule of inference to replace that premise. Nevertheless, this technical maneuver is usually employed in practice only when the universal premise has the status of a law which we are not prepared to abandon merely because occasionally there are apparent exceptions to it. For when such a premise is replaced by a rule of inference, we are along the road to transforming the meanings of some of the terms employed in the premise, so that its empirical content is gradually absorbed into the meanings of those terms. Thus, in the above example, the statement that copper is a good electrical conductor is assumed to be a factual one, in the sense that possession of high conductivity is not one of the defining traits of what it is to be copper, so that empirical evidence is required for establishing the statement. On the other hand, when that statement is replaced by a rule of inference, electrical conductivity tends to be taken as a more or less "essential" trait of copper, so that in the end no thing may come to be classified as copper unless the object is a good conductor. As has already been noted, this tendency helps to account for the view that genuine laws express relations of logical necessity. But in any event, when this tendency has run its full course, the discovery of a poorly conducting substance that is in other respects like copper would require a reclassification of substances with a corresponding revision in the meanings associated with such terms as 'copper.' That is why the transformation of an ostensibly empirical law into a rule of inference occurs usually only when the law is assumed to be so well-established that quite overwhelming evidence is needed for dislocating it. Accordingly, although to call a universal conditional a law it is not required that we must be disposed to reinterpret apparently negative evidence so as to retain the statement as an integral part of our knowledge, many statements are classified as laws in part because we do have such an attitude toward them.

IV.   *Contrary-to-fact Universals*

There are thus four types of considerations which seem relevant in classifying statements as laws of nature: (1) syntactical considerations relating to the form of lawlike statements; (2) the logical relations of statements to other statements in a system of explanations; (3) the functions assigned to lawlike statements in scientific inquiry; and (4) the cognitive attitudes manifested toward a statement because of the nature of the available evidence. These considerations overlap in part, since, for example, the logical position of a statement in a system is related to the role the statement can play in inquiry, as well as to the kind of evidence that can be obtained for it. Moreover, the conditions mentioned in these considerations are not asserted to be sufficient (or perhaps, in some cases, even necessary) for affixing the label "law of nature" to statements. Undoubtedly statements can be manufactured which satisfy these conditions but which would ordinarily not be called laws, just as statements sometimes called laws may be found which fail to satisfy one or more of these conditions. For reasons already stated, this is inevitable, for a precise explication of the meaning of "law of nature" which will be in agreement with every use of this vague expression is not possible. Nevertheless, statements satisfying these conditions appear to escape the objections raised by critics of a Humean analysis of nomic universality. This claim requires some defense; and something must also be said about the related problem of the logical status of contrary-to-fact conditionals.

1.   Perhaps the most impressive current criticism of Humean analyses of nomic universality is the argument that *de facto* universals cannot support subjunctive conditionals. Suppose we know that there never has been a raven that was not black, that there is at present no raven that is not black, and that there never will be a raven that will not be black. We are then warranted in asserting as true the unrestricted accidental universal S: 'All ravens are black.' It has been argued, however, that S does not express what we would usually call a law of nature.[14] For suppose that in point of fact no raven has ever lived or will live in polar

[14] William Kneale, "Natural Laws and Contrary-to-Fact Conditionals," *Analysis*, Vol. 10 (1950), p. 123. Cf. also William Kneale, *Probability and Induction*, Oxford, 1949, p. 75. The impetus to much recent Anglo-American discussion of nomological universals and subjunctive as well as "contrary-to-fact" (or "counterfactual") conditionals was given by Roderick M. Chisholm, "The Contrary-to-fact Conditional," *Mind*, Vol. 55 (1946), pp. 289-307, and Nelson Goodman, "The Problem of Counterfactual Conditionals," *Journal of Philosophy*, Vol. 44 (1947), pp. 113-28, the latter also reprinted in Nelson Goodman, *Fact, Fiction, and Forecast*, Cambridge, Mass., 1955.

regions. But suppose further that we do not know whether or not dwelling in polar regions affects the color of ravens, so that as far as we know the progeny of ravens that might migrate into such regions may grow white feathers. Accordingly, though S is true, this truth may be only a consequence of the "historical accident" that no ravens ever live in polar regions. In consequence, the accidental universal S does not support the subjunctive conditional that if inhabitants of polar regions were ravens they would be black; and since a law of nature must, by hypothesis, support such conditionals, S cannot count as a law. In short, unrestricted universality does not explicate what we mean by nomic universality.

But though the argument may establish this latter point, it does not follow that S is not a law of nature because it fails to express an irreducible nomic necessity. For despite its assumed truth, S may be denied the status of law for at least two reasons, neither of which has anything to do with questions of such necessity. In the first place, the evidence for S may coincide with S's scope of predication, so that to anyone familiar with that evidence S cannot perform the functions which statements classified as laws are expected to perform. In the second place, though the evidence for S is by hypothesis logically sufficient to establish S as true, the evidence may be exclusively direct evidence; and one may refuse to label S as a law, on the ground that only statements for which indirect evidence is available (so that statements must occupy a certain logical position in the corpus of our knowledge) can claim title to the label.

But another consideration is no less relevant in this connection. The failure of S to support the subjunctive conditional mentioned above is a consequence of the fact that S is asserted to be true within a context of assumptions which themselves make dubious the subjunctive conditional. For example, S is asserted in the knowledge that no ravens inhabit polar regions. But it has already been suggested that we know enough about birds to know that the color of their plumage is not invariant for every species of birds. And though we do not know at present the precise factors upon which the color of plumage depends, we do have grounds for believing that the color depends at least in part on the genetic constitution of birds; and we also know that this constitution can be influenced by the presence of certain factors (e.g., high-energy radiations) which may be present in special environments. Accordingly, S does not support the cited subjunctive conditional, not because S is incapable of supporting *any* such conditional, but because the total knowledge at our command (and not only the evidence for S itself) does not warrant *this particular* conditional. It may be plausible to suppose that S does validate the subjunctive conditional that were any inhabitant of polar regions a raven not exposed to X-ray radiations, that raven would be black.

The point to be noted, therefore, is that whether or not S supports a given subjunctive conditional depends not only on the truth of S but also on other knowledge we may possess—in effect on the state of scientific inquiry. To see the point more clearly, let us apply the criticism under discussion to a statement generally counted as a law of nature. Suppose there are (omnitemporally) no physical objects that do not attract each other inversely as the square of their distances from each other. We are then entitled to assert as true the unrestricted universal S': 'All physical bodies attract each other inversely as the square of the distance between them.' But suppose also that the dimensions of the universe are finite, and that no physical bodies are ever separated by a distance greater than, say, 50 trillion light-years. Does S' support the subjunctive conditional that if there were physical bodies at distances from each other greater than 50 trillion light-years, they would attract each other inversely as the square of the distance between them? According to the argument under consideration, the answer must presumably be no. But is this answer really plausible? Is it not more reasonable to say that no answer is possible, either in the affirmative or negative—unless indeed some further assumptions are made? For in the absence of such additional assumptions, how can one adjudicate any answer that might be given? On the other hand, if such further assumptions were made—for example, if we assume that the force of gravity is independent of the total mass of the universe—it is not inconceivable that the correct answer may be an affirmative one.

In sum, therefore, the criticism under discussion does not undermine the Humean analysis of nomic universality. The criticism does bring into clearer light, however, the important point that a statement is usually classified as a law of nature because the statement occupies a distinctive position in the system of explanations in some area of knowledge, and because the statement is supported by evidence satisfying certain specifications.

2. When planning for the future or reflecting on the past, we frequently carry on our deliberations by making assumptions that are contrary to the known facts. The results of our reflections are then often formulated as contrary-to-fact conditionals (or "counterfactuals"), having the forms 'If a were P, then b would be Q,' or 'If a had been P, then b would have been (or would be) Q.' For example, a physicist designing an experiment may at some point in his calculations assert the counterfactual C: 'If the length of pendulum a were shortened to one-fourth its present length, its period would be half its present period.' Similarly, in at-

tempting to account for the failure of some previous experiment, a physicist can be imagined to assert the counterfactual C': 'If the length of pendulum a had been shortened to one-fourth its actual length, its period would have been half its actual period.' In both conditionals, the antecedent and consequent clauses describe suppositions presumably known to be false.

What has come to be called the "problem of counterfactuals" is the problem of making explicit the logical structure of such statements and of analyzing the grounds upon which their truth or falsity may be decided. The problem is closely related to that of explicating the notion of nomic universality. For a counterfactual cannot be translated in a straightforward way into a conjunction of statements in the indicative mood, using only the standard non-modal connectives of formal logic. For example, the counterfactual C' tacitly asserts that the length of pendulum a was not in fact shortened to one-fourth its actual length. However, C' is not rendered by the statement: 'The length of a was not shortened to a fourth of its actual length and if the length of a was shortened to one-fourth of its present length then its period was half its present period.' The proposed translation is unsatisfactory, because, since the antecedent clause of the indicative conditional is false, it follows by the rules of formal logic that if the length of a was shortened to a fourth of its present length, its period was *not* half its present period —a conclusion certainly not acceptable to anyone who asserts C'.[15] In consequence, critics of Humean analyses of nomic universality have argued that a distinctive type of nonlogical necessity is involved not only in universals of law but also in contrary-to-fact conditionals.

The content of counterfactuals can nevertheless be plausibly explicated without recourse to any unanalyzable modal notions. For what the physicist who asserts C' is saying can be rendered more clearly though more circuitously as follows. The statement 'The period of the pendulum a was half its present period' *follows logically* from the supposition 'The length of a was one-fourth its present length,' when this supposition is conjoined with the law that the period of a simple pendulum is proportional to the square root of its length, together with a number of further assumptions about initial conditions for the law (e.g., that a is a simple pendulum, that air resistance is negligible). Moreover, though the supposition and the statement deduced from it with the help of the assumptions mentioned are admittedly both false, their falsity is not included among the premises of the deduction. Accordingly, it does *not*

---

[15] This conclusion follows because of the logical rule governing the use of the connective "if-then." According to this rule both a statement of the form 'If S_1 then S_2' and the statement of the form 'If S_1 then not S_2' are true on the hypothesis that S_1 is false, no matter what S_2 may be.

follow from those premises that if *a*'s length was a fourth of its present length then *a*'s period was a half of its present period. In short, the counterfactual *C′* is thus asserted within some context of assumptions and special suppositions; and when these are laid bare, the introduction of modal categories other than those of formal logic is entirely gratuitous. More generally, a counterfactual can be interpreted as an implicit *metalinguistic* statement (i.e., a statement about *other* statements, and in particular about the logical relations of these other statements) asserting that the indicative form of its consequent clause follows logically from the indicative form of its antecedent clause, when the latter is conjoined with some law and the requisite initial conditions for the law.[16]

In consequence, disputes as to whether or not a given counterfactual is true can be settled only when the assumptions and suppositions on which it is based are made explicit. A counterfactual which is unquestionably true on one set of such premises may be false on another set, and may have no determinate truth-value on some third set. Thus, a physicist might reject *C′* in favor of the counterfactual 'If the length of pendulum *a* had been shortened to a fourth of its present length, the period of *a* would have been significantly more than half its present period.' He would be warranted in doing so if he is assuming, for example, that the arc of vibration of the shortened pendulum is more than 60° and if he also is assuming a modified form of the law for the periods of pendulums stated above (which is asserted only for pendulums with quite small arcs of vibration). Again, a tyro in experimental design may declare *C′* to be true, though he assumes among other things not only that the circular bob of the pendulum is three inches in diameter, but also that the apparatus enclosing the pendulum has an opening just a hairsbreadth wider than three inches at the place where the bob of the shortened pendulum has its center. It is obvious, however, that *C′* is now false because under the stated assumptions the shortened pendulum does not vibrate at all.

The various assumptions under which a counterfactual is asserted are not stated in the counterfactual itself. The evaluation of the validity of a counterfactual may therefore be quite difficult—sometimes because we do not know the assumptions under which it is asserted or because we are not clear in our minds what tacit assumptions we are making,

---

[16] Although the position adopted in the text has been reached independently, its present formulation is indebted to the views expressed in Henry Hiz, "On the Inferential Sense of Contrary-to-Fact Conditionals," *Journal of Philosophy*, Vol. 48 (1951), pp. 586-87; Julius R. Weinberg, "Contrary-to-Fact Conditionals," *Journal of Philosophy*, Vol. 48 (1951), pp. 17-22; Roderick M. Chisholm, "Law Statements and Counterfactual Inference," *Analysis*, Vol. 15 (1955), pp. 97-105; and John C. Cooley, "Professor Goodman's 'Fact, Fiction, and Forecast,'" *Journal of Philosophy*, Vol. 54 (1957), pp. 293-311.

and sometimes because we simply lack the skill to assess the logical import even of the assumptions that we make explicit. Such difficulties frequently confront us, especially in connection with counterfactuals asserted in the course of everyday affairs or even in the writings of historians. Consider, for example, the counterfactual 'If the Versailles Treaty had not imposed burdensome indemnities on Germany, Hitler would not have come into power.' This assertion has been a controversial one, not only because those participating in the discussion of it adopt different explicit assumptions, but also because much of the dispute has been conducted on the basis of implicit premises that no one has fully brought into light. In any event, it is certainly not possible to construct a general formula which will prescribe just what must be included in the assumptions upon which a counterfactual can be adequately grounded. Attempts to construct such a formula have been uniformly unsuccessful; and those who see the problem of counterfactuals as that of constructing such a formula are destined to grapple with an insoluble problem.

V. *Causal Laws*

Something must finally be said about causal laws. It would be an ungrateful and pointless task to canvass even partially the variety of senses that have been attached to the word 'cause'—varying from the ancient legal associations of the word, through the popular conception of causes as efficient agents, to the more sophisticated modern notions of cause as invariable functional dependence. The fact that the term has this wide spectrum of uses immediately rules out the possibility that there is just one correct and privileged explication for it. It is nevertheless both possible and useful to identify one fairly definite meaning associated with the word in many areas of science as well as in ordinary discourse, with a view to obtaining from this perspective a rough classification of laws that serve as premises in explanations. On the other hand, it would be a mistake to suppose that, because in one meaning of the word the notion of cause plays an important role in some field of inquiry, the notion is indispensable in all other fields—just as it would be an error to maintain that, because this notion is useless in certain parts of science, it cannot have a legitimate role in other divisions of scientific study.

The sense of 'cause' we wish to identify is illustrated by the following example. An electric spark is passed through a mixture of hydrogen and oxygen gas; the explosion that follows the passage of the spark is accompanied by the disappearance of the gases and the condensation of water vapor. The disappearance of the gases and the formation of water in this experiment are commonly said to be the effects that are caused by the spark. Moreover, the generalization based on such experiments (e.g., 'Whenever a spark passes through a mixture of hydrogen and oxygen gas, the gases disappear and water is formed') is called a "causal law."

The law is said to be a causal one apparently because the relation it formulates between the events mentioned supposedly satisfies four conditions. In the first place, the relation is an invariable or uniform one, in the sense that whenever the alleged cause occurs so does the alleged effect. There is, moreover, the common tacit assumption that the cause constitutes both a necessary and a sufficient condition for the occurrence of the effect. In point of fact, however, most of the causal imputations made in everyday affairs, as well as most of the causal laws frequently mentioned, do not state the sufficient conditions for the occurrence of the effect. Thus, we often say that striking a match is the cause of its bursting into flame, and tacitly assume that other conditions without which the effect would not occur (e.g., presence of oxygen, a dry match) are also present. The event frequently picked out as the cause is normally an event that completes the set of sufficient conditions for the occurrence of the effect, and that is regarded for various reasons as being "important." In the second place, the relation holds between events that are spatially contiguous, in the sense that the spark and the formation of water occur in approximately the same spatial region. Accordingly, when events spatially remote from each other are alleged to be causally related, it is tacitly assumed that these events are but termini in a cause-and-effect chain of events, where the linking events are spatially contiguous. In the third place, the relation has a temporal character, in the sense that the event said to be the cause precedes the effect and is also "continuous" with the latter. In consequence, when events separated by a temporal interval are said to be causally related, they are also assumed to be connected by a series of temporally adjacent and causally related events. And finally, the relation is asymmetrical, in the sense that the passage of the spark through the mixture of gases is the cause of their transformation into water, but the formation of the water is not the cause of the passage of the spark.

The ideas in terms of which this notion of cause are stated have been frequently criticized as being vague; and telling objections have been made in particular against the common-sense conceptions of spatial and temporal continuity, on the ground that they contain a nest of confusions. It is undoubtedly true, moreover, that in some of the advanced sciences such as mathematical physics this notion is quite superfluous; and it is even debatable whether the four conditions just mentioned are in fact fulfilled in alleged illustrations of this notion of cause (such as the above example), when the illustrations are analyzed in terms of modern phys-

The Logical Character of Scientific Laws   **75**

ical theories. Nevertheless, however inadequate this notion of cause may be for the purposes of theoretical physics, it continues to play a role in many other branches of inquiry. It is a notion that is firmly embodied in the language we employ, even when abstract physical theories are used in the laboratory as well as in practical affairs for obtaining various results through the manipulation of appropriate instrumentalities. Indeed, it is because some things can be manipulated so as to yield other things, but not conversely, that causal language is a legitimate and convenient way of describing the relations of many events.

On the other hand, not all laws of nature are causal in the indicated sense of this term. A brief survey of types of laws that are used as explanatory premises in various sciences will make this evident.

1. As has already been mentioned, a basic and pervasive type of law is involved in the assumption that there are "natural kinds" or "substances." Let us understand by a "determinable" a property such as color or density, which has a number of specific or "determinate" forms. Thus, among the determinate forms of the determinable color are red, blue, green, yellow, etc.; among the determinate forms of the determinable density are the density with magnitude 0.06 (when measured in some standard fashion), the density with magnitude 2, the density with magnitude 12, etc. The determinate forms of a given determinable thus constitute a "related family" of properties such that every individual of which the determinable property can be significantly predicated must, of logical necessity, have one and only one of the determinate forms of the determinable.[17] A law of the type under consideration (e.g., 'There is the substance rock salt') then asserts that there are objects of various kinds, such that every object of a given kind is characterized by determinate forms of a set of determinable properties, and such that objects belonging to different kinds will differ in at least one (but usually more than one) determinate form of a common determinable. For example, to say that a given object *a* is rock salt is to say that there is a set of determinable properties (crystalline structure, color, melting point, hardness, etc.) such that under standard conditions *a* has a determinate form of each of these determinables (*a* has cubical crystals, it is colorless, it has a density of 2.163, a melting point of 804° C, the degree of hardness 2 on Mohs' scale, etc.). Moreover, *a* differs from an object belonging to a different kind, for example talc, in at least one (and in fact in a great many) determinate forms of these determinables. Accordingly, laws of this type assert that there is an invariable concomitance of determinate

---

[17] For this terminology, cf. W. E. Johnson, *Logic*, Vol. 1, Cambridge, England, 1921, Chapter 11; and Rudolf Carnap, *Logical Foundations of Probability*, Chicago, 1950, Vol. 1, p. 75.

properties in every object that is of a certain kind. It will be clear, however, that laws of this type are not causal laws—they do not assert, for example, that the density of rock salt precedes (or follows) its degree of hardness.

2.   A second type of law asserts an invariable sequential order of dependence among events or properties. Two subordinate types can be distinguished. One of these is the class of causal laws, such as the law about the effect of a spark in a mixture of hydrogen and oxygen, or the law that stones thrown into water produce a series of expanding concentric ripples. A second subordinate type is the class of "developmental" (or "historical") laws, such as the law 'The formation of lungs in the human embryo never precedes the formation of the circulatory system' or the law 'Consumption of alcohol is always followed by a dilation of the blood vessels.' Both subordinate types are frequent in areas of study in which quantitative methods have not been extensively introduced, although as the examples indicate such laws are encountered elsewhere as well. Developmental laws can be construed to have the form 'If x has the property P at time t, then x has the property Q at time t' later than t.' They are commonly not regarded as causal laws, apparently for two reasons. In the first place, though developmental laws may state a necessary condition for the occurrence of some event (or complex of events), they do not state the sufficient conditions. Indeed, we usually have only the vaguest sort of knowledge as to what these sufficient conditions are. In the second place, developmental laws generally state relations of sequential order between events separated by a temporal interval of some duration. In consequence, such laws are sometimes regarded as representing only an incomplete analysis of the facts, on the ground that, since something may intervene after the earlier event to prevent the realization of the later one, the sequential order of events is not likely to be invariable. Nevertheless, whatever may be the limitations of developmental laws and however desirable it may be to supplement them by laws of another sort, both causal and developmental laws are extensively used in the explanatory systems of current science.

3.   A third type of law, common in the biological and social sciences as well as in physics, asserts invariable statistical (or probabilistic) relations between events or properties. One example of such a law is: 'If a geometrically and physically symmetrical cube is repeatedly tossed, the probability (or relative frequency) that the cube will come to rest with a given face uppermost is $\frac{1}{6}$'; other examples have been previously mentioned. Statistical laws do not assert that the occurrence of one event is *invariably* accompanied by the occurrence of some other event.

They assert only that, in a sufficiently long series of trials, the occurrence of one event is accompanied by the occurrence of a second event with an *invariable relative frequency*. Such laws are manifestly not causal, though they are not incompatible with a causal account of the facts they formulate. Indeed, the above statistical law about the behavior of a cube can be deduced from laws that are sometimes said to be causal ones, if suitable assumptions are made about the statistical distribution of initial conditions for the application of those causal laws. On the other hand, there are statistical laws even in physics for which at present no causal explanations are known. Moreover, even if one assumes that "in principle" all statistical laws are the consequences of some underlying "causal order," there are areas of inquiry—in physics as well as in the biological and social sciences —in which the explanation of many phenomena in terms of strictly universal causal laws is not likely to be feasible practically. It is a reasonable presumption that however much our knowledge may increase, statistical laws will continue to be used as the proximate premises for the explanation and prediction of many phenomena.

4. A fourth type of law, characteristic of modern physical science, asserts a relation of functional dependence (in the mathematical sense of "function") between two or more variable magnitudes associated with stated properties or processes. Two subtypes can be distinguished.

a. In the first place, there are numerical laws stating an interdependence between magnitudes such that a variation in any of them is concurrent with variations in the others. An example of such a law is the Boyle-Charles' law for ideal gases, that $pV = aT$, where p is the pressure of the gas, V its volume, T its absolute temperature, and a a constant that depends on the mass and the nature of the gas under consideration. This is not a causal law. It does not assert, for example, that a change in the temperature is followed (or preceded) by some change in the volume or in the pressure; it asserts only that a change in T is concurrent with changes in p or V or in both. Accordingly, the relation stated by the law must be distinguished from the sequential order of the events that may occur when the law is being tested or used for making predictions. For example, in testing the law in a laboratory, one may diminish the volume of an ideal gas in such a way that its temperature remains constant, and then note that its pressure increases. But the law says nothing about the order in which these magnitudes may be varied, nor about the temporal sequence in which the changes may be observed. Laws of this subtype can nevertheless be used for predictive as well as explanatory purposes. For example, if in the case of a suitably "isolated" system the magnitudes mentioned in such a law satisfy the indicated relation between them at one instant, they will satisfy this relation at some future instant, even though the magnitudes may have undergone some change in the interim.

b.   A second subtype consists of numerical laws asserting in what manner a magnitude varies with the time, and more generally how a change in a magnitude per unit of time is related to other magnitudes (in some cases, though not always, to temporal durations). Galileo's law for freely falling bodies in a vacuum is one illustration of such a law. It says that the distance d traversed by a freely falling body is equal to $gt^2/2$, where g is constant and t is the duration of the fall. An equivalent way of stating Galileo's law is to say that the change in the distance per unit time of a freely falling body is equal to gt. In this formulation, it is evident that a time-rate of change in one magnitude is related to a temporal interval. Another example of a law belonging to this subtype is the law for the velocity of the bob of a simple pendulum along the path of its motion. The law says that, if v_0 is the velocity of the bob at the lowest point of its motion, h the height of the bob above the horizontal line through this point, and k a constant, then at any point along the arc of its motion the bob has a velocity v such that $v^2 = v_0^2 - kh^2$. Since the velocity v is the change in distance per unit of time, the law thus says that the change in the distance of the bob along its path per unit of time is a certain mathematical function of its velocity at the lowest point of its swing and of its altitude. In this case, the time-rate of change in one magnitude is not given as a function of the time. Laws that belong to this subtype are often called "dynamical laws" because they formulate the structure of a temporal process and are generally explained on the assumption that a "force" is acting on the system under consideration. Such laws are sometimes assimilated in causal laws, although in fact they are not causal in the specific sense distinguished earlier in this section. For the relation of dependence between the variables mentioned in the law is symmetrical, so that a state of the system at a given time is determined as completely by a later state as by an earlier one. Thus, if we know the velocity of the bob of a simple pendulum at any given instant, then provided there is no external interference with the system, the above law enables us to calculate the velocity at any other time, whether it is earlier or later than the given instant.

The preceding classification of laws is not proposed as an exhaustive one; and in any event, later chapters will discuss more fully the structures of certain types of law. The classification does indicate, however, that not all the laws recognized in the sciences are of one type, and that a scientific explanation is often regarded as satisfactory even though the laws cited in the premises are not "causal" in any customary sense.

Law Statements and
Counterfactual Inference

Roderick M. Chisholm

Reprinted from *Analysis,* 15 (Apr., 1955), 97–105, with permission of Basil Blackwell, Publisher.

LAW STATEMENTS AND COUNTERFACTUAL INFERENCE[1]

By RODERICK M. CHISHOLM

THE problems I have been invited to discuss arise from the fact that there are two types of true synthetic universal statement : statements of the one type, in the context of our general knowledge, seem to warrant counterfactual inference and statements of the other type do not. I shall call statements of the first type " law statements " and statements of the second type " non-law statements". Both law and nonlaw statements may be expressed in the general form, " For every x, if x is S, x is P ". Law statements, unlike nonlaw statements, seem to warrant inference to statements of the form, "If *a*, which is not S, *were* S, *a* would be P " and " For every x, if x *were* S, x would be P ". I shall discuss (I) this distinction between law and non-law statements and (II) the related problem of interpreting counterfactual statements.[2]

I

Let us consider the following as examples of law statements :

L1. Everyone who drinks from this bottle is poisoned.

L2. All gold is malleable.

And let us consider the following as examples of nonlaw statements :

N1. Everyone who drinks from —— bottle wears a necktie.

N2. Every Canadian parent of quintuplets in the first half of the twentieth century is named ' Dionne '.

Let us suppose that L1 and N1 are concerned with the same bottle (perhaps it is one of short duration and has contained

[1] Read at the Western Division meeting of the American Philosophical Association, University of Illinois, May 7, 1954.
[2] Detailed formulations of this problem are to be found in the following works : W. E. Johnson, *Logic*, Vol. III, chapter I; C. H. Langford, review of W. B. Gallie's "An Interpretation of Causal Laws ", *Journal of Symbolic Logic*, Vol. VI (1941), p. 67 ; C. I. Lewis, *An Analysis of Knowledge and Valuation*, Part II; Roderick M. Chisholm, " The Contrary-to-fact Conditional ", *Mind*, Vol. 55 (1946), pp. 289–307 (reprinted in H. Feigl and W. S. Sellars, *Readings in Philosophical Analysis*); Nelson Goodman, " The Problem of Counterfactual Conditionals ", *Journal of Philosophy*, Vol. 44 (1947), pp. 113–128 (reprinted in L. Linsky, *Semantics and the Philosophy of Language*); F. L. Will, " The Contrary-to-fact Conditional ", *Mind*, Vol. 56 (1947), pp. 236–249; and William Kneale, " Natural Laws and Contrary to Fact Conditionals ", ANALYSIS, Vol. 10 (1950), pp. 121–125. See further references below and in Erna Schneider, "Recent Discussion of Subjunctive Conditionals ", *Review of Metaphysics*, Vol. VI (1953), pp. 623–647. My paper, referred to above, contains some serious errors,

only arsenic.) Let us suppose, further, that the blank in N1 is replaced by property terms which happen to characterize the bottle uniquely (perhaps they describe patterns of fingerprints). I shall discuss certain philosophical questions which arise when we make the following " preanalytic " assumptions. From L1 we can infer.

> L1.1   If Jones had drunk from this bottle, he would have been poisoned.

and from L2 we can infer

> L2.1   If that metal were gold, it would be malleable.

But from N1 we cannot infer

> N1.1   If Jones had drunk from —— bottle, he would have worn a necktie.

and from N2 we cannot infer

> N2.1   If Jones, who is Canadian, had been parent of quintuplets during the first half of the twentieth century, he would have been named ' Dionne '.

I shall not defend these assumptions beyond noting that, in respects to be discussed, they correspond to assumptions which practically everyone does make.

There are two preliminary points to be made concerning the interpretation of counterfactual statements. (1) We are concerned with those counterfactuals whose antecedents, " if a were S," may be interpreted as meaning the same as " if a had property S". There is, however, another possible interpretation: " if a were S " could be interpreted as meaning the same as " if a were identical with something which in fact does have property S ".[1] Given the above assumptions, N2.1 is false according to the first interpretation, which is the interpretation with which we are concerned, but it is true according to the second (for if Jones were identical with one of the Dionnes, he would be named ' Dionne '). On the other hand, the statement

> N2.2   If Jones, who is Canadian, had been parent of quintuplets during the first half of the twentieth century, there would have been at least two sets of Canadian quintuplets.

is true according to the first interpretation and false according to the second. (2) It should be noted, secondly, that there is a respect—to be discussed at greater length below—in which our counterfactual statements may be thought of as being elliptical. If we assert L1.1, we might, nevertheless, accept the following qualification : " Of course, if Jones had emptied the bottle,

---

[1] Compare K. R. Popper, "A Note on Natural Laws and so-called ' Contrary-to-fact conditionals ' ", *Mind*, vol. 58 (1949), pp. 62–66.

cleaned it out, filled it with water, and *then* drunk from it, he might not have been poisoned." And, with respect to L2.1, we might accept this qualification : " If that metal were gold it would be malleable—provided, of course, that what we are supposing to be contrary-to-fact is that statement ' That metal is not gold ' and *not* the statement 'All gold is malleable '."

Can the relevant difference between law and non-law statements be described in familiar terminology without reference to counterfactuals, without use of modal terms such as " causal necessity ", " necessary condition ", " physical possibility ", and the like, and without use of metaphysical terms such as " real connections between matters of fact " ? I believe no one has shown that the relevant difference *can* be so described. I shall mention three recent discussions.

(1) It has been suggested that the distinction between law statements and nonlaw statements may be made with respect to the universality of the nonlogical terms which appear in the statements. A term may be thought of as being universal, it has been suggested, if its meaning can be conveyed without explicit reference to any particular object ; it is then said that law statements, unlike nonlaw statements, contain no nonlogical terms which are not universal.[1] (These points can be formulated more precisely.) This suggestion does not help, however, if applied to what we have been calling " law statements " and " nonlaw statements ", for L1 is a law statement containing the *non*universal nonlogical term " this bottle " and N1 (we have supposed) is a nonlaw statement all of whose nonlogical terms *are* universal. It may be that, with respect to ordinary usage, it is incorrect to call L1 a " law statement " ; this point does not affect our problem, however, since we are assuming that L1, whether or not it would ordinarily be called a " law statement ", does, in the context of our general knowledge, warrant the inference to L1.1

(2) It has been suggested that the two types of statement might be distinguished epistemologically. P. F. Strawson, in his *Introduction to Logical Theory*, suggests that in order to *know*, or to have good evidence or good reason for believing, that a

[1] Compare C. G. Hempel and Paul Oppenheim, " Studies in the Logic of Explanation ", *Philosophy of Science*, Vol. 15, 1948, pp. 135–175 (reprinted in H. Feigl and M. Brodbeck, *Readings in the Philosophy of Science*). It should be noted that these authors (i) attempt to characterize laws with respect only to formalized languages, (ii) concede that "the problem of an adequate definition of purely qualitative (universal) predicates remains open ", and (iii) propose a distinction between " derived " and " fundamental " laws. The latter distinction is similar to a distinction of Braithwaite, discussed below. See also Elizabeth Lane Beardsley, " Non-Accidental and Counterfactual Sentences ", *Journal of Philosophy*, Vol. 46 (1949), pp. 573–591 ; review of the latter by Roderick M. Chisholm, *Journal of Symbolic Logic*, Vol. XVI (1951), pp. 63–64.

given nonlaw statement is true, it is necessary to know that all of its instances have in fact been observed ; but in order to know, or to have good evidence or good reason for believing, that a given law statement is true, it is *not* necessary to know that all of its instances have been examined. (We need not consider the problem of defining " instance " in this use.) "An essential part of our grounds for accepting " a nonlaw statement must be " evidence that there will be no more " instances and " that there never were more than the limited number of which observations have been recorded " (p. 199). Possibly this suggestion is true, but it leaves us with our problem. For the suggestion itself requires use of a modal term ; it refers to what a man *needs* to know, or what it is *essential* that he know, in order to know that a law statement is true. But if we thus allow ourselves the use of modal terms, we could have said at the outset merely that a law statement describes what is " physically necessary ", etc., and that a nonlaw statement does not.

(3) R. B. Braithwaite, in *Scientific Explanation*, suggests that a law statement, as distinguished from a nonlaw statement is one which " appears as a deduction from higher-level hypotheses which have been established independently of the statement (p. 303). " To consider whether or not a scientific hypothesis would, if true, be a law of nature is to consider the way in which it could enter into an established scientific deductive system " (Ibid). In other words, the question whether a statement is law-like may be answered by considering certain logical, or epistemological, relations which the statement bears to certain *other* statements. Our nonlaw statement N2, however, is deducible from the following two statements : (i) " Newspapers which are generally reliable report that all parents of quintuplets during the first half of the twentieth century are named ' Dionne ', " and (ii) " If newspapers which are generally reliable report that all parents of quintuplets during the first half of the twentieth century are named ' Dionne ', then such parents are named ' Dionne '." Statements (i) and (ii) may be considered as " higher level " parts of a " hypothetical-deductive system " from which the nonlaw statement N2 can be deduced ; indeed (i) and (ii) undoubtedly express the grounds upon which most people accept N2. It is not enough, therefore, to describe a nonlaw statement as a statement which " appears as a deduction from higher level hypotheses which have been established *i*ndependently ". (I suggest, incidentally, that it is only at an *a*dvanced stage of inquiry that one regards a synthetic universal *s*tatement as being a *non*law statement.)

LAW STATEMENTS AND COUNTERFACTUAL INFERENCE 101

II

Even if we allow ourselves the distinction between law statements and nonlaw statements and characterize the distinction philosophically, by reference, say, to physical possibility (e.g. "All S is P" is a law statement provided it is not physically possible that anything be both S and not P, etc.), we find that contrary-to-fact conditionals still present certain difficulties of interpretation.[1] Assuming that the distinction between law statement and nonlaw statement is available to us, I shall now make some informal remarks which I hope will throw light upon the ordinary use of these conditionals.

Henry Hiz has suggested that a contrary-to-fact conditional might be interpreted as a metalinguistic statement, telling us something about what can be inferred in a given system of statements. " It says that, if something is accepted in this system to be true, then something else can be accepted in this system to be true."[2] This suggestion, I believe, can be applied to the ordinary use of contrary-to-fact conditionals, but it is necessary to make some qualifying remarks concerning the relevant " systems of statements ".

Let us consider one way of justifying the assertion of a contrary-to-fact conditional, " If *a* were S, *a* would be P ". The antecedent of the counterfactual is taken, its indicative form, as a *supposition* or *assumption*.[3] One says, in effect, " Let us *suppose* that *a* is S ", even though one may believe that *a* is not S. The indicative form of the consequent of the counterfactual— viz., " *a* is P "—is then shown to follow logically from the antecedent taken with certain other statements already accepted. This demonstration is then taken to justify the counterfactual. The point of asserting the counterfactual may be that of *calling attention to, emphasizing,* or *conveying,* one or more of the premises which, taken with the antecedent, logically imply the consequent.

In simple cases, where singular counterfactuals are asserted, we may thus think of the speaker : (i) as having deduced the consequences of a singular supposition, viz., the indicative form of the counterfactual antecedent, taken with a statement he

---

[1] Modal analyses of law statements are suggested by Hans Reichenbach, *Elements of Symbolic Logic*, Ch. VIII, and Arthur Burks, " The Logic of Causal Propositions ", *Mind*, Vol. LX (1951), pp. 363–382.

[2] Henry Hiz, " On the Inferential Sense of Contrary-to-fact Conditionals ", *Journal of Philosophy*, Vol. 48 (1949), pp, 586–587.

[3] Compare S. Jaskowski, " On the Rules of Suppositions in Formal Logic ", *Studia Logica*, No. 1 (Warsaw, 1934), and A. Meinong, *Über Annahmen,* concerning this use of " assumption."

interprets as a law statement; and (ii) as being concerned in part to call attention to, emphasize, or convey, the statement interpreted as a law statement. We can usually tell, from the context of a man's utterance, what the supposition is and what the other statements are with which he is concerned. He may say, " If that were gold, it would be malleable "; it is likely, in this case, that the statement interpreted as a law statement is L2, "All gold is malleable "; it is also likely that this is the statement he is concerned to emphasize.

F. H. Bradley suggested, in his *Principles of Logic*, that when a man asserts a singular counterfactual " the real judgment is concerned with the individual's *qualities*, and asserts no more than a connection of adjectives."[1] Bradley's suggestion, as I interpret it, is that the *whole* point of asserting a singular counter-factual, normally, is to call attention to, emphasize, or convey the statement interpreted as a law statement. It might be mis-leading, however, to say that the man is *affirming* or *asserting* what he takes to be a law statement, or statement describing a " con-nection of adjectives ", for he has not formulated it explicitly. It would also be misleading to say, as Bradley did (p. 89), that the man is merely *supposing* the law statement to be true, for the law statement is something he *believes*, and not merely supposes, to be true. If he were merely supposing "All gold is malleable," along with " That is gold ", then it is likely he would include this supposition in the antecedent of his counterfactual and say " If that were gold and if all gold were malleable, then that would be malleable ". Let us say he is *presupposing* the law statement.

We are suggesting, then, that a man in asserting a counter-factual is telling us something about what can be deduced from some " system of statements " when the indicative version of the antecedent is added to this system as a *supposition*. We are referring to the statements of this system (other than the indica-tive version of the antecedent) as the *presuppositions* of his assertion. And we are suggesting that, normally, at least part of the point of asserting a counterfactual is to *call attention to, emphasize,* or *convey*, one or more of these presuppositions.

The statements a man presupposes when he asserts a counter-factual will, presumably, be statements he accepts or believes. But they will not include the denial of the antecedent of his counterfactual (even if he believes this denial to be true) and

---

[1] Op. cit., p. 90. Compare D. J. O'Connor, " The Analysis of Conditional Sentences ", *Mind*, Vol. LX (1951), p. 360; Robert Brown and John Watling, " Counterfactual Con-ditionals ", *Mind*, Vol. LXI (1952), p. 226.

LAW STATEMENTS AND COUNTERFACTUAL INFERENCE 103

they will not include any statements he would treat as nonlaw statements.[1] And normally there will be many other statements he believes to be true which he will deliberately exclude from his presuppositions. The peculiar problem of interpreting ordinary counterfactual statements is that of specifying which, among the statements the asserter believes, he intends to *exclude* from his presuppositions. What statements he will exclude will depend upon what it is he is concerned to call attention to, emphasize, or convey.

Let us suppose a man accepts the following statements, taking the universal statements to be law statements : (1) All gold is malleable ; (2) No cast-iron is malleable ; (3) Nothing is both gold and cast-iron ; (4) Nothing is both malleable and not malleable ; (5) That is cast-iron ; (6) That is not gold ; and (7) That is not malleable. We may contrast three different situations in which he asserts three different counterfactuals having the same antecedents.

First, he asserts, pointing to an object his hearers don't know to be gold and don't know not to be gold, " If that *were* gold, it would be malleable ". In this case, he is supposing the denial of (6) ; he is excluding from his presuppositions (5), (6), and (7) ; and he is concerned to emphasize (1).

Secondly, he asserts, pointing to an object he and his hearers agree to be cast-iron, " If *that* were gold, then some gold things would not be malleable ". He is again supposing the denial of (6) ; he is excluding (1) and (6), but he is no longer excluding (5) or (7) ; and he is concerned to emphasize either (5) or (2).

Thirdly, he asserts, " If that were gold, then some things would be both malleable and not malleable ". He is again supposing the denial of (6) ; he is now excluding (3) and no longer excluding (1), (5), (6), or (7) ; and he is now concerned to emphasize (1), (2), or (5).

Still other possibilities readily suggest themselves.

If, then, we were to ask " What if that were gold? " our question would have a number of possible answers—e.g., the subjunctive forms of the denial of (7), the denial of (1), and the denial of (4). Any one of these three answers might be appropriate, but they would not *all* be appropriate in conjunction. Which answer is the appropriate one will depend upon what we wish to know. If, in asking " What if that were gold ? ", we wish to know of some law statement describing gold, the denial

---

[1] Instead of saying his presuppositions include no statement he treats as a law statement, it might be more accurate to say this : if his presuppositions include any statement N he would interpret as a nonlaw statement, then N and the man's supposition cannot be so formulated that the supposition constitutes a substitution-instance of N's antecedent.

of (7) is appropriate ; if we wish to know what are the properties of the thing in question, the denial of (1) is appropriate ; and if we wish to know whether the thing has properties such that a statement saying nothing gold has those properties is a law statement, the denial of (4) is appropriate. The counterfactual question, "What if that were gold? ", is, therefore, clearly ambiguous. But in each case, the question could be formulated clearly and unambiguously.

Counterfactuals are similar to *probability* statements in that each type of statement is, in a certain sense, elliptical. If we ask, "What is the probability that this man will survive ? ", our question is incompletely formulated ; a more explicit formulation would be, "With respect to such-and-such evidence, what is the probability that this man will survive? " Similarly, if we ask, "What would American policy in Asia be if Stevenson were President ", our question is incompletely formulated ; a more explicit formulation would be, " Supposing that Stevenson were President, and presupposing so-and-so, but not so-and-so, what would be the consequences with respect to American policy in Asia? " But there is an important respect in which counterfactual statements *differ* from such probability statements. If a man wishes to know what is the probability of a certain statement, i.e., if he wishes to know the truth of a categorical probability statement, then, we may say, he should take into consideration *all* the relevant evidence available to him ; the premises of his probability inference should omit no relevant statement which he is justified in believing.[1] But this " requirement of total evidence " cannot be assumed to hold in the case of counterfactual inference. If a man asks, "What would American policy in Asia be, if Stevenson were President? ", and if his question may be interpreted in the way in which it ordinarily would be interpreted, then there are many facts included in his store of knowledge which we would expect him to *overlook*, or *ignore*, in answering his question ; i.e., there are many facts which we would expect him deliberately to *exclude* from his presuppositions. Normally we would expect him to exclude the fact that Eisenhower's program is the one which has been followed since 1953 ; another is the fact that Mr. Dulles is Secretary of State. But there are other facts, which may also be included in the man's store of knowledge, whose status is more questionable. Does he intend to exclude the fact that Congress was Republican; does he intend to exclude those Asiatic events which have occurred as a result of Eisenhower's policies ; does

---

[1] Compare Rudolf Carnap, *Logical Foundations of Probability*, p. 211 ff.

he intend to exclude the fact that Stevenson went to Asia in 1953? There is no point in insisting either that he consider or that he exclude these facts. But, if he wishes to be understood, he should tell us which are the facts that he is considering, or presupposing, and which are the ones he is excluding.

Bradley suggested the ambiguity of some counterfactual statements may be attributed to the fact that " the supposition is not made evident " (*op. cit.* p. 89). In our terminology, it would be more accurate to say that the *presupposition* is not made evident ; for the supposition is usually formulated explicitly in the antecedent of the counterfactual statement. (But when a man says, " If that thing, which is not S, were S . . . . . , " the subordinate indicative clause expresses neither a supposition nor a presupposition.) Ideally it might be desirable to formulate our counterfactuals in somewhat the following way : " Supposing that that is S, and presupposing so-and-so, then it follows that that is P." In practice, however, it is often easy to tell, from the context in which a counterfactual is asserted, just what it is that is being presupposed and what it is that is being excluded[1]

Although I have been using the terms " counterfactual " and " contrary-to-fact " throughout this discussion, it is important to note that, when a man arrives at a conditional statement in the manner we have been discussing, his supposition—and thus also the antecedent of his conditional—need *not* be anything he believes to be false. For example, a man in deliberating will consider the consequences of a supposition, taken along with certain presuppositions, and he will also consider the consequences of its denial, taken along with the same presuppositions. It is misleading to say, therefore, that the conditionals he may then affirm are " counterfactual ", or " contrary-to-fact ", for he may have no beliefs about the truth or falsity of the respective antecedents and one of these antecedents will in fact be true.[2] A better term might be " suppositional conditional " or, indeed, " hypothetical statement ".

Brown University, U.S.A.

[1] " The Contrary-to-fact Conditional " (pp. 303–304 ; Feigl-Sellars, p. 494) I discuss what I take to be certain conventions of ordinary language pertaining to this point.
[2] Compare Alan Ross Anderson, "A Note on Subjunctive and Counterfactual Conditionals ", Analysis, Vol. 12 (1951), pp. 35–38; Roderick M. Chisholm, review of David Pears' " Hypotheticals ", *Journal of Symbolic Logic*, Vol. 15 (1950), pp. 215–216.

The Problem of
Counterfactual Conditionals

Nelson Goodman

I

THE PROBLEM OF COUNTERFACTUAL CONDITIONALS[1]

1. The Problem in General

The analysis of counterfactual conditionals is no fussy little grammatical exercise. Indeed, if we lack the means for interpreting counterfactual conditionals, we can hardly claim to have any adequate philosophy of science. A satisfactory definition of scientific law, a satisfactory theory of confirmation or of disposition terms (and this includes not only predicates ending in "ible" and "able" but almost every objective predicate, such as "is red"), would solve a large part of the problem of counterfactuals. Conversely, a solution to the problem of counterfactuals would give us the answer to critical questions about law, confirmation, and the meaning of potentiality.

I am not at all contending that the problem of counterfactuals is logically or psychologically the first of these related problems. It makes little difference where we start if we can go ahead. If the study of counterfactuals has up to now failed this pragmatic test, the alternative approaches are little better off.

---

[1] My indebtedness in several matters to the work of C. I. Lewis has seemed too obvious to call for detailed mention.

· COUNTERFACTUAL CONDITIONALS ·

What, then, is the *problem* about counterfactual conditionals? Let us confine ourselves to those in which antecedent and consequent are inalterably false—as, for example, when I say of a piece of butter that was eaten yesterday, and that had never been heated,

If that piece of butter had been heated to 150° F., it would have melted.

Considered as truth-functional compounds, all counterfactuals are of course true, since their antecedents are false. Hence

If that piece of butter had been heated to 150° F., it would not have melted

would also hold. Obviously something different is intended, and the problem is to define the circumstances under which a given counterfactual holds while the opposing conditional with the contradictory consequent fails to hold. And this criterion of truth must be set up in the face of the fact that a counterfactual by its nature can never be subjected to any direct empirical test by realizing its antecedent.

In one sense the name "problem of counterfactuals" is misleading, because the problem is independent of the form in which a given statement happens to be expressed. The problem of counterfactuals is equally a problem of factual conditionals, for any counterfactual can be transposed into a conditional with a true antecedent and consequent; e.g.,

Since that butter did not melt, it wasn't heated to 150° F.

The possibility of such transformation is of no great importance except to clarify the nature of our problem. That

4

· COUNTERFACTUAL CONDITIONALS ·

"since" occurs in the contrapositive shows that what is in question is a certain kind of connection between the two component sentences; and the truth of statements of this kind—whether they have the form of counterfactual or factual conditionals or some other form—depends not upon the truth or falsity of the components but upon whether the intended connection obtains. Recognizing the possibility of transformation serves mainly to focus attention on the central problem and to discourage speculation as to the nature of counterfacts. Although I shall begin my study by considering counterfactuals as such, it must be borne in mind that a general solution would explain the kind of connection involved irrespective of any assumption as to the truth or falsity of the components.

The effect of transposition upon conditionals of another kind, which I call "semifactuals", is worth noticing briefly. Should we assert

Even if the match had been scratched, it still would not have lighted,

we would uncompromisingly reject as an equally good expression of our meaning the contrapositive,

Even if the match lighted, it still wasn't scratched.

Our original intention was to affirm not that the non-lighting could be inferred from the scratching, but simply that the lighting could not be inferred from the scratching. Ordinarily a semifactual conditional has the force of denying what is affirmed by the opposite, fully counterfactual conditional. The sentence

Even had that match been scratched, it still wouldn't have lighted

· COUNTERFACTUAL CONDITIONALS ·

is normally meant as the direct negation of

Had the match been scratched, it would have lighted.

That is to say, in practice full counterfactuals affirm, while semifactuals deny, that a certain connection obtains between antecedent and consequent.[2] Thus it is clear why a semifactual generally has not the same meaning as its contrapositive.

There are various special kinds of counterfactuals that present special problems. An example is the case of 'counteridenticals', illustrated by the statements

If I were Julius Caesar, I wouldn't be alive in the twentieth century,

and

If Julius Caesar were I, he would be alive in the twentieth century.

Here, although the antecedent in the two cases is a statement of the same identity, we attach two different consequents which, on the very assumption of that identity, are incompatible. Another special class of counterfactuals is that of the 'countercomparatives', with antecedents such as

If I had more money, ...

The trouble with these is that when we try to translate the counterfactual into a statement about a relation between

---

[2] The practical import of a semifactual is thus different from its literal import. Literally a semifactual and the corresponding counterfactual are not contradictories but contraries, and both may be false (cf. Note I.9 below). The presence of the auxiliary terms "even" and "still", or either of them, is perhaps the idiomatic indication that a not quite literal meaning is intended.

6

· COUNTERFACTUAL CONDITIONALS ·

two tenseless, non-modal sentences, we get as an antecedent something like

If "I have more money than I have" were true, . . . ,

which wrongly represents the original antecedent as self-contradictory. Again there are the 'counterlegals', conditionals with antecedents that either deny general laws directly, as in

If triangles were squares, . . . ,

or else make a supposition of particular fact that is not merely false but impossible, as in

If this cube of sugar were also spherical, ...

Counterfactuals of all these kinds offer interesting but not insurmountable special difficulties.[3] In order to concentrate upon the major problems concerning counterfactuals in general, I shall usually choose my examples in such a way as to avoid these more special complications.

As I see it, there are two major problems, though they are not independent and may even be regarded as aspects of a single problem. A counterfactual is true if a certain connection obtains between the antecedent and the con-

---

[3] Of the special kinds of counterfactuals mentioned, I shall have something to say later about counteridenticals and counterlegals. As for countercomparatives, the following procedure is appropriate:—Given "If I had arrived one minute later, I would have missed the train", first expand this to "($\exists t$). t is a time. I arrived at t. If I had arrived one minute later than t, I would have missed the train". The counterfactual conditional constituting the final clause of this conjunction can then be treated, within the quantified whole, in the usual way. Translation into "If 'I arrive one minute later than t' were true, then 'I miss the train' would have been true" does not give us a self-contradictory component.

· COUNTERFACTUAL CONDITIONALS ·

sequent. But as is obvious from examples already given, the consequent seldom follows from the antecedent by logic alone. (1) In the first place, the assertion that a connection holds is made on the presumption that certain circumstances not stated in the antecedent obtain. When we say

If that match had been scratched, it would have lighted,

we mean that conditions are such—i.e. the match is well made, is dry enough, oxygen enough is present, etc.—that "That match lights" can be inferred from "That match is scratched". Thus the connection we affirm may be regarded as joining the consequent with the conjunction of the antecedent and other statements that truly describe relevant conditions. Notice especially that our assertion of the counterfactual is *not* conditioned upon these circumstances obtaining. We do not assert that the counterfactual is true *if* the circumstances obtain; rather, in asserting the counterfactual we commit ourselves to the actual truth of the statements describing the requisite relevant conditions. The first major problem is to define relevant conditions: to specify what sentences are meant to be taken in conjunction with an antecedent as a basis for inferring the consequent. (2) But even after the particular relevant conditions are specified, the connection obtaining will not ordinarily be a logical one. The principle that permits inference of

That match lights

from

That match is scratched. That match is dry enough. Enough oxygen is present. Etc.

8

· COUNTERFACTUAL CONDITIONALS ·

is not a law of logic but what we call a natural or physical or causal law. The second major problem concerns the definition of such laws.

2. *The Problem of Relevant Conditions*

It might seem natural to propose that the consequent follows by law from the antecedent and a description of the actual state-of-affairs of the world, that we need hardly define relevant conditions because it will do no harm to include irrelevant ones. But if we say that the consequent follows by law from the antecedent and *all* true statements, we encounter an immediate difficulty:— among true sentences is the negate of the antecedent, so that from the antecedent and all true sentences everything follows. Certainly this gives us no way of distinguishing true from false counterfactuals.

We are plainly no better off if we say that the consequent must follow from *some* set of true statements conjoined with the antecedent; for given any counterfactual antecedent *A*, there will always be a set *S*—namely, the set consisting of *not-A*—such that from *A·S* any consequent follows. (Hereafter I shall regularly use the following symbols: "*A*" for the antecedent; "*C*" for the consequent; "*S*" for the set of statements of the relevant conditions or, indifferently, for the conjunction of these statements.)

Perhaps then we must exclude statements logically incompatible with the antecedent. But this is insufficient; for a parallel difficulty arises with respect to true statements which are not logically but are otherwise incompatible with the antecedent. For example, take

If that radiator had frozen, it would have broken.

9

· COUNTERFACTUAL CONDITIONALS ·

Among true sentences may well be (*S*)

That radiator never reached a temperature below 33° F.

Now we have as true generalizations both

All radiators that freeze but never reach below 33° F. break,

and also

All radiators that freeze but never reach below 33° F. fail to break;

for there are no such radiators. Thus from the antecedent of the counterfactual and the given *S*, we can infer any consequent.

The natural proposal to remedy this difficulty is to rule that counterfactuals cannot depend upon empty laws; that the connection can be established only by a principle of the form "All *x*'s are *y*'s" when there are some *x*'s. But this is ineffectual. For if empty principles are excluded, the following non-empty principles may be used in the case given with the same result:

Everything that is either a radiator that freezes but does not reach below 33° F., or that is a soap bubble, breaks;

Everything that is either a radiator that freezes but does not reach below 33° F., or is powder, does not break.

By these principles we can infer any consequent from the *A* and *S* in question.

The only course left open to us seems to be to define relevant conditions as the set of all true statements each of which is both logically and non-logically compatible with *A* where non-logical incompatibility means violation of a

· COUNTERFACTUAL CONDITIONALS ·

non-logical law.[4] But another difficulty immediately appears. In a counterfactual beginning

If Jones were in Carolina, . . .

the antecedent is entirely compatible with

Jones is not in South Carolina

and with

Jones is not in North Carolina

and with

North Carolina plus South Carolina is identical with Carolina;

but all these taken together with the antecedent make a set that is self-incompatible, so that again any consequent would be forthcoming.

Clearly it will not help to require only that for *some* set S of true sentences, $A \cdot S$ be self-compatible and lead by law to the consequent; for this would make a true counterfactual of

If Jones were in Carolina, he would be in South Carolina,

and also of

If Jones were in Carolina, he would be in North Carolina,

which cannot both be true.

It seems that we must elaborate our criterion still further, to characterize a counterfactual as true if and only if there is some set S of true statements such that $A \cdot S$ is self-compatible and leads by law to the consequent, while there

---

[4] This of course raises very serious questions, which I shall come to presently, about the nature of non-logical law.

· COUNTERFACTUAL CONDITIONALS ·

is no such set S' such that $A \cdot S'$ is self-compatible and leads by law to the negate of the consequent.[5] Unfortunately even this is not enough. For among true sentences will be the negate of the consequent: $-C$. Is $-C$ compatible with A or not? If not, then A alone without any additional conditions must lead by law to C. But if $-C$ is compatible with A (as in most cases), then if we take $-C$ as our S, the conjunction $A \cdot S$ will give us $-C$. Thus the criterion we have set up will seldom be satisfied; for since $-C$ will normally be compatible with A, as the need for introducing the relevant conditions testifies, there will normally be an S (namely, $-C$) such that $A \cdot S$ is self-compatible and leads by law to $-C$.

Part of our trouble lies in taking too narrow a view of our problem. We have been trying to lay down conditions under which an A that is known to be false leads to a C that is known to be false; but it is equally important to make sure that our criterion does not establish a similar connection between our A and the (true) negate of C. Because our S together with A was to be so chosen as to give us C, it seemed gratuitous to specify that S must be compatible with C; and because $-C$ is true by supposition, S would necessarily be compatible with it. But we are testing whether our criterion not only admits the true counterfactual we are concerned with but also excludes the

-----

[5] Note that the requirement that $A \cdot S$ be self-compatible can be fulfilled only if the antecedent is self-compatible; hence the conditionals I have called "counterlegals" will all be false. This is convenient for our present purpose of investigating counterfactuals that are not counterlegals. If it later appears desirable to regard all or some counterlegals as true, special provisions may be introduced.

opposing conditional. Accordingly, our criterion must be modified by specifying that S be compatible with both C and $-C$.[6] In other words, S by itself must not decide between C and $-C$, but S together with A must lead to C but not to $-C$. We need not know whether C is true or false.

Our rule thus reads that a counterfactual is true if and only if there is some set S of true sentences such that S is compatible with C and with $-C$, and such that $A \cdot S$ is self-compatible and leads by law to C; while there is no set S' compatible with C and with $-C$, and such that $A \cdot S'$ is self-compatible and leads by law to $-C$.[7] As thus stated, the rule involves a certain redundancy; but simplification is not in point here, for the criterion is still inadequate.

The requirement that $A \cdot S$ be self-compatible is not strong enough; for S might comprise true sentences that although *compatible with A*, were such that *they would*

---

[6] It is natural to inquire whether for similar reasons we should stipulate that S must be compatible with both A and $-A$, but this is unnecessary. For if S is incompatible with $-A$, then A follows from S; therefore if S is compatible with both C and $-C$, then $A \cdot S$ cannot lead by law to one but not the other. Hence no sentence incompatible with $-A$ can satisfy the other requirements for a suitable S.

[7] Since the first edition of this book, W. T. Parry has pointed out that no counterfactual satisfies this formula; for one can always take $-(A \cdot -C)$ as S, and take $-(A \cdot C)$ as S'. Thus we must add the requirement that neither S nor S' follows by law from $-A$. Of course this does not alleviate the further difficulties explained in the following paragraphs of the text above. (See Parry's 'Reexamination of the Problem of Counterfactual Conditionals', *Journal of Philosophy*, vol. 54 [1957], pp. 85–94, and my 'Parry on Counterfactuals', same journal, same volume, pp. 442–5.)

· COUNTERFACTUAL CONDITIONALS ·

not be true if A were true. For this reason, many statements that we would regard as definitely false would be true according to the stated criterion. As an example, consider the familiar case where for a given match m, we would affirm

(i) If match m had been scratched, it would have lighted,

but deny

(ii) If match m had been scratched, it would not have been dry.[8]

According to our tentative criterion, statement (ii) would be quite as true as statement (i). For in the case of (ii), we may take as an element in our S the true sentence

Match m did not light,

which is presumably compatible with A (otherwise nothing would be required along with A to reach the opposite as the consequent of the true counterfactual statement (i)). As our total $A \cdot S$ we may have

Match m is scratched. It does not light. It is well made. Oxygen enough is present . . . etc.;

and from this, by means of a legitimate general law, we can infer

It was not dry.

And there would seem to be no suitable set of sentences S' such that $A \cdot S'$ leads by law to the negate of this conse-

---

[8] Of course, some sentences similar to (ii), referring to other matches under special conditions, may be true; but the objection to the proposed criterion is that it would commit us to many such statements that are patently false. I am indebted to Morton G. White for a suggestion concerning the exposition of this point.

· COUNTERFACTUAL CONDITIONALS ·

quent. Hence the unwanted counterfactual is established in accord with our rule. The trouble is caused by including in our *S* a true statement which though compatible with *A* would not be true if *A* were. Accordingly we must exclude such statements from the set of relevant conditions; *S*, in addition to satisfying the other requirements already laid down, must be not merely compatible with *A* but 'jointly tenable' or *cotenable* with *A*. *A* is cotenable with *S*, and the conjunction *A·S* self-cotenable, if it is not the case that *S* would not be true if *A* were.[9]

Parenthetically it may be noted that the relative fixity of conditions is often unclear, so that the speaker or writer has to make explicit additional provisos or give subtle verbal clues as to his meaning. For example, each of the following two counterfactuals would normally be accepted:

If New York City were in Georgia, then New York City would be in the South.

If Georgia included New York City, then Georgia would not be entirely in the South.

Yet the antecedents are logically indistinguishable. What happens is that the direction of expression becomes important, because in the former case the meaning is

---

[9] The double negative cannot be eliminated here; for ". . . if *S* would be true if *A* were" actually constitutes a stronger requirement. As we noted earlier (Note I.2), if two conditionals having the same counterfactual antecedent are such that the consequent of one is the negate of the consequent of the other, the conditionals are contraries and both may be false. This will be the case, for example, if every otherwise suitable set of relevant conditions that in conjunction with the antecedent leads by law either to a given consequent or its negate leads also to the other.

· COUNTERFACTUAL CONDITIONALS ·

If New York City were in Georgia, and the boundaries of Georgia remained unchanged, then . . . ,

while in the latter case the meaning is

If Georgia included New York City, and the boundaries of New York City remained unchanged, then . . . .

Without some such cue to the meaning as is covertly given by the word-order, we should be quite uncertain which of the two consequents in question could be truly attached. The same kind of explanation accounts for the paradoxical pairs of counteridenticals mentioned earlier.

Returning now to the proposed rule, I shall neither offer further corrections of detail nor discuss whether the requirement that S be cotenable with A makes superfluous some other provisions of the criterion; for such matters become rather unimportant beside the really serious difficulty that now confronts us. In order to determine the truth of a given counterfactual it seems that we have to determine, among other things, whether there is a suitable S that is cotenable with A and meets certain further requirements. But in order to determine whether or not a given S is cotenable with A, we have to determine whether or not the counterfactual "If A were true, then S would not be true" is itself true. But this means determining whether or not there is a suitable S_1, cotenable with A, that leads to $-S$ and so on. Thus we find ourselves involved in an infinite regressus or a circle; for cotenability is defined in terms of counterfactuals, yet the meaning of counterfactuals is defined in terms of cotenability. In other words to establish any counterfactual, it seems that we first have to determine the truth of another. If so, we can never explain a counterfactual except in terms of others, so that the problem of counterfactuals must remain unsolved.

Though unwilling to accept this conclusion, I do not at present see any way of meeting the difficulty. One naturally thinks of revising the whole treatment of counterfactuals in such a way as to admit first those that depend on no conditions other than the antecedent, and then use these counterfactuals as the criteria for the cotenability of relevant conditions with antecedents of other counterfactuals, and so on. But this idea seems initially rather unpromising in view of the formidable difficulties of accounting by such a step-by-step method for even so simple a counterfactual as

If the match had been scratched, it would have lighted.

3. The Problem of Law

Even more serious is the second of the problems mentioned earlier: the nature of the general statements that enable us to infer the consequent upon the basis of the antecedent and the statement of relevant conditions. The distinction between these connecting principles and relevant conditions is imprecise and arbitrary; the 'connecting principles' might be conjoined to the condition-statements, and the relation of the antecedent-conjunction $(A \cdot S)$ to the consequent thus made a matter of logic. But the same problems would arise as to the kind of principle that is capable of sustaining a counterfactual; and it is convenient to consider the connecting principles separately.

In order to infer the consequent of a counterfactual from the antecedent A and a suitable statement of relevant conditions S, we make use of a general statement; namely,

· COUNTERFACTUAL CONDITIONALS ·

the generalization[10] of the conditional having $A \cdot S$ for antecedent and C for consequent. For example, in the case of

If the match had been scratched, it would have lighted

the connecting principle is

Every match that is scratched, well made, dry enough, in enough oxygen, etc., lights.

But notice that *not* every counterfactual is actually sustained by the principle thus arrived at, *even* if that principle is *true*. Suppose, for example, that all I had in my right pocket on VE day was a group of silver coins. Now we would not under normal circumstances affirm of a given penny P

If P had been in my pocket on VE day, P would have been silver,[11]

even though from

P was in my pocket on VE day

---

[10] The sense of "generalization" intended here is that explained by C. G. Hempel in 'A Purely Syntactical Definition of Confirmation', *Journal of Symbolic Logic*, vol. 8 (1943), pp. 122–43. See also III.3, below.

[11] The antecedent in this example is intended to mean "If P, while remaining distinct from the things that were in fact in my pocket on VE day, had also been in my pocket then", and *not* the quite different, counteridentical "If P had been identical with one of the things that were in my pocket on VE day". While the antecedents of most counterfactuals (as, again, our familiar one about the match) are—literally speaking—open to both sorts of interpretation, ordinary usage normally calls for some explicit indication when the counteridentical meaning is intended.

· COUNTERFACTUAL CONDITIONALS ·

we can infer the consequent by means of the general statement

Everything in my pocket on VE day was silver.

On the contrary, we would assert that if P had been in my pocket, then this general statement would not be true. The general statement will *not* permit us to infer the given consequent from the counterfactual assumption that P was in my pocket, because the general statement will not itself withstand that counterfactual assumption. Though the supposed connecting principle is indeed general, true, and perhaps even fully confirmed by observation of all cases, it is incapable of sustaining a counterfactual because it remains a description of accidental fact, not a law. The truth of a counterfactual conditional thus seems to depend on whether the general sentence required for the inference is a law or not. If so, our problem is to distinguish accurately between causal laws and casual facts.[12]

The problem illustrated by the example of the coins is closely related to that which led us earlier to require the cotenability of the antecedent and the relevant conditions, in order to avoid resting a counterfactual on any statement that would not be true if the antecedent were true. For decision as to the cotenability of two sentences depends partly upon decisions as to whether certain general statements are laws, and we are now concerned directly with

---

[12] The importance of distinguishing laws from non-laws is too often overlooked. If a clear distinction can be defined, it may serve not only the purposes explained in the present paper but also many of those for which the increasingly dubious distinction between analytic and synthetic statements is ordinarily supposed to be needed.

· COUNTERFACTUAL CONDITIONALS ·

the latter problem. Is there some way of so distinguishing
laws from non-laws, among true universal statements of
the kind in question, that laws will be the principles that
will sustain counterfactual conditionals?

Any attempt to draw the distinction by reference to a
notion of causative force can be dismissed at once as un-
scientific. And it is clear that no purely syntactical criterion can be adequate, for even the most special descriptions of particular facts can be cast in a form having any
desired degree of syntactical universality. "Book *B* is
small" becomes "Everything that is Q is small" if "Q"
stands for some predicate that applies uniquely to *B*. What
then does distinguish a law like

All butter melts at 150° F.

from a true and general non-law like

All the coins in my pocket are silver ?

Primarily, I would like to suggest, the fact that the first is
accepted as true while many cases of it remain to be determined, the further, unexamined cases being predicted
to conform with it. The second sentence, on the contrary,
is accepted as a description of contingent fact *after* the
determination of all cases, no prediction of any of its instances being based upon it. This proposal raises innumerable problems, some of which I shall consider presently;
but the idea behind it is just that the principle we use to
decide counterfactual cases is a principle we are willing to
commit ourselves to in deciding unrealized cases that are
still subject to direct observation.

As a first approximation then, we might say that a law is
a true sentence used for making predictions. That laws are

· COUNTERFACTUAL CONDITIONALS ·

used predictively is of course a simple truism, and I am not proposing it as a novelty. I want only to emphasize the Humean idea that rather than a sentence being used for prediction because it is a law, it is called a law because it is used for prediction; and that rather than the law being used for prediction because it describes a causal connection, the meaning of the causal connection is to be interpreted in terms of predictively used laws.

By the determination of all instances, I mean simply the examination or testing by other means of all things that satisfy the antecedent, to decide whether all satisfy the consequent also. There are difficult questions about the meaning of "instance", many of which Professor Hempel has investigated. Most of these are avoided in our present study by the fact that we are concerned with a very narrow class of sentences: those arrived at by generalizing conditionals of a certain kind. Remaining problems about the meaning of "instance" I shall have to ignore here. As for "determination", I do not mean final discovery of truth, but only enough examination to reach a decision as to whether a given statement or its negate is to be admitted as evidence for the hypothesis in question.

Our criterion excludes vacuous principles as laws. The generalizations needed for sustaining counterfactual conditionals cannot be vacuous, for they must be supported by evidence.[13] The limited scope of our present problem

---

[13] Had it been sufficient in the preceding section to require only that $A \cdot S$ be self-*compatible*, this requirement might now be eliminated in favor of the stipulation that the generalization of the conditional having $A \cdot S$ as antecedent and C as consequent should be non-vacuous; but this stipulation would not guarantee the self-*cotenability* of $A \cdot S$.

· COUNTERFACTUAL CONDITIONALS ·

makes it unimportant that our criterion, if applied generally to all statements, would classify as laws many statements—e.g., true singular predictions—that we would not
normally call laws.

For convenience, I shall use the term "lawlike" for sentences that, whether they are true or not, satisfy the other
requirements in the definition of law. A law is thus a sentence that is both lawlike and true, but a sentence may be
true without being lawlike, as I have illustrated, or lawlike
without being true, as we are always learning to our dis-
may.

Now if we were to leave our definition as it stands, lawlikeness would be a rather accidental and ephemeral
property. Only statements that happen actually to have
been used for prediction would be lawlike. And a true
sentence that had been used predictively would cease to be
a law when it became fully tested—i.e., when none of its
instances remained undetermined. The definition, then,
must be restated in some such way as this: A general statement is lawlike if and only if it is acceptable prior to the
determination of all its instances. This is immediately objectionable because "acceptable" itself is plainly a dispositional term; but I propose to use it only tentatively, with
the idea of eliminating it eventually by means of a non-
dispositional definition. Before trying to accomplish that,
however, we must face another difficulty in our tentative
criterion of lawlikeness.

Suppose that the appropriate generalization fails to sustain a given counterfactual because that generalization,
while true, is unlawlike, as is

Everything in my pocket is silver.

22

· COUNTERFACTUAL CONDITIONALS ·

All we would need to do to get a law would be to broaden the antecedent strategically. Consider, for example, the sentence

Everything that is in my pocket or is a dime is silver.

Since we have not examined all dimes, this is a predictive statement and—since presumably true—would be a law. Now if we consider our original counterfactual and choose our S so that $A \cdot S$ is

P is in my pocket. P is in my pocket or is a dime,

then the pseudo-law just constructed can be used to infer from this the sentence "P is silver". Thus the untrue counterfactual is established. If one prefers to avoid an alternation as a condition-statement, the same result can be obtained by using a new predicate such as "dimo" to mean "is in my pocket or is a dime".[14]

The change called for, I think, will make the definition of lawlikeness read as follows: A sentence is lawlike if its acceptance does not depend upon the determination of any given instance.[15] Naturally this does not mean that

---

[14] Apart from the special class of connecting principles we are concerned with, note that under the stated criterion of lawlikeness, any statement could be expanded into a lawlike one; for example: given "This book is black" we could use the predictive sentence "This book is black and all oranges are spherical" to argue that the blackness of the book is the consequence of a law.

[15] So stated, the definition counts vacuous principles as laws. If we read instead "given class of instances", vacuous principles will be non-laws since their acceptance depends upon examination of the null class of instances. For my present purposes the one formulation is as good as the other.

· COUNTERFACTUAL CONDITIONALS ·

acceptance is to be independent of all determination of instances, but only that there is no particular instance on the determination of which acceptance depends. This criterion excludes from the class of laws a statement like

That book is black and oranges are spherical

on the ground that acceptance requires knowing whether the book is black; it excludes

Everything that is in my pocket or is a dime is silver

on the ground that acceptance demands examination of all things in my pocket. Moreover, it excludes a statement like

All the marbles in this bag except Number 19 are red, and Number 19 is black

on the ground that acceptance would depend on examination of or knowledge gained otherwise concerning marble Number 19. In fact the principle involved in the proposed criterion is a rather powerful one and seems to exclude most of the troublesome cases.

We must still, however, replace the notion of the acceptability of a sentence, or of its acceptance *depending* or *not depending* on some given knowledge, by a positive definition of such dependence. It is clear that to say that the acceptance of a given statement depends upon a certain kind and amount of evidence is to say that given such evidence, acceptance of the statement is in accord with certain general standards for the acceptance of statements that are not fully tested. So one turns naturally to theories of induction and confirmation to learn the distinguishing factors or circumstances that determine whether or not a sentence is acceptable without complete evidence. But

· COUNTERFACTUAL CONDITIONALS ·

publications on confirmation not only have failed to make clear the distinction between confirmable and non-confirmable statements, but show little recognition that such a problem exists.[16] Yet obviously in the case of some sentences like

Everything in my pocket is silver

or

No twentieth-century president of the United States will be between 6 feet 1 inch and 6 feet 1½ inches tall,

not even the testing with positive results of all but a single instance is likely to lead us to accept the sentence and predict that the one remaining instance will conform to it; while for other sentences such as

All dimes are silver

or

All butter melts at 150° F.

or

All flowers of plants descended from this seed will be yellow,

positive determination of even a few instances may lead us to accept the sentence with confidence and make predictions in accordance with it.

There is some hope that cases like these can be dealt with by a sufficiently careful and intricate elaboration of current confirmation theories; but inattention to the problem

---

[16] The points discussed in this and the following paragraph have been dealt with a little more fully in my 'A Query on Confirmation', *Journal of Philosophy*, vol. xliii (1946), pp. 383–5.

· COUNTERFACTUAL CONDITIONALS ·

of distinguishing between confirmable and non-confirmable sentences has left most confirmation theories open to more damaging counterexamples of an elementary kind.

Suppose we designate the 26 marbles in a bag by the letters of the alphabet, using these merely as proper names having no ordinal significance. Suppose further that we are told that all the marbles except d are red, but we are not told what color d is. By the usual kind of confirmation theory this gives strong confirmation for the statement

Ra. Rb. Rc. Rd. . . . Rz

because 25 of the 26 cases are known to be favorable while none is known to be unfavorable. But unfortunately the same argument would show that the very same evidence would equally confirm

Ra. Rb. Rc. Re. . . . Rz. —Rd,

for again we have 25 favorable and no unfavorable cases. Thus "Rd" and "—Rd" are equally and strongly confirmed by the same evidence. If I am required to use a single predicate instead of both "R" and "—R" in the second case, I will use "P" to mean:

is in the bag and either is not d and is red, or is d and is not red.

Then the evidence will be 25 positive cases for

All the marbles are P

from which it follows that d is P, and thus that d is not red. The problem of what statements are confirmable merely becomes the equivalent problem of what predicates are projectible from known to unknown cases.

So far, I have discovered no way of meeting these diffi-

26

· COUNTERFACTUAL CONDITIONALS ·

culties. Yet as we have seen, some solution is urgently wanted for our present purpose; for only where willingness to accept a statement involves predictions of instances that may be tested does acceptance endow that statement with the authority to govern counterfactual cases, which cannot be directly tested.

In conclusion, then, some problems about counterfactuals depend upon the definition of cotenability, which in turn seems to depend upon the prior solution of those problems. Other problems require an adequate definition of law. The tentative criterion of law here proposed is reasonably satisfactory in excluding unwanted kinds of statements, and in effect, reduces one aspect of our problem to the question how to define the circumstances under which a statement is acceptable independently of the determination of any given instance. But this question I do not know how to answer.

A Theory of Conditionals

Robert Stalnaker

Reprinted with permission of the editor and the author from *Studies in Logical Theory,*
American Philosophical Quarterly Monograph Series, No. 2, ed. Nicholas Rescher (Oxford:
Basil Blackwell, Publisher, 1968), pp. 98–112.

IV

A Theory of Conditionals

ROBERT C. STALNAKER*

I. INTRODUCTION

A conditional sentence expresses a proposition which is a function of two other propositions, yet not one which is a *truth* function of those propositions. I may know the truth values of "Willie Mays played in the American League" and "Willie Mays hit four hundred" without knowing whether or not Mays would have hit four hundred if he had played in the American League. This fact has tended to puzzle, displease, or delight philosophers, and many have felt that it is a fact that calls for some comment or explanation. It has given rise to a number of philosophical problems; I shall discuss three of these.

My principal concern will be with what has been called the *logical problem of conditionals*, a problem that frequently is ignored or dismissed by writers on conditionals and counterfactuals. This is the task of describing the formal properties of the *conditional function*: a function, usually represented in English by the words "if . . . then," taking ordered pairs of propositions into propositions. I shall explain informally and defend a solution, presented more rigorously elsewhere, to this problem.[1]

The second issue—the one that has dominated recent discussions of contrary-to-fact conditionals—is the *pragmatic problem of counterfactuals*. This problem derives from the belief, which I share with most philosophers writing about this topic, that the formal properties of the conditional function, together with all of the *facts*, may not be sufficient for determining the truth value of a counterfactual; that is,

* I want to express appreciation to my colleague, Professor R. H. Thomason, for his collaboration in the formal development of the theory expounded in this paper, and for his helpful comments on its exposition and defense.

The preparation of this paper was supported in part by a National Science Foundation grant, GS–1567.

[1] R. C. Stalnaker and R. H. Thomason, "A Semantic Analysis of Conditional Logic" (forthcoming). In this paper, the formal system, C2, is proved sound and semantically complete with respect to the interpretation sketched in the present paper. That is, it is shown that a formula is a consequence of a class of formulas if and only if it is derivable from the class in the formal system, C2.

different truth valuations of conditional statements may be consistent with a single valuation of all nonconditional statements. The task set by the problem is to find and defend criteria for choosing among these different valuations.

This problem is different from the first issue because these criteria are pragmatic, and not semantic. The distinction between semantic and pragmatic criteria, however, depends on the construction of a semantic theory. The semantic theory that I shall defend will thus help to clarify the second problem by charting the boundary between the semantic and pragmatic components of the concept. The question of this boundary line is precisely what Rescher, for example, avoids by couching his whole discussion in terms of conditions for belief, or justified belief, rather than truth conditions. Conditions for justified belief are pragmatic for any concept.[2]

The third issue is an epistemological problem that has bothered empiricist philosophers. It is based on the fact that many counter-factuals seem to be synthetic, and contingent, statements about unrealized possibilities. But contingent statements must be capable of confirmation by empirical evidence, and the investigator can gather evidence only in the actual world. How are conditionals which are both empirical and contrary-to-fact possible at all? How do we learn about possible worlds, and where are the facts (or counterfacts) which make counterfactuals true? Such questions have led philosophers to try to analyze the conditional in non-conditional terms[3]—to show that conditionals merely appear to be about unrealized possibilities. My approach, however, will be to accept the appearance as reality, and to argue that one can sometimes have evidence about nonactual situations.

In Sects. II and III of this paper, I shall present and defend a theory of conditionals which has two parts: a formal system with a primitive conditional connective, and a semantical apparatus which provides general truth conditions for statements involving that connective. In Sects. IV, V and VI, I shall discuss in a general way the relation of the theory to the three problems outlined above.

[2] N. Rescher, *Hypothetical Reasoning* (Amsterdam, 1964).

[3] Cf. R. Chisholm, "The Contrary-to-fact Conditional," *Mind*, vol. 55 (1946), pp. 289–307, reprinted in *Readings in Philosophical Analysis*, ed. by H. Feigl and W. Sellars (New York, 1949), pp. 482–497. The problem is sometimes posed (as it is here) as the task of analyzing the *subjunctive* conditional into an indicative statement, but I think it is a mistake to base very much on the distinction of mood. As far as I can tell, the mood tends to indicate something about the attitude of the speaker, but in no way effects the propositional content of the statement.

II. THE INTERPRETATION

Eventually, I want to defend a hypothesis about the truth conditions for statements having conditional form, but I shall begin by asking a more practical question: how does one evaluate a conditional statement? How does one decide whether or not he believes it to be true? An answer to this question will not be a set of truth conditions, but it will serve as a heuristic aid in the search for such a set.

To make the question more concrete, consider the following situation: you are faced with a true-false political opinion survey. The statement is, "If the Chinese enter the Vietnam conflict, the United States will use nuclear weapons." How do you deliberate in choosing your response? What considerations of a logical sort are relevant? I shall first discuss two familiar answers to this question, and then defend a third answer which avoids some of the weaknesses of the first two.

The first answer is based on the simplest account of the conditional, the truth functional analysis. According to this account, you should reason as follows in responding to the true-false quiz: you ask yourself, first, will the Chinese enter the conflict? and second, will the United States use nuclear weapons? If the answer to the first question is no, *or* if the answer to the second is yes, then you should place your *X* in the "true" box. But this account is unacceptable since the following piece of reasoning is an obvious *non sequitur*: "I firmly believe that the Chinese will stay out of the conflict; *therefore* I believe that the statement is true." The falsity of the antecedent is never sufficient reason to affirm a conditional, even an indicative conditional.

A second answer is suggested by the shortcomings of the truth-functional account. The material implication analysis fails, critics have said, because it leaves out the idea of *connection* which is implicit in an if-then statement. According to this line of thought, a conditional is to be understood as a statement which affirms that some sort of logical or casual connection holds between the antecedent and the consequent. In responding to the true-false quiz, then, you should look, not at the truth values of the two clauses, but at the relation between the propositions expressed by them. If the "connection" holds, you check the "true" box. If not, you answer "false."

If the second hypothesis were accepted, then we would face the task of clarifying the idea of "connection," but there are counter-examples even with this notion left as obscure as it is. Consider the following case: you firmly believe that the use of nuclear weapons by the United States in this war is inevitable because of the arrogance of power, the bellicosity of our president, rising pressure from congressional hawks, or other *domestic* causes. You have no opinion about future Chinese actions, but you do not think they will make much difference one way or another to nuclear escalation. Clearly, you believe the opinion survey statement to be true even though you believe the antecedent and consequent to be logically and casually independent of each other. It seems that the presence of a "connection" is not a necessary condition for the truth of an if-then statement.

The third answer that I shall consider is based on a suggestion made some time ago by F. P. Ramsey.[4] Consider first the case where you have no opinion about the statement, "The Chinese will enter the Vietnam war." According to the suggestion, your deliberation about the survey statement should consist of a simple thought experiment: add the antecedent (hypothetically) to your stock of knowledge (or beliefs), and then consider whether or not the consequent is true. Your belief about the conditional should be the same as your hypothetical belief, under this condition, about the consequent.

What happens to the idea of connection on this hypothesis? It is sometimes relevant to the evaluation of a conditional, and sometimes not. If you believe that a casual or logical connection exists, then you will add the consequent to your stock of beliefs along with the antecedent, since the rational man accepts the consequences of his beliefs. On the other hand, if you already believe the consequent (and if you also believe it to be causally independent of the antecedent), then it will remain a part of your stock of beliefs when you add the antecedent, since the rational man does not change his beliefs without reason. In either case, you will affirm the conditional. Thus this answer accounts for the relevance of "connection" when it is relevant without making it a necessary condition of the truth of a conditional.

Ramsey's suggestion covers only the situation in which you have no opinion about the truth value of the antecedent. Can it be generalized? We can of course extend it without problem to the case where you believe or know the antecendent to be true; in this case, no changes need be made in your stock of beliefs. If you already believe that the Chinese will enter the Vietnam conflict, then your belief about the conditional will be just the same as your belief about the statement that the U.S. will use the bomb.

---

[4] F. P. Ramsey, "General Propositions and Causality" in Ramsey, *Foundations of Mathematics and other Logical Essays* (New York, 1950), pp. 237–257. The suggestion is made on p. 248. Chisholm, *op. cit.*, p. 489, quotes the suggestion and discusses the limitations of the "connection" thesis which it brings out, but he develops it somewhat differently.

What about the case in which you know or believe the antecedent to be false? In this situation, you cannot simply add it to your stock of beliefs without introducing a contradiction. You must make adjustments by deleting or changing those beliefs which conflict with the antecedent. Here, the familiar difficulties begin, of course, because there will be more than one way to make the required adjustments.[5] These difficulties point to the pragmatic problem of counterfactuals, but if we set them aside for a moment, we shall see a rough but general answer to the question we are asking. This is how to evaluate a conditional:

> First, add the antecedent (hypothetically) to your stock of beliefs; second, make whatever adjustments are required to maintain consistency (without modifying the hypothetical belief in the antecedent); finally, consider whether or not the consequent is then true.

It is not particularly important that our answer is approximate—that it skirts the problem of adjustments—since we are using it only as a way of finding truth conditions. It is crucial, however, that the answer not be restricted to some particular context of belief if it is to be helpful in finding a definition of the conditional function. If the conditional is to be understood as a function of the propositions expressed by its component clauses, then its truth value should not in general be dependent on the attitudes which anyone has toward those propositions.

Now that we have found an answer to the question, "How do we decide whether or not we believe a conditional statement?" the problem is to make the transition from belief conditions to truth conditions; that is, to find a set of truth conditions for statements having conditional form which explains why we use the method we do use to evaluate them. The concept of a *possible world* is just what we need to make this transition, since a possible world is the ontological analogue of a stock of hypothetical beliefs. The following set of truth conditions, using this notion, is a first approximation to the account that I shall propose:

> Consider a possible world in which *A* is true, and which otherwise differs minimally from the actual world. "*If A, then B*" is *true (false) just in case B is true (false) in that possible world.*

[5] Rescher, *op. cit.*, pp. 11–16, contains a very clear statement and discussion of this problem, which he calls the problem of the ambiguity of belief-contravening hypotheses. He argues that the resolution of this ambiguity depends on pragmatic considerations. Cf. also Goodman's problem of relevant conditions in N. Goodman, *Fact, Fiction, and Forecast* (Cambridge, Mass., 1955), pp. 17–24.

A THEORY OF CONDITIONALS   103

An analysis in terms of possible worlds also has the advantage of providing a ready made apparatus on which to build a formal semantical theory. In making this account of the conditional precise, we use the semantical systems for modal logics developed by Saul Kripke.[6] Following Kripke, we first define a *model structure*. Let M be an ordered triple (K,R,λ). K is to be understood intuitively as the set of all possible worlds; R is the relation of relative possibility which defines the structure. If α and β are possible worlds (members of K), then $\alpha R\beta$ reads "β is possible with respect to α." This means that, where α is the actual world, β is a possible world. R is a reflexive relation; that is, every world is possible with respect to itself. If your modal intuitions so incline you, you may add that R must be transitive, or transitive and symmetrical.[7] The only element that is not a part of the standard modal semantics is λ, a member of K which is to be understood as the *absurd world*—the world in which contradictions and all their consequences are true. It is an isolated element under R; that is, no other world is possible with respect to it, and it is not possible with respect to any other world. The purpose of λ is to allow for an interpretation of "If A, then B" in the case where A is impossible; for this situation one needs an impossible world.

In addition to a model structure, our semantical apparatus includes a *selection function, f*, which takes a proposition and a possible world as arguments and a possible world as its value. The *s*-function selects, for each antecedent A, a particular possible world in which A is true. The *assertion* which the conditional makes, then, is that the consequent is true in the world selected. A conditional is true in the actual world when its consequent is true in the selected world.

Now we can state the semantical rule for the conditional more formally (using the corner, $>$, as the conditional connective):

$A>B$ is true in α if B is true in $f(A,\alpha)$;
$A>B$ is false in α if B is false in $f(A,\alpha)$.

The interpretation shows conditional logic to be an extension of modal logic. Modal logic provides a way of talking about what is true in the actual world, in all possible worlds, or in at least one, unspecified world. The addition of the selection function to the semantics and

---

[6] S. Kripke, "Semantical Analysis of Modal Logics, I," *Zeitschrift für mathematische Logik und Grundlagen der Mathematik*, vol. 9 (1963), pp. 67–96.

[7] The different restrictions on the relation R provide interpretations for the different modal systems. The system we build on is von Wright's M. If we add the transitivity requirement, then the underlying modal logic of our system is Lewis's S4, and if we add both the transitivity and symmetry requirements, then the modal logic is S5. Cf. S. Kripke, *op. cit.*

the conditional connective to the object language of modal logic provides a way of talking also about what is true in *particular* non-actual possible situations. This is what counterfactuals are: statements about particular counterfactual worlds.

But the world selected cannot be just any world. The s-function must meet at least the following conditions. I shall use the following terminology for talking about the arguments and values of s-functions: where $f(A,\alpha)=\beta$, A is the *antecedent*, α is the *base world*, and β is the *selected world*.

(1) For all antecedents A and base worlds α, A must be true in $f(A,\alpha)$.

(2) For all antecedents A and base worlds α, $f(A,\alpha)=\lambda$ only if there is no world possible with respect to α in which A is true.

The first condition requires that the antecedent be true in the selected world. This ensures that all statements like "if snow is white, then snow is white" are true. The second condition requires that the absurd world be selected only when the antecedent is impossible. Since everything is true in the absurd world, including contradictions, if the selection function were to choose it for the antecedent A, then "If A, then B and not B" would be true. But one cannot legitimately reach an impossible conclusion from a consistent assumption.

The informal truth conditions that were suggested above required that the world selected *differ minimally* from the actual world. This implies, first, that there are no differences between the actual world and the selected world except those that are required, implicitly or explicitly, by the antecedent. Further, it means that among the alternative ways of making the required changes, one must choose one that does the least violence to the correct description and explanation of the actual world. These are vague conditions which are largely dependent on pragmatic considerations for their application. They suggest, however, that the selection is based on an ordering of possible worlds with respect to their resemblance to the base world. If this is correct, then there are two further formal constraints which must be imposed on the s-function.

(3) For all base worlds α and all antecedents A, if A is true in α, then $f(A,\alpha)=\alpha$.

(4) For all base worlds α and all antecedents B and B', if B is true in $f(B',\alpha)$ and B' is true in $f(B,\alpha)$, then $f(B,\alpha)=f(B',\alpha)$.

The third condition requires that the base world be selected if it is among the worlds in which the antecedent is true. Whatever the criteria for evaluating resemblance among possible worlds, there is

A THEORY OF CONDITIONALS   105

obviously no other possible world as much like the base world as the base world itself. The fourth condition ensures that the ordering among possible worlds is consistent in the following sense: if any selection established β as prior to β' in the ordering (with respect to a particular base world α), then no other selection (relative to that α) may establish β' as prior to β.[8] Conditions (3) and (4) together ensure that the s-function establishes a total ordering of all selected worlds with respect to each possible world, with the base world preceding all others in the order.

These conditions on the selection function are necessary in order that this account be recognizable as an explication of the conditional, but they are of course far from sufficient to determine the function uniquely. There may be further formal constraints that can plausibly be imposed on the selection principle, but we should not expect to find semantic conditions sufficient to guarantee that there will be a unique s-function for each valuation of non-conditional formulas on a model structure. The questions, "On what basis do we select a selection function from among the acceptable ones?" and "What are the criteria for ordering possible worlds?" are reformulations of the pragmatic problem of counterfactuals, which is a problem in the application of conditional logic. The conditions that I have mentioned above are sufficient, however, to define the semantical notions of validity and consequence for conditional logic.

III. THE FORMAL SYSTEM

The class of valid formulas of conditional logic according to the definitions sketched in the preceding section, is coextensive with the class of theorems of a formal system, C2. The primitive connectives of C2 are the usual $\supset$ and $\sim$ (with v, &, and $\equiv$ defined as usual), as well as a conditional connective, $>$ (called the corner). Other modal and conditional concepts can be defined in terms of the corner as follows:

$\Box A =_{\mathrm{DF}} \sim A > A$

$\Diamond A =_{\mathrm{DF}} \sim (A > \sim A)$

$A \gtrless B =_{\mathrm{DF}} (A >)B \ \& \ (B > A)$

The rules of inference of C2 are *modus ponens* (if A and $A \supset B$ are theorems, then B is a theorem) and the Gödel rule of necessitation (If A is a theorem, then $\Box A$ is a theorem). There are seven axiom schemata:

---

[8] If $f(A, \alpha) = \beta$, then β is established as prior to all worlds possible with respect to α in which A is true.

(a1) Any tautologous wff (well-formed formula) is an axiom.

(a2) $\Box(A \supset B) \supset (\Box A \supset \Box B)$

(a3) $\Box(A \supset B) \supset (A > B)$

(a4) $\Diamond A \supset .(A > B) \supset \sim(A > \sim B)$

(a5) $A > (B \vee C) \supset .(A > B) \vee (A > C)$

(a6) $(A > B) \supset (A \supset B)$

(a7) $A \gtrless B \supset . \ (A > C) \supset (B > C)$

The conditional connective, as characterized by this formal system, is intermediate between strict implication and the material conditional, in the sense that $\Box(A \supset B)$ entails $A > B$ by (a3) and $A > B$ entails $A \supset B$ by (a6). It cannot, however, be analyzed as a modal operation performed on a material conditional (like Burks' causal implication, for example).[9] The corner lacks certain properties shared by the two traditional implication concepts, and in fact these differences help to explain some peculiarities of counterfactuals. I shall point out three unusual features of the conditional connective.

(1) Unlike both material and strict implication, the conditional corner is a non-transitive connective. That is, from $A > B$ and $B > C$, one cannot infer $A > C$. While this may at first seem surprising, consider the following example: *Premises.* "If J. Edgar Hoover were today a communist, then he would be a traitor." "If J. Edgar Hoover had been born a Russian, then he would today be a communist." *Conclusion.* "If J. Edgar Hoover had been born a Russian, he would be a traitor." It seems reasonable to affirm these premises and deny the conclusion.

If this example is not sufficiently compelling, note that the following rule follows from the transitivity rule: From $A > B$ to infer $(A \& C) > B$. But it is obvious that the former rule is invalid; we cannot always strengthen the antecedent of a true conditional and have it remain true. Consider "If this match were struck, it would light," and "If this match had been soaked in water overnight *and* it were struck, it would light."[10]

(2) According to the formal system, the denial of a conditional is equivalent to a conditional with the same antecedent and opposite

---

[9] A. W. Burks, "The Logic of Causal Propositions," *Mind*, vol. 60 (1951), pp. 363–382. The causal implication connective characterized in this article has the same structure as strict implication. For an interesting philosophical defense of this modal interpretation of conditionals, see B. Mayo, "Conditional Statements," *The Philosophical Review*, vol. 66 (1957), pp. 291–303.

[10] Although the transitivity inference fails, a related inference is of course valid. From $A > B$, $B > C$, and A, one can infer C. Also, note that the biconditional connective is transitive. From $A \gtrless B$ and $B \gtrless C$, one can infer $A \gtrless C$. Thus the biconditional is an equivalence relation, since it is also symmetrical and reflexive.

consequent (provided that the antecedent is not impossible). That is, $\Diamond A-\sim(A > B)\equiv(A > \sim B)$. This explains the fact, noted by both Goodman and Chisholm in their early papers on counterfactuals, that the normal way to contradict a counterfactual is to contradict the consequent, keeping the same antecedent. To deny "If Kennedy were alive today, we wouldn't be in this Vietnam mess," we say, "If Kennedy were alive today, we would so be in this Vietnam mess."

(3) The inference of contraposition, valid for both the truth-functional horseshoe and the strict implication hook, is invalid for the conditional corner. $A > B$ may be true while $\sim B > \sim A$ is false. For an example in support of this conclusion, we take another item from the political opinion survey: "If the U.S. halts the bombing, then North Vietnam will not agree to negotiate." A person would believe that this statement is true if he thought that the North Vietnamese were determined to press for a complete withdrawal of U.S. troops. But he would surely deny the contrapositive, "If North Vietnam agrees to negotiate, then the U.S. will not have halted the bombing." He would believe that a halt in the bombing, and much more, is required to bring the North Vietnamese to the negotiating table.[11]

Examples of these anomalies have been noted by philosophers in the past. For instance, Goodman pointed out that two counterfactuals with the same antecedent and contradictory consequents are "normally meant" as direct negations of each other. He also remarked that we may sometimes assert a conditional and yet reject its contrapositive. He accounted for these facts by arguing that semifactuals—conditionals with false antecedents and true consequents—are for the most part not to be taken literally. "In practice," he wrote, "full counterfactuals affirm, while semifactuals deny, that a certain connection obtains between antecedent and consequent. . . . The practical import of a semifactual is thus different from its literal import."[12] Chisholm also suggested paraphrasing semifactuals before analyzing them. "Even if you were to sleep all morning, you would be tired" is to be read "It is false that if you were to sleep all morning, you would not be tired."[13]

A separate and nonconditional analysis for semi-factuals is necessary to save the "connection" theory of counterfactuals in the face of the anomolies we have discussed, but it is a baldly *ad hoc*

---

[11] Although contraposition fails, *modus tolens* is valid for the conditional: from $A > B$ and $\sim B$, one can infer $\sim A$.

[12] Goodman, *op. cit.*, pp. 15, 32.

[13] Chisholm, *op. cit.*, p. 492.

maneuver. Any analysis can be saved by paraphrasing the counter-examples. The theory presented in Sect. II avoids this difficulty by denying that the conditional can be said, in general, to assert a connection of any particular kind between antecedent and consequent. It is, of course, the structure of inductive relations and casual connections which make counterfactuals and semifactuals true or false, but they do this by determining the relationships among possible worlds, which in turn determine the truth values of conditionals. By treating the relation between connection and conditionals as an indirect relation in this way, the theory is able to give a unified account of conditionals which explains the variations in their behavior in different contexts.

IV. The Logical Problem: General Considerations

The traditional strategy for attacking a problem like the logical problem of conditionals was to find an *analysis*, to show that the unclear or objectionable phrase was dispensable, or replaceable by something clear and harmless. Analysis was viewed by some as an *unpacking*—a making manifest of what was latent in the concept; by others it was seen as the *replacement* of a vague idea by a precise one, adequate to the same purposes as the old expression, but free of its problems. The semantic theory of conditionals can also be viewed either as the construction of a concept to replace an unclear notion of ordinary language, or as an *explanation* of a commonly used concept. I see the theory in the latter way: no recommendation or stipulation is intended. This does not imply, however, that the theory is meant as a description of linguistic usage. What is being explained is not the rules governing the use of an English word, but the structure of a concept. Linguistic facts—what we would say in this or that context, and what sounds odd to the native speaker—are relevant as evidence, since one may presume that concepts are to some extent mirrored in language.

The "facts," taken singly, need not be decisive. A recalcitrant counterexample may be judged a deviant use or a different sense of the word. We can claim that a paraphrase is necessary, or even that ordinary language is systematically mistaken about the concept we are explaining. There are, of course, different senses and times when "ordinary language" goes astray, but such *ad hoc* hypotheses and qualifications diminish both the plausibility and the explanatory force of a theory. While we are not irrevocably bound to the linguistic facts, there are no "don't cares"—contexts of use with which we are not concerned, since any context can be relevant as evidence for or against an analysis. A general interpretation which avoids dividing senses and accounts for the behavior of a concept in many contexts fits the familiar pattern of scientific explanation in which diverse, seemingly unlike surface phenomena are seen as deriving from some common source. For these reasons, I take it as a strong point in favor of the semantic theory that it treats the conditional as a univocal concept.

V. Pragmatic Ambiguity

I have argued that the conditional connective is semantically unambiguous. It is obvious, however, that the context of utterance, the purpose of the assertion, and the beliefs of the speaker or his community may make a difference to the interpretation of a counterfactual. How do we reconcile the ambiguity of conditional sentences with the univocity of the conditional concept? Let us look more closely at the notion of ambiguity.

A sentence is ambiguous if there is more than one proposition which it may properly be interpreted to express. Ambiguity may be syntactic (if the sentence has more than one grammatical structure), semantic (if one of the words has more than one meaning), or pragmatic (if the interpretation depends directly on the context of use). The first two kinds of ambiguity are perhaps more familiar, but the third kind is probably the most common in natural languages. Any sentence involving pronouns, tensed verbs, articles or quantifiers is pragmatically ambiguous. For example, the proposition expressed by "L'état, c'est moi" depends on who says it; "Do it now" may be good or bad advice depending on when it is said; "Cherchez la femme" is ambiguous since it contains a definite description, and the truth conditions for "All's well that ends well" depends on the domain of discourse. If the theory presented above is correct, then we may add conditional sentences to this list. The truth conditions for "If wishes were horses, then beggers would ride" depend on the specification of an *s*-function.[14]

The grounds for treating the ambiguity of conditional sentences as pragmatic rather than semantic are the same as the grounds for treating the ambiguity of quantified sentences as pragmatic: simplicity and systematic coherence. The truth conditions for quantified statements vary with a change in the domain of discourse, but there is

---

[14] I do not wish to pretend that the notions needed to define ambiguity and to make the distinction between pragmatic and semantic ambiguity (e.g., "proposition," and "meaning") are precise. They can be made precise only in the context of semantic and pragmatic theories. But even if it is unclear, in general, what pragmatic ambiguity is, it is clear, I hope, that my examples are cases of it.

a single structure to these truth conditions which remains constant for every domain. The semantics for classical predicate logic brings out this common structure by giving the universal quantifier a single meaning and making the domain a parameter of the interpretation. In a similar fashion, the semantics for conditional logic brings out the common structure of the truth conditions for conditional statements by giving the connective a single meaning and making the selection function a parameter of the interpretation.

Just as we can communicate effectively using quantified sentences without explicitly specifying a domain, so we can communicate effectively using conditional sentences without explicitly specifying an *s*-function. This suggests that there are further rules beyond those set down in the semantics, governing the use of conditional sentences. Such rules are the subject matter of a *pragmatics* of conditionals. Very little can be said, at this point, about pragmatic rules for the use of conditionals since the logic has not advanced beyond the propositional stage, but I shall make a few speculative remarks about the kinds of research which may provide a framework for treatment of this problem, and related pragmatic problems in the philosophy of science.

(1) If we had a functional logic with a conditional connective, it is likely that $(\forall x)(Fx > Gx)$ would be a plausible candidate for the form of a law of nature. A law of nature says, not just that every actual F is a G, but further that for every possible F, if it were an F, it would be a G. If this is correct, then Hempel's confirmation paradox does not arise, since "All ravens are black" is not logically equivalent to "All non-black things are non-ravens." Also, the relation between counterfactuals and laws becomes clear: laws support counterfactuals because they entail them. "If this dove were a raven, it would be black" is simply an instantiation of "All ravens are black."[15]

(2) Goodman has argued that the pragmatic problem of counterfactuals is one of a cluster of closely related problems concerning induction and confirmation. He locates the source of these difficulties in the general problem of projectability, which can be stated roughly as follows: when can a predicate be validly projected from one set of cases to others? or when is a hypothesis confirmed by its positive instances? Some way of distinguishing between natural predicates

[15] For a discussion of the relation of laws to counterfactuals, see E. Nagel, *Structure of Science* (New York, 1961), pp. 47–78. For a recent discussion of the paradoxes of confirmation by the man who discovered them, see C. G. Hempel, "Recent Problems of Induction" in *Mind and Cosmos*, ed. by R. G. Colodny (Pittsburgh, 1966), pp. 112–134.

A THEORY OF CONDITIONALS 111

and those which are artificially constructed is needed. If a theory of projection such as Goodman envisions were developed, it might find a natural place in a pragmatics of conditionals. Pragmatic criteria for measuring the inductive properties of predicates might provide pragmatic criteria for ordering possible worlds.[16]

(3) There are some striking structural parallels between conditional logic and conditional probability functions, which suggests the possibility of a connection between inductive logic and conditional logic. A probability assignment and an *s*-function are two quite different ways to describe the inductive relations among propositions; a theory which draws a connection between them might be illuminating for both.[17]

VI. CONCLUSION: EMPIRICISM AND POSSIBLE WORLDS

Writers of fiction and fantasy sometimes suggest that imaginary worlds have a life of their own beyond the control of their creators. Pirandello's six characters, for example, rebelled against their author and took the story out of his hands. The skeptic may be inclined to suspect that this suggestion is itself fantasy. He believes that nothing goes into a fictional world, or a possible world, unless it is put there by decision or convention; it is a creature of invention and not discovery. Even the fabulist Tolkien admits that Faërie is a land "full of wonder, but not of information."[18]

For similar reasons, the empiricist may be uncomfortable about a theory which treats counterfactuals as literal statements about non-actual situations. Counterfactuals are often contingent, and contingent statements must be supported by evidence. But evidence can be gathered, by us at least, only in this universe. To satisfy the empiricist, I must show how possible worlds, even if the product of convention, can be subjects of empirical investigation.

There is no mystery to the fact that I can partially define a possible world in such a way that I am ignorant of some of the determinate truths in that world. One way I can do this is to attribute to it features

---

[16] Goodman, *op. cit.*, especially Ch. IV.

[17] Several philosophers have discussed the relation of conditional propositions to conditional probabilities. See R. C. Jeffrey, "If," *The Journal of Philosophy*, vol. 61 (1964), pp. 702–703, and E. W. Adams, "Probability and the Logic of Conditionals" in *Aspects of Inductive Logic*, ed. by J. Hintikka and P. Suppes (Amsterdam, 1966), pp. 265–316. I hope to present elsewhere my method of drawing the connection between the two notions, which differs from both of these.

[18] J. R. Tolkien, "On Fairy Stories" in *The Tolkien Reader* (New York, 1966), p. 3.

of the actual world which are unknown to me. Thus I can say, "I am thinking of a possible world in which the population of China is just the same, on each day, as it is in the actual world." *I* am making up this world—it is a pure product of my intentions—but there are already things true in it which I shall never know.

Conditionals do implicitly, and by convention, what is done explicitly by stipulation in this example. It is because counterfactuals are generally about possible worlds which are very much like the actual one, and defined in terms of it, that evidence is so often relevant to their truth. When I wonder, for example, what would have happened if I had asked my boss for a raise yesterday, I am wondering about a possible world that I have already roughly picked out. It has the same history, up to yesterday, as the actual world, the same boss with the same dispositions and habits. The main difference is that in that world, yesterday I asked the boss for a raise. Since I do not know everything about the boss's habits and dispositions in the actual world, there is a lot that I do not know about how he acts in the possible world that I have chosen, although I might find out by watching him respond to a similar request from another, or by asking his secretary about his mood yesterday. These bits of information about the actual world would not be decisive, of course, but they would be relevant, since they tell me more about the non-actual situation that I have selected.

If I make a conditional statement—subjunctive or otherwise—and the antecedent turns out to be true, then whether I know it or not, I have said something about the actual world, namely that the consequent is true in it. If the antecedent is false, then I have said something about a particular counterfactual world, even if I believe the antecedent to be true. The conditional provides a set of conventions for selecting possible situations which have a specified relation to what actually happens. This makes it possible for statements about unrealized possibilities to tell us, not just about the speaker's imagination, but about the world.

Yale University

II. The Activity Theory

Causation

R. G. Collingwood

Reprinted with permission of the publisher from R. G. Collingwood, *An Essay on Metaphysics* (Oxford: The Clarendon Press, 1940), pp. 285–327.

XXIX

THREE SENSES OF THE WORD 'CAUSE'

CONFORMABLY to the historical nature of metaphysics, any discussion of a metaphysical difficulty must be historically conducted. One major difficulty, or group of difficulties, now exercising students of metaphysics is connected with the idea of causation. I do not hope in the present part of my essay to offer a complete solution for this difficulty or group of difficulties; all I propose to do is to show what I mean by saying that it ought to be discussed historically.

I shall confine myself to making two main points.

1. That the term 'cause', as actually used in modern English and other languages, is ambiguous. It has three senses; possibly more; but at any rate three.

Sense I. Here that which is 'caused' is the free and deliberate act of a conscious and responsible agent, and 'causing' him to do it means affording him a motive for doing it.

Sense II. Here that which is 'caused' is an event in nature, and its 'cause' is an event or state of things by producing or preventing which we can produce or prevent that whose cause it is said to be.

Sense III. Here that which is 'caused' is an event or state of things, and its 'cause' is another event or state of things standing to it in a one-one relation of causal priority: i.e. a relation of such a kind that (*a*) if the cause happens or exists the effect also must

286 THREE SENSES OF THE WORD 'CAUSE'

happen or exist, even if no further conditions are fulfilled, (*b*) the effect cannot happen or exist unless the cause happens or exists, (*c*) in some sense which remains to be defined, the cause is prior to the effect; for without such priority there would be no telling which is which. If C and E were connected merely by a one-one relation such as is described in the sentences (*a*) and (*b*) above, there would be no reason why C should be called the cause of E, and E the effect of C, rather than vice versa. But whether causal priority is temporal priority, or a special case of temporal priority, or priority of some other kind, is another question.

Sense I may be called the *historical* sense of the word 'cause', because it refers to a type of case in which both C and E are human activities such as form the subject-matter of history. When historians talk about causes, this is the sense in which they are using the word, unless they are aping the methods and vocabulary of natural science.

Sense II refers to a type of case in which natural events are considered from a human point of view, as events grouped in pairs where one member in each pair, C, is immediately under human control, whereas the other, E, is not immediately under human control but can be indirectly controlled by man because of the relation in which it stands to C. This is the sense which the word 'cause' has in the *practical sciences of nature*, i.e. the sciences of nature whose primary aim is not to achieve theoretical knowledge about nature but to enable man to enlarge his control

THREE SENSES OF THE WORD 'CAUSE' 287
of nature. This is the sense in which the word 'cause'
is used, for example, in engineering or medicine.

Sense III refers to a type of case in which an
attempt is made to consider natural events not practically, as things to be produced or prevented by human
agency, but theoretically, as things that happen independently of human will but not independently of
each other: causation being the name by which this
dependence is designated. This is the sense which
the word has traditionally borne in physics and
chemistry and, in general, the *theoretical sciences of
nature*.

The difficulties to which I referred at the beginning
of this chapter are all connected with sense III. The
other two senses are relatively straightforward and
easy to understand. They give rise to no perplexities.
The only perplexities that ever occur in connexion
with them are such as arise from a confusion of
sense I with sense II, or from a confusion of either
with sense III. But sense III, as I shall show, raises
difficult problems quite by itself, and apart from any
confusion with other senses. These problems are
due to internal conflict. The various elements which
go to make up the definition of sense III are mutually
incompatible. This incompatibility, at the lowest
estimate, constitutes what I called in Chapter VII a
'strain' in the current modern idea of causation, and
therefore in the whole structure of modern natural
science in so far as modern natural science is based
on that idea.

I have called I, II, and III different 'senses' of the

288 THREE SENSES OF THE WORD 'CAUSE'

word 'cause'. A technical objection might be lodged against this expression on any of three grounds, if no more.

(*a*) 'What you have distinguished are not three senses of the word "cause", but three types of case to any one of which that word is appropriate, the sense in which it is used being constant.' But, as I shall try to show, if you ask what exactly you mean by the word on each type of occasion you will get three different answers.

(*b*) 'What you have distinguished is three kinds of causation.' But the three definitions of causation referred to in the foregoing paragraph are not related to each other as species of any common genus; nor is there any fourth definition, the definition of cause in general, of which the three 'kinds' of causation are species.

(*c*) 'One of your three so-called senses of the word "cause" is the only proper sense; the other two represent metaphorical usages of the word.' In order to show how baseless this objection is, it would be necessary to show that the distinction between 'proper' and 'metaphorical' senses of words is illusory. The contradictory of 'proper' is not 'metaphorical' but 'improper'. A proper usage of a word is one which as a matter of historical fact occurs in the language to which the word belongs. The contradictory of 'metaphorical' is 'literal'; and if the distinction between literal and metaphorical usages is a genuine distinction, which in one sense it is, both kinds of usage are equally proper. There is another sense in which all

THREE SENSES OF THE WORD 'CAUSE' 289
language is metaphorical; and in that sense the objection to certain linguistic usages on the ground that they are metaphorical is an objection to language as such, and proceeds from an aspiration towards what Charles Lamb called the uncommunicating muteness of fishes. But this topic belongs to the theory of language, that is, to the science of aesthetic, with which this essay is not concerned.[1]

At the same time I do not wish to imply that the distinction between I, II, and III is an example of what Aristotle calls 'accidental equivocation'.[2] It is not mere equivocation, for there is a continuity between the three things distinguished, though this continuity is not of the kind suggested in any of the three objections I have quoted. And the differences between them are not accidental; they are the product of an historical process; and to the historian historical processes are not accidental, because his business is to understand them, and calling an event accidental means that it is not capable of being understood. This brings me to my second main point.

2. That the relation between these three senses of the word 'cause' is an historical relation: No. I being the earliest of the three, No. II a development from it, and No. III a development from that.

---

[1] The main questions involved, as I see them, are discussed in my *Principles of Art*, especially Chapter XI.

[2] *Eth. Nic.* 1096ᵇ 26–7: (although the various goodnesses of honour, wisdom, and pleasure are not identical in definition but differ *qua* goodnesses) 'the case does not resemble one of accidental equivocation', οὐκ ἔοικε τοῖς γε ἀπὸ τύχης ὁμωνύμοις.

XXX

CAUSATION IN HISTORY

IN sense I of the word 'cause' that which is caused is the free and deliberate act of a conscious and responsible agent, and 'causing' him to do it means affording him a motive for doing it. For 'causing' we may substitute 'making', 'inducing', 'persuading', 'urging', 'forcing', 'compelling', according to differences in the kind of motive in question.

This is a current and familiar sense of the word (together with its cognates, correlatives, and equivalents) in English, and of the corresponding words in other modern languages. A headline in the *Morning Post* in 1936 ran, 'Mr. Baldwin's speech causes adjournment of House'. This did not mean that Mr. Baldwin's speech compelled the Speaker to adjourn the House whether or no that event conformed with his own ideas and intentions; it meant that on hearing Mr. Baldwin's speech the Speaker freely made up his mind to adjourn. In the same sense we say that a solicitor's letter causes a man to pay a debt or that bad weather causes him to return from an expedition.

I have heard it suggested that this is a secondary sense of the word 'cause', presupposing and derived from what I call sense III. The relation here described as 'presupposing' or 'being derived from' might, I take it, be understood either (1) as an historical relation, where '*b* presupposes *a*' means that a state of things *a* has given rise by an historical

CAUSATION IN HISTORY 291

process into a state of things *b*, as a state of the English language in which 'cat' means an animal with claws gives rise by an historical process to a state in which it also means a kind of whip that lacerates the flesh of its victim; or (2) as a logical relation, where '*b* presupposes *a*' means that a state of things *a* exists contemporaneously with a state of things *b*, and *a* is an indispensable condition of *b*; as a state of the English language in which 'cat' still means an animal exists contemporaneously with a state in which it means a whip, and is an indispensable condition of it.

1. Sense I is not historically derived from sense III. On the contrary, when we trace the historical changes in the meaning of the word 'cause' in English and other modern languages, together with the Latin *causa* and the Greek αἰτία, we find that sense I is not only an established modern sense, it is also of great antiquity. In English it goes back, as the quotations in the *Oxford English Dictionary* show, to the Middle Ages. In Latin it is the commonest of all the senses distinguished by Lewis and Short, and also the oldest. In Greek, as the articles αἰτία, αἴτιος in Liddell and Scott show, the word which in Latin is translated *causa* meant originally 'guilt', 'blame', or 'accusation', and when first it began to mean 'cause', which it sometimes does in fifth-century literature, it was used in sense I, for the cause of a war or the like. In fact, the historical relation between these senses is the opposite of what has been suggested. Sense I is the original sense, and senses II and III have been derived from it by a process I shall trace in the sequel.

2. Sense I does not logically presuppose sense III. On the contrary, as I shall show in the following chapters, both sense II and sense III logically presuppose sense I; and any attempt to use the word in sense II or III without the anthropomorphic implications belonging to sense I must result either in a misuse of the word cause (that is, its use in a sense not consistent with the facts of established usage), or in a redefinition of it so as to make it mean what in established usage it does not mean: two alternatives which differ only in that established usage is defied with or without a formal declaration of war.

A cause in sense I is made up of two elements, a *causa quod* or efficient cause and a *causa ut* or final cause. The *causa quod* is a situation or state of things existing; the *causa ut* is a purpose or state of things to be brought about. Neither of these could be a cause if the other were absent. A man who tells his stockbroker to sell a certain holding may be caused to act thus by a rumour about the financial position of that company; but this rumour would not cause him to sell out unless he wanted to avoid being involved in the affairs of an unsound business. And *per contra* a man's desire to avoid being involved in the affairs of an unsound business would not cause him to sell his shares in a certain company unless he knew or believed that it was unsound.

The *causa quod* is not a mere situation or state of things, it is a situation or state of things known or believed by the agent in question to exist. If a prospective litigant briefs a certain barrister because of

CAUSATION IN HISTORY   293

his exceptional ability, the *causa quod* of his doing so
is not this ability simply as such, it is this ability as
something known to the litigant or believed in by
him.

The *causa ut* is not a mere desire or wish, it is an
intention. The *causa ut* of a man's acting in a certain
way is not his wanting to act in that way, but his
meaning to act in that way. There may be cases
where mere desire leads to action without the intermediate phase of intention; but such action is not
deliberate, and therefore has no cause in sense I of
the word.

Causes in sense I of the word may come into
operation through the act of a second conscious and
responsible agent, in so far as he (1) either puts the
first in a certain situation in such a way that the first
now believes or knows himself to be in that situation,
or alternatively informs or persuades the first that he
is in a certain situation; or (2) persuades the first to
form a certain intention. In either of these two cases,
the second agent is said to cause the first to do a
certain act, or to 'make him do it'.

The act so caused is still an act; it could not be
done (and therefore could not be caused) unless the
agent did it of his own free will. If A causes B to do
an act β, β is B's act and not A's; B is a free agent in
doing it, and is responsible for it. If β is a murder,
which A persuaded B to commit by pointing out
certain facts or urging certain expediencies, B is the
murderer. There is no contradiction between the
proposition that the act β was caused by A, and

the proposition that B was a free agent in respect of β, and is thus responsible for it. On the contrary, the first proposition implies the second.

Nevertheless, in this case A is said to 'share the responsibility' for the act β. This does not imply that a responsibility is a divisible thing, which would be absurd; it means that, whereas B is responsible for the act β, A is responsible for his own act, α, viz. the act of pointing out certain facts to B or urging upon him certain expediencies, whereby he induces him to commit the act β. When a child accused of a misdeed rounds on its accuser, saying, 'You made me do it', he is not excusing himself, he is implicating his accuser as an accessory. This is what Adam was doing when he said, 'The woman whom thou gavest to be with me, she gave me of the tree, and I did eat'.

A man is said to act 'on his own responsibility' or 'on his sole responsibility' when (1) his knowledge or belief about the situation is not dependent on information or persuasion from any one else, and (2) his intentions or purposes are similarly independent. In this case (the case in which a man is ordinarily said to exhibit 'initiative') his action is not uncaused. It still has both a *causa quod* and a *causa ut*. But because he has done for himself, unaided, the double work of envisaging the situation and forming the intention, which in the alternative case another man (who is therefore said to cause his action) has done for him, he can now be said to cause his own action as well as to do it. If he invariably acted in that way the total complex of his activities could

CAUSATION IN HISTORY   295

be called self-causing (*causa sui*); an expression which refers to absence of persuasion or inducement on the part of another, and is hence quite intelligible and significant, although it has been denounced as nonsensical by people who have not taken the trouble to consider what the word 'cause' means.

XXXI

CAUSATION IN PRACTICAL NATURAL SCIENCE

In sense I of the word 'cause' that which is caused is a human action (including under that name actions of other, non-human, agents, if there are any, which act in the same conscious, deliberate, and responsible way which is supposed to be characteristic of human beings). That which causes may, as we have seen, come into operation through the activity of a second human agent.

In sense II that which is caused is an event in nature; but the word 'cause' still expresses an idea relative to human conduct, because that which causes is something under human control, and this control serves as means whereby human beings can control that which is caused. In this sense, the cause of an event in nature is the handle, so to speak, by which human beings can manipulate it. If we human beings want to produce or prevent such a thing, and cannot produce or prevent it immediately (as we can produce or prevent certain movements of our own bodies), we set about looking for its 'cause'. The question 'What is the cause of an event *y*?' means in this case 'How can we produce or prevent *y* at will?'

This sense of the word may be defined as follows. *A cause is an event or state of things which it is in our power to produce or prevent, and by producing or preventing which we can produce or prevent that whose*

PRACTICAL NATURAL SCIENCE   297

cause it is said to be. When I speak of 'producing' something I refer to such occasions as when one turns a switch and thus produces the state of things described by the proposition 'the switch is now at the ON position'. By preventing something I mean producing something incompatible with it, e.g. turning the switch to the OFF position.

Turning a switch to one or other position by finger-pressure is an instance of producing a certain state of things (the ON or OFF position of the switch) immediately, for it is nothing but a certain complex of bodily movements all immediately produced. These movements are not our means of turning the switch, they are the turning of the switch. Subject to certain indispensable conditions, the turning of the switch is our 'means' of producing a further state of things, viz. incandescence or its absence in a certain filament. What is immediately produced (the position of the switch) is the 'cause' in sense II of what is thus mediately produced.

The search for causes in sense II is natural science in that sense of the phrase in which natural science is what Aristotle calls a 'practical science', valued not for its truth pure and simple but for its utility, for the 'power over nature' which it gives us: Baconian science, where 'knowledge is power' and where 'nature is conquered by obeying her'. The field of a 'practical science' is the contingent, or in Aristotle's terminology 'what admits of being otherwise'. The light, for example, is on, but it admits of being off; i.e. I find by experiment that I am able to extinguish

298 CAUSATION IN PRACTICAL

it by turning the switch to the OFF position. To discover that things are contingent is to discover that we can produce and prevent them.

Before the above definition of sense II is accepted, a preliminary question must be answered. I will put the question by distinguishing between two ideas, the idea of a 'practical' science of nature and the idea of an 'applied' science of nature, and asking to which of these ideas sense II belongs. By a 'practical' science of nature I mean one whose relation to practice is more intimate than that of means to end: one whose practical utility is not an ulterior end for whose sake it is valued, but its essence. By an 'applied' science of nature I mean one whose essence *qua* science is not practical utility but theoretical truth, but one which, in addition to being true, is useful as providing the solution for practical problems by being 'applied' to them. The Aristotelian and Baconian formulae might be understood as covering either of these two cases; but my present inquiry demands that they should be distinguished.

Sense II of the word 'cause' is bound up with the idea of a 'practical' science. An 'applied' science, being *qua* science not practical but theoretical, uses the word cause in sense III: a sense in which it is only an 'accident' (in the vocabulary of traditional logic) that knowing a cause enables some one to produce the effect, and in which, therefore, the statement '*x* causes *y*' would be in no way invalidated by the statement that *x* is a thing of such a kind as cannot be produced or prevented by human beings. I am

NATURAL SCIENCE   299

not here denying that there is such a sense. What I
am doing is to assert that there is another sense,
recognizable in actual and long-established usage, in
which it is not accidental but essential to the idea of
causation that knowing the cause should enable some
one to produce the effect, and in which the statement
'*x* causes *y*' would be flatly contradicted by the statement that *x* is a thing of such a kind as cannot be
produced or prevented by human beings.

This usage, representing sense II of the word
'cause', can be recognized by two criteria: the thing
described as a cause is always conceived as something
in the world of nature or physical world, and it is
always something conceived as capable of being produced or prevented by human agency. Here are
some examples. The cause of malaria is the bite of
a mosquito; the cause of a boat's sinking is her being
overloaded; the cause of books going mouldy is their
being in a damp room; the cause of a man's sweating
is a dose of aspirin; the cause of a furnace going out
in the night is that the draught-door was insuffi-
ciently open; the cause of seedlings dying is that
nobody watered them.

In any one of the above cases, for example the
first, the question whether the effect can be produced
or prevented by producing or preventing the cause
is not a further question which arises for persons
practically interested when the proposition that (for
example) malaria is due to mosquito-bites has been
established; it is a question which has already been
answered in the affirmative by the establishment of

that proposition. This affirmative answer is in fact what the proposition means. In other words: medicine (the science to which the proposition belongs) is not a theoretical science which may on occasion be applied to the solution of practical problems, it is a practical science. The causal propositions which it establishes are not propositions which may or may not be found applicable in practice, but whose truth is independent of such applicability; they are propositions whose applicability is their meaning.

Consider a (hypothetical) negative instance. A great deal of time and money is being spent on 'cancer research', that is, on the attempt to discover 'the cause of cancer'. I submit that the word 'cause' is here used in sense II; that is to say, discovering the cause of cancer means discovering something which it is in the power of human beings to produce or prevent, by producing or preventing which they can produce or prevent cancer. Suppose some one claimed to have discovered the cause of cancer, but added that his discovery would be of no practical use because the cause he had discovered was not a thing that could be produced or prevented at will. Such a person would be ridiculed by his colleagues in the medical profession. His 'discovery' would be denounced as a sham. He would not be allowed to have done what he claimed to have done. It would be pointed out that he was not using the word 'cause' in the established sense which it bears in a medical context. To use my own terminology, it would be pointed out that he was thinking of medicine as an

NATURAL SCIENCE   301

applied science, whereas it is a practical science; and using the word cause in sense III, whereas in medicine it bears sense II.

This usage of the word is not exclusively modern. It can be traced back through Middle English usages to familiar Latin usages of the word *causa*, and thence to the Greek αἰτία and its equivalent πρόφασις in, for example, the Hippocratic writings of the fifth century before Christ.

A cause in sense II is never able by itself to produce the corresponding effect. The switch, as I said, only works the light subject to certain indispensable conditions. Among these are the existence of an appropriate current and its maintenance by insulation and contacts. These are called *conditiones sine quibus non*. Their existence, over and above the cause, constitutes one of the differences between sense II and sense III of the word 'cause'. As we shall see in the next chapter, a cause in sense III requires no such accompaniment. A cause in sense II is conditional, a cause in sense III is unconditional. This distinction was correctly understood by John Stuart Mill, whose formal definition of the term 'cause' is a definition of sense III, but who recognizes that ordinarily when people speak of a cause they are using the word in sense II. A cause, he tells us, is the invariable unconditional antecedent of its effect. This antecedent, he thinks, is always complex, and any one of the elements that go to make it up is called a condition. But what people ordinarily call a cause is one of these conditions, arbitrarily selected, and dignified by a mere abuse of language with a name that properly belongs to the whole set.[1]

Mill deserves great credit for seeing that the word 'cause' was used in these two different ways. But his account of the relation between a cause in sense II and the conditions that accompany it is not quite satisfactory. Closer inspection would have shown him that the 'selection' of one condition to be dignified by the name of cause is by no means arbitrary. It is made according to a principle. The 'condition' which I call the cause (in sense II) of an event in which I take a practical interest is the condition I am able to produce or prevent at will. Thus, if my car fails to climb a steep hill, and I wonder why, I shall not consider my problem solved by a passer-by who tells me that the top of a hill is farther away from the earth's centre than its bottom, and that consequently more power is needed to take a car uphill than to take her along the level. All this is quite true; what the passer-by has described is one of the conditions which together form the 'real cause' (Mill's phrase; what I call the cause in sense III) of my car's stopping; and

[1] 'Since then, mankind are accustomed with acknowledged propriety so far as the ordinances of language are concerned, to give the name of cause to almost any one of the conditions of a phenomenon, or any portion of the whole number, *arbitrarily selected*, without excepting even those conditions which are purely negative, and in themselves incapable of causing anything; it will probably be admitted without longer discussion, that no one of the conditions has more claim to that title than another, and that *the real cause of the phenomenon is the assemblage of all its conditions.*' (J. S. Mill, *System of Logic*, Book III, chap. v, § 3; ed. 1, vol. i, p. 403, my italics.)

NATURAL SCIENCE 303

as he has 'arbitrarily selected' one of these and called it the cause, he has satisfied Mill's definition of what the word ordinarily means. But suppose an A.A. man comes along, opens the bonnet, holds up a loose high-tension lead, and says: 'Look here, sir, you're running on three cylinders'. My problem is now solved. I know the cause of the stoppage. It is *the* cause, just because it has not been 'arbitrarily selected'; it has been correctly identified as the thing that I can put right, after which the car will go properly. If I had been a person who could flatten out hills by stamping on them the passer-by would have been right to call my attention to the hill as the cause of the stoppage; not because the hill was a hill but because I was able to flatten it out.

To be precise, the 'condition' which is thus 'selected' is in fact not 'selected' at all; for selection implies that the person selecting has before him a finite number of things from among which he takes his choice. But this does not happen. In the first place the conditions of any given event are quite possibly infinite in number, so that no one could thus marshal them for selection even if he tried. In the second place no one ever tries to enumerate them completely. Why should he? If I find that I can get a result by certain means I may be sure that I should not be getting it unless a great many conditions were fulfilled; but so long as I get it I do not mind what these conditions are. If owing to a change in one of them I fail to get it, I still do not want to know what they all are; I only want to know what the one is that has changed.

304   CAUSATION IN PRACTICAL

From this a principle follows which I shall call 'the relativity of causes'. Suppose that the conditions of an event y include three things, a, β, γ; and suppose that there are three persons A, B, C, of whom A is able to produce or prevent a and only a; B is able to produce or prevent β and only β; and C is able to produce or prevent γ and only γ. Then if each of them asks 'What was the cause of y?' each will have to give a different answer. For A, a is the cause; for B, β; and for C, γ. The principle may be stated by saying that *for any given person the cause in sense II of a given thing is that one of its conditions which he is able to produce or prevent.*

For example, a car skids while cornering at a certain point, strikes the kerb, and turns turtle. From the car-driver's point of view the cause of the accident was cornering too fast, and the lesson is that one must drive more carefully. From the county surveyor's point of view the cause was a defect in the surface or camber of the road, and the lesson is that greater care must be taken to make roads skid-proof. From the motor-manufacturer's point of view the cause was defective design in the car, and the lesson is that one must place the centre of gravity lower.

If the three parties concerned take these three lessons respectively to heart accidents will become rarer. A knowledge of the causes of accidents will be gained in such a sense that knowledge is power: causes are causes in sense II, and knowledge of the cause of a thing we wish to prevent is (not merely brings, but is) knowledge how to prevent it. As in

NATURAL SCIENCE   305

the science of medicine so in the study of 'accidents',
where 'accident' means something people wish to
prevent, the word 'cause' is used in sense II.

As in medicine, therefore, so in the study of 'accidents' the use of the word in any other sense, or its
use by some one who fails to grasp the implications
of this sense, leads to confusion. If the driver, the
surveyor, and the manufacturer agreed in thinking
they knew the cause of the accident I have described,
but differed as to what it was, and if each thought that
it was a thing one of the others could produce or
prevent, but not himself, the result would be that
none of them would do anything towards preventing
such accidents in future, and their so-called knowledge of the cause of such accidents would be a
'knowledge' that was not, and did not even bring,
power. But since in the present context the word
'cause' is used in sense II, the reason why their
'knowledge' of the 'cause' of such accidents does not
enable them to prevent such accidents is that it is
not knowledge of their cause. What each of them
mistakes for such knowledge is the following nonsense proposition: 'the cause of accidents like this is
something which somebody else is able to produce
or prevent, but I am not.' Nonsense, because 'cause'
means 'cause in sense II', and owing to the relativity
of causes 'the cause of this accident' means 'that one
of its conditions which I am able to produce or
prevent'. Hence the folly of blaming other people in
respect of an event in which we and they are together
involved. Every one knows that such blame is foolish;

but without such an analysis of the idea of causation as I am here giving it is not easy to say why.

In medicine the principle of the relativity of causes means that, since any significant statement about the cause of a disease is a statement about the way in which that disease can be treated, two persons who can treat the same disease in two different ways will make different statements as to its cause. Suppose that one medical man can cure a certain disease by administering drugs, and another by 'psychological' treatment. For the first the 'cause' of the disease will be definable in terms of bio-chemistry; for the second in terms of psychology. If the disease itself is defined in terms of bio-chemistry, or in terms that admit of explanation or analysis in bio-chemical language, the definition of its cause in terms of psychology may be thought to imply an 'interactionist' theory of the relation between body and mind; and may be thought objectionable in so far as such theories are open to objection. But this would be a mistake. Definition of its cause in terms of psychology implies no theory as to the relation between body and mind. It simply records the fact that cases of the disease have been successfully treated by psychological methods, together with the hope that psychological methods may prove beneficial in future cases. To speak of this as 'evidence for an interactionist theory' would be to talk nonsense.

A corollary of the relativity principle is that *for a person who is not able to produce or prevent any of its conditions a given event has no cause in sense II at all,*

NATURAL SCIENCE   307

and any statement he makes as to its cause in this sense of the word will be a nonsense statement. Thus the managing director of a large insurance company once told me that his wide experience of motor accidents had convinced him that the cause of all accidents was people driving too fast. This was a nonsense statement; but one could expect nothing better from a man whose practical concern with these affairs was limited to paying for them. In sense II of the word 'cause' only a person who is concerned with producing or preventing a certain kind of event can form an opinion about its cause. For a mere spectator there are no causes. When Hume tried to explain how the mere act of spectation could in time generate the idea of a cause, where 'cause' meant the cause of empirical science, that is, the cause in sense II, he was trying to explain how something happens which in fact does not happen.

If sciences are constructed consisting of causal propositions in sense II of the word 'cause', they will of course be in essence codifications of the various ways in which the people who construct them can bend nature to their purposes, and of the means by which in each case this can be done. Their constituent propositions will be (*a*) experimental, (*b*) general.

(*a*) In calling them experimental I mean that they will be established by means of experiment. No amount of observation will serve to establish such a proposition; for any such proposition is a declaration of ability to produce or prevent a certain state of things by the use of certain means; and no one knows what he can do, or how he can do it, until he tries. By observing and thinking he may form the opinion that he can probably do a given thing that resembles one he has done in the past; he may, that is, form an opinion as to its cause; but he cannot acquire knowledge.

(b) Because the proposition 'x causes y', in sense II of the word 'cause', is a constituent part of a practical science, it is essentially something that can be applied to cases arising in practice; that is to say, the terms x and y are not individuals but universals, and the proposition itself, rightly understood, reads 'any instance of x is a thing whose production or prevention is means respectively of producing or preventing some instance of y'. It would be nonsense, in this sense of the word 'cause', to inquire after the cause of any individual thing as such. It is a peculiarity of sense II that every causal proposition is a general proposition or 'propositional function'. In sense I every causal proposition is an individual proposition. In sense III causal propositions might equally well be either individual or general.

If the above analysis of the cause-effect relation (in sense II) into a means-end relation is correct, why do people describe this means-end relation in cause-effect terminology? People do not choose words at random; they choose them because they think them appropriate. If they apply cause-effect terminology to things whose relation is really that of means and end the reason must be that they want to apply to those things some idea which is conveyed by the

NATURAL SCIENCE 309

cause-effect terminology and not by the means-end terminology. What is this idea? The answer is not doubtful. The cause-effect terminology conveys an idea not only of one thing's leading to another but of one thing's forcing another to happen or exist; an idea of power or compulsion or constraint.

From what impression, as Hume asks, is this idea derived? I answer, from impressions received in our social life, in the practical relations of man to man; specifically, from the impression of causing (in sense I) some other man to do something when, by argument or command or threat or the like, we place him in a situation in which he can only carry out his intentions by doing that thing; and conversely, from the impression of being caused to do something.

Why, then, did people think it appropriate to apply this idea to the case of actions in which we achieve our ends by means, not of other human beings, but of things in nature?

Sense II of the word 'cause' is especially a Greek sense; in modern times it is especially associated with the survival or revival of Greek ideas in the earlier Renaissance thinkers; and both the Greeks and the earlier Renaissance thinkers held quite seriously an animistic theory of nature. They thought of what we call the material or physical world as a living organism or complex of living organisms, each with its own sensations and desires and intentions and thoughts. In Plato's *Timaeus*, and in the Renaissance Platonists whose part in the formation of modern natural science was so decisive, the constant use of language with

310   CAUSATION IN PRACTICAL

animistic implications is neither an accident nor a metaphor; these expressions are meant to be taken literally and to imply what they seem to imply, namely that the way in which men use what we nowadays call inorganic nature as means to our ends is not in principle different from the way in which we use other men. We use other men by assuming them to be free agents with wills of their own, and influencing them in such a way that they shall decide to do what is in conformity with our plans. This is 'causing' them so to act in sense I of the word 'cause'. If 'inorganic nature' is alive in much the same way as human beings, we must use it according to much the same principles; and therefore we can apply to this use of it the same word 'cause', as implying that there are certain ways in which natural things behave if left to themselves, but that man, being more powerful than they, is able to thwart their inclination to behave in these ways and make them behave not as they like but as he likes.

To sum up. Sense II of the word 'cause' rests on two different ideas about the relation between man and nature.

1. The anthropocentric idea that man looks at nature from his own point of view; not the point of view of a thinker, anxious to find out the truth about nature as it is in itself, but the point of view of a practical agent, anxious to find out how he can manipulate nature for the achieving of his own ends.

2. The anthropomorphic idea that man's manipulation of nature resembles one man's manipulation

NATURAL SCIENCE   311

of another man, because natural things are alive in much the same way in which men are alive, and have therefore to be similarly handled.

The first idea is admittedly part of what civilized and educated European men nowadays think about their relations with nature. The second idea is part of what they notoriously did think down to (say) four centuries ago. How they began to get rid of this idea, and how completely they have even now got rid of it, are questions I shall not raise. My point is that even to-day, when they use the word 'cause' in sense II, they are talking as if they had not yet entirely got rid of it. For if the vocabulary of practical natural science were overhauled with a view to eliminating all traces of anthropomorphism, language about causes in sense II would disappear and language about means and ends would take its place.

Fifty years ago, anthropologists were content to note the fact that 'survivals' occur. Since then, they have seen that the occurrence of such things constitutes a problem, and a difficult one. 'Students have made some progress in ascertaining what causes folklore to decay, but what causes the surviving elements to survive? What vacuum does the survival fill? . . . These questions . . . remain a problem for the future.'[1] What causes the survival of language which taken literally implies the survival of supposedly obsolete thought-forms is, I submit, the fact that these thought-forms are not so dead as they are supposed to be. It is certainly true that modern

[1] Charlotte S. Burne, *Folklore*, vol. xxii (1911), p. 37.

312   PRACTICAL NATURAL SCIENCE

natural science has tried very hard to expel anthropomorphic elements from its conception of nature.
Among natural scientists to-day it is orthodox to take
the will for the deed. For the historical metaphysician
it is a question how far this anti-anthropomorphic
movement has been successful. The continued use
of the word 'cause' in sense II is prima-facie evidence
that its success has not been complete.

XXXII

CAUSATION IN THEORETICAL NATURAL SCIENCE

SENSE III of the word 'cause' represents an attempt to apply it not to a 'practical' but to a 'theoretical' science of nature. I shall first explain the characteristics which would belong to this sense if the attempt were successful, and then consider certain difficulties which in the long run prove fatal to it.

In the contingent world to which sense II belongs a cause is contingent (*a*) in its existence, as depending for its existence on human volition, (*b*) in its operation, as depending for the production of its effect on *conditiones sine quibus non*. In the necessary world to which sense III belongs a cause is necessary (*a*) in its existence, as existing whether or no human beings want it to exist, (*b*) in its operation, as producing its effect no matter what else exists or does not exist. There are no *conditiones sine quibus non*. The cause leads to its effect by itself, or 'unconditionally'; in other words the relation between cause and effect is a one-one relation. There can be no relativity of causes, and no diversity of effects due to fulfilment or non-fulfilment of conditions.

I propose to distinguish the one-many and many-one[1] character of the cause-effect relation in sense II

---

[1] One-many, because a cause in sense II leads to its effect only when the *conditiones sine quibus non* are fulfilled. Many-one, because of the relativity of causes (see p. 304).

from its one-one character in sense III by calling these senses *loose* and *tight* respectively. A loose cause requires some third thing other than itself and its effect to bind the two together, namely a group of *conditiones sine quibus non*; a tight cause is one whose connexion with its effect is independent of such adventitious aids.

In order to illustrate the implications of sense III, I will refer to the contradiction between the traditional denial of *actio in distans* (which, I suppose, would hold as against action across a lapse of time no less than across a distance in space) and the assumption, commonly made nowadays, that a cause precedes its effect in time. I shall argue that *actio in distans* is perfectly intelligible in sense II but nonsense in sense III.

If I set fire to one end of a time-fuse, and five minutes later the charge at its other end explodes, there is said to be a causal connexion between the first and second events, and a time-interval of five minutes between them. But this interval is occupied by the burning of the fuse at a determinate rate of feet per minute; and this process is a *conditio sine qua non* of the causal efficacy ascribed to the first event. That is to say, the connexion between the lighting of the fuse and the detonation of the charge is causal in the loose sense, not the tight one. If in the proposition '*x* causes the explosion' we wish to use the word 'cause' in the tight sense, *x* must be so defined as to include in itself every such *conditio sine qua non*. It must include the burning of the whole fuse; not its burning until 'just

NATURAL SCIENCE   315

before' that process reaches the detonator, for then there would still be an interval to be bridged, but its burning until the detonator is reached. Only then is the cause in sense III complete; and when it is complete it produces its effect, not afterwards (however soon afterwards) but then. Cause in sense III is simultaneous with effect.

Similarly, it is coincident with its effect in space. The cause of the explosion is where the explosion is. For suppose x causes y, and suppose that x is in a position p_1 and y in a position p_2, the distance from p_1 to p_2 being δ. If 'cause' is used in sense II, δ may be any distance, so long as it is bridged by a series of events which are *conditiones sine quibus non* of x causing y. But if 'cause' is used in sense III, δ must $= 0$. For if it did not, p_2 would be any position on the surface of a sphere whose centre was p_1 and whose radius would $= \delta$; so the relation between p_1 and p_2 would be a one-many relation. But the relation between x and y, where x causes y in sense III, is a one-one relation. Therefore, where δ does not $= 0$, x cannot cause y in sense III.

The denial of *actio in distans*, spatial or temporal, where the 'agent' is a cause in sense III, is therefore not a 'prejudice'[1] but is logically involved in the definition of sense III.

The main difficulty about sense III is to explain what is meant by saying that a cause 'produces' or 'necessitates' its effect. When similar language is used of senses I and II we know what it means. In sense I

[1] As Russell calls it: *Mysticism and Logic*, cit., p. 192.

it means that *x* affords somebody a motive for doing *y*; in sense II, that *x* is somebody's means of bringing *y* about. But what (since it cannot mean either of these) does it mean in sense III?

There are two well-known answers to this question, which may be called the rationalist and empiricist answers respectively.

(i) The rationalist answer runs: 'necessitation means implication'. A cause, on this view, is a 'ground', and its relation to its effect is the relation of ground to consequent, a logical relation. When some one says that *x* necessitates *y* he means on this view that *x* implies *y*, and is claiming the same kind of insight into *y* which one has (for example) into the length of one side of a triangle given the lengths of the other two sides and the included angle. Whatever view one takes as to the nature of implication, one must admit that in such a case the length of the third side can be ascertained without measuring it and even without seeing it, e.g. when it lies on the other side of a hill. The implication theory, therefore, implies that 'if the cause is given the effect follows', not only in the sense that whenever the cause actually exists the effect actually follows, but that from the thought of the cause the thought of the effect follows logically. That is to say, any one who wishes to discover the effect of a given thing *x* can discover the answer by simply thinking out the logical implications of *x*. Nothing in the nature of observation or experiment is needed.

This is in itself a tenable position in the sense that, if any one wants to construct a system of science in which the search for causes means a search for grounds, there is nothing to prevent him from trying. This was in fact what Descartes tried to do. His projected 'universal science' was to be a system of grounds and consequents. And if, as is sometimes said, modern physics represents a return in some degree to the Cartesian project, it would seem that the attempt is being made once more. But the rationalist theory of causation, however valuable it may be as the manifesto of a particular scientific enterprise, cannot be regarded as an 'analysis' of the causal propositions asserted by natural science as it has existed for the last few centuries. If it were accepted, these propositions would have to be abandoned as untrue. For no one believes that they can be established by sheer 'thinking', that is, by finding the so-called effects to be logically implied in the so-called causes. It is just because this is impossible that the questions what causes a given effect and what effect a given cause produces have to be answered by observation and experiment. Hence the result of establishing a science of the Cartesian type would be not an analysis of propositions of the type 'x causes y' into propositions of the type 'x implies y' but the disuse of causal propositions in that kind of science and the use of implicational propositions instead; while in the sciences of observation and experiment causal propositions not analysable into implicational propositions would still be used; the meaning of 'necessity' in these causal propositions being still doubtful.

318   CAUSATION IN THEORETICAL

This situation would not be illuminated by alleging that the sciences in which causal propositions occur are 'backward' or 'immature sciences'. Such a statement would imply that the idea of causation is a half-baked idea which when properly thought out will turn into the different idea of implication. This I take to be the Hegelian theory of the dialectic of concepts, and if any one wishes to maintain it I do not want to forbid him; but I must observe that it does not excuse him from answering the question what the half-baked idea is *an sich*, that is, before its expected transformation has happened.

(ii) I turn to the empiricist answer: 'necessitation means observed uniformity of conjunction'. Like the former answer this one cannot be taken literally; for no one, I think, will pretend that the proposition '*x* necessitates *y*' means merely 'all the observed *x*'s have been observed to be conjoined with *y*'s', and does not also mean '*x*'s observed in the future will also be conjoined with *y*'s'. In fact the question (so urgent for, e.g., Hume and Mill) how we proceed from the mere experience of conjunction to the assertion of causal connexion resolves itself into the question how we pass from the first of these to the second. For Hume and Mill the proposition 'all the observed *x*'s have been observed to be conjoined with *y*'s' is not what we mean by saying '*x* necessitates *y*', it is only the empirical evidence on the strength of which we assert the very different proposition '*x* necessitates *y*'. Thus, if any one says 'necessitation means observed uniformity of conjunction', it must be supposed either that he is talking without thinking; or that he is carelessly expressing what, expressed more accurately, would run: 'necessitation is something we assert on the strength of observed uniformity of conjunction', without telling us what he thinks necessitation to be; or, thirdly, that he is expressing still more carelessly what should run: 'in order to assert a necessitation we must pass from the first of the above propositions to the second; now I cannot see how this is possible; therefore I submit that we ought never to assert necessitations, but on the occasions when we do assert them we ought to be asserting something quite different, namely observed conjunction'. Necessitation being again left undefined.

(iii) A third answer to our question has been given by Earl Russell, in a paper[1] of very great importance, to which I have already referred; but I want here and now to express my great admiration for it and my great indebtedness to it. He says: '*necessary* is a predicate of a propositional function meaning that it is true for all possible values of its argument or arguments'. This I will call the 'functional' answer. In so far as it amounts to saying that causation in sense III implies a one-one relation between cause and effect, I entirely agree. But I find myself, very reluctantly, unable to accept all of what I take Earl Russell to mean. I will give two examples.

(a) How, on the functional theory, could any one ever know a causal proposition to be true, or even know that the facts in his possession tended to justify

[1] 'On the Notion of Cause', referred to on p. 69, above.

a belief in it? Only, so far as I can see, if there is a relation of implication between x and y. For 'all *possible* values' of x may be an infinite number; and, even if they are not, it may not be practicable to examine them individually. If a, b, c are the sides of any triangle, we know that $a+b-c$ will always be a positive quantity, because that is implied in the definition of a triangle. Thus the functional theory presupposes the rationalistic or implicational theory, which I have already given reasons for rejecting.

(β) I do not know whether Earl Russell, in the sentence quoted above, wished to be understood as meaning that the word 'necessary' has no other meaning than that which he there ascribes to it. If so, he was mistaken. It has another meaning, which is in fact its original meaning. Just as the original sense of the word 'cause' is what I have called the historical sense, according to which that which is caused is the act of a conscious and responsible agent, so the original sense of the word 'necessary' is an historical sense, according to which it is necessary for a person to act in a certain way: deciding so to act and acting therefore freely and responsibly, yet (in a sense which in no wise derogates from his responsibility) 'necessitated' to act in that way by certain 'causes', in sense I of the word 'cause'.

Even if Earl Russell does not wish to deny that the word 'necessary' has this historical sense, I cannot think that his failure to mention it is well advised. This original sense of the word 'necessary' is just as much the foundation on which the other senses of the

NATURAL SCIENCE 321

word 'necessary' have been built, as the corresponding sense of the word 'cause' (sense I, the 'historical' sense) is the foundation on which have been built the other senses of the word 'cause'. Between the respective histories of these two words there is not only parallelism, there is interconnexion. It is therefore very natural that Earl Russell should appeal to the word 'necessary' in his attempt to clear up the meaning of the word 'cause'. But the metaphysical problems connected with the idea of causation are historical problems, not to be solved except by historical treatment; and if the history of the word 'necessary' has run on parallel lines to the history of the word 'cause', the appeal from the latter to the former is scientifically barren, because it takes us not from one problem to the solution of that problem, but from one unsolved problem to another unsolved problem of the same kind.

Most people think that when we use the word 'causation' in sense III we mean to express by it something different from logical implication, and something more than uniformity of conjunction, whether observed only, or observed in the past and also expected in the future; and that this 'something different' and 'something more' is in the nature of compulsion. On the historical issue of what has actually been meant when words have actually been used, this is correct.

Earl Russell (op. cit., p. 190) argues that people cannot mean this because (as he very truly says) 'where desire does not come in, there can be no

322   CAUSATION IN THEORETICAL

question of compulsion'. All the same, as I shall now try to show, they do mean this. Causation in sense III is an anthropomorphic idea. Natural scientists have tried to use it as a weapon for attacking anthropomorphic conceptions of nature; but it has been a treacherous weapon. It has led them unawares to reaffirm the view they were attacking. And that may be why, in Earl Russell's own words, 'physics has ceased to look for causes' (op. cit., p. 180).

We found the idea of compulsion present in sense II of the word 'cause'. From what impression, we then asked, is this idea derived? We now find it present in sense III, and we must ask the same question, and answer it in the same way. The idea of compulsion, as applied to events in nature, is derived from our experience of occasions on which we have compelled others to act in certain ways by placing them in situations (or calling their attention to the fact that they are in situations) of such a kind that only by so acting can they realize the intentions we know or rightly assume them to entertain: and conversely, occasions in which we have ourselves been thus compelled. Compulsion is an idea derived from our social experience, and applied in what is called a 'metaphorical' way not only to our relations with things in nature (sense II of the word 'cause') but also to the relations which these things have among themselves (sense III). Causal propositions in sense III are descriptions of relations between natural events in anthropomorphic terms.

The reason why we are in the habit of using these

anthropomorphic terms is, of course, that they are traditional. Inquiry into the history of the tradition shows that it grew up in connexion with the same animistic theory of nature to which I referred in discussing sense II of the word 'cause', but that in this case the predominant factor was a theology of Neoplatonic inspiration.

If a man can be said to cause certain events in nature by adopting certain means to bringing them about, and if God is conceived semi-anthropomorphically[1] as having faculties like those of the human mind but greatly magnified, it will follow that God also will be regarded as bringing about certain things in nature by the adoption of certain means.

Now comes a step in the argument which, if we tried to reconstruct it without historical knowledge, we should probably reconstruct wrongly. If x is a thing in nature produced by God as a means of producing y, we might fancy x to be a purely passive instrument in God's hand, having no power of its own, but 'inert', as Berkeley in the true spirit of post-Galilean physics insists that matter must be. And in

---

[1] I distinguish an anthropomorphic conception of God (cf. p. 185) from a semi-anthropomorphic. An anthropomorphic God would be simply what Matthew Arnold called a 'magnified non-natural man'. His attributes would be merely the attributes of man, enlarged. For example, he would be liable to anger, but his anger would be a more formidable thing than man's. A semi-anthropomorphic God would be the result of criticizing this childish idea in the light of the reflection that, if God is really greater than man, he cannot have those attributes which in man are due to man's littleness; e.g. anger, which comes of being thwarted.

that case God alone would possess that compulsive force which is expressed by the word 'cause'; that word would not be given as a name to *x*, and God would be the sole cause.

Actually, God is for medieval thinkers not the sole cause but the first cause. This does not mean the first term in a series of efficient causes (a barbarous misinterpretation of the phrase), but a cause of a peculiar kind, as distinct from 'secondary causes'. The *Liber de Causis*, a Neoplatonic Arabic work of the ninth century, whose influence on medieval cosmology was at this point decisive, lays it down that God in creating certain instruments for the realization of certain ends confers upon these instruments a power in certain ways like his own, though inferior to it.

Thus endowed with a kind of minor and derivative godhead, these instruments accordingly acquire the character of causes, and constitute that division of nature which, according to John the Scot, 'both is created and creates'. Their causality is thus a special kind of causality existing wholly within nature, whereby one thing in nature produces or necessitates another thing in nature. The words 'produces' and 'necessitates' are here used literally and deliberately to convey a sense of volition and compulsion; for the anthropomorphic account of natural things is taken as literally true; the activity of these secondary causes is a scaled-down version of God's and God's is a scaled-up version of man's.

This idea of God is only semi-anthropomorphic,

because it implies the ascription to God of a power not belonging to man, the power of creating instruments of His will which are themselves possessed of will.

This was the atmosphere in which our modern conception of nature took shape. For in the sixteenth and seventeenth centuries, when the animistic conception of nature was replaced among scientists and philosophers by a mechanistic one, the word 'cause' was not a novelty; it was a long-established term, and its meaning was rooted in these Neoplatonic notions.

Thus when we come to Newton, and read (e.g.) the *Scholium* appended to his Definitions, we find him using as a matter of course a whole vocabulary which, taken literally, ascribes to 'causes' in nature a kind of power which properly belongs to one human being inducing another to act as he wishes him to act. Causes are said, in the twelfth paragraph of that *Scholium*, to be 'forces impressed upon bodies for the generation of motion. True motion is neither generated nor altered, but by some force impressed upon the body moved.' The cause, for Newton, is not that which impresses the force, it is the force itself.

Here and throughout his treatment of the subject it is perfectly clear that for him the idea of causation is the idea of force, compulsion, constraint, exercised by something powerful over another thing which if not under this constraint would behave differently; this hypothetical different behaviour being called by contrast 'free' behaviour. This constraint of one thing in nature by another is the secondary causation of medieval cosmology.

Taken *au pied de la lettre*, Newton is implying that a billiard-ball struck by another and set in motion would have liked to be left in peace; it is reluctant to move, and this reluctance, which is called inertia, has to be overcome by an effort on the part of the ball that strikes it. This effort costs the striker something, namely part of its own momentum, which it pays over to the sluggard ball as an inducement to move. I am not suggesting that this reduction of physics to social psychology is the doctrine Newton set out to teach; all I say is that he expounded it, no doubt as a metaphor beneath which the truths of physics are concealed.

I have already reminded the reader that in Newton there is no law of universal causation. He not only does not assert that every event must have a cause, he explicitly denies it; and this in two ways.

(i) In the case of a body moving freely (even though its motion be what he calls 'true' motion as distinct from relative motion), there is uncaused motion; for caused means constrained, and free means unconstrained. If a body moves freely from p_1 to p_2 and thence to p_3, the 'event' which is its moving from p_2 to p_3 is in no sense caused by the preceding 'event' of its moving from p_1 to p_2; for it is not caused at all. Newton's doctrine is that any movement which happens according to the laws of motion is an uncaused event; the laws of motion are in fact the laws of free or causeless motion.

(ii) He asserts that there is such a thing as relative motion; but, as he puts it, 'relative motion may be generated or altered without any force impressed upon the body'. If, therefore, it were possible to show either that all motion is 'free', that is to say, takes place according to laws having the same logical character as the Newtonian laws of motion; or that all motion is 'relative'; then on Newton's own principles it would follow that no motion is caused, and the cat would be out of the bag. It would have become plain that there is no truth concealed beneath the animistic metaphor; and that 'the idea of causation' is simply a relic of animism foisted upon a science to which it is irrelevant.

This is what modern physics has done. Developing the Newtonian doctrine in the simplest and most logical way, it has eliminated the notion of cause altogether. In place of that notion, we get a new and highly complex development of the Newtonian 'laws of motion'. Of the two Newtonian classes of events, (*a*) those that happen according to law (*b*) those that happen as the effects of causes, class (*a*) has expanded to such an extent as to swallow up (*b*). At the same time, the survival of the term 'cause' in certain sciences other than physics, such as medicine, is not a symptom of their 'backwardness', because in them the word 'cause' is not used in the same sense. They are practical sciences, and they accordingly use the word in sense II.

Causation and Recipes

Douglas Gasking

Reprinted from *Mind*, 64 (1955), 479–487, with permission of Basil Blackwell, Publisher.

III.—CAUSATION AND RECIPES

By Douglas Gasking

We sometimes speak of one thing, or of one sort of thing, causing another—of the second as being the result of or due to the former. In what circumstances do we do so ?

If we start with some typical statements of causal connection— " The train-smash was due to a buckled rail " ; " Vitamin B deficiency causes beri-beri "—two things are likely to strike us. First, the effect is something that comes into being after the cause, and secondly, we suppose that anyone fully conversant with the circumstances and the relevant causal laws could, from a knowledge of the cause, predict the effect. So it is very natural to suggest, as an answer to our question : We say that A causes B whenever a person with the requisite empirical information could infer from the occurrence of A to the subsequent occurrence of B. Or we might put it : We say that A causes B whenever B regularly follows A.

But this " regular succession " notion will not do. For there are cases where we would speak of A causing B where it is not the case that from the occurrence of A we may infer the subsequent occurrence of B.

An example to illustrate this : Iron begins to glow when its temperature reaches a certain point. I do not know what that temperature is : for the sake of the illustration I will suppose it to be 1,000°C., and will assume that iron never glows except at or above this temperature. Now, if someone saw a bar of iron glowing and, being quite ignorant of the physical facts, asked : " What makes that iron glow ? What causes it to glow ? " we should answer : " It is glowing because it is at a temperature of 1,000°C. or more." The glowing, B, is caused by the high temperature, A. And here the B that is caused is not an event subsequent to the cause A. Iron reaches 1,000°C. and begins glowing at the same instant. Another example : current from a battery is flowing through a variable resistance, and we have a voltmeter connected to the two poles of the battery to measure the potential difference. Its reading is steady. We now turn the knob of our variable resistance and immediately the voltmeter shows that the potential difference has increased. If someone now asks : What caused this increase ?, we reply : " the increase of the resistance in the circuit ". But here again the effect was not something subsequent to the cause, but simultaneous.

So perhaps our account should be emended so as to read : We speak of A as causing B when the occurrence of B may be inferred from the occurrence of A and the occurence of B is either subsequent to or simultaneous with the occurrence of A.

But this will not do either, For there are, first of all, cases where from the occurrence of A we may infer the subsequent occurrence of B, yet would not speak of A as causing B. And secondly there are cases where from the occurrence of A we may infer the simultaneous occurrence of B, yet would not speak of A as causing B.

Here is an example of the first case. Given (A) that at t_1 a body freely falling *in vacuo* is moving at a speed of 32 feet per second we can infer (B) that at t_2, one second later, it will be moving at 64 feet per second. We might be prepared to say that this inference was in some sense or other a causal inference. But it would be a most unnatural and 'strained' use of the word 'cause' to say that the body's movement at 64 feet per second at t_2 was caused by its moving at 32 feet per second at t_1. It would be even more unnatural, to take a famous example, to say that the day that will be here in twelve hours' time is caused by the fact that it is now night. Yet from the present fact we can certainly infer that in twelve hours' time it will be day.

An example to illustrate the second point. From the fact that a bar of iron is now glowing we can certainly infer (and it will be a causal inference) that it is now at a temperature of 1,000°C. or over. Yet we should not say that its high temperature was caused by the glowing : we say that the high temperature causes the glowing, not *vice-versa*. Another example : watching the voltmeter and battery in the electrical circuit previously described we see that the needle suddenly jumps, showing that the potential difference has suddenly increased. From this we infer that the electrical resistance of the circuit has, at that moment, increased. But we should not say that the rise in potential difference caused the increase in resistance : rather that the rise in resistance caused a rise in the potential difference. Or again, knowing the properties of a certain sort of wax, we infer from the fact that the wax has melted that, at that very moment, it reached such and such a temperature. Yet we should not say that the wax's melting caused it to reach the critical temperature : rather that its reaching that temperature caused it to melt. Why do we speak of 'cause' in some cases in which we can infer from A to B, but not in others ?

The reason is not always of the same sort. Sometimes in such a case it would be nonsense to speak of A causing B, sometimes it would merely be false. Our very last example is a rather trivial instance of the first sort of reason. It is nonsense to speak of the melting of the wax causing the high temperature of the wax because " x melts " means " high temperature causes x to become liquid ". So " the melting of the wax caused the high-temperature of the wax " is equivalent to the absurdity " The high temperature of the wax's causing of the wax to become liquid caused the high temperature of the wax ".

But it is not for this sort of reason that we do not say that the glowing of the iron causes the high temperature of the iron. " Melting " is by definition an effect and not a cause of an increase in temperature, but the same is not true of " glowing ". It is not logically absurd to say that the glowing of a piece of iron causes its high temperature ; it is merely untrue. It is possible to imagine and to describe a world in which it would have been true. Here is an account of such an imaginary world.

" Our early ancestors many millennia ago discovered that you could make a large range of substances (wood, water, leaves, etc.) glow first blue, then purple, then red by a process of alternately covering them so as to exclude light, then rapidly letting light fall on them, then quickly covering them again, and so on. Wood, for instance, starts glowing after about six minutes of this treatment, and reaches the red stage in about ten minutes. If it is then left in constant daylight or in constant darkness it gradually fades through purple to blue and then ceases glowing. A number of other substances behave similarly, though the time needed to produce the glowing effect differs somewhat from substance to substance. None of the things that early man thus learnt to make glow, however, suffered any change of temperature in the process. Then, about 1000 B.C. men got hold of samples of fairly pure iron, for the first time. They tried the covering-uncovering technique on it to see if it too, like wood and water, but unlike certain sorts of rock, would glow if manipulated in this way. They found that it would, but that, unlike other substances, iron began to get hot when it started glowing, got hotter still at the purple stage, and when glowing red was very hot indeed. Precise measurements in modern times showed that on reaching the red stage the temperature of iron was 1,000°C. In other respects this imaginary world is just like our world, except that when you put a poker or other non-combustible object in a fire it does not begin to glow, however hot it gets."

Who can doubt that in this imaginary world we should have said that the glowing of the iron caused its temperature to rise, and not *vice-versa* ? What, then, are the essential differences between this world and ours, which would lead us to say one thing in one world and another in another ?

Human beings can make bodily movements. They do not move their arms, fingers, mouths and so on by doing anything else ; they just move them. By making bodily movements men can manipulate things : can lift them, hold them in certain positions, squeeze them, pull them, rub them against each other, and so on. Men discovered that whenever they manipulated certain things in certain ways in certain conditions certain things happened. When you hold a stone in your hand and make certain complex movements of arm and fingers the stone sails through the air approximately in a parabola. When you manipulate two bits of wood and some dry grass for a long time in a certain way the grass catches fire. When you squeeze an egg, it breaks. When you put a stone in the fire it gets hot. Thus men found out how to produce certain effects by manipulating things in certain ways : how to make an egg break, how to make a stone hot, how to make dry grass catch fire, and so on.

We have a general manipulative technique for making anything hot : we put it on a fire. We find that when we manipulate certain things in this way, such as water in a vessel, it gets hot but does not begin to glow. But we find, too, that certain other things, such as bars of iron, when manipulated in this way do not only get hot, they also, after a while, start to glow. And we have no general manipulative technique for making things glow : the only way to make iron glow is to apply to it the general technique for making things hot. We speak of making iron glow by making it hot, *i.e.* by applying to it the usual manipulative technique for making things hot, namely, putting on a fire, which in this special case, also makes it glow. We do not speak of making iron hot by making it glow, for we have no general manipulative technique for making things glow. And we say that the high temperature causes the glowing, not *vice-versa*.

In our imaginary world there is a general manipulative technique for making things glow—namely, rapidly alternating exposure to light and shielding from light. There is no other way of making them glow. In general, things manipulated in this way glow, but do not get hot. Iron, however, glows and gets hot. In this world we speak of making iron hot by making it glow, *i.e.* by applying to it the usual manipulative technique for making things glow which, in this special case, also makes it hot. We do not speak of making iron glow by making it hot, for the general manipulative technique of putting things on fires, which makes them hot, does not, in this world, also make things glow.

And in this world, we should say that the glowing causes the high temperature, not *vice-versa*.

What this example shows is the following : When we have a general manipulative technique which results in a certain sort of event A, we speak of producing A by this technique. (Heating things by putting them on a fire.) When in certain cases application of the general technique for producing A also results in B we speak of producing B by producing A. (Making iron glow by heating it.)   And in such a case we speak of A causing B, but not *vice-versa*. Thus the notion of causation is essentially connected with our manipulative techniques for producing results.   Roughly speaking : " A rise in the temperature of iron causes it to glow " means " By applying to iron the general technique for making things hot you will also, in this case, make it glow ".   And " The glowing of iron causes its temperature to rise " means " By applying to iron the general technique for making things glow you will also, in this case, make it hot ". This latter statement is, as it happens, false, for there is no general technique for making things glow, let alone one which, applied to iron, also makes it hot.

Thus a statement about the cause of something is very closely connected with a recipe for producing it or for preventing it. It is not exactly the same, however.   One often makes a remark of the form " A causes B " with the practical aim of telling someone how to produce or prevent B, but not always.   Sometimes one wishes to make a theoretical point.   And one can sometimes properly say of some particular happening, A, that it caused some other particular event, B, even when no-one could have produced A, by manipulation, as a means of producing B. For example, one may say that the rise in mean sea-level at a certain geological epoch was due to the melting of the Polar ice-cap.   But when one can properly say this sort of thing it is always the case that people can produce events of the first sort as a means to producing events of the second sort.   For example, one can melt ice in order to raise the level of water in a certain area.   We could come rather closer to the meaning of " A causes B " if we said : " Events of the B sort can be produced by means of producing events of the A sort."

This account fits in with the principle that an event, A, at time t_2 cannot be the cause of an event B at an earlier time, t_1.   It is a logical truth that one cannot alter the past.   One cannot, therefore, by manipulations at t_2 which produce A at t_2 also produce B retrospectively at t_1.

Let us turn now to the cases where, although from a state of affairs A we can infer a later state of affairs B, we nevertheless would not say that A causes B ; *e.g.* to the case where from the speed of a freely falling body at t_1 we can infer its speed at t_2, or infer coming darkness from present daylight. These are cases where a process is taking place whose law we know, so that we can infer from one stage in the process a later stage. Our inference presupposes that nothing happens to interfere with the process ; the falling body will not encounter an obstruction, the earth's spinning will not be stopped by, say, our sun becoming a super-nova. The difference between the earth's spinning and the body's falling is that in the latter case we can set the process going and arrange that nothing shall thereafter interfere with it for a certain time ; in the former case we cannot. It is the same sort of difference as there is between melting ice in a bucket and the water-level rising in the bucket and melting Polar ice-caps and sea-level rising. We cannot set the earth spinning, but we can set a top spinning.

Imagine a world in which there is an exact correlation between the colour and the temperature of everything. Anything at a certain low temperature is a certain shade of, say, blue. If an object becomes warmer its colour changes to purple, then red, then orange, then yellow and finally to white. Cold (or blue) objects can be made hot (or red) by putting them in a fire ; after a long time in a very big fire they become very hot (yellow). In such a world we should very probably not have had two sets of words : " cold ", " warm ", " hot ", " very hot " and also " blue ", " purple ", " red ", " yellow "—but only one set—say the words " blue ", " purple ", " red ", and so on. We should have spoken of things " looking purple ", or " being purple to the eyes " and of their " feeling purple " or " being purple to the touch ". (In our actual world we talk of things being round or square whether we apprehend their shapes by the eye or by the touch : we do not have a special word meaning " round to the eye " and another quite different word meaning " round to the touch ", since there is a correlation between these.)

In such a world we should speak of making purple things red by putting them on a fire, but should not normally speak of making something " red to the eye " (*i.e.* what we mean by " red ") by putting it on a fire ; nor of making something " red to the touch " (*i.e.* what we mean by " hot ") by this method. Still less should we speak of making something " red to the eye " by making it " red to the touch ", or of making it " red to the touch " by making it " red to the eye ". (In our actual world we do not speak of making things " visibly round " by making them

CAUSATION AND RECIPES   485

" tangibly round ", nor *vice versa*.)   When a single manipulation on our part invariably produces two effects A and B, we do not speak of producing one by producing the other, nor do we speak of one as a cause of the other.   (The visible roundness is neither cause nor effect of the tangible roundness of a penny.)   It is only when we have a technique for producing A which in some circumstances but not in all also produces B that we speak of producing B by producing A, and speak of A as causing B.

When we set a process going—drop a stone from a tower, set a top spinning—we set the stage, see that nothing shall interfere (for a certain time at least) with the process we are about to start, and then set things going.   After that, things take their own course without further intervention on our part—the stone gathers speed, the top loses it.   There are successive stages in the process.   At stage A at t_1 the stone is moving fairly fast, at a later stage B at t_2 the stone is going very fast.   But, on the presupposition that the process continues undisturbed, the very same initial stage-setting and send-off, C, which will produce fairly fast motion at t_1 (A), will always produce very fast motion at t_2 (B), and the initial stage-setting and send-off C which will produce very fast motion at t_2 (B) will always produce fairly fast motion at t_1 (A).   That is, the process being undisturbed, an initial send-off C will always produce both A and B : there is not a general technique for producing A which in some circumstances also produces B.   Hence we do not speak of producing B by producing A.   There is not a general technique for bringing it about that, one second after the start, a stone is falling at 32 feet per second, which in some circumstances can also be used to bring it about that two seconds after the start it is falling at 64 feet per second.   Hence we do not speak of achieving the latter by means of the former, and do not speak of the former as causing the latter.

Of course one could, by attaching a rocket to the falling body, which fires one second after the start, secure that a body which is moving at 32 feet per second one second after departure is one second later travelling much faster then 64 feet per second. But this would contradict our presupposition that the process, after being started, was left uninterfered with.   It is on this presupposition only that C always produces both A and B.

I have made two points :

First : that one says " A causes B " in cases where one could produce an event or state of the A sort as a means to producing one of the B sort.   I have, that is, explained the " cause-effect " relation in terms of the " producing-by-means-of " relation.

486   D. GASKING :

Second : I have tried to give a general account of the producing-by-means-of relation itself : what it is to produce B by producing A.   We learn by experience that whenever in certain conditions we manipulate objects in a certain way a certain change, A, occurs.   Performing this manipulation is then called : " producing A ".   We learn also that in certain special cases, or when certain additional conditions are also present, the manipulation in question also results in another sort of change, B.   In these cases the manipulation is also called " producing B ", and, since it is in general the manipulation of producing A, in this case it is called " producing B by producing A ".   For example, one makes iron glow by heating it.   And I discussed two sorts of case where one does not speak of " producing B by producing A ".   (1) Where the manipulation for producing A is the general technique for producing B, so that one cannot speak of " producing B by producing A " but only *vice-versa*.   (2) Where the given manipulation invariably produces both A and B, so that the manipulation for producing B is not a special case only of that for producing A.

The notion of " cause " here elucidated is the fundamental or primitive one.   It is not the property of scientists ; except for those whose work most directly bears on such things as engineering, agriculture or medicine, and who are naturally interested in helping their practical colleagues, scientists hardly ever make use of the notion.   A statement about causes in the sense here outlined comes very near to being a recipe for producing or preventing certain effects.   It is not simply an inference-licence. Professional scientists, when they are carefully stating their findings, mostly express themselves in functional laws, which are pure inference-licences, with nothing of the recipe about them (explicitly at least).   Thus the formula $1 = \dfrac{E}{R}$ tells you how to infer the current in a given circuit, knowing the electro-motive force and the resistance ; it tells you how to infer the electro-motive force, knowing the resistance and current ; and how to infer the resistance from current and electro-motive force.   All these three things it tells you ; and no one of them any more specially than any other—it works all ways, as an inference-licence.   But while one might say a current of 3 amps. was caused by an e.m.f. of 6 volts across a resistance of 2 ohms, one would hardly say that a resistance of 2 ohms in the circuit was caused by an e.m.f. of 6 volts and a current of 3 amps.   Why not ?   Given an e.m.f. of 6 volts one could make 3 amps. flow by making the resistance equal to 2 ohms.   But one could not, given an e.m.f. of 6 volts, make the resistance of the circuit equal to 2 ohms by making a current of 3 amps. flow.

From one point of view the progress of natural science can be viewed as resulting from the substitution of pure inference-licences for recipes.

There is, however, what might be called a " popular science " use of " cause " which may not exactly fit the account given— a use of the word by laymen who know some science and by some scientists in their less strictly professional moments.   I have in mind such a locution as " Gravity causes unsupported bodies to fall ".   Such a statement is not quite on a par, logically, with " Great heat causes steel to melt ".   It would be fair to say, I think, that the use of the word " cause " here is a sophisticated extension from its more primitive and fundamental meaning. It is the root notion that I have been concerned with.

In accounts of causation given by philosophers in the past a specially fundamental role was often played by the motion of bodies.   Every kind of change and every kind of natural law was often supposed to be " ultimately reducible to " or to be explicable in terms of it.   In this account, too, though in a rather different way, the motion of bodies occupies a special position.   Central to this account is the notion of a manipulation to produce A and thereby to produce B.   When we manipulate things we control the motion of bodies, *e.g.* by rubbing sticks together (motion of bodies) men made them hot and thereby caused them to ignite. At least all those causal chains that are initiated by human beings go back to manipulations, that is, to matter in motion.

University of Melbourne.

III. The Logical Entailment Theory

Necessity in Causation

Brand Blanshard

Reprinted with permission of the publisher from Brand Blanshard, *Reason and Analysis* (La Salle, Ill.: Open Court Publishing Co., 1962), pp. 444–471.

CHAPTER XI

NECESSITY IN CAUSATION

1. Causation is only one strand in the network of relations that holds things together, and any one of these relations might in theory be singled out by the philosopher for special attention. Most of them have in fact been passed over as of minor importance. But a few of them have held a continued fascination for both the scientific and the speculative mind. Among this select few causation is perhaps the most conspicuous member. Why is this? There are several reasons.

(1) It is a relation, as Hume pointed out, to which we have to appeal if we are to take one step beyond the given into the world of physical things, or to past or future. If we perceive a voice as a wife's or a friend's, or assume that the postman has left the mail in the hall, or expect the floor to hold us up when we walk, we are depending on causal relations. If there were no such relations, we should have no reason for believing that there were any physical things or that anything would behave in one way rather than another. Causation is the lifeline connecting us with the world.

(2) It is also our instrument of *control*. Our intellectual interest, as Dewey has emphasized, tends to follow our practical needs, and science to enlist in the service of technology. A grasp of the causes of things will give us command over them if anything can. As long as the causes of malaria and yellow fever were unknown, we were helpless about them; once their causes were brought to light, we could see what must be done to eradicate them. If such other plagues of mankind as cancer, juvenile delinquency and senile decay are to be eliminated, the first step is to master their causes.

(3) But science does not aim merely at control; its primary aim is at *understanding*. It considers that the understanding of a thing or event has been achieved when the laws that govern it have been formulated. Not all these laws, indeed, are causal laws. The laws of motion, the laws that all mammals are vertebrates, the law that all ruminating animals have cloven hooves, the law that light travels at a certain speed, are not statements of causal connection. Nevertheless, causal laws are the staple of science. They are laws that would

NECESSITY IN CAUSATION   445

have first mention as examples of scientific explanation, for they carry with them the strongest sense of understanding. When we ask the question Why? about any event—a disease, a tidal wave, a war, a motor 'accident'—what we are asking for is an explanation in terms of its causes. In natural science that is what explanation normally means.

(4) If the mastery of causal laws gives control and understanding, it is because such laws are more than devices of our own. They belong to nature; they are part of the network, the set of objective ties, that bind events together. The scientist's traditional assumption has been that nothing happens by accident, that whether he knows the cause of an event or not, it is there to be found and is the condition of the event's occurrence. Indeed every event seems to be implicated with every other. Not only does each event have a precursor in a line that stretches backward without beginning and forward without end, but these lines of causation intercross. My use of a pen at this moment would seem to have no causal connection with someone's eating his lunch at the same moment in Los Angeles. And this is no doubt true if one means a connection in a straight temporal line. But there are indirect causal lines. After all, it is not fancy but highly probable fact that the occurrence of either event depends on another celebrated event that happened at Marathon some twenty-five centuries earlier, so that each of the present events is connected through a common cause with the other. The universe itself may be regarded as one gigantic congeries of events linked directly or indirectly by a network of causal laws. And since the strands that form this network belong to the nature of things no less than the items linked, philosophers have often felt that to understand them fully would be to grasp the necessary order of the universe.

2. The philosophy of science that has been most popular in recent years denies that there is any such order. A causal law is a statement that an event of the kind A is regularly followed by an event of the kind B. That is the end of the matter; the question *why* B should follow is an idle question; it asks for what cannot be given because it is not there. Here Russell and Wittgenstein returned to Hume. According to Hume, 'we may define a cause to be an object followed by another, and where all the objects similar to the first are followed by objects similar to the second'.[1] We know that a billiard ball, when struck by another, does in fact roll away; a child knows, after sticking

[1] *Inquiry Concerning Human Understanding*, Sec. VII, Pt. 2.

446   REASON AND ANALYSIS

its finger in a candle flame, that the flame does in fact burn; that is all
we know in either case and, in principle, all we shall ever know.

   This doctrine, when first announced, was a shock to both common
sense and philosophy, and rumblings of discontent continue in both
quarters. There was no objection to holding that causality did involve
regular sequence; the objection from both parties was that the
regular-sequence view left out something that was plainly there and
was of prime importance. The missing element, however, was not the
same for the two parties. What common sense thought had been left
out was the element of constraint or compulsion. When one billiard
ball struck another, it surely gave it a push; it compelled it to move
by exerting force on it. For ordinary thought, this is surely the
essential element in the case, and to ignore it seemed perverse. On
the other hand, what philosophers particularly objected to was the
exclusion of necessity. They had been in the habit of thinking that
one could *reason* from effect to cause, that the two were so related
that, given the first, one could with sufficient acumen *deduce* the
second. Aquinas thought that, given the existence of the world, he
could deduce its Creator; Spinoza that, given the existence of a
pebble, he could deduce an absolute substance; Locke that, given his
percept of a sphere, he could deduce a physical thing that caused it
and was like it. If such reasoning was illicit, much that had passed as
sound metaphysics would have to be discarded. Plain men and
philosophers were thus united in feeling that a causality from which
force and necessity were omitted was a mere shell of itself.

3. The genius of Hume is apparent in the persuasive clearness with
which he met these objections. Never perhaps, except by Berkeley,
has a major metaphysical upset been effected with arguments so
simple. In causation, rightly seen, he held, there is no trace of either
compulsion or necessity, and without these all that is left is regular
sequence. To the contention that the cause exercises force or compulsion he replied that this supposed force is really our own experience wrongly projected into things. It is true that when we push
a table we feel sensations of strain and resistance, but the billiard ball
that strikes another has no such sensations. It is true that when, after
repeatedly seeing a ball roll away upon being struck, we next see a
ball rolling toward another, there is a felt tendency to expect the
second to roll away. To that extent there exists in our minds a gentle
feeling of constraint. It is natural and easy to project this constraint,
belonging only to our habit of thought, into the action of the outward
cause. But the projection is plainly illicit. Does it follow that when a

NECESSITY IN CAUSATION   447

hammer strikes a nail or a bolt of lightning splits an oak, we speak uncritically in ascribing to the cause any exercise of force? Yes, Hume would reply, the inference is not to be escaped. The only force we know is a kind of sensation. There is no such sensation in the hammer that strikes the nail or the bolt that splits the oak. To place it there is a regression to animism.

4. As for the element of necessity in causation, Hume dismisses it in a similar though slightly more complicated way. He bases his argument on the assumption that ideas are copies of sensations, and that if we claim to have a certain idea, we must be prepared to point to the sensation or sensations from which it is derived. Now rationalists had said that when the flame produced the burn, or one ball made another roll, there was a logical *must* in the situation; the effect *had* to happen; we could see that once the cause occurred, the result *could* not have been otherwise.

Hume's reply was threefold. (1) If it is true that we have this idea of necessity, we must be able to point to the sensation that gave rise to it. Now a logical relation of this kind is not the sort of thing that could be seen or heard or smelt or otherwise sensed at all. Hence, never having sensed it, we have no copy of it in the way of an idea. We only delude ourselves if we think we have. (2) Hume undertook to confirm this view by means of a rapid survey. There were three types of situation in which causality appeared, and he sought to show that necessity was to be found in none of them. (*a*) Cause and effect might both be physical, as when the rolling of one ball made another roll. We have seen already how he handled this. What we are experiencing is the fact of sequence, not the necessity of it; the necessity ascribed only reflects the firmness of our habit of expectation. (*b*) Cause and effect may both be mental; the thought of Theodore Roosevelt 'suggests by association' the thought of Franklin Roosevelt. But in such association of ideas, which is no doubt a fact, is there any logical necessity? If we think of the first Roosevelt, *must* we go on to think of the second? Obviously not, and of course we often do not in fact. (*c*) A physical event may cause a mental one, or a mental a physical one. (i) A flame, to take our former example, may cause a burning sensation. Now we have no doubt that flames have been followed by burning sensations, or that they will continue to be. But do we see that they *must* produce them, in the same transparent way in which we can see that the diameter of a circle must cut it in equal halves? Clearly not. The question why?, asked about this latter statement, would be pointless, since we have already reached the necessity which the question why? is asking. But between the action of the flame on the finger and the feeling of a burning sensation there is a long series of intermediate steps about any one of which, let alone the series as a whole, we could perfectly well ask why. And if we did, we should not get a glimmering of an answer. Why a change in the skin on our fingertips should be followed by the mental event called pain lies in total darkness. (ii) Nor do we seem to be better off as to the action of mind on body. We will to lift our hand and the hand comes up, and it may be thought captious to make a mystery of it. But after all, familiarity is not intelligibility. Hume pointed out that if the volition was to make our arm move, it must somehow affect the motion of the atoms in our heads, and that there was no profounder mystery in the world than how it did this; we are as ignorant of the process as we should be if our wish were to move mountains or enable beggars to ride.

(3) Hume offered a third argument which he thought clinched the case completely. This was a *reductio ad absurdum* designed to show that the cause-effect relation could not possibly contain the ground-consequent or implying relation. Take any case of logical implication, for example that in which being the diameter of a given circle implies that it cuts the circle in half. If you know that the 'halves' of the circle before you are not equal, you know that the line cannot be a diameter; in logical jargon, $(p \supset q.\sim q) \supset \sim p$; to deny the consequent and still affirm the antecedent is held to be self-contradiction. Now is there any self-contradiction in saying that the effect in a causal sequence might not have occurred, while the cause occurred nevertheless? None whatever. There is no contradiction in supposing that I make the same volition that has always caused my arm to rise, and that nothing happens. If this were self-contradictory, it would be strictly inconceivable, whereas it is perfectly easy to conceive; indeed it is what actually occurs when the man with paralysis wills to lift his arm. Can the effect equally be conceived without the cause? Undoubtedly, Hume would reply. It is entirely conceivable that the second billiard ball should roll away by itself, or should suddenly secede from the universe, or start talking Hebrew. To say that this is improbable is to miss the point. What is alleged is that it is logically impossible, and this it clearly is not, since such an impossibility could not be conceived, and this quite obviously can.

For Hume and his many followers, such considerations were decisive. It seemed clear to them that causation had no necessity about it. The linkage that it supplies between events is not intelligible in the sense that entailment is intelligible; that two events should accompany

NECESSITY IN CAUSATION   449

each other is just as little necessary as the chance that two dice should both fall with a six up. The man who argued that because one die showed a six the next must do so too would be regarded as absurd; and he would really be arguing with equal absurdity if he held that because one event happens any other event *must* happen. Nor does the fact that, so far as we know, events of this kind have always gone together make any difference in principle. The fact that snow has always been white does not make it more intelligible *why* it is white, or less thinkable that it should be black or purple. Regularities we can admit. But there is no ground whatever for converting these regularities into necessities. All that we can sensibly mean by saying that A causes B is that whenever there occurs an event of the kind A—defined as precisely as possible—it is followed by an event of the kind B—defined with similar care. And this is what is meant by the 'uniform-sequence' view.

What are we to say of this defence? It evidently depends on three propositions: first, that all our ideas come from sense; second, that we never apprehend necessity as having a part in causation; third, that cause and effect may be dissociated without contradiction. I may as well say at once that no one of these arguments, as stated, seems to me convincing.

5. (1) No doubt Hume is right that a relation of necessity cannot be touched, seen, or tasted, indeed is not a sense content of any kind. But the conclusion that we never find it in our experience of nature does not follow unless in conjunction with the further premise that our experience of nature is wholly sense experience. And to say that is to beg the question. For the contention of the non-Humians is that they do in fact apprehend (if not by sense, then by some other appropriate faculty such as reason or intelligence) necessary connections between certain sensibly presented qualities. It is no sufficient answer to this to say that experience is confined to sense qualities. Whether it is so confined is precisely the point at issue.

The question, then, is whether we do find in experience non-sensible necessities. And it seems plain enough that we do. Here are six or eight of them chosen at random: that this scarlet patch is more like this crimson patch than like that azure patch; that this surface cannot at once be blue and red; that this pink shade is a colour; that the space between the ends of this ruler can be divided without limit; that any two leaves on that tree and any other two make four; that these two lines do not enclose a space; that if this triangle has equal sides it has equal angles; that this sweet taste is different from that sour one. This last example is extremely simple, and if admitted, it will carry necessity right through our perceptual world. And does it not have to be admitted? What we mean by 'sweet' is not the same as not being sour, but if any taste is sweet it excludes sourness, not in fact merely, but necessarily. The world of perceptual experience is honeycombed with necessary involvements and exclusions. Hume's suggestion that since ideas come from experience, they must all come from sense experience turns on a pre-judgment of what experience is like.

6. (2) It will be convenient to look next at the third argument. This is that if causality involves necessity, then a denial of the consequent would, as in hypothetical reasoning, commit us to denying the antecedent, whereas in this case it does not. We can perfectly well imagine the second billiard ball's not rolling while supposing the first to behave normally, or the failure of our arm to rise, though we make the customary volition. If the cause entailed the effect, we should see that, given the antecedent, the consequent *had* to happen; to say this and also to admit that sometimes it does not happen should be merely to contradict oneself. Yet no such contradiction is involved.

Now note, to begin with, that the argument is stated, following Hume, in terms of imagination. We can *imagine* the first ball's rolling without the second doing so; we can *imagine* resolving to lift an arm and the arm's not rising. But the question whether, given a set of conditions, something might have happened other than what did happen is not to be settled by asking whether we can imagine it to have happened. It is likely enough that we can, but that proves nothing beyond the liveliness of our imagination. I can imagine myself stealing off to a work-room in the cellar and emerging with a perpetual motion machine; I can imagine myself spending an evening over figures and diagrams and showing the world next morning that at last the circle has been squared. But the ability to imagine such events does not show that they are in fact possible. This depends on whether they are consistent with certain conditions, consistent in the second instance with the postulates of geometry and in the first instance with the laws of mechanics. It may be said that the laws of mechanics at least are themselves empirical only, so there would be no inconsistency in supposing them suspended. But whether they are or not is hardly a point to be settled by appeal to the imagination. If a scientist maintained that there was something in the nature of matter that rendered Newton's three laws of motion necessary, we could not refute him by imagining a ball to cease rolling when there is no obstruction or to turn suddenly into a cow and leap over the moon.[1]

7. Whether causality involves necessity can be tested only by a case in which the cause and the effect are conceived clearly and distinctly and one then asks oneself whether the first conception entails the second. A causal law, whether stating a uniform sequence or an entailment, is always a statement that something of the *kind* A causes something of the *kind* B, and a kind is something conceived rather than imagined, as is also the linkage of kinds. Now just as the disproof that such linkage is necessary is not to be found in imagination, so also it is not to be found in actual cases. At first we seem to have such a case in the paralysed man who wills to lift his arm without result. If the cause entails the effect, it is argued, we should be able to see that the arm *must* rise, but since it does not, we have here a clear case in which the cause does not necessitate the effect. But the example proves nothing. For if the arm does not rise, then even in the uniform-sequence view, what we have is not a case of cause and effect at all; the failure of the 'effect' to follow shows that the sequence is not uniform, and therefore not causal. Indeed the uniform-sequence theory cannot hope to disprove the entailment theory by instances in which cause and effect are disjoined, for if they are thus disjoined, they are *ipso facto* not cause and effect.

If the entailment theory is to be disproved, then, it must be not through an imagined or actual disjoining of cause and effect, but through a conceived disjoining. The critic must produce a case in which two events are admitted to be causally related and in which we have a clear and complete apprehension of the connected terms; and we must then be able to see that no necessity connects them. In the abstract, this test may seem easy to apply. Unfortunately it is very hard to apply, for the reason that the full and clear grasp of either cause or effect is itself so difficult to achieve. The critic produces a sample in which cause and effect, though never disjoined in fact, seem divorceable in theory, only to find, when challenged, that the true cause or effect or both have not yet been arrived at. It is not improbable, indeed, that one ground for doubt whether A is really the cause is the inability to see any reason why it should produce B. At any rate, as long as there remains an interval not bridged by any

---

[1] Speaking strictly, we must admit that the logically impossible is unimaginable as well as inconceivable. If Flatland or a square equal in area to a given circle is not logically possible, one cannot imagine it in full detail. I am using 'imagination' here in its looser popular sense.

visible necessity, the reflective mind continues to look further. Perhaps the commonest of these intervals are those presented, on the one hand, by space and time, and on the other, by the increasing complexity of the cause as we study it.

8. Consider how we reject an antecedent as the cause until it achieves approximate identity with the effect. A man gets malaria, and we say that he has been bitten by an anopheles mosquito. Of course there is nothing in such a bite, so far as we can see, to make malaria necessary. But then are we quite clear that the bite *is* the cause? It clearly happens at times without an ensuing malaria. The disease must be caused by something nearer to it in time and space. This would seem to be the pouring into the bloodstream, by means of the bite, of a mass of parasites called *plasmodia*. But we cannot stop here either. The mere presence of the parasites in the bloodstream is not the cause; they may be present while their host shows no sign of the disease. They must not only be present; they must attack the red blood corpuscles in the stream. But even this is not the proximate cause, for there is still a temporal interval between it and the appearance of the recognized forms of the disease. Following the attacks of the parasites, the blood corpuscles are systematically drained of their haemoglobin. Is this, then, the cause? It is natural enough to say so, but we might still intelligibly ask, Could not this happen and the disease still not happen? So we again move nearer to the effect. Since haemoglobin is the means by which oxygen is conveyed to the tissues, its disappearance means that these tissues are starved and cannot function. Here at last we have reached a condition which cannot occur without the occurrence of the disease. But then this condition *is* the disease; this starvation of bodily tissues is the essential constitutive factor in it. As long as the series of changes presents us merely with state A followed unintelligibly by a different state B, we continue to hunt for a cause that will somehow bridge the gap in both necessity and time.

9. Consider again how, with reflection, we broaden the scope of the cause. We begin by taking it as the efficient or precipitating cause, that is, the one change occurring immediately before the effect and in proximity with it. What caused the gun to go off was pulling the trigger; what caused the window to break was the impact of the stone; what caused malaria was the bite of the mosquito, or some other event known to physicians that preceded the disease more closely. But if the cause of an event includes that without which the

NECESSITY IN CAUSATION   453

event would not have happened, it includes much besides the efficient cause. 'The real cause of the phenomenon,' as Mill recognized, 'is the assemblage of all its conditions.'[1] A man's contracting malaria has many conditions that no one would think worth mentioning, but are as essential to what happened as anything that an expert would point out. If the patient had no air to breathe, if gravitation did not hold him to the earth, if the sun did not provide him with a certain amount of warmth, if any one of dozens of co-operating organs in his body were not functioning in its normal way, if his prevailing cast of mind were more sanguine or melancholic, the course of his disease would not be precisely what it is. Each one of these is what is called a necessary condition of the disease's occurring as it did. When all of them are put together, they form the sufficient condition. And it is the sufficient condition that is here meant by the cause.

It will now perhaps be apparent why it is so difficult to show that causality does not involve necessity, even if it does not in fact. The critic would have to ascertain and clearly conceive the sufficient cause on the one hand and the total proximate effect on the other, and he would have to show that though these two were never in fact dissociated from each other, there were no reasons why they should not be, since there was no necessity lurking within this uniformity or behind it. This is an impossible undertaking. It would require one to prove a negative by exhausting in thought the nature of the cause and the effect, and we have just seen two reasons why this is impracticable. We never reach the proximate cause of anything, since between any alleged cause and effect an intermediate state exists, and since the cause as the sum of the conditions is too complex to be exhausted. Hume's argument, then, to show that causation excludes necessity carries little conviction. That argument was that whereas in a case of genuine necessity the denial of the consequent committed us by clear necessity to denying the antecedent, in a case of cause and effect we could always deny the effect and see that there was *no* necessity constraining us to deny the cause. But any such negative insight would require a knowledge of the terms and their sequence that we do not in fact possess.

10. (3) It is possible that our knowledge, while unable to support a sweeping negative, might still suffice to show positive traces of a necessary connection. Hume's remaining argument is aimed at this possibility and attempts to explain all such traces away. They are really projections upon the object of a habit or tendency in our own

[1] *System of Logic*, Bk. III, Ch. 5, Sec. 3.

mind, which has no necessity about it. This projection theory has so often been effectively dealt with that I do not propose to linger over it.[1] I shall follow another line that has seldom been taken. Critics of Hume have often held that he was wrong about the projection, but right about what was projected, since there was really no necessity to project. I think the reverse is the truth, that in the sequence of our ideas a genuine necessity can often be found, and that it is legitimate to surmise something like it in the sequence of physical events.

11. Consider a case of inference in which one arrives at a new conclusion following logically from the premises. The emergence of the conclusion in our thought is of course an event with causes and conditions, which are as little exhaustible as those of a physical event. But there is a striking feature in such a sequence: we can see that the logical relation connecting premise with conclusion is also one of the conditions that govern the temporal succession; it had a part in the emergence of the conclusion as a psychical event. Take a very simple case. A person is presented with an arc of regular curvature and asked to complete it. He completes it into a circle; why? He could have drawn a hundred other lines, but he may not even feel tempted to do so, and may go straight to his result. If asked to explain why he chose this line rather than others, he will probably say that he had no alternative, that if he were to continue the curve he started with, he could do so in only one way. On the logical point he is clearly right; the curve he started with did appoint its continuation in the sense that if its curvature were to be maintained, it could be extended in one way only. But it may be held that this necessary relation between the two segments of the curve had nothing whatever to do with the emergence in his mind of the pattern of its completion. Such a denial seems to me at odds with introspectable fact. The natural thing to say is that he completed the curve as he did because the character of the given curve *required* it. And this 'because' is not a merely logical because. It conditioned the factual sequence itself. The logical nexus had something to do with channeling the thought in one direction rather than another. This supplies the most natural and enlightening answer to the question why the line was continued as it was.

It may be objected that this is not a typical inference, since the conclusion is only implicit in the act of extending the line, and that an example of explicit and full blown inference would be more

---

[1] For an older criticism, see T. H. Green's *Works*, Vol. I, 270 ff. For a more recent criticism, see C. J. Ducasse, *Nature, Mind and Death*, Ch. 7.

NECESSITY IN CAUSATION   455

helpful. Very well, let us take such an example.[1] One is presented with two straight lines crossing each other at any angle. Are the opposite angles, say A and B in the figure below, equal, or are they not? They may look equal, but are they really so? One begins to

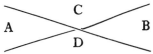

reflect. The line on which A and C are angles is a straight line, and therefore A and C add up to 180 degrees. The other line, on which C and B are angles, is also straight, and therefore C and B add up to 180 degrees. A equals 180 degrees minus C. B also equals 180 degrees minus C. That means that they must be equal. The equality of the angles has emerged as a new and necessary insight from the data before us.

Now the steps in this reasoning are a succession of judgments occurring in time. Each asserts a proposition and the logical relations that link these propositions with the conclusions are valid timelessly. Does it make sense to say that timeless relations holding between the propositions asserted in a succession of judgments actually affect the course of that succession? Each person must decide this for himself. Let him suppose himself to be trying to answer the problem set, and to have the succession of simple insights we have described. He comes to see that angles A and B are less than 180 degrees by exactly the same amount, namely by the size of the angle C. It leaps into his mind that if that is true, then A and B themselves are equal. Why the leap to this particular conclusion? Present-day Humians tell us that the logical relation between the last step and the next to the last had nothing whatever to do with that last step's being taken; if the question Why? is a request for necessity, we are as much in the dark as to why the thinker took it as if he had made a judgment about the Spanish Armada or the rising cost of butter. What seems to me odd about this view is its firm refusal to decide the matter empirically; no one would say this kind of thing who took his cue from the observed facts of his own thinking rather than from an antecedent theory. When, having reached the final step, he asks himself why he took it, the only natural answer is that he took it because the preceding step led to it logically.

Why has this answer been so strenuously denied? Perhaps because it is seen as the thin edge of a rationalist wedge. At any rate it will be well to set out and briefly consider the main objections.

[1] It has been suggested by Max Wertheimer; cf. his *Productive Thinking*, 79 ff.

12. (1) First it is objected that the explanation is insufficient. Even if logical necessity does link the propositions asserted and even if this necessity somehow works, the emergence of the conclusion is surely conditioned by much else—for example the thinker's state of freshness or fatigue, his interest in the problem, and the normal functioning of his brain. This is true enough, but it quite mistakes the thesis that is being maintained. That thesis is not the absurd one that an abstract relation between propositions is the *sufficient* cause for a concrete event. It is the comparatively modest one that this relation is a *necessary* condition, which means that, except for this relation, that precise event would not have happened as it did.

The same objection is sometimes put in another way by saying that causation is being confused with causal law. An actual event is a concrete occurrence whose attributes and relations are inexhaustible, and its cause must be as concrete as itself; a causal law is a connection between attributes abstracted from these concrete wholes. To suppose that when one has stated an abstract law governing the occurrence of malaria, one has explained the actual event, is an illusion, for the obvious reason that there are so many features in the concrete event that the law leaves out. True enough again. But we shall not get very far if we reject every partial explanation on the ground that it does not explain wholly. The scientist thinks that he has gone some way towards explaining an event when he can bring it under a law that states a mere conjunction; we have certainly gone farther if we can see in that law a filament of necessity; but even here the event as a concrete whole is not explained. This we grant. But what follows? That we should accept nothing because we cannot have all? To see a necessary link between partial features is surely an insight worth achieving. It does explain so far as it goes.

13. (2) It has been objected that causality links events, and that a timeless relation is no event. When we say that A causes B, we normally mean by A some event that precedes B; any component of that cause will also be something that precedes B; and we are changing the meaning of 'cause' if we include in it timeless relations. There is some pith in this semantic comment. It may be that both the plain man and the scientist most commonly mean by 'cause' the efficient cause, the only conspicuous *change* occurring in the temporal and spatial neighbourhood of the effect. And of course if we begin by so defining 'cause', necessity will be excluded by stipulation. But such stipulation, as Mill pointed out, is highly arbitrary. It sacrifices to the dramatic what reflection shows to be essential. The stroke of the

NECESSITY IN CAUSATION 457

cue makes the billiard ball roll as it does; but neither would it roll in this way if the table were not level, or the air were not of a certain density, or gravitation were not exerting its normal pull. It is perfectly legitimate to use the word 'cause' in its philosophically more interesting sense of the sum of the conditions given which the effect will occur; and in the absence of any of which it will not occur. And if we do use the word in this sense, then the necessities linking the objects of our thought cannot be omitted. Granted that they do not provide the same *kind* of condition as antecedent events, or the presence of permanent bodies like the earth and the sun, still if they are *conditiones sine quibus non*, they belong as truly among the essential conditions as efficient causes themselves.

14. (3) It has been objected that what channels the inferential movement is not the logical relation itself, but our grasp or apprehension of that relation. If Socrates is a man and all men are mortal, then Socrates must be mortal; it is not because the premises entail this last proposition that we go on to assert it, but because we *see* that they entail it. This objection, sensible enough at first glance, is seen at a second glance to be worthless. We are trying to explain why a certain conclusion should present itself, and we are offered an explanation which assumes that the conclusion has presented itself already. To see that p implies q, we must clearly have q in mind as well as p. And when the question before us is how q came to appear there, it is no help to say it appeared there because it had already made its appearance. The explanation is circular.

15. (4) A cognate objection has been offered by Professor Hempel, who thinks the ascription of a causal role to logical relations 'an inherently obscure idea'. 'Surely Mr Blanshard must be using a metaphor—and I think a misleading one—when he speaks of an abstract, non-temporal ideal as getting hold of an artist and moulding his work, or of a timeless relation serving as the condition of a temporal passage.' We must look for the determinants of a man's line of thought to agencies within himself. What moves him to follow a logical line is not the logical connections in the subject matter, but a 'certain disposition, namely that of acting in accordance with the standard'.[1] Now in turning from necessities to dispositions are we really moving from obscurity into light? I doubt it. 'Disposition' may mean various things. (*a*) In our case of the intersecting lines, to say that I have a disposition to think of the angles A and B as equal may

---

[1] *Determinism and Freedom*, ed. by Sidney Hook, 162.

mean that in point of fact I always, or usually, think this thought after I have taken the preceding steps. No doubt I do, but the question still remains, Why? It is not enough to offer in explanation the fact to be explained. (*b*) To explain through a disposition may mean that as a result of repetition I have acquired a *habit* of passing to the final thought upon completion of the earlier steps. The disposition at work will then be of the same type as leads me, after saying 'do, re, mi' to go on with 'fa'. This sort of explanation was once accepted by associationists, even for a priori thinking, and it amounts to a denial that such thinking takes place at all. It has been dealt with so often that we do not feel called upon to traverse the ground again.[1] And it would be particularly needless to do so here, since Professor Hempel rejects this antiquated empiricism as emphatically as any rationalist would. (*c*) A disposition may mean a capacity. The disposition to infer the equality of the angles from the preceding propositions would be the power to make the inference, once the figure is presented and the problem set. Unfortunately this does not help either. The fact that one *can* do something does not help to explain why one does it, and is equally consistent with one's not doing it. The question is: Granted that a man has the requisite intelligence, why is it that when he is set a geometrical problem he may never have faced before, he comes up with one special and valid answer rather than any one of a thousand others? If he does it, we know of course that he can do it, that he has the requisite intelligence to do it. But our question remains unanswered. We want to know what guided that intelligence down the particular track it took. And how could we answer more faithfully to fact than by saying that his intelligence was responding to, and following, certain necessities in its subject-matter. He did not fabricate these himself. He may attend or not attend, but he cannot make them otherwise by any act of will; they are in some sense there to be apprehended and adhered to. His intelligence, that is, his capacity for apprehending them, is indeed a condition of his thinking as he does, but this intelligence would have no direction if cut off from the structures that form its objects.

(*d*) The only other relevant sense of 'disposition' I can think of is drawn from *Gestalt* psychology. Experimenters of this school have shown that our interest in certain regular figures like circles and squares is not due to association merely, but is in a sense inborn. When presented a field of dots or stars distributed at random, we tend to find in them these simple patterns, and if given fragments of

[1] One need only refer to the names of Green, Bradley, and Cook Wilson. I have tried to set out the argument in some detail in *The Nature of Thought*, II, Chap. 28.

NECESSITY IN CAUSATION 459

the patterns we tend to complete them into these regular wholes. Now the 'disposition' to do such things is again ambiguous. If it means a native or unacquired interest in some figures rather than others, it has no obvious bearing on our problem. If it means a tendency to complete fragments into certain types of whole because of this natural interest, it looks as if it might have a bearing. But we must distinguish once again. To complete a fragment into a pattern because one likes or prefers that pattern is not reasoning, nor is it very plausible to say that our reasoning in logic and mathematics reduces to a large-scale indulgence of instinctive pattern-preferences. If this were true, it would be a puzzle why such reasoning should give us knowledge, and why one should not cultivate opposite preferences if one wished. But it is clear that not all Gestaltist dispositions are of this kind. In genuine reasoning, necessity is not the plaything of non-rational preferences; there is a genuine 'requiredness' in the object of thought, and inference is under the constraint of this requiredness. Wertheimer has described many cases in which the thinker is really doing what he would naturally say he was doing, namely following the argument where it leads. If such guidance of the steps of inference is to be included in the work of dispositions, we should agree with Mr Hempel in using them as the chief element in our explanation. But, so conceived, they are not alternatives to necessity. They include it; indeed without it they are as blind as moles.

16. (5) Several critics of the necessity view have offered an argument which has been very clearly stated by Professor Pap:

> . . . if implications have such causative force—directing the movement of thought the way a river bed directs the flow of water—they must have it whether the thinker sees them or not. Yet it is notorious that we may think of a set of premises and not see what follows from them or draw the wrong conclusion from them.'[1]

One can only think that this criticism has been made under a misapprehension, since it invites so obvious a reply. This misapprehension we have met already in the first criticism above, and we must try again to scotch it. If the necessity linking premise and conclusion were offered as the *sufficient* condition of the conclusion's appearance, then the failure of that appearance, or the occurrence of

[1] Arthur Pap in *Determinism and Freedom*, ed. by S. Hook, 204. Cf. *ibid.*, 169 (Mr Hook), 162 (Mr Hempel), and E. Nagel, *Sovereign Reason*, 287–8.

some other judgment instead, would of course refute the theory decisively. And for all I know, this theory may have been urged by someone; I can only plead not guilty myself. To make necessity the sufficient condition of a train of thought is to make the thinker a disembodied intellectual machine controlled by the drive-wheels of logic. No such monster has ever existed. If Archimedes at a triumphant moment cried, 'Eureka', it may have been in part because he had had a good night or a large draught of the Syracusan equivalent of coffee. If these were necessary conditions for the achieving of his insight, the famous cry would not have been heard without them, even though all the data for the solution were there. But what does this prove? Only that other conditions besides the necessities in his subject-matter were needed if his thought were to function effectively. This no one would deny. It has no tendency to show that when he did reach the solution, its entailment by the data before him had nothing to do with his reaching it. In short, the criticism assumes that if necessity plays any part in inference it must play the whole part; and there is no good ground for this whatever.

What if the thinker draws the wrong conclusion? The answer is the same. There are other factors at work besides the necessity in the subject-matter, and when inference goes astray, these are in control. There is nothing in this inconsistent with saying that necessity sometimes *is* in control. To draw a wrong conclusion is, strictly speaking, not to reason wrongly, but not to reason at all; it is to engage in a process that simulates reasoning while following the track of association or prejudice—an unhappily common experience. 'Man thinks not always', as Locke said, even when he seems to be doing so. But the fact that some idea-sequences are irrational does not show that all of them are. It merely attests that, as human beings, we are still brokenly and imperfectly rational.

This criticism becomes more important if interpreted in another way, which most critics of the theory seem to have missed. In a world in which causality involves necessity, how could errors and inconsequences occur at all? Suppose that someone makes an untrue judgment. This judgment is an event; as such, it has been caused; and on our theory the event follows by necessity from preceding events. The false judgment, then, is as genuinely necessary as the true. If John says that p is true, and James says that it is false, both judgments are necessary, and both are necessitated by the nature of things. Both, therefore, must be true. And this is self-contradiction.

I do not think it is. The appearance of contradiction lies in the confusion of a necessary proposition with a necessary judgment, the

NECESSITY IN CAUSATION   461

necessitation of a proposition with that of a psychical event. In the first case, interpreted in our way, two propositions, a premise and a conclusion, are linked by implication, and because of this linkage, when the first presents itself in the mind of the thinker it facilitates his passage to the second. The necessary nexus does, to be sure, link the two judgments as psychical events, but solely through linking their cognitive objects. If the inference is really determined by the implication thus linking its objects, it will be valid, and if its premises are true, its conclusion must be true. Now turn to the other case, in which a false judgment has been made. It is possible that this too has arisen through valid inference, this time from a false premise. But either in the judgment or in the premise we shall find ourselves with something whose appearance must be explained on different principles from that of the conclusion just described, namely a judgment that is not a *conclusion* at all. It is not a judgment that has arisen under constraint from any cognitive necessity, but one whose chief roots lie in the psycho-physical organism and may well be involved with a tangled mass of likes, antipathies, and desires. So far as a man judges falsely, we say that he is not under the influence of reason, or that his thought is determined not by reasons but by causes. This puts the matter helpfully. What should be added, on our theory, is that these causes are not in principle unintelligible. If we knew enough, we could see that, given James's heredity, his past experience, his thyroid deficiency, and so on, the cropping up of that stupid suggestion in his mind was necessary. It is thus correct to say that John's true judgment and James's false judgment are both necessitated. There is no contradiction in saying so because the necessitation in the two cases operates from different bases, one of which does not require the truth of the consequent. The necessitation in the first case operates from presumably true premises to produce a conclusion through valid inference. In the second case it operates, not from premises, but from 'non-rational' factors, perhaps deeply buried from knowledge in the body and mind of the agent, to produce what we call an 'irrational' belief. Though the judgments are contradictory, our account of their origins is not.

17. (6) The most popular argument against the necessity view is, as one might expect, that it confuses implication with inference.[1] Of course the two are profoundly different. Implication is a timeless relation connecting propositions. Inference is a temporal, psychological

---

[1] It is offered, for example, by Ernest Nagel, *Sovereign Reason*, 288–9 by Durant Drake, *Invitation to Philosophy*, 372, and by many others.

passage from one judgment to another. Implication is objective, in the sense that it holds whether we recognize it or not. Inference is subjective, in the sense that it is a process in our own mind. The items linked by implication are not, in the ordinary sense, existents; the propositions of Euclid, for example, are neither things nor events. On the other hand, the items linked by inference, commonly called judgments, are actual mental occurrents. No one will accuse us, so far, of confusing the two kinds of connection. What is it exactly that provokes the charge? It is our contention that implication, though different from inference, may serve as a causal component within it. We hold that the necessity linking propositions together does sometimes account causally for the inference's taking one path rather than another, and that the explanation of the temporal passage is therefore not complete unless this timeless relation is introduced. There is no evident confusion here, though some confusion does seem to be discernible in the minds of critics. They offer examples of a proposition's presenting itself without being followed by an implied sequel, of the consequent's appearing with no antecedent announcing it, and of both presenting themselves successively without any inferential passage; and they say that these things could not possibly be if implication ever really participated in inference. We freely admit that all these things take place, and add merely that the admission leaves our theory intact. To elaborate this after all that has been said would only bore the reader. The charge of confusion between implication and inference itself rests on a confusion as to the identity of the culprit.

18. (7) One final point before leaving this debate. When I briefly stated the necessity view in my book on *The Nature of Thought*, I added that unless this view were true, 'no conclusions are ever arrived at *because* the evidence requires them', and that this was inconsistent with an assumption we always make in arguing with men supposed to be reasonable. We set before them the evidence that has constrained us to accept a proposition and assume that it will, or at least may, move them to a like acceptance. Professor Nagel agrees with me as to the importance of this kind of reasonableness, but thinks it possible to hold to it without going to the extreme of assigning necessity an actual part in the causal process.

'A man who first notes a premise *A*, and then perceives that *A* logically implies *B*, *is* moved by reasons when he accepts *B* on the evidence of the premise—even if the causal sequence, the thought of

NECESSITY IN CAUSATION 463

A, the perception of the connection between *A* and *B*, the assertion of *B*, is a logically contingent one. Such a thinker might not assert *B* did he not *perceive* the connection between *A* and *B*; and his *perception* of this connection is doubtless one of the factors which causally determine his thought and acceptance of *B*. But is there any reason for maintaining that if the connection between this factor and the effect attributed to it is a logically contingent one, its manifest operation is illusory?'[1]

Let us see what the theory here suggested involves. A man is engaged in a process of reasoning; starting with a belief that A is true, he sees that A entails B, and therefore accepts B; then that B entails C, and therefore accepts C; then that C entails D; and therefore accepts D. Mr Nagel's theory of the process appears to be this: thought leaps in a contingent way from point to point in its advance, but once it has reached a new point, it can look back and see that between its present position and the point just left there is a necessary connection. As a result of seeing this connection, it accepts the new proposition; then uses it as the base for another contingent leap which will be similarly seen to be justified on arrival and review. There are two comments to be made.

(*a*) When, by a process in which necessity has played no part, the thought of A has given rise to the thought of B, the thinker sees that A entails B, and because of this insight, we are told, he accepts B; 'his *perception* of this connection is doubtless one of the factors which causally determine his thought and acceptance of B'. This can hardly be correct. It cannot be the perception of the connection that 'determines his *thought*' of B; for he cannot perceive a connection between A and B without having the thought of B already; we have paid our respects earlier to this circular explanation. Leaving this aside, however, we read that it is the grasp of this connection which determines his *acceptance* of B. Now his acceptance of B is a psychological act, and the presentation of a timeless logical connection is said to have 'determined' this act. This concedes in principle the main point that is being demurred to, namely that a timeless necessity can determine a psychological event. It may be replied that what determined the acceptance was not the necessity apprehended but the apprehension of it. This might mean (i) that when a thought works causally, it is the bare contentless act of apprehension that works, and hence that it makes no difference what the thought is about. I do not think this is plausible or that Mr Nagel would so

[1] *Sovereign Reason*, 290.

regard it. If what works in the mind is the apprehension of necessity, then the necessity apprehended must be one element of what works. Without this element the mere apprehension would neither be what it is nor work as it does. Or what might be meant is (ii) that if the content or object is taken into account, it must be the ostensible object only; it need not be real necessity that is present, but only what appears to us as necessity. This too will not bear examination. It would mean that when we accept, for example, 2 + 2 as equalling 4, we never do so because 2 + 2 are really equal to 4, but only because they seem to be so. Such a theory would indeed imply that we never grasp necessity at all—the necessity that really links concepts and propositions. It is never this necessity that moves our acceptance or works in our minds, but some surrogate of it confined to the psychological order. This theory would lead to a profound sort of scepticism which I cannot think that Mr Nagel would care to embrace. But if he is to avoid it, I see no alternative to the admission that non-temporal necessities contribute to the causing of temporal events.

(*b*) Still, all he would have admitted, even so, is that a seen necessity contributes to our *acceptance* of B. He has not admitted that the necessity linking A with B has contributed to B's following A in our thought. He would hold, I take it, that if we are asked to continue the sequence 2, 4, 8, 16, in accord with the rule of this series, and we answer with '32', the logical necessity of 32 as the next step in the series had nothing to do with our leap to the thought of that number; the leap is wholly contingent. *After* we have reached the number by this contingent leap, we can see that it really is next in the series and can accept it as such. Then, using it as a new basis, and seeking to go on, we manage to say '64', though again we must say that it is as strictly unintelligible how we got there as if we had said '1776' or 'the Queen of Sheba'. To explain in terms of habit would not render the connection intelligible, even if such an explanation were generally available in these cases, which it is not. What is Mr Nagel's own explanation of the inferential movement? He hints that in such a sequence the thinker is really carried along 'by the happy working of his own body', and he is content to think that in this 'happy working' there is nothing but contingency. One can only envy him the ownership of so co-operative a body. It continues in accommodating fashion, though always by pure contingency, to throw up suggestions which when examined are found to be connected necessarily with premises just entertained, but since there are no necessities at work in the body, the fact that one judgment follows on another logically as well as temporally must be set down as happy accident. In spite

NECESSITY IN CAUSATION 465

of his modest avowals, I cannot believe that Mr Nagel's thinking is composed of such a chapter of accidents; it seems to me more firmly directed than that. How one would *prove* to him that he is not the beneficiary of so large a bounty of mere fortune I do not know. All one can do is to urge him to examine his thought at first hand and to report what he actually sees, not what he ought to see on the assumptions of a naturalistic metaphysic.

19. We have dealt at such length with necessity in inference because this is the region in which we can most clearly see it at work in causation. Not that we are wholly in the dark as to why causation moves as it does in other regions of the mind; I do not think it is utterly unintelligible, for example, why a person should fear death, or why he should grieve at the loss of a friend. But we must surely admit Hume's contention that through the larger part of the known world—he would say all of it—the nature of the causal process is at present impenetrable to us. We do not know why a volition moves a muscle, or why a burn hurts, or why a nail sinks at the blow of a hammer. Is it reasonable to believe that there is necessity in such behaviour, in spite of our failure to detect it? I think it is, and shall try to state the chief grounds for thinking so.

20. (1) The first is that, hard as it may be to accept the necessity thesis, it is still harder to accept the alternative. Scientists sometimes say that uniformity is all they need or want. Perhaps it is; their interest is in the discovery of laws, not in the explanation of why laws should be what they are. Nevertheless uniformity cannot by itself be the whole story, for if it were, there would not be even that. Let us suppose for a moment that between two events, A and B, there is no sort of constraint or inner connection, no reason why B should follow rather than anything else. If this were true, B's regular attendance upon A would be a miracle. With no ground for its appearance in the nature of anything preceding it, B's occurrence along with A would be a matter of chance, and if we made any calculations about it, they would have to be based on the theory of chance. This theory is clear enough in simple cases. Suppose we throw a die and get a 3. We then ask what the chances are that we shall get a 3 on the next throw. They are 1 in 6. What are the chances that we shall get two successive 3's? They are 1 in 36. The probability that we should get any of the numbers on the die n times in succession is $\frac{1}{6n}$, and it is obvious that this fraction dwindles with enormous speed as one goes on. In an actual game with dice where it was important to get 3's, how long should we be willing to assume that nothing but chance was involved if an opponent continued to get them? Suppose he got 3's three times in succession. The odds against that are 215 to 1, and we should regard him as remarkably lucky. Suppose he got five 3's running; the odds against that are 7775 to 1, and we should certainly grow suspicious. A few more such successes, and we should be confident that either he or the dice or both were in need of rigorous inspection.

Now suppose that one billiard ball hits another which rolls away, and suppose there is no link whatever between these events but chance conjunction. If that were true, the likelihood that the second ball would behave in that way again when struck by the first will have to be calculated, if at all, by the theory of chances. It is true that since the ball could behave not in one of six ways only but in any one of an unlimited number of ways, the chances are not definitely calculable; but we can see that the odds against a single repetition would be enormous, and the odds against this repetition continuing would be enormous beyond conception. Yet it is just this constant repetition that we actually find. It continues not merely for a few cases, or a few hundred ones, but so far as we can see, through an inexhaustible series of cases. To suggest that this constant accompaniment is a matter of chance is to abuse the meaning of the word. If it were a matter of chance in the strict sense, the lawfulness we find in nature would simply not be there. Something more is clearly at work.

21. (2) If asked what this is, we can only say that it is some kind of necessity. Here we shall probably meet the question, 'How can you insist that necessity is present and also admit that you cannot see it? When you say that the diameter bisects a circle or that what has shape has size, you can say that necessity is present because you do see it; you are laying hold of what is self-evident. When you say that the causal connection is necessary, one assumes that you can point to something that is similarly self-evident. But you have just admitted that causal connections throughout the physical and psycho-physical realm are entirely opaque to us.'

We have granted, it is true, that we cannot generally see why the effect follows the cause. But that is not the same as to say that we wholly lack a priori insight into causation. I am inclined to follow Professor Broad in holding that we do have such insight. He thinks we know a priori several propositions that apply to the causation of

NECESSITY IN CAUSATION   467

changes generally.[1] (*a*) 'Every change has a cause.' It is perhaps not self-evident that the mere continuance of a process requires a special explanation—the continued resting of a ball, for example; but if anyone were to suggest to us that at some point the ball began to move, or increased the speed of its movement without any cause at all, we should say he must certainly be mistaken. (*b*) The second proposition goes on to say something about the natures of A and B, though what it says remains highly abstract. It says that 'the cause of any *change* contains a change as a factor. This seems to me as evident,' Broad adds, 'as any proposition that I have ever met with.' A change cannot come from nothing at all; *ex nihilo nihil fit*. Nor could it come from a state that remained unchanged through time, for then there would be nothing to account for its appearance at one time rather than another. We are convinced that there must be something to account for this, and that it can only be another change. Thirdly (*c*) 'if a change issues from a moment *t*, then all changes which are factors in its cause are changes which enter into *t*'. 'I think,' says Broad, 'that this proposition is the accurate expression of the common dictum that a cause must precede its effect and be continuous with it in time.'[2] (*d*) To these propositions I would add another, namely that the cause and the effect are linked through their characters, that it is in virtue of A's being a change of the character *a* that it produces B with the character *b*. This does not exclude the possibility of alternative causes of B. It does imply that if there are such causes, it is something in the nature of each of the alternate causes in virtue of which the effect is produced.

I am inclined to think that these are all a priori insights into causality. If they are, it is untrue to say that the causal relation is wholly opaque and impenetrable to us. Even if we do not know why a particular change produced another, we do have necessary knowledge about the causation of changes generally.

22. (3) Can we say anything more about the nature of this necessary knowledge? Here again we may start from Broad. 'It may be noticed,' he writes, 'that in English we have the three sentences, "Nothing has

---

[1] *Examination of McTaggart's Philosophy*, I, 232–235. In *The Philosophy of C. D. Broad* (ed. by P. A. Schilpp), 741–744, he offers a further analysis of some of these propositions.

[2] *Examination*, I, 233. Broad adds a fourth proposition about causality that seems to him self-evident: 'A given change in a given process issuing from a given moment cannot have more than one total cause.' But upon further analysis of this proposition in *The Philosophy of Broad*, 744, he writes that it seems not impossible that a change should have several co-existing total causes. I doubt therefore whether he would wish to hold to his original proposition.

φ and lacks ψ", "Nothing can have φ and lack ψ", and "Nothing could have had φ and lacked ψ". The first expresses a Universal of Fact, the second a Universal of Law, and the third an Absolute Necessity.'[1] The universal of fact, 'nothing has φ and lacks ψ', would be exemplified, I suppose, by the observation made by Darwin that tom-cats that are white and blue-eyed are also deaf. The universal of law, 'nothing can have φ and lack ψ', Broad illustrates by 'anything that had inertial mass would have gravitational mass'. Absolute necessity he illustrates by the proposition, 'anything that had shape would have extension'. To which of these types does a causal statement belong?

Suppose I decide to lift my arm, and the arm moves; here we should say that the decision caused the movement. Regarding this sort of sequence Broad says, 'I *know* that *this* change would not have issued from that moment unless *that* decision had entered into that moment.' If it is objected that my body might have been electrically stimulated to such behaviour, the statement may be amended by the addition 'if the other conditions were as I believed them to be'. Two points about this case should be noted, for when put together they make it clear why causality is such a puzzle to philosophers. On the one hand, the way mind acts on body is as mysterious as anything in our experience. On the other hand, if one can say, as Broad does, and perhaps most people would, 'I *know* that *this* change would not have issued from that moment unless *that* decision had entered into that moment', then one is claiming a very different kind of knowledge from that of a 'universal of fact'. To say of a tom-cat simply on the ground of its not being deaf, 'I *know* that it is not white and blue-eyed', would seem presumptuous, since between these characters we see no linkage except that they have in certain cases been found together. To say that I know that my arm would not have moved as it did if I had not decided to move it is certainly to claim more than that such events have regularly accompanied each other; it is to claim that the decision was a *necessary* condition of the movement. What sort of necessity belongs to such a condition?

Broad suggests only two types of necessity in terms of which it could be understood, the 'universal of law' and 'absolute necessity'. The universal of law he illustrates, as we have seen, by the connection between inertial mass and gravitational mass. What distinguishes this necessity from absolute necessity is that it is contingent in the following sense: though, given the structure of the actual world, a thing could not have the one kind of mass without having the other, still there *might have been* a world in which the one appeared without

[1] *Examination of McTaggart's Philosophy*, I, 243.

NECESSITY IN CAUSATION 469

the other, whereas if the characters were connected by absolute necessity, there *could not have been* a world in which a thing had the one character (e.g. shape) without the other (e.g. extension).

Now it seems to me that the notion of contingent necessity is a half-way house in which we cannot rest. To be sure, it is a notion continually used in scientific and other explanation; to explain a fact, we bring it under a law; to explain the law, we show that it follows necessarily from a more general law, and the more general the better. But the necessity here lies merely in the linkage between the propositions, not in the propositions themselves; if the more general law is true, the less general follows, but there is no implication that the general law is itself a necessary truth, nor therefore that the derived truth is. Such explanation is of course valid, but it leaves the question of chief interest unanswered. Suppose we have traced our derivative laws back to ultimate laws; we explain the fall of a particular raindrop in the end by appeal to the law of gravitation. These ultimate laws will state principles on which the universe is constructed. To say that they are themselves contingently necessary would be meaningless, since there is nothing further on which they could be contingent. Of the three types of universal statement with which Broad provides us, then, only two are available; these ultimate principles must be either universals of fact, presumed to be mere conjunctions, or absolute necessities.

23. Confronted with this choice, we hold them to be absolute necessities. We cannot show them to be so by simple appeal to self-evidence. But there is other evidence available. Let us look again at the fourth of our a priori causal propositions. This was that if A produces B, it was in virtue of a linkage between the characters *a* and *b*. Now what could be meant by saying that A produces B *in virtue of* its character unless the character of A *determined* what was to emerge?

'If two plants, whose nature is really the same, can determine the growth of totally different seeds, how can we call either the seed *of* that plant at all? Grant that a seed may sometimes be produced by a plant of its own kind, and sometimes by a plant of another kind, without any difference of circumstances, and merely because causes do not act uniformly, and you have really granted that anything may produce anything; flint and steel may produce seed instead of a spark, and oil raise the waves or quench a conflagration. But to say that anything may produce anything is to empty the word "produce" of all its meaning. For the causal relation is a necessary relation, such that if you have one thing you *must* have another. To add that it does not matter what that other is, destroys the force of the *must*.'[1]

The point here is a simple one. To say that A produces B in virtue of its special nature *is* to assert necessity. If it is in virtue of a certain character in A and not of something else that B comes into being, then if B was not there, A was not there, and could not have been there. If it was in virtue of being belladonna that something dilated the pupil yesterday, then you know that if, under circumstances otherwise the same, something does not dilate the pupil today, it *cannot* be belladonna; to say that it might be would be to deny that belladonna *as such* acts in a certain way, which is what our causal statement meant. We should be saying that though it was of the nature of belladonna to dilate the pupil, nevertheless, since it sometimes fails to do so, it is *not* of its nature to do so. That is mere incoherence.

Joseph goes so far as to hold that to deny necessity in causation is to deny the law of identity itself. 'To assert a causal connection between *a* and *x* implies that *a* acts as it does because it is what it is; because, in fact, it is *a*. So long therefore as it is *a*, it must act thus; nd to assert that it may act otherwise on a subsequent occasion is to assert that what is *a* is something else than the *a* which it is declared to be.'[2] Now this is obviously true if the causal properties of a thing are introduced into its nature by definition. We often conceive things in terms of such properties. 'Glass is brittle, fusible, transparent, hard; gold is malleable, soluble in *aqua regia*, of a certain specific gravity, etc. Matter is impenetrable, mobile, etc. A man is wise, benevolent, quick-tempered, etc.'[3] These may all be taken as causal properties. If gold did not dissolve on being placed in *aqua regia* we should not call it gold because its so behaving is taken as a defining property of gold. But as Professor Stebbing pointed out, we do not commonly include in the nature of a thing all its causal properties.[4] A billiard ball has the causal property of being able to initiate motion in another billiard ball if it strikes it with a certain velocity, but this causal property, Miss Stebbing would say, forms no part of the nature of the ball as we ordinarily think of it. In this she seems to me right. She then goes on to argue that, for all we can see, it is a

[1] H. W. B. Joseph, *Introduction to Logic*, 2nd ed., 407.
[2] *Ibid.*, 408.
[3] G. F. Stout, *Studies in Philosophy and Psychology*, 305.
[4] *A Modern Introduction to Logic*, 285 ff.

NECESSITY IN CAUSATION 471

completely external relation, that is, that the ball could still be precisely what it is if it did not have this property. Here I think she is mistaken. To include a causal property in the definition of a term is not the only way of arguing for its internality. Even if a thing *is* not its behaviour, still if we say that it behaves in this way in virtue of having this nature, that it is *such as* to behave in this way, then we are saying, I suggest, that it *could not* lack the causal property while possessing this nature. The roundness of the ball is a constitutive, not a behavioural property, but if it is in virtue of its roundness that the ball rolls, then a ball that was unable to roll would not be a ball.

24. I do not think that any of the three arguments we have offered, or all of them together, *prove* that the link between a particular cause and a particular effect involves necessity. It is just conceivable that the regularities in the world, though infinitely improbable on the theory of chances, are what Montague calls 'an outrageous run of luck'. It is conceivable that while we have some self-evident knowledge of causality generally, there remain enclaves of contingency in the occurrence of particular events. It seems barely possible that we are suffering from a deep and distorting illusion in thinking that A's acting as it does follows from its being what it is. We should be adducing more impressive evidence—granted—if we could show in a particular case of hammer and nail that the cause entails the effect, as we can show that being a triangle entails having angles equal to 180 degrees. This we cannot do. But 'C may perfectly well entail E without our being able to see that it does so, and we may have general grounds for assuming the presence of a logical necessity which we cannot grasp ourselves, or at least see that this assumption is really presupposed in all our scientific reasoning'.[1] It is the part of reasonableness to accept a conclusion, even when indemonstrable, if it makes sense of things and no alternative does.

---

[1] A. C. Ewing, *Idealism*, 167. For another defence of the view that 'natural laws are principles of necessitation', see W. Kneale, *Probability and Induction*, 70 ff.

A. The Nonlogical Entailment Version

The Logic of Causal Propositions

Arthur Burks

Reprinted from *Mind*, 60 (1951), 263–282, with permission of Basil Blackwell, Publisher.

VIII.—THE LOGIC OF CAUSAL PROPOSITIONS

By Arthur W. Burks

1. *Introduction*

IT is characteristic of a science that growth in its content is accompanied by an increase in the technicality of its language. This is no accident, for the achievements of a well-developed science cannot be completely expressed in the vague, ambiguous, and weak terminology of its early stages. For example, the language of pre-Galilean physics is inadequate to express the modern conceptions of force and energy.

Unfortunately the remark just made about scientific languages does not generally apply to philosophical ones. The notable exceptions are to be found in the fields of logic, both deductive and inductive, where the techniques of symbolic logic have been employed to give precise and technical definitions of such concepts as 'valid inference', 'constructibility', 'intensional', and 'degree of confirmation'. This paper is intended as a contribution along the same lines : it seeks to develop a language for expressing *causal propositions* (contrary-to-fact conditionals, statements of causal laws, assertions of causal necessity and possibility, etc.) which is more precise, explicit, and formal than the language of everyday discourse.

The new language is called the 'logic of causal propositions'. It will be developed by the following procedure. In section 2 various types of causal propositions will be analysed as they occur in ordinary usage. To resolve ambiguities and vaguenesses as well as to simplify the treatment, a new symbolism will be introduced and the sentences being analysed translated into it. The logical principles governing inferences among causal and other propositions will then be formulated. Finally, in section 3, the resultant symbolic language will be organized into a formal system.

It should be made clear at the outset that we are concerned with the deductive interrelations of causal and non-causal propositions, and that hence this is not a study in the logic of confirmation or the theory of probability. As the traditional division of logic into inductive logic and deductive logic recognizes, there are two different kinds of relations into which causal propositions enter. In other words, to define 'cause', 'causal law', etc., completely, we must formulate both the deductive and the inductive properties of these concepts. In this paper we will deal only with the former.

It might seem that we could best achieve our objective of a technical language for discussing causality by ignoring present usage and starting *ab initio*. This is not the case, however, since the primary motive for constructing a new language is to help answer questions (see the example in the next paragraph) which hitherto have been of necessity phrased in the old language. Unless there is continuity between the new and the old we shall not be answering the original questions but different ones. On the other hand, despite this continuity, there must be important differences between the two languages, else one could not be more technical than the other. Basically, in developing a technical language out of a vague and ambiguous one we must make certain somewhat arbitrary decisions. Also, the symbols of the new language should be chosen so as to be convenient from a formal point of view, whether or not they correspond directly to the basic symbols of ordinary language; though of course the new symbolism should be sufficiently rich to make possible definitions of the old symbols (insofar as they are clear and precise) in terms of them.

The relations which obtain between a technical language and the language of which it is an outgrowth may be illustrated by the following example. Consider the question: Can causal propositions be adequately translated into an extensional language (*e.g.*, that of *Principia Mathematica*)? The first point to note is that this question is a technical reformulation of a very old metaphysical one: Can the concept of causal connexion be defined in terms of ideas of matter-of-fact and constant conjunction, *i.e.*, can causal potentialities be reduced to actualities? This issue was argued by the medieval nominalists and realists, but it is important from our point of view that stating it as they did in a non-technical language they fused and confused it with many other issues: questions concerning the ontological status and value character of properties and concepts, of mathematical principles, and of ethical laws. The second point to note is that just as symbolic logic aids in separating out this one issue of causal laws from all the others, it can profitably be employed to help solve it. For the logic of causal propositions tells us some of the properties of causal propositions, and hence provides criteria for judging any proposed extensional translation.

There is a matter related to this second point which warrants attention.   If the question stated in the previous paragraph has an affirmative answer, *i.e.*, if causal propositions are extensional, a knowledge of the extensional analysis of causal propositions would make the development of the proposed logic unnecessary. So it might seem that the answer to the given question should be regarded as a means to the proposed logic, rather than the reverse.   Such is not the case, however, as the question under consideration admits of no easy answer.   For example, the simple translation of a law in terms of universal quantification and material implication is inadequate (*cf.* 2.4).   That an extensional translation, if it exists, is complicated, is shown by the following considerations.

The ultimate data on which causal laws and theories rest— statements reporting the results of observations and experiments —can certainly be expressed in an extensional language.   To determine whether or not causal laws and theories are themselves extensional we must examine the relation between them and their evidence.   Since the relation between empirical evidence and a law of nature is inductive rather than deductive in character this kind of consideration brings in all the complexities of inductive logic and probability theory.   Hence it seems reasonable to begin with a study of the deductive properties of causal propositions.

2. *Analysis of Causal Propositions* [1]

In this section we shall analyse causal propositions and their relations to *extensional propositions* (material implications, ordinary disjunctions, conjunctions, quantified statements, etc.) and *logical propositions* (strict implications, assertions of logical necessity, possibility, impossibility, etc.).   The results will be given in the form of logical principles which in section 3 will be organized into a formal system.   We shall introduce in this section only those principles governing causal propositions which are not included in the ordinary machinery of existing logic. We intend these new principles merely to supplement those of existing logic, and shall construct the deductive system of section 3 so that it contains both.

[1] In these analyses I am indebted to private discussions with C. H. Langford, Paul Henle, and Irving M. Copi.

2.1. *Contrary-to-Fact Implication*

Consider a hypothetical, contrary-to-fact statement about the past, expressed in the subjunctive mood ; *e.g.*, someone says of a person coming out of a gas-filled basement : ' If he had lit a match the whole house would have exploded '. This is clearly a compound sentence of the ' if . . . then . . .' form. It should not, however, be analysed as ' If (he had lit a match) then (the whole house would have exploded)', for the antecedent and consequent of this sentence are subjunctive rather than indicative and hence are not amenable to existing logics. Rather, the subjunctive element should be placed in the connective, giving ' If it had been the case that (he lit a match) then it would have been the case that (the whole house exploded) '.

The logical manipulation of sentences is simplified if the temporal reference is made by means of a fixed co-ordinate system rather than by the use of verb tenses. Let ' L ' and ' H ' designate the repeatable properties of ' lighting a match ' and ' exploding a house ' and ' a ' the approximate, extended spatio-temporal region referred to. Since the kind of implication involved in this sentence is neither material nor strict (we call it ' contrary-to-fact implication ' or ' counterfactual implication ') a new symbol ' *s* ' is introduced for it. The sentence then becomes ' La *s* Ha '.

There are two important points to note about our symbol ' *s* '. In the first place, we stipulate that ' *s* ' always represents a certain state as a fact, and is never used to express an attitude of wishing or the like. (Contrast in this connexion the subjunctive sentences ' O were he only here ', ' May he return soon ', and ' Part we in friendship from your land '.) In the second place, ' *s* ' is always counterfactual. In contrast, ordinary subjunctive sentences are sometimes counterfactual and sometimes not. The sentence ' if the criminal had come by automobile he would have left tracks ' uttered by a detective as he approaches the scene of a crime is an example of the non-counterfactual subjunctive, as is the sentence ' If they should miss the train they would have to wait an hour at the station '. Since we do not wish our symbolism to be subject to such ambiguity we stipulate that ' *s* ' is always counterfactual and introduce another symbol in 2.2 for the non-counterfactual uses of the subjunctive. We can express the counterfactual character of ' *s* ' by stating that the following is a valid logical principle :

$$(P_1) \quad p \, s \, q \, . \supset \, \sim p.$$

Further valid rules for ' *s* ' can best be stated in connexion with

THE LOGIC OF CAUSAL PROPOSITIONS   367

the concept of ' causal implication ', and hence will be given in a later subsection (2.3).

It is the function of logic to classify and formulate fallacious forms of argumentation as well as valid ones. Ordinarily this is done by some systematic method ; *e.g.*, the use of truth-tables for the propositional calculus. At this stage in the development of the logic of causal propositions, however, such a method is by the nature of the case excluded. Hence we shall employ the older method of listing invalid argument forms (formal fallacies). For example, ' La *s* Ha ' implies neither that ' Ha ' is true nor that it is false, for while ' La *s* Ha ' implies that under the circumstances the truth of ' La ' would have been *sufficient* to insure the truth of ' Ha ' it does not imply that it was necessary (*cf.* 2.2). *E.g.*, the house could have been exploded by the spark from a starting motor. Hence the following statement forms are fallacious (not universally valid) :

$$(\text{F}_1) \quad \text{p } s \text{ q} \, . \, \supset \, \sim \text{q},$$
$$(\text{F}_2) \quad \text{p } s \text{ q} \, . \, \supset \, . \, \text{q } s \text{ p}.$$

2.2. *Causal Implication*

Consider the following statement of a causal law : ' A beam of electrons moving in a vacuum perpendicular to a magnetic field is deflected '. While we commonly symbolize such a sentence by means of material implication this is not correct (*cf.* 2.4). The implication involved in a causal law is different from both material implication and strict implication. We shall call it ' causal implication ' and introduce the symbol ' *c* ' for it. The given sentence may then be symbolized by ' (x)(Ex *c* Dx)'. We shall call any statement of the form ' (x)(Ex *c* Dx) ' a *causal universal*. Causal implications also occur in statements that are not universal, as ' Ea *c* Da '. A non-counterfactual subjunctive (' If he should release that eraser it would fall ', ' If he were to strike me I would strike him ') is also translated as a causal implication. In such cases there is no strictly logical difference between a sentence expressed in the indicative mood (' If he releases that eraser it will fall ') and the corresponding subjunctive sentence, so (in contrast to ordinary languages) we will use the same symbolic form for them.

It should be noted that those symbolically simple predicates which designate ' dispositions ', ' potentialities ', or ' powers ' contain causal implications implicitly. Thus ' That diamond was hard ' implies ' If an attempt had been made to scratch that diamond with, *e.g.*, steel, it would have failed ' and ' That table is green' implies 'If white light were shone on the table green light would be reflected'. All predicates except those designating immediately experienced qualities (*e.g.*, as in 'This book appears red now ') are of this kind.

We intend 'Ea *c* Da ' to assert that the conditions expressed by 'Ea ' are *causally sufficient* to make 'Da' true. By 'sufficient conditions' we mean a set of conditions, complete with respect to negative properties as well as positive ones (*i.e.*, counteracting causes must be explicitly mentioned) sufficient to cause the state of affairs expressed by the consequent. Thus '(x)(Ex *c* Dx)' should be interpreted as 'A beam of electrons moving in a vacuum perpendicular to a magnetic field *and subject to no other forces* is deflected '. There are a number of consequences of the fact that '*c*' means 'causally sufficient' that need to be noted.

The first is that the argument from 'Ea *c* Da ' to 'Da *c* Ea ' is fallacious, and hence also

$$(F_3) \quad p\, c\, q \,.\, \supset \,.\, q\, c\, p.$$

The second consequence is that the antecedent may contain superfluous or even irrelevant conditions ; *e.g.*, 'A beam of electrons of *one* milliampere intensity moving in a vacuum perpendicular to a magnetic field and *parallel* to a nearby wooden rod is deflected ' ['(x)(ExOxPx . *c* Dx)'] is true. In fact, on this interpretation of the symbolism these are valid inferences :

$$\text{Ea}\, c\, \text{Da.} \quad \therefore \quad \text{EaOa} \,.\, c\, \text{Da.}$$

$$(x)(\text{Ex}\, c\, \text{Dx}). \quad \therefore \quad (x)(\text{ExPx} \,.\, c\, \text{Dx}).$$

The leading principles of these inferences are

$$(P_2). \quad p\, c\, q \,.\, \supset : \text{pr} \,.\, c\, q,$$

$$(P_3). \quad (x)(\text{fx}\, c\, \text{gx}) \supset (x)(\text{fxhx} \,.\, c\, \text{gx}).$$

Because of these two principles '*c*' may not correspond to the ordinary use of 'cause' in certain respects. Thus the phrase 'causal law' is probably not customarily applied to a true causal universal such as '(x)(ExOxPx . *c* Dx)' since the antecedent contains superfluous and irrelevant conditions. Also, by (P_2) we can validly infer 'Ea $\sim$ Ea . *c* Da ' from the true statement 'Ea *c* Da ', and it is doubtful whether ordinary usage would sanction this inference (*cf.* 2.5). Fortunately it is not necessary for us to decide exactly what ordinary usage is on these points, for whatever the utility of the ordinary concept of 'causal law' in everyday affairs it has neither the precision nor the logical simplicity requisite for a basic concept in our system.

The third consequence of the fact that '*c*' means 'causally sufficient' is that it expresses a transitive relation :

THE LOGIC OF CAUSAL PROPOSITIONS   369

(P_4).   p c q . q c r : $\supset$. p c r,

(P_5).   (x)(fx c gx) . (x)(gx c hx) : $\supset$ (x)(fx c hx).

Note that the acceptance of these principles allows us to predicate the relation of causal implication of events which are not contiguous in time and space. (In such cases, of course, there is a certain oversimplification in our use of the same individual variable or constant in both the antecedent and the consequent of an implication.) In fact, we do not intend ' c ' to connote temporal sequence at all ; *i.e.*, it may be used to express causal relations of a non-temporal sort (*e.g.*, Ohm's Law, the Exclusion Principle). As a result transposition is valid :

(P_6)   p c q . $\supset$. $\sim$ q c $\sim$ p,

for if a cause is sufficient to produce an effect then the effect is a causally necessary condition of the cause and the absence of the effect causally implies the absence of the cause. Similarly we have :

(P_7)   pq . c r : $\supset$: p $\sim$ r . c $\sim$ q.

Because of these deviations some of the arguments which are valid by the rules of the logic of causal propositions do not sound valid when expressed in ordinary languages. Thus ' If it rains he'll wear his raincoat ; therefore if he doesn't wear his raincoat it won't rain ' sounds invalid ; rain could cause him to wear a raincoat but his not wearing a raincoat has no causal influence on the weather. Nevertheless if he does not wear a raincoat we can infer on causal grounds from the given premise that it won't rain. The matter is further complicated by the fact that such assertions of causal implication are elliptical, many of the relevent conditions being omitted from the antecedent ; this point will be taken up later in this section.

The fourth consequence of the fact that ' c ' means ' causally sufficient ' has to do with the validity of the principle of exportation.[1] Suppose two conditions are causally sufficient to produce an effect. For example, if an object satisfies the two conditions of being heavier than air and being released, it falls

$$[(x)(HxRx . c Fx)].$$

It does not follow either causally or materially from the fact that one condition is satisfied that the second is causally sufficient to produce the effect. Thus

HaRa . c Fa, Ha. $\therefore$ Ra c Fa

[1] A. W. Burks, and I. M. Copi, " Lewis Carroll's Barber Shop Paradox ", MIND, vol. 59 (1950), pp. 219-222.

is an invalid argument, and so this statement form is fallacious :

$$(\text{F}_4) \quad pq \cdot c\,r : \supset : p \supset \cdot q\,c\,r.$$

On the other hand,

$$(\text{P}_8) \quad pq \cdot c\,r : \supset : p\,c \cdot q \supset r$$

is a valid statement form, for it does follow, and on causal grounds, that where the first condition is satisfied the second will in fact produce the effect.

An important implication is that statements of ordinary usage involving causal implication must be construed as elliptical to avoid this fallacy. Suppose someone asserts ' If this object is released here and now (a) then (causally) it will fall ', when in fact it is true that ' Ha '. It might seem that we should translate this statement into ' Ra c Fa ' and regard it as having been derived from the premises ' HaRa . c Fa ' and ' Ha '. But the suggested argument commits fallacy (F$_4$). To avoid this fallacy we must regard the English sentence as elliptical for a longer statement whose antecedent mentions or refers to conditions sufficient to bring about the consequent. An elliptical sentence is necessarily vague, so that it is impossible to decide with certainty what its meaning is. A plausible translation of ' If this object is released here and now (a) then (causally) it will fall ' is ' HaRa . c Fa '; *i.e.*, the given sentence is elliptical for a statement which explicitly states conditions sufficient to cause the consequent. It seems clear that most ordinary assertions of causal implication are elliptical in this or a closely similar way.

2.3. *Causal Implication and Contrary-to-Fact Implication*

We can further explicate the meanings of ' c ' and ' s ' by considering their interrelations. A typical use of a causal law is to infer a contrary-to-fact implication from it :

$$(x)(\text{E}x \, c \, \text{D}x), \quad \sim \text{Ea} \quad \therefore \quad \text{Ea} \, s \, \text{Da}.$$

Thus there is a valid form of inference involving the denial of the antecedent of a causal implication :

$$(\text{P}_9) \quad p\,c\,q \cdot \sim p : \supset \cdot p\,s\,q.$$

Similarly,

$$\sim \text{Ea}, \quad \sim (\text{Ea} \, s \, \text{Da}) \quad \therefore \quad \sim (x)(\text{E}x \, c \, \text{D}x)$$

and

$$(\text{P}_{10}) \quad \sim \text{fy} \cdot \sim (\text{fy} \, s \, \text{gy}) : \supset \, \sim (x)(\text{fx} \, c \, \text{gx})$$

are valid.

It is natural to ask : Does the converse of (P$_9$) hold ? Equivalently, is it a valid principle that

$$(\text{P}_{11}) \quad p\,s\,q \cdot \equiv : \sim p \cdot p\,c\,q \, ?$$

It does seem that when we use the subjunctive in the counter-factual sense (' s ') we mean to be asserting both a causal relation (' c ') and to be denying that the antecedent is true. A more general sort of confirmation of the validity of (P_{11}) is to be found in the intuitively acceptable character of the various principles that it implies. We note first that it does not conflict with any of the previous valid or invalid statement forms involving ' s '. Also, (P_{11}) leads to the following transitivity relations which seem intuitively correct :

$$(P_{12}) \quad p\,s\,q \,.\, q\,s\,r : \supset .\, p\,s\,r,$$

$$(P_{13}) \quad p\,s\,q \,.\, q\,c\,r : \supset .\, p\,s\,r.$$

Further consequences will be developed later.

We saw before (2.2) that most ordinary uses of causal implica-tion are elliptical. (P_{11}) implies that the same must be true of contrary-to-fact implication. As before, it is impossible to decide exactly what the meaning of an elliptical sentence is, but a plausible translation of such a sentence as ' If this object had been released then and there (a) it would have fallen ' is ' If this object had been released then and there and had been heavier than air it would have fallen ' [' HaRa . s Fa ']. Another possible translation is ' ' Ra ' and some of the true propositions about the particular situation (a) imply ' Fa ' in a *special contrary-to-fact* sense ', where the italicized phrase is defined as follows. An antecedent implies a consequent in this special contrary-to-fact sense when (1) the antecedent is false, (2) the antecedent causally implies (c) the consequent, (3) the ante-cedent does not strictly imply the consequent (*cf.* 2.5), and (4) the antecedent is causally possible and the consequent is not causally necessary (*cf.* 2.5).[1]

A similar problem of translation obtains with respect to sub-junctive sentences of the form ' If f had been the case, g would have been the case anyway ' or ' Even if f had been the case g would have been the case ' ; *e.g.*, ' Even if this object had been blue at a it would have fallen '. Such a sentence is asserted when it is believed that sufficient conditions would have been fulfilled to cause the phenomenon even if the one in question had been different. Thus a plausible translation of it is ' If this released object had been heavier than air and blue it would have fallen ' [' HaRaBa . s Fa ']. Note that this follows from ' HaRa . s Fa ', for (P_{11}) and (P_2) imply by ordinary logical rules

$$(P_{14}) \quad p\,s\,q \,.\, \supset : pr \,.\, s\,q.$$

[1] In this connexion see Nelson Goodman, " The Problem of Counter-factual Conditionals ", *The Journal of Philosophy*, vol. 44 (1947), pp. 113-128, part II.

Other possible translations are ' HaRaBa . *s* Fa : Fa $\sim$ Ba ' and
' $\sim$ (Ba *s* $\sim$ Fa) . $\sim$ Ba '. The first of these, together with the
assertion that ' HaRaBa ' is causally possible (*cf.* 2.5), implies
the second (by the calculus of section 3). It should be emphasized that we are suggesting only plausible translations of the
English sentences under consideration, and are not attempting
to give a precise analysis of them. Precise analysis is not
required for our purpose, since the analyses we give are sufficiently close to correct usage to satisfy the continuity requirement stated in section 1.

2.4. *Causal Implication and Material Implication*

A very common use of a causal universal is to make predictions
from it. For example,

$$(x)(Ex \, c \, Dx), \quad Ea \quad \therefore \, Da$$

and

$$(x)(Ex \, c \, Dx), \quad \sim Da \quad \therefore \sim Ea$$

are valid arguments. And of course these are valid whether
' a ' refers to the future, as in the case of a prediction, or to the
past. When a prediction is disconfirmed the causal universal is
thereby refuted :

$$Ea, \quad \sim Da \quad \therefore \sim (x)(Ex \, c \, Dx).$$

These arguments can all be validated by the principle that a
causal implication implies a material implication :

$$(P_{15}) \quad p \, c \, q \, . \, \supset \, . \, p \supset q.$$

This implies

$$(P_{16}) \quad (x)(fx \, c \, gx) \supset (x)(fx \supset gx) \, ;$$

in our terminology : a causal universal implies the corresponding
material universal.

It is natural to ask : Do the converses of (P_{15}) and (P_{16}) hold ?
Note that if they did, a causal implication would be equivalent
to a material implication and a causal universal would be equivalent to the corresponding material universal, with the result
that the logic of causal propositions would reduce in immediate
and simple fashion to an extensional logic (*cf.* section 1). Good
arguments can be advanced, however, to show that these equiva-
lences are fallacious :

$$(F_5) \quad p \, c \, q \, . \, \equiv \, . \, p \supset q,$$

$$(F_6) \quad (x)(fx \, c \, gx) \equiv (x)(fx \supset gx).$$

This is the case even though these distinctions are not reflected
by ordinary grammatical form. Thus the English 'if . . .
then . . .' may be used indifferently for causal implication and

material implication (as well as for strict implication) ; the kind of implication involved is determined from the content of the sentence or its context.

The argument to show that (F_5) is invalid is simple. For if (F_5) were valid a false proposition would causally imply any proposition, and hence by (P_9) counterfactually imply any proposition. *E.g.*, ' This glass was not released ' would imply both '(Releasing this glass) c (it exploded) ' and '(Releasing this glass) c (it didn't explode) ', and hence both ' If this glass had been released it would have exploded ' and ' If this glass had been released it would not have exploded '. A separate argument is required to establish the invalidity of (F_6). For one could hold that a causal universal is equivalent to the corresponding material universal, but still hold that something more is meant by a causal implication than a mere material implication. *E.g.*, one could hold that ' Ea c Da ' is true if and only if ' $(x)(Ex \supset Dx)$ ' is true. Such a position appears logically arbitrary, to be sure, but it is a possible one. To show that (F_6) is invalid we point out two unacceptable consequences which follow from the assumption of its validity.

(1) Consider the following true proposition : ' All the books on this desk are in German '. It is clearly a mere summary of facts, a universal proposition true by accident, not by law, so we would naturally symbolize it by ' $(x)(Bx \supset Gx)$ ' rather than by ' $(x)(Bx\, c\, Gx)$ '. Moreover, we would say that since it is true by accident and not by law the corresponding *contingent universal* ' $(x)(Bx \supset Gx) . \sim (x)(Bx\, c\, Gx)$ ' is true. But on the theory that a causal universal is equivalent to the corresponding material universal the quoted statement is self-contradictory !

(2) Suppose next that ' Russell's *Principles* is not a book on this desk ' [' $\sim$ Ba '] is also true. Under the proposed equivalence we could validly conclude ' If Russell's *Principles* were on this desk it would be in German ' [' Ba s Ga ']. For we would be given ' $(x)(Bx \supset Gx)$ ', and that it is equivalent to ' $(x)(Bx\, c\, Gx)$ ', so we could infer by ordinary logical rules ' $(x)(Bx\, c\, Gx)$ '. We could specify this to get ' Ba c Ga ' which we could combine with ' $\sim$ Ba ' to get ' Ba c Ga . $\sim$ Ba '. Then by (P_9) we could infer ' Ba s Ga '. Hence if (F_6) were valid we would be unable to distinguish those cases where we can validly deduce contrary-to-fact implications (*cf.* 2.3) from those where such a deduction cannot be validly made.

There is one feature of the examples just employed in (1) and (2) which merits attention. Consider the sentence ' All the books on this desk are in German '. It was translated as

374   ARTHUR W. BURKS:

' $(x)(Bx \supset Gx)$ ', where the predicate ' B ' means ' being a book on *this* desk *now* '. This predicate makes reference to a particular place and time, and in this respect is to be contrasted with such a predicate as ' E ' [' being an electron beam '] which need not include in its definition any restriction to a particular spatiotemporal region. On this basis we call ' B ' an *indexical predicate* and ' E ' a *symbolic predicate*.[1] The relevance of this distinction to the matter at hand is that one might argue that though (F_6) is a fallacy in general, it is a valid principle in a language which contains no indexical predicates. (This would mean that it would be a valid principle in a scientific language, for since science investigates only repeatable qualities a scientific language need contain no indexical predicates.)

We can, however, construct examples to show that (F_6) is a fallacy even when the predicates involved are non-indexical. Thus we could modify the above example by replacing the indexical predicate ' B ' by a complicated symbolic predicate ' $\bar{B}$ ' such as ' being a book on a desk which is of such a size and shape, which is five feet from an individual with such and such a history, . . ., . . .'. By making this description sufficiently complicated we could make it highly probable that it was unique to this particular desk. Then ' $(x)(\bar{B}x \supset Gx)$ ' would very probably be true, while ' $(x)(\bar{B}x \, c \, Gx)$ ' would very probably be false. The fact that we could not be certain of the uniqueness of the property defined does not destroy the example, because the truth of either a causal universal or a material universal is never known with more than probability.

2.5. *Causal Implication and Strict Implication*

A causal implication implies a material implication (P_{15}) but not *vice versa* (F_5) ; in contrast, a strict implication implies a causal implication but not *vice versa*.[2] These facts are expressed by the principle

$$(P_{17}) \quad p \prec q \, . \supset . \, p \, c \, q,$$

and the fallacy

$$(F_7) \quad p \prec q \, . \equiv . \, p \, c \, q.$$

It should be noted that because of (P_{17}), ' c ' differs in meaning

---

[1] For an elaboration of this distinction see A. W. Burks, " Icon, Index, and Symbol ", *Philosophy and Phenomenological Research*, vol. 9 (1948-49), pp. 673-689.

[2] For logics of strict implication see C. I. Lewis and C. H. Langford, *Symbolic Logic ;* Ruth C. Barcan, " A Functional Calculus of First Order Based on Strict Implication ", *The Journal of Symbolic Logic*, vol. 11 (1946), pp. 1-16 ; and Rudolf Carnap, *Meaning and Necessity*.

THE LOGIC OF CAUSAL PROPOSITIONS   375

from the ordinary usage of ' cause ' in that the ordinary usage signifies that the implication is causal (in our sense of ' c ') but not strict, *i.e.*, the ordinary meaning of ' p causally implies q ' should probably be symbolized as ' p c q . $\sim$ (p $\dashv$ q) '. Our reasons for introducing this principle—apart from its intrinsic plausibility—are as follows.

Adding (P_{17}) to our already existing logical machinery is the simplest way of handling those contrary-to-fact implications and non-counterfactual uses of the subjunctive that are based on strict implications. Thus any statement of the form ' If the premises had been true the conclusion would have been true ' follows from the validity of the argument and the falsity of the premises. Likewise, in deducing the practical consequences of a belief we may say ' If this were true than such and such would be the case ', which is probably best symbolized by means of ' c '. Again, such a sentence as ' If the Rock of Gibraltar were a man it would be rational ' [' G s R '] can be dealt with by means of (P_{17}), for it would follow from the strict implication ' G $\dashv$ R ' (assuming the traditional definition of ' man ') and the factual premise ' $\sim$ G ' by (P_{17}) and (P_{11}).

A second reason for introducing (P_{17}) is that it takes the place of several more specialized principles. Consider, for example,

$$p\,s\,q\,.\,q\,\dashv\,r : \supset .\,p\,s\,r,$$
$$p\,s\,q\,.\supset : p\,s\,.\,pq.$$

These principles are intuitively valid, and by means of them we can validate the argument : ' If Russell's *Principles* were placed on this desk it would not be in German. $\therefore$ If Russell's *Principles* were placed on this desk it would not be the case that all the books on this desk are in German '

[' Ba $s \sim$ Ga, $\therefore$ Ba $s \sim$ (x)(Bx $\supset$ Gx) '].

For the second principle allows us to infer ' Ba s . Ba $\sim$ Ga ' from the premise, and since

' Ba $\sim$ Ga . $\dashv$ $\sim$ (x)(Bx $\supset$ Gx) '

is true, the conclusion follows by the first principle. But this argument can also be validated by making use of the more general principles (P_{17}) and the first of the following two valid principles of distribution.

(P_{18}) p c q . p c r : $\equiv$: p c . qr,

(P_{19}) p $\vee$ q . c r : $\equiv$: p c r . q c r.

The line of argument is then as follows. By (P_{17}) we infer ' Ba c Ba ' from ' Ba $\dashv$ Ba '. By (P_{11}) we infer ' $\sim$ Ba ' and ' Ba $c \sim$ Ga ' from the premise. ' Ba c Ba ' and ' Ba $c \sim$ Ga '

give ' Ba c . Ba $\sim$ Ga ' by (P$_{18}$), and this with ' $\sim$ Ba ' gives
' Ba s . $Ba \sim$ Ga ' by (P$_{11}$).   Using (P$_{17}$) again we infer
' Ba $\sim$ Ga . $c \sim$ (x)(Bx $\supset$ Gx) ' from the corresponding strict
implication.   The conclusion follows by (P$_{13}$).

One consequence of (P$_{17}$) which must be noted is that it introduces causal paradoxes derivable from the so-called paradoxes
of strict implication.   Thus because a contradiction strictly
implies anything ' Ba $\sim$ Ba . $\prec$ Ga ' is true and hence by (P$_{17}$)
' Ba $\sim$ Ba . c Ga ' is true ; since ' $\sim$ (Ba $\sim$ Ba) ' is true on
logical grounds we may infer ' Ba $\sim$ Ba . s Ga ' by (P$_{11}$).   Similarly, ' Ba c . Ga $\mathbf{v} \sim$ Ga ' is true.   These results have a certain
sanction in ordinary usage ; *e.g.*, ' If Russell's *Principles* were
placed on this desk it would either be in German or not in
German ' does not seem an unreasonable consequence of
' Russell's *Principles* is not on this desk '.   In any event, as we
have previously noted there is considerable arbitrariness inherent
in the symbolic formulation of any common-sense idea.   Once
a case of vagueness is posed clearly by means of a precise symbolism its resolution should be determined by convenience.   It
is on this basis that we adopt (P$_{17}$).

There is a consequence of introducing the paradoxes of strict
implication into the logic of causal propositions which is of considerable importance.   Because of these paradoxes statements
of the form ' $p\,c\,q$ ' and ' $p\,c \sim q$ ' are not simple contraries ;
e.g., ' Ba $\sim$ Ba . c Ga ' and ' Ba $\sim$ Ba . $c \sim$ Ga ' are both true.
Thus it is a fallacy that

$$(\mathbf{F_8})\quad p\,c\,q . \supset \sim (p\,c \sim q).$$

Similarly it is a fallacy that

$$(\mathbf{F_9})\quad p\,s\,q . \supset \sim (\rho\,s \sim q).$$

In order to state the circumstances under which ' $p\,c\,q$ ' and
' $p\,c \sim q$ ' (and ' $p\,s\,q$ ' and ' $p\,s \sim q$ ') are contraries it might
seem that we should qualify the above statement forms by
stipulating that they hold only if the antecedent of each causal
(or contrary-to-fact) implication is logically possible (not self-
contradictory) and the consequent of each such implication is
not logically necessary.   This qualification would exclude the
cases we have been considering so far.   But there are also
"paradoxical" cases to be considered which are not derived
from the paradoxes of strict implication though they are parallel
to them.

Corresponding to the implications with logically impossible
antecedents there are implications with causally impossible antecedents, *i.e.*, antecedents which can never be exemplified because

THE LOGIC OF CAUSAL PROPOSITIONS   377

they contradict existing laws. *E.g.*, assuming ' (x)(RxHx . *c* Fx) ' to be true, ' RaHa $\sim$ Fa . *s* Wa ' [' If this released, heavier than air, object had not fallen it would have been white '] and ' RaHa $\sim$ Fa . *c* Wa ' are such implications. Similarly, corresponding to the implications with logically necessary consequents there are implications with causally necessary consequents, *i.e.*, consequents true by virtue of a causal law. Under the same assumption as before ' Wa *c* : RaHa . ⊃ Fa ' [' If this object is white then (causally) if it is released and is heavier than air it will fall '] is such an implication. It seems desirable to count these statements as true, rather than false, just as we count the corresponding strict implications true. We shall do this, though we emphasize that there is a certain arbitrariness in this procedure.

Thus there are " paradoxes " of causal implication analogous to the paradoxes of strict implication : a causally impossible antecedent causally implies any consequent and a causally necessary consequent is causally implied by any antecedent. To state these principles symbolically we introduce symbols for the concepts of causal possibility ('◈') and causal necessity ('ⓒ '),[1] corresponding to the concepts of logical possibility ('◇') and logical necessity ('□ '). The " paradoxes " of causal implication are then

$$(P_{20}) \quad \sim ◈p ⊃ . \, p \, c \, q,$$

$$(P_{21}) \quad p ⊃ . \, q \, c \, p.$$

With these causally modal concepts we can also state the principles of contraries for causal and contrary-to-fact implications :

$$(P_{22}) \quad ◈p ⊃ \sim (p \, c \, q . \, p \, c \sim q),$$

$$(P_{23}) \quad ◈p ⊃ \sim (p \, s \, q . \, p \, s \sim q).$$

(It is unnecessary to require that ' p ' be logically possible as well as causally possible, for as we shall see by (P_{28}) that which is causally possible is also logically possible.)

Lewis Carroll's barber shop paradox [2] provides an example of the use of the causal modalities. The owner of the barber shop lays down the following rules : (1) ' If Carr and Allen are out, then Brown must be in ' [' CA . *c* $\sim$ B '], and (2) ' If Allen goes out Brown must accompany him ' [' A *c* B ']. Carroll's argument is as follows : (a) the first rule implies ' C ⊃ . A *c* $\sim$ B ', (b) the second rule implies ' $\sim$ (A *c* $\sim$ B) ', and (c) by *modus tollens*

[1] These are what Hans Reichenbach (*Elements of Symbolic Logic*, p. 392) calls physical modalities.   [2] Burks and Copi, *op. cit.*

these results imply ' $\sim$ C '; *i.e.*, the given rules imply that Carr can never go out ! Step (a) is of course invalid by (F_4) and step (b) is valid only if the true premise ' $\diamondsuit$ A ' is assumed (*cf.* P_{22}). It should be noted that ' AC ', together with the two rules, implies a contradiction by (P_{15}) and the usual rules of logic. ' AC ' is clearly logically possible ; therefore it must be causally impossible. Hence we have the valid principle

$$(P_{24}) \quad pq \cdot c\,r : p\,c \sim r : . \supset \sim \diamondsuit(pq).$$

Thus the troublesome feature of Carroll's example is that the rules are such that the antecedent of one represents a causal impossibility. (Of course, this is true only on the assumption that the rules laid down are obeyed, and hence our symbolization of Carroll's rules is not completely adequate. If they do obey the rules, the barbers have certain causal dispositions—as is shown by the fact that counterfactual propositions may under appropriate circumstances be inferred—so that an adequate symbolization will be of the general form given.)

The concepts of causal necessity and possibility can be related to the concept of causal implication, just as the corresponding ideas of logical possibility and necessity can be related to the concept of strict implication. Thus we have

$$(P_{25}) \quad \boxed{c}(p \supset q) \equiv . \, p\,c\,q.$$

Causal possibility is related to causal necessity in this way :

$$(P_{26}) \quad \diamondsuit p \equiv \sim \boxed{c} \sim p .$$

When (P_{25}) is applied to a causal universal the symbol for causal necessity (' $\boxed{c}$ ') appears inside the scope of a universal quantifier in the resultant expression. *E.g.*, ' (x)(Ex c Dx) ' becomes ' (x) $\boxed{c}$ (Ex $\supset$ Dx) '. The question arises as to the proper interpretation of this result. Now to say that for every spatio-temporal region ' Ex $\supset$ Dx ' is true on causal grounds is logically equivalent to saying that ' (x)(Ex $\supset$ Dx) ' is true on causal grounds. Thus we have [1]

$$(P_{27}) \quad (x)\boxed{c}fx \equiv \boxed{c}(x)fx.$$

We are now in a position to compare the properties of the causal symbols we have introduced with those of the corresponding logical symbols. The first point to note is that while a causal implication or necessity is implied by the corresponding strict implication or logical necessity, it implies the corresponding material implication or assertion without a modal operator.

---

[1] *Cf.* Carnap, *op. cit.*, pp. 178-179, 186.

THE LOGIC OF CAUSAL PROPOSITIONS 379

This is exemplified by (P_{15}) and (P_{17}) and also by

(P_{28}) $\Box p \supset \boxed{c} p$,

(P_{29}) $\boxed{c} p \supset p$.

(Note that by (P_{28}) the paradoxes of strict implication become special cases of the paradoxes of causal implication.) In the second place, the deductive interrelations of 'c', '$\boxed{c}$', and '$\diamondsuit\!\!\!c$' are quite similar to those of '$\dashv$', '$\Box$', and '$\diamondsuit$'. This has already been illustrated by the parallelism of the causal modalities and the logical modalities. It is further verified by the fact that this hypothesis accounts for all the rules of the present section (as we shall show in section 3) and for all the fallacies (in the sense that the fallacies are not theorems). Thus it would seem that causal propositions have a certain modal character, despite the fact that they are empirical rather than rational. This suggests that the formalized logic of causal propositions should be a double modal logic. We now turn to the construction of such a system.

3. *The Calculus of Causal Propositions*

In this section we shall develop an applied functional calculus of first order which will formalize the results of section 2. This calculus is patterned after Church's formulation of a functional calculus of first order and Fitch's development of a modal logic with quantifiers.[1]

The limitations of our language should perhaps be commented on. A language of first order is clearly inadequate to state the statistical and quantitative theories of a well-developed science. We believe, however, that besides being a first step toward achieving a truly adequate language, the present formulation is of intrinsic interest because many of the questions about causality traditionally considered by philosophers (*e.g.*, Bacon, Hume, Mill, and Keynes) concern universal (non-statistical), qualitative laws.

3.1. *Vocabulary and Formation Rules*

The extensional part of the primitive vocabulary consists of the logical constants $\sim$, $\supset$, parentheses, and the universal quantifier; and of infinite lists of propositional constants and variables, individual constants and variables, and functional constants and variables of all degrees. This is supplemented by

[1] Alonzo Church, *Introduction to Mathematical Logic*, part I, and F. B. Fitch, "Intuitionistic Modal Logic with Quantifiers", *Portugaliae Mathematica*, vol. 7 (1948), pp. 113-118. Consult these works for historical references to the methods employed.

the non-extensional primitive symbols $\square$ and $\boxed{c}$. Symbols of the object language will generally be used autonomously as in the preceding sentences. Capital Roman letters and lower-case Greek letters, with or without numerical subscripts, will be used as variables in the syntax language, Roman letters taking formulas of the calculus as values and Greek letters taking individual variables as values unless otherwise specified.

A formula is any finite sequence of primitive symbols. The recursive definition of ' well-formed formula ' (' w.f.f.') is :

A propositional variable or constant alone is w.f.

If β is a functional variable or constant of degree n and α_1, α_2, ..., α_n are individual variables or constants, $\beta\,(\alpha_1, \alpha_2, \ldots \alpha_n)$ is w.f.

If A and B are w.f., $\sim$A, (A $\supset$ B), (α)A, $\square$A and $\boxed{c}$A are w.f.

No formula is w.f. unless its being so follows from these rules. Hereafter the Roman letter syntactic variables will take as values only w.f.f. Parentheses will be omitted or replaced by dots whenever this simplifies the punctuation without introducing ambiguity. An occurrence of an individual variable α in a w.f.f. A will be called ' a bound occurrence ' if it is in a w.f. part of the form (α)B ; otherwise it will be called ' a free occurrence '.

It should be noted that by these formation rules formulas with modal operators operating on modal operators are w.f., *e.g.*, ' $\boxed{c}(\square p \supset \boxed{c}p)$ '. In connexion with the interpretation of these formulas it should be remembered that because of (P_{17}) and (P_{28}) $\boxed{c}$ is not to be interpreted as ' it is true on causal grounds ' but rather as ' it is true on either causal or logical grounds '. Examples of sentences with causal modalities operating on causal modalities are sentences which assert that the appearance of one dispositional property causes the appearance of another, or that if a certain causal law were false such-and-such would be the case, or that it is a causal law that a given kind of habit or resolution arises under certain circumstances.

The definitions are :

$$
\begin{aligned}
(A \vee B) &=_{df} & (\sim A \supset B) \\
(A \,.\, B) &=_{df} & \sim(\sim A \vee \sim B) \\
(A \equiv B) &=_{df} & ((A \supset B)\,.\,(B \supset A)) \\
(A \,\text{-}3\, B) &=_{df} & \square(A \supset B) \\
(A\,c\,B) &=_{df} & \boxed{c}(A \supset B) \\
(A\,s\,B) &=_{df} & (\sim A \,.\, (A\,c\,B)) \\
(\exists\alpha)A &=_{df} & \sim(\alpha)\sim A \\
\Diamond A &=_{df} & \sim\square\sim A \\
\boxed{\Diamond} A &=_{df} & \sim\boxed{c}\sim A
\end{aligned}
$$

THE LOGIC OF CAUSAL PROPOSITIONS 381

3.2. *Axioms and Primitive Rule of Inference.*

Primitive rule :

(I) From A and A ⊃ B to infer B (*modus ponens*).

The axioms are determined by the following schemata and rules :—

(1) A ⊃ . B ⊃ C : ⊃ : A ⊃ B . ⊃ . A ⊃ C.

(2) A ⊃ . B ⊃ A.

(3) ∼A ⊃ ∼B . ⊃ . B ⊃ A.

(4) $(\alpha)(A \supset B) \supset . A \supset (\alpha) B$ if α is not free in A.

(5) $(\alpha)A \supset B$ where α is an individual variable, β is an individual variable or constant, no free occurrence of α in A is in a w.f. part of A of the form $(\beta)C$, and B results from the substitution of β for all free occurrences of α in A.

(6) □A ⊃ ⓒA.

(7) ⓒA ⊃ A.

(8) $(\alpha)(A \supset B) \supset . (\alpha)A \supset (\alpha)B$.

(9) □(A ⊃ B) ⊃ . □A ⊃ □B.

(10) ⓒ(A ⊃ B) ⊃ . ⓒA ⊃ ⓒB.

(11) (α)□A ⊃ □(α)A.

(12) (α)ⓒA ⊃ ⓒ(α)A.

(II) If A is an axiom, so is (α)A.

(III) If A is an axiom, so is □A.

Axiom schemata (9) and (11) are not used in establishing the principles of section 2, but are included for the sake of completeness. By means of them the strict implication analogues of our theorems can be proved. Hence this calculus contains a system of strict implication as well as both an extensional system and a system of causal implication.

3.3 *Theorems*

' Theorem ' is defined as follows. A proof of a formula B on hypotheses $A_1, A_2, \ldots, A_n$, is a finite sequence of formulas such that each member of the sequence is an axiom or is one of the hypotheses or follows by (I) from preceding members of the sequence, and such that the last member of the sequence is B. Any formula for which there exists a proof without hypotheses is a theorem. To assert that there is a proof of B on hypotheses $A_1, A_2, \ldots, A_n$ we write $A_1, A_2, \ldots, A_n \vdash B$, and to assert that there is a proof of B without hypotheses we write ⊢ B.

All the principles of section 2 are theorems of the calculus just constructed. We will not show this in detail but will instead state some metatheorems by means of which this result can easily be established.

Note first that every theorem of the propositional calculus is a theorem of this system and that the results of making proper substitutions of w.f.f. of the calculus of causal propositions for the variables of the theorems of the propositional calculus are likewise theorems of the system. Hence the machinery of the propositional calculus can be employed in proving the principles of section 2. Note also that the Deduction Theorem holds for the calculus of causal propositions.[1]

In addition, the following metatheorems or derived rules of inference hold for the calculus of causal propositions.

(IV) If $A_1, A_2, \ldots, A_n \vdash B$, then

$$\boxed{c}A_1, \boxed{c}A_2, \ldots, \boxed{c}A_n \vdash \boxed{c}B.$$

Proof :[2] Let $B_1, B_2, \ldots, B_n$ (where B_n is B) be the given proof of B on the given hypotheses. To make the desired proof operate on the given proof as follows :

(*a*) Replace each hypothesis A_i by $\boxed{c}A_i$;

(*b*) Replace each axiom C by $\Box C$, $\Box C \supset \boxed{c}C$ and $\boxed{c}C$;

(*c*) Replace any B_i that is neither an axiom nor an hypothesis by $\boxed{c}(B_j \supset B_i) \supset . \boxed{c}B_j \supset \boxed{c}B_i$, $\boxed{c}B_j \supset \boxed{c}B_i$, and $\boxed{c}B_i$; where $B_j \supset B_i$ and B_j are the premises from which B_i was inferred in the given proof.

The resulting sequence is the desired proof by virtue of (I), (III), (6), and (10).

(V) If $A_1, A_2, \ldots, A_n \vdash B$, then

$$(\alpha)A_1, (\alpha)A_2, \ldots, (\alpha)A_n \vdash (\alpha)B.$$

Proof : Similar to that of (IV) but using (I), (II) and (8).

(VI) If $\vdash A \supset B$, then $\vdash \boxed{c}A \supset \boxed{c}B$.

Proof : By means of (IV), (I), and (10).

(VII) If $\vdash A \supset B$, then $\vdash (\alpha)A \supset (\alpha)B$.

Proof : Similar to that of (VI), but using (V) and (8) with (I).

University of Michigan.

---

[1] *Cf.* Church, *op. cit.*, sections 2.4 and 1.9 respectively.
[2] This proof is based on one of Fitch's, *op. cit.*, p. 117.

B. The Necessary-and-Sufficient Condition Version

Causation

Richard Taylor

Reprinted with permission of the publisher and the author from *The Monist,* 47, no. 2 (1963), 287–313.

CAUSATION

Metaphysicians, theologians and philosophers generally once thought of an efficient cause as something that *produces* something. That which was produced, according to this ancient idea, was a new being. In the case the new being was a substance—a soul, for example, or matter, or any substance at all—then the causation of that being was considered an act of creation. It is in this sense that God was quite naturally thought of as the creator of the world, and also, as its efficient cause. If, on the other hand, the new being was simply a modification of an existing substance, then there was no creation, in the strict sense, but only what Aristotle called generation. When a sculptor, for instance, fabricates a statue, he does not create anything, but simply imposes changes upon what already exists. Still, he does produce a new being—namely, a statue— even though this new being is only the modification of a substance that already existed. This is the way Plato, in contrast to later Christian theologians, thought of God's relation to the world. God, or the demiurge, according to this idea, was the cause of the world only in the sense that he converted chaos into a universe. He did not create the chaos with which he began.

Now this original idea of an efficient cause had no necessary connection with the ideas of uniformity, constancy or law. It was always supposed that, given the cause, the effect must follow; but this was not usually understood to mean that, given the same cause, the same effect must always follow. A particular sculptor, for example, was considered the efficient cause of a particular statue, but it was not supposed that this sculptor could do nothing but make statues. The necessity of an effect, given its cause, was thought to be a consequence of the *power* of the cause to produce it, and not of any invariance between that cause and that effect. Thus, if a sculptor has the power to make a statue, and exercises that power upon marble, then the marble cannot help but become a statue; the effect must follow, given its cause. Thus arose the idea, so clear to our predecessors but so obscure and implausible to us, that a cause must be as great or greater than its effect; the greater cannot be produced by the lesser. It is also this idea of the power of a cause to produce its effect which gave rise to the common distinction between acting and being acted upon, and the kindred distinctions between agent and patient, activity and passivity. A sculptor *acts* in creating, or causing, a statue, but the marble upon which he acts, or exercises his power, does not act; it is a purely passive recipient of changes imposed by an active cause.

We thus find in this ancient idea of an efficient cause two closely related concepts, that of *power* or *efficacy,* and that of *necessity* or *compulsion,* both of which concepts modern philosophers have been eager to eschew if they can. The idea of efficacy is, of course, part of the very etymology of "efficient cause."

Power.—An efficient cause was thought to produce its effect by virtue of its power to do so. Berkeley considered this so obvious that he used it as an important argument to prove that our ideas cannot be caused by other ideas, but must be produced by an active being. Ideas, he said, are altogether inert or passive things, without the power to cause anything. God, of course, has always been thought of by theologians and philosophers as a being of such power that he can produce a world. This is essentially what was meant by calling God a "first cause"—namely, that everything ultimately depends for its existence upon his power, whereas he depends upon the power of nothing except himself. It was in the same way that statues, temples and other human artifacts were considered the expression of human power. The very movements of men and animals were thought to be the expression of the power of such creatures over their own bodies, leading Aristotle to describe animals as self-moved. When philosophers eventually came to analyze this idea of power within the presuppositions of empiricism they became involved, of course, in enormous difficulties. The longest part of Locke's *Essay* is devoted to a tortuous and inconclusive discussion of it. Thomas Reid finally affirmed that the idea of the active power of a cause—as exemplified, for instance, in the power of a man over his own voluntary movements—cannot be analyzed or defined at all, though it seemed to him perfectly clear and intelligible.

This is but an intimation of the importance that the idea of causal power once had in philosophy and metaphysics. It is seldom any longer referred to, being now assumed to be, at best, a derivative concept, with the result that much traditional metaphysics is simply incomprehensible to modern students.

There is, however, one element in this notion of causal power or efficacy that has never been doubted, and is even still a part of everyone's conception of causation; namely, that the power of an efficient cause never extends to things past. This priority of efficient causes to their effects is not, moreover, a mere convention of speech, but a metaphysical necessity. The power of a cause to produce an effect has a fixed temporal direction that results, not from the connotations of words, but from its very nature as an efficient cause. Nothing past is within the power of anything, either to do or undo. Aristotelians might express this by saying that the past contains no potentialities or real possibilities; everything past can only be what it actually is. Things present, on the other hand, are capable of becoming a variety of things, depending on what they are converted to by the causes that act upon them. It is in this sense, according to this way of looking at things, that the future, unlike the past, contains alternative and mutually incompatible possibilities, and is thus within the power of men and other efficient causes and movers to determine in this way and that.

Necessity. The second concept involved in this original idea of an efficient cause, it was noted, is that of *necessity* or *compulsion.* The efficient cause, it was always thought, *makes* its effect happen, the relation between cause and effect being such that, given the former, the latter cannot fail to occur. There was never thought to be any necessitation or compulsion in the reverse direction, however; that is, an effect was never thought of as compelling the occurrence of its cause, despite the fact that the cause could be as certainly inferred from the effect as the effect from the cause. Thus, a man vanquishes his foe by making him die; that is, by doing something which renders it impossible for him to live. But despite the fact that one can infallibly infer a cause from such an effect, it was never thought that the effect compelled the occurence of the cause. Similarly, a man, in raising his arm, makes it move upwards, the arm being the passive recipient of changes wrought by an active cause. Or, to take an example from inanimate nature, the sun warms a stone, or makes it become warmer, in a manner in which it cannot be said that the stone, in becoming warmer, makes the sun shine upon it.

A return to the metaphysics of causation. This ancient idea of an efficient cause that I have very loosely sketched is generally considered by contemporary philosophers to be metaphysical and obscure, and quite plainly erroneous. We have, it is generally thought, long since gotten rid of such esoteric concepts as power and compulsion, reducing causation to simple, empirically discoverable relationships such as succession and uniformity. I believe, on the contrary, that while this older metaphysical idea of an efficient cause is not an easy one to grasp, it is nonetheless superior and far closer to the truth of things than the conceptions of causation that are now usually taken for granted.

It is the aim of this discussion to defend this claim. I shall do so by showing that the attempts of modern philosophy to expurgate the ideas of necessity and power from the concept of causation, and to reduce causation to constancy of sequence, have failed, and that the ideas of power and necessity are essential to that concept. Many philosophers are now apparently agreed that causation cannot be described without in one way or another introducing modal concepts, which amounts to re-establishing the necessity which Hume was once thought to have gotten rid of, but hardly anyone, apparently, has noticed that we need also the idea of power or efficacy. If, as I believe, both of these ideas are indispensable, then it will be found that the advance of contemporary philosophy over the metaphysics of our predecessors is much less impressive than we had supposed.

Necessity vs. invariable sequence. Let the letters A, B, C . . . etc., designate events, states of affairs, conditions, or substances which, we assume, *have* existed. These symbols, in other words, shall designate anything we please that was ever real. This stipulation excludes from our consideration not only things future, but also things that might have but in fact did not exist, as well as impossible things, kinds or classes of things as distinguished from things themselves, and so on. Now we want to consider true assertions of the form "A was the cause of B," wherein we assume that A was in fact, as asserted, the cause of B.

Let A, for example, be the beheading of Anne Boleyn, and B her subsequent death, and assume that the former was the cause of the latter. What, then, is asserted by that statement? Does it mean that A and B are constantly conjoined, B following upon A? Plainly not, for the event A, like B, occurred only once in the history of the universe. The assertion that A and B are constantly conjoined—that the one never occurs without the other—is therefore true, but not significant. Each is also constantly conjoined with every other event that has occurred only once. Nor do we avoid this obvious difficulty by saying that B must follow immediately upon A in order to be the effect of A; for there were numberless things that followed immediately upon A. At the moment of Anne's death, for instance, numberless persons were being born here and there, others were dying, and, let us suppose, some bird was producing a novel combination of notes from a certain twig, any of which events we may assume not to have happened before or since. Yet the beheading of that queen had nothing to do with these. Mere constancy of conjunction, then, even with temporal contiguity, does not constitute causation.

Here there is an enormous temptation to introduce classes or kinds, and to say, after the fashion familiar to all students of philosophy, that A was the cause of B, provided A was immediately followed by B, and that things similar to A are always in similar circumstances followed by things similar to B. This, however, only allows us to avoid speaking of necessary connections by exploiting the vagueness in the notion of similarity. When confronted with counter examples, one can always say that the requisite similarity was lacking, and thus avoid having to say that the necessary connection was lacking. What does "similar" mean in this context? If we construe it to mean *exactly* similar, then the class of things similar to A and the class of things similar to B have each only one member, namely, A and B, and we are back where we started. The only thing exactly similar to the beheading of Anne Boleyn, for instance, is the beheading of Anne Boleyn, and the only thing exactly similar to her death is her death. Other things are only more or less similar to these—similar, that is, in some respects, and dissimilar in others. If, however, we allow the similarity to be one of degree, then the statement that things similar to A are always followed by things similar to B is not true. A stage dramatization of the beheading of Anne Boleyn is similar—perhaps very similar—to the beheading of Anne Boleyn, but it is not followed by anything very similar to her death. Here it is tempting to introduce the idea of relevance, and say that things similar to A in all relevant respects are followed by things similar to B in all relevant respects; but this just gives the whole thing away. "Relevant respects," it soon turns out, are nothing but those features of the situation that have some causal connection with each other. Or consider another example. Suppose we have two pairs of matches. The first pair are similar to each other in all respects, let us suppose, except only that one is red and the other blue. The other pair are likewise similar in all respects, except only that one is wet and the other dry. Now the degree of similarity between the members of each pair is the same. One of the differences, however, is "relevant" to the question of what happens when the matches are rubbed, while the other is not. Whether the match is red or blue is irrelevant, but whether it is wet or dry is not. But all this means, obviously, is that the dryness of a match is casually connected to its igniting, while its color is not.

Laws. Sometimes difficulties of the kind suggested have been countered by introducing the idea of a *law* into the description of casual connections. For instance, it is sometimes suggested that a given A was the cause of a given B, provided there is a law to the effect that whenever A occurs in certain circumstances, it is followed by B. This appears, however, to involve the same problems of uniqueness and similarity that we have just considered. There can be no law connecting just two things. It can be no law, for example, that if Anne Boleyn is beheaded, *she* dies, or whenever a particular match is rubbed, *it* ignites.

One could, perhaps, overcome these difficulties by embodying in the statement of the law precisely those respects in which things must be similar in order to behave similarly under certain specified conditions, all other similarities and differences being disregarded as irrelevant. For example, there could be a law to the effect that whenever *any* match of such and such precisely stated chemical composition is treated in a certain specified way, under certain specified conditions, then it ignites. Any match of that description would, of course, be similar to any other fitting the same description, and any other similarities and differences between such matches, however conspicuous, would be "irrelevant" i.e., not mentioned in the law.

That overcomes the difficulty of specifying how similar two causes must be in order to have similar effects. They must, according to this suggestion, be exactly similar in certain respects only, and can be as dissimilar as one pleases in other respects. But here we shall find that, by introducing the idea of a law, we have tacitly re-introduced the idea of a necessary connection between cause and effect —precisely the thing we were trying to avoid. A general statement counts as a *law* only if we can use it to infer, not only what does happen, but what would happen if something else were to happen, and this we can never do from a statement that is merely a true general statement.

To make this clear, assume that there is a true statement to the effect that any match having a certain set of properties ignites when rubbed in a certain manner under certain conditions. Such a statement, though true, need not be a law. We could easily take a handful (or a car full) of matches, and give all of them some set of properties that distinguished them from all other matches that ever have existed or ever will exist. For example, we could put the same unique combination of marks on the sticks. Having done so, we could then rub each in a certain way and, if all of them in fact ignited, it would then be *true* that *any* match that has those properties ignites when rubbed in that fashion. But this, though a true statement, would be no law, simply because there is no necessary connection between a match's having those properties and behaving as it does when rubbed. If, contrary to fact, another match were to have those properties, but lacked, say, the property of dryness, it might not ignite. For a true general statement of this kind to count as a law, then, we must be able to use it to infer what would happen if something else, which does not happen, were to happen; for instance, that a certain match which lacks some property would ignite if only it had that property. This, however, expresses some necessary, and not merely *de facto,* connection between properties and events. There is some connection between a match's being dry and igniting when rubbed. There is not the same connection between its being decorated in a certain way and igniting when rubbed—even though it may be true that every match so decorated does ignite when rubbed. But this only means that the decoration on its stick does not have anything to do—has no necessary connection—with a match's igniting when rubbed, while its being dry does.[1]

Causes as necessary and sufficient conditions. In the light of the foregoing we can now set forth our problem more clearly in the following way.

Every event occurs under innumerable and infinitely complex conditions. Some of these are relevant to the occurrence of the event in question, while others have nothing to do with it. This means, that some of the conditions under which a given event occurs are such that it would not have occurred, had those conditions been absent, while others are such that their presence or absence makes no difference.

Suppose, for instance, that a given match has ignited, and assume that this was caused by something. Now it would be impossible to set forth all the conditions under which this occurred, for they are numberless. A description of them would be incomplete if it were not a description of the entire universe at that moment. But among

---

[1] This point was suggested by R. M. Chisholm's "Law Statements and Counterfactual Inference," *Analysis,* 15 (1955), pp. 97-105.

those conditions there were, let us suppose, those consisting
of (a) the match's being dry (b) its being rubbed in a
certain way, (c) its being of such and such chemical composition, (d) the rubbing surface being of such and such
roughness, (e) the presence of dust motes in the air nearby,
(f) the sun shining, (g) the presence of an observer named
Smith, and so on. Now some of these conditions—namely,
(a) through (d), and others as well—had something to do
with the match igniting, while others—such as (e), for instance—had no casual connection with it. This we have
learned from experience. Our problem, then, is not to
state how we *know* which were the causal conditions of its
igniting and which were not. The answer to this is obvious
—we know by experience and induction. Our problem is,
rather, to state just what relationship those causal conditions had to the match igniting, but which the numberless irrelevant conditions had not; to state, for example,
what connection the match's being rubbed had to its igniting, but which the presence of dust motes had not.

The most natural way of expressing this connection is
to say that had the match not been rubbed, then it would
not have ignited, given all the other conditions that occurred, but only those that occurred, whereas, given those
other conditions that occurred, including the match's being
rubbed as it was, it would still have ignited, even had the
dust motes been absent. This appears to be exactly what
one has in mind in saying that the friction on the match
head had something to do with its igniting, while the
presence of the dust motes did not—the latter condition
was not at all necessary for the igniting of the match,
whereas the former was. This, however, is simply a way of
saying that the friction was a *necessary condition* of the
match igniting, given the other conditions that occurred

but no others, whereas the presence of dust motes was not.

If this is correct, then we can simply assert that the cause, A, of an event, B, is that totality of conditions, from among all those, but only those, that occurred, each of which was necessary for the occurrence of B. Now if this set of conditions, A, is thus understood, as it should be, to include *every* condition, out of that totality that occurred, that was necessary for the occurence of B, then we can say that the set of conditions, A, is also *sufficient* for B, since no other condition was necessary. We can, accordingly, understand the relationship between any set of conditions A, and any set B, expressed in the statement that A was the cause of B, to be simply described in this fashion: That A was the set, from among all those conditions that occurred, each of which was necessary, and the totality of which was sufficient, for the occurrence of B. This appears to be exactly what distinguishes the causal conditions of any event from all those that occurred but which were not causally connected with the event in question.

It is now evident that this reintroduces the concept of necessity which Hume was once so widely believed to have gotten rid of. For to say of any condition that a certain event would not have occurred if that condition had been absent is exactly equivalent to saying that this condition was necessary for its occurrence, or, that it was such that the event in question would not have occurred without it, given only those other conditions that occurred. There seems, however, as we have seen, to be no other way of distinguishing the causal conditions of any event from those infinitely numerous and complex other conditions under which any given event occurs. We cannot distinguish them by introducing the concept of a law, unless we understand the law to be, not merely a statement of what does happen,

CAUSATION   299

but what must happen; for we can find true statements of
what does happen, and happens invariably, which are not
laws. The conjunction of properties and events can be as
constant as we please, with no exception whatever, without
there being any causal connections between them. It is not
until we can say what would have happened, had something else happened which did not happen, that we leave
the realm of mere constancy of conjunction and find ourselves speaking of a causal connection; and as soon as we
speak in this fashion, we are speaking of necessary connections.

Now to say of a given event that it would not have
occurred without the occurrence of another is the same as
saying that the occurrence of the one without the other
was causally, though not logically, impossible; or, that in
a non-logical sense, the one without the other could not
have occurred. We can accordingly define the concepts of
necessity and sufficiency in the following way.

To say of any condition or set of conditions, *x*, that it
was *necessary* for the occurrence of some event, E, means
that, within the totality of other conditions that occurred,
but only those, the occurrence of E without *x* was impossible, or could not obtain. Similarly, to say of any condition
or set of conditions, *x*, that it was *sufficient* for some event,
E, means that, within the totality of other conditions that
occurred, but only those, the occurrence of *x* without E
was impossible, or could not obtain. The expression "was
impossible" in these definitions has, of course, the same
sense as "could not have occurred" in the discussion preceding and not the sense of *logical* impossibility. There
are, we can grant at once, no logically necessary connections
between causes and effects. In terms of our earlier example,
we can say that Anne Boleyn could not live long after being

beheaded, or that it was impossible for her to do so, without maintaining that this was logically impossible.

The concepts of necessity and sufficiency, as thus defined, are of course the converses of each other, such that if any condition or set of conditions is necessary for another, that other is sufficient for it, and vice versa. The statement, that x is necessary for E, is logically equivalent to saying the E is sufficient for x, and similarly, the statement that x is sufficient for E is logically equivalent to saying that E is necessary for x. This fact enables us now to introduce a very convenient notation, as follows. If we let x and E represent any conditions, events or sets of these, we can symbolize the expression, "x is sufficient for E," with an arrow in this way:

$$x \longrightarrow E.$$

Similarly, we can symbolize the expression "x is necessary for E'" with a reverse arrow, in this way:

$$x \longleftarrow E.$$

Since, moreover, the expression "x is sufficient for E" is exactly equivalent to "E is necessary for x," we can regard as exactly equivalent the following representations of this relationship:

$$x \longrightarrow E.$$
$$E \longleftarrow x,$$

since the first of these means that the occurence of x without E is impossible, and the second means exactly the same thing. It should be noted, however, that the arrows symbolize no temporal relations whatever.

With this clear and convenient way of symbolizing these relationships, we can now represent the conception of causation at which we have arrived in the following way.

Consider again a particular event that has occurred at a particular time and place, such as the igniting of a particular match, and call this E. Now E, we can be sure, occurred under a numerous set of conditions, which we can represent as $a, b, c \ldots n$. Let a, for instance, be the condition consisting of the match's being dry, b its being rubbed, c its being of such and such chemical composition, d the rubbing surface being of such and such roughness, e the presence of dust motes in the air, f the sun shining, and so on, *ad infinitum*. Now some of these conditions—namely, a, b, c and d—were presumably necessary for E, in the sense that E would not have occurred in the absence of any of them, given only the other conditions that occurred, whereas others, such as e and f, had nothing to do with E. If, furthermore, as we can assume for illustration, a, b, c and d were jointly sufficient for E, the relations thus described can be symbolized as follows:

$$a \longleftarrow E$$
$$b \longleftarrow E$$
$$c \longleftarrow E$$
$$d \longleftarrow E$$
$$e$$
$$f$$
$$abcd \longrightarrow E$$

And since a, b, c and d are each individually necessary for E, it follows that E is sufficient for all of them, and we can accordingly symbolize this:

$$abcd \longleftarrow E.$$

And this permits us to express the causal relation, in this example, with the utmost simplicity as follows:

$$abcd \rightleftharpoons E,$$

which means, simply, that the cause of E was that set of conditions, within the totality, only, of those that actually occurred, that was necessary and sufficient for E.

It is at this point that our metaphysical difficulties

really begin, but before turning to those, two points of clarification must be made.

The first point is, that this analysis does not exactly express the "ordinary use" of the word "cause," and does not purport to. The reason for this is not that the analysis itself is unprecise, but rather that ordinary usage is, in such cases. Most persons, for example, are content to call "the cause" of any event some one condition that is conspicuous or, more commonly, whatever part of the causal conditions that is novel. In the example we have been using, for example, the rubbing of the match would normally be regarded as "the cause" of its igniting, without regard to its dryness, its chemical composition, and so on. But the reason for this, quite obviously, is that these other conditions are taken for granted. They are not mentioned, not because they are thought to have nothing to do with the match igniting, but rather, because they are presupposed. Philosophically, it makes no difference at all whether we say that, given the other conditions necessary for the match's igniting, it was then caused to ignite by being rubbed, or whether we say that its being rubbed was, together with these other conditions, the cause of its igniting. Its being rubbed has neither more nor less to do with its igniting than does, say, its being dry. The only difference is that it was, presumably, dry all the while and, in that state, was rubbed. It might just as well have been rubbed all the while and, in that state, suddenly rendered dry, in which case we could say that it was ignited by suddenly becoming dry.

The second point is, that there is a perfectly natural point of view from which perhaps no condition is ever really necessary for the occurrence of any event, nor any set of conditions sufficient for it, from which one could derive the absurd result that, on the analysis suggested, events do not have any causes. We said, for instance, that the match's being rubbed was a necessary condition for its igniting. But, it might at first seem, that is not a necessary condition at all, since there are other ways of igniting matches—touching them to hot surfaces, for instance. Similarly, we said that rubbing the match was, together with certain other conditions, sufficient for its igniting. But this might seem false, since it would be possible to prevent it from igniting, even under these conditions—by applying a fire extinguisher, for instance.

This objection overlooks an essential qualification in the analysis, however. We said that the cause of an event E is that set of conditions that were, within the totality of those other conditions, only, that in fact occurred, individually necessary and jointly sufficient for E. If, in terms of our example, that totality of other conditions that in fact occurred did not, in fact, include some such condition as the match's being in contact with a hot surface, nor the application of any fire extinguisher, etc., then, within the totality of conditions that did occur, its being rubbed *was* necessary for its igniting, and was also, together with certain other conditions that occurred, sufficient for its igniting.

Time and efficacy. Our analysis of the causal relationship, as it now stands, has one strange consequence that is immediately obvious; namely, that it does not enable us to draw any distinction between cause and effect. We have suggested that the cause of an event is that set of conditions, among all those that occur, which is necessary and sufficient for that event, from which it of course follows that if any condition or set of conditions, A, is the cause of another, B, then B is automatically also the cause of A.

For concerning any A and any B, if A is necessary and sufficient for B, and therefore, on our analysis, the cause of B, then it logically follows that B is necessary and sufficient for A, and therefore the cause of A. This is quite plainly absurd. One cannot possibly say that a match's igniting is the cause of its being rubbed, that a stone's being warm is the cause of the sun's shining upon it, or that a man's being intoxicated is the cause of his having alcohol in his blood, despite the fact that the relationships of necessity and sufficiency between cause and effect are the same in both directions.

Earlier metaphysicians took it for granted that the difference between cause and effect was one of power or efficacy or, what amounts to the same thing, that the cause of anything was always something active, and its effect some change in something that is passive. Thus, the sun has the power to warm a stone, but the stone has no power to make the sun shine; it is simply the passive recipient of a change wrought by the sun. Similarly, alcohol in the blood has the power to produce feelings of intoxication, but a man cannot by having such feelings, produce alcohol in his blood.

Modern philosophers, on the contrary, have almost universally supposed that the difference between cause and effect is not to be found in anything so esoteric as power or efficacy, but is simply a temporal difference, nothing more. The cause of an event, it is now almost universally supposed, is some condition or set of conditions that precedes some other, its effect, in time. Thus, if our analysis of the causal relationship is otherwise correct, then it should, according to this prevalent view, have some qualification added about time, such as to require that the cause should occur before its effect.

I believe this to be the profoundest error in modern philosophy, and the source of more misconceptions than any other. By this simple expedient of introducing considerations of time, philosophers imagine that they no longer need to talk metaphysically of causal power or efficacy. In fact, of course, philosophers, like everyone else, do still speak freely of power and efficacy—of the power of various substances to corrode, to dissolve, to cause intoxication, to cause death, and so on. But in their philosophies, they imagine that such terms express only ideas of *time*, and that they can be omitted from any exact description of causal connections, just by the simple device of introducing temporal qualifications.

I intend to prove that this is an error, by showing, first, that in many perfectly clear instances of causation, causes do not precede their effects in time, but are entirely contemporaneous with them, and second, that the causal conditions of an event cannot, in fact, precede that event in time.

Before doing this, however, let us consider a question that is meant to give some intimation that what I have called a profound error is an error indeed.

Let us suppose, for now, that there is a temporal interval between a cause and its effect, such that it is true to say that one occurs *before* the other. Now if the relationships between the two are otherwise identical—namely, are simply the relationships of necessity and sufficiency set forth above, or, for that matter, any other relationships whatever—the question can be asked, *why* it should be thought so important to regard only the prior condition or set of conditions as the cause of the subsequent one, and never the subsequent one as the cause of the prior one. There is, certainly, an absurdity in saying that a man's dying is the cause of his being shot, or that a man's being intoxicated is the cause of his having imbibed alcohol, rather than the other way around; but what *kind* of absurdity is it? Is it merely a verbal error, a wrong choice of vocabulary, or is it a metaphysical absurdity? Compare it with the following simple example. If one were to point out that a son cannot exist before his father, he would probably not be *merely* calling attention to a point of vocabulary. He would be stating an obvious truth of biology. If, on the other hand, one were to say that one's brother's sons cannot be his nieces, but must be his nephews, he would obviously be making only a point about language, about the use of certain words. Now then, when one says that a cause cannot come after its effect, which kind of point is he making? Is he *merely* calling attention to a matter of vocabulary, or is he saying something metaphysically significant about causes and their effects?

It seems fairly clear that there is something metaphysically absurd, and not merely an inept choice of words, in supposing that efficient causes might work backwards. There is surely some reason why nothing can produce an effect in the past, and the reason cannot just be, that if it did, we would not then *call* it a cause.

Consider the following illustration.[2] There is a variety of ways in which one might ensure that a certain man— say, some political rival—is dead on a certain day. One way would be to shoot him the day before. We can assume that this, together with all the other conditions prevailing, is sufficient for his being dead the next day, and further, that in case conditions are such that he would not have died had he not been shot, then it is also necessary for his being dead then. But another, equally good way of en-

---

[2] This example was suggested by R. M. Chisholm.

suring that he is dead on that day would be to attend his funeral later on. This would surely be sufficient for his prior death and, in case conditions are such that his being dead is sufficient for somene's attending his funeral, then it is also a necessary condition of his prior death. Suppose, then, that one man shoots him, and another attends his funeral, and that both of these acts are related to that man's death in exactly the same way, except only for the difference in time; that is, that each act is, given only those other conditions that occur, both necessary and sufficient for his being dead on the day in question. Why should one man be blamed more than the other, or held any more responsible for the death? Each man, equally with the other, did something necessary and sufficient for that man's death. Either act guarantees the death as well as the other. The thing to note is, that this question is *not* answered by merely observing that one of these acts occurred before the death, and the other after; that is already quite obvious. Nor is it answered by noting that we do not, as it happens, *call* the subsequent event the cause. That is obvious and irrelevant; the word "cause" was not even used in the example. We do not hold a man responsible for any event, unless something he does is a necessary and sufficient *prior* condition of it. That is granted. But merely stating that fact does not answer the question, Why not? It cannot be a mere question of vocabulary whether, for example, a certain man should be hanged for what he has done.

The correct answer to this question, I believe, is that no cause exerts any power over the past. The same idea is expressed, more metaphysically, by saying that all past things are actual, and never at some later time potentially what they are not then actually, whereas a present thing can be actually one thing but potentially another. This would be expressed in terms of our example by saying that a man who shoots another acts upon him, or does something to him, or is an agent, whereas the man who is thus killed does not, in dying, act upon his assassin, but is the passive recipient, or patient, of the other's causal activity. The man who merely attends the funeral, on the other hand, does not act upon him who is already dead. He is merely the passive observer of what has already been done.

This metaphysical way of conceiving these relationships seems, moreover, to be the way all men do think of causes and effects, and it explains the enormous absurdity in the supposition that causes might act so as to alter things already past. For anything to be a cause it must act upon something and, as a matter of fact—indeed, of metaphysical necessity—nothing past can be acted upon by anything. The profound error of modern philosophy has been to suppose that, in making that point, one is making only a point about language.

Contemporaneous causes and effects. If we can cite clear examples of causal connections, wherein those conditions that constitute the cause and those that constitute the effect are entirely contemporaneous, neither occurring before the other, then it will have been proved that the difference between a cause and its effect cannot be a temporal one, but must consist of something else.

In fact, such examples are not at all hard to find. Consider, for instance, a locomotive that is pulling a caboose, and to make it simple, suppose this is all it is pulling. Now here the motion of the locomotive is sufficient for the motion of the caboose, the two being connected in such a way that the former cannot move without the latter mov-

ing with it. But so also, the motion of the caboose is sufficient for the motion of the locomotive, for, given that the
two are connected as they are, it would be impossible for
the caboose to be moving without the locomotive moving
with it. From this it logically follows that, conditions being
such as they are—viz., both objects being in motion, there
being no other movers present, no obstructions to motion,
and so on—the motion of each object is also necessary for
the motion of the other. But is there any temporal gap between the motion of one and the motion of the other?
Clearly, there is not. They move together, and in no sense
is the motion of one followed by the motion of the other.

Here it is tempting to say that the locomotive must
start moving before the caboose can start moving, but this
is both irrelevant and false. It is irrelevant, because the
effect we are considering is not the caboose's *beginning* to
move, but its moving. And it is false because we can suppose the two to be securely connected, such that as soon
as either begins to move the other must move too. Even if
we do not make this supposition, and suppose, instead, that
the locomotive does begin moving first, and moves some
short distance before overcoming the looseness of its connection with the caboose, still, it is no cause of the motion
of the caboose until that looseness is overcome. When that
happens, and not until then, the locomotive imparts its
motion to the caboose. Cause and effect are, then, perfectly
contemporaneous.

Again, consider the relationships between one's hand
and a pencil he is holding while writing. We can ignore
here the difficult question of what causes the *hand* to move.
It is surely true, in any case, that the motion of the pencil
is caused by the motion of the hand. This means, first, that
conditions are such that the motion of the hand is sufficient

for the motion of the pencil. Given precisely those conditions, however, the motion of the pencil is sufficient for the motion of the hand; neither can move, under the conditions assumed—that the fingers are grasping the pencil, etc.—without the other moving with it. It follows, then, that under these conditions the motion of either is also necessary for the motion of the other. And, quite obviously, both motions are contemporaneous; the motion of neither is *followed* by the motion of the other.

Or again, consider a leaf that is being fluttered by the wind. Here it would be quite clearly erroneous to say that the wind currents impinge upon the leaf, and then, some time later, the leaf flutters in response. There is no gap in time at all. One might want to say that the leaf, however light, does offer some resistance to the wind, and that the wind must overcome this slight resistance before any fluttering occurs. But then we need only add, that the wind is no cause of the leaf's motion until that resistance is overcome. Cause and effect are again, then, contemporaneous.

What, then, distinguishes cause and effect in the foregoing examples? It is not the time of occurence, for both occur strictly together. It is not any difference in the relations of necessity and sufficiency, for these are identical both ways. But there is one thing which, in all these cases, appears to distinguish the cause from the effect; namely, that the cause acts upon something else to produce some change. The locomotive pulls the caboose, but the caboose does not push the locomotive; it just follows passively along. The hand pushes the pencil, and imparts motion to it, while the pencil is just passively moved. The wind acts upon the leaf, to move it; but it is no explanation of the wind's blowing to say that the leaf is moving. In

all these cases, to be sure, what has been distinguished as
the cause is itself moved by something else—the locomotive
by steam in its cylinders, the hand by a man, the wind by
things more complex and obscure; but that only calls attention to the fact that causes can themselves be the effects
of other causes. Whether all causes must be such, or whether, on the contrary, something can be a "first cause" or
a "prime mover" is something that need not concern us
here. One can, in any case, see why it has seemed plausible,
and even necessary, to some thinkers.

The examples just considered suggest our final point;
namely, that there not only is no temporal gap between
cause and effect in certain examples that come readily to
mind, but that there is in fact never any such gap in any
example that one carefully considers.[3] This will be seen, I
think, if we consider a clear example of causation wherein
the cause seems, at first, to precede its effect, and then find
that, even in such a case, there is no such temporal priority
at all.

Consider, then, the case of a window breaking as a
result of a stone being thrown against it. Here it is tempting to say that the stone is first thrown, and then the window
breaks, implying that the cause occurs before the effect.
But that is not a good description of what happens. It is
not enough that the stone should be thrown; it must hit
the window. Even then, it must overcome the resistance
of the window. Only then does the window break; cause
and effect are simultaneous. Nor does one avoid this conclusion by the familiar device of conceiving of both cause
and effect as events, both having duration in time, and
being such that the effect begins to occur as soon as the

---

[3] A similar point is made by Bertrand Russell, "On the Notion of Cause,"
in *Mysticism and Logic* (London: Allen and Unwin, 1950).

cause ceases. It is, at best, simply arbitrary how one divides any process up into events. But even if one does permit himself to do this, and regards a cause, for instance, as a change occurring over a length of time, it is obvious that not all that change can be counted as the cause of some other change following it in time. In the example we are considering, for instance, it is the impact of the stone against the glass that causes the shattering; it is not what the stone was doing before then. Had the stone behaved exactly as it did up to that moment, but then made no contact with the glass, or had it then struck the glass with a force insufficient to break it, the glass would not have shattered. The behavior of the stone up to that moment was, accordingly, not sufficient for the effect in question. Similarly, had the stone behaved entirely differently up to that moment, but then somehow, at that moment, exerted upon the glass the pressure that it did exert, the glass would have broken as it did anyway. The behavior of the stone up to that moment was, accordingly, neither necessary nor sufficient for the effect in question. What *was* necessary and sufficient, on the other hand, was that the stone should at that moment only have exerted the pressure it did; and, given that condition, then the window breaks—not a day or two later, and not a second or two later, but at that very moment. The shattering of the glass can also, of course, be conceived as a process that takes time; but here we need only note that the only part of that shattering that is caused by the impact of the stone is that part that occurs at the moment of impact. The subsequent behavior of the glass is the effect of what happens after the glass has been struck.

Here again, then—and, I believe, in any example one closely considers—cause and effect are contemporaneous.

It is therefore no priority in time that distinguishes the cause from the effect, nor is it, again, any difference in the relations of necessity and sufficiency, these being, as always, identical either way. What does seem to distinguish cause from effect is that the former is something that acts upon the glass to produce its shattered condition. Of course the glass acts upon the stone, too, to produce, for example, its retarded velocity, but that is a different effect, and a different cause, and these are also contemporaneous. To point this out is only, in any case, to call attention to the fact that causes, in acting, can sometimes be acted upon. Whether this is always so is a question, important to theology and to the problem of free will, that need not concern us.

RICHARD TAYLOR

BROWN UNIVERSITY

Causes and Conditions

J. L. Mackie

Reprinted with permission of the editor and the author from the *American Philosophical Quarterly*, 2, no. 4 (Oct., 1965), 245–264.

CAUSES AND CONDITIONS

J. L. MACKIE

Asked what a cause is, we may be tempted to say that it is an event which precedes the event of which it is the cause, and is both necessary and sufficient for the latter's occurrence; briefly, that a cause is a necessary and sufficient preceding condition. There are, however, many difficulties in this account. I shall try to show that what we often speak of as a cause is a condition not of this sort, but of a sort related to this. That is to say, this account needs modification, and can be modified, and when it is modified we can explain much more satisfactorily how we can arrive at much of what we ordinarily take to be causal knowledge; the claims implicit within our causal assertions can be related to the forms of the evidence on which we are often relying when we assert a causal connection.

§ 1. SINGULAR CAUSAL STATEMENTS

Suppose that a fire has broken out in a certain house, but has been extinguished before the house has been completely destroyed. Experts investigate the cause of the fire, and they conclude that it was caused by an electrical short-circuit at a certain place. What is the exact force of their statement that this short-circuit caused this fire? Clearly the experts are not saying that the short-circuit was a necessary condition for this house's catching fire at this time; they know perfectly well that a short-circuit somewhere else, or the overturning of a lighted oil stove, or any one of a number of other things might, if it had occurred, have set the house on fire. Equally, they are not saying that the short-circuit was a sufficient condition for this house's catching fire; for if the short-circuit had occurred, but there had been no inflammable material nearby, the fire would not have broken out, and even given both the short-circuit and the inflammable material, the fire would not have occurred if, say, there had been an efficient automatic sprinkler at just the right spot. Far from being a condition both necessary and sufficient for the fire, the short-circuit was, and is known to the experts to have been, neither necessary nor sufficient for it. In what sense, then, is it said to have caused the fire?

At least part of the answer is that there is a set of conditions (of which some are positive and some are negative), including the presence of inflammable material, the absence of a suitably placed sprinkler, and no doubt quite a number of others, which combined with the short-circuit constituted a complex condition that was sufficient for the house's catching fire — sufficient, but not necessary, for the fire could have started in other ways. Also, of *this* complex condition, the short-circuit was an indispensable part: the other parts of this condition, conjoined with one another in the absence of the short-circuit, would not have produced the fire. The short-circuit which is said to have caused the fire is thus an indispensable part of a complex sufficient (but not necessary) condition of the fire. In this case, then, the so-called cause is, and is known to be, an *insufficient* but *necessary* part of a condition which is itself *unnecessary* but *sufficient* for the result. The experts are saying, in effect, that the short-circuit is a condition of this sort, that it occurred, that the other conditions which conjoined with it form a sufficient condition were also present, and that no other sufficient condition of the house's catching fire was present on this occasion. I suggest that when we speak of the cause of some particular event, it is often a condition of this sort that we have in mind. In view of the importance of conditions of this sort in our knowledge of and talk about causation, it will be convenient to have a short name for them: let us call such a condition (from the initial letters of the words italicized above), an INUS condition.[1]

This account of the force of the experts' statement about the cause of the fire may be confirmed by reflecting on the way in which they will have reached this conclusion, and the way in which anyone who disagreed with it would have to challenge it. An important part of the investigation will have consisted in tracing the actual course of the fire; the experts will have ascertained that no other condition sufficient for a fire's breaking out and taking this course was present, but that the short-circuit did occur and that conditions were present which in conjunction with it were sufficient for the fire's breaking out and taking the course that it did. Provided that there is some necessary and sufficient condition of the fire — and this is an assumption that we commonly make in such contexts — anyone who wanted to deny the experts' conclusion would have to challenge one or another of these points.

---

[1] This term was suggested by D. C. Stove, who has also given me a great deal of help by criticizing earlier versions of this article.

We can give a more formal analysis of the statement that something is an INUS condition. Let A stand for the INUS condition — in our example, the occurrence of a short-circuit at that place — and let B and $\overline{C}$ (that is, not-C, or the absence of C) stand for the other conditions, positive and negative, which were needed along with A to form a sufficient condition of the fire — in our example, B might be the presence of inflammable material, $\overline{C}$ the absence of a suitably placed sprinkler. Then the conjunction $AB\overline{C}$ represents a sufficient condition of the fire, and one that contains no redundant factors; that is, $AB\overline{C}$ is a minimal sufficient condition for the fire.[2] Similarly, let $D\overline{E}F$, $\overline{G}\overline{H}I$, etc., be all the other minimal sufficient conditions of this result. Now, provided that there is some necessary and sufficient condition for this result, the disjunction of all the minimal sufficient conditions for it constitutes a necessary and sufficient condition.[3] That is, the formula "$AB\overline{C}$ or $D\overline{E}F$ or $\overline{G}\overline{H}I$ or ..." represents a necessary and sufficient condition for the fire, each of its disjuncts, such as $AB\overline{C}$, represents a minimal sufficient condition, and each conjunct in each minimal sufficient condition, such as A, represents an INUS condition. To simplify and generalize this, we can replace the conjunction of terms conjoined with A (here $B\overline{C}$) by the single term X, and the formula representing the disjunction of all the other minimal

---

[2] The phrase "minimal sufficient condition" is borrowed from Konrad Marc-Wogau, "On Historical Explanation," *Theoria*, vol. 28 (1962), pp. 213–233. This article gives an analysis of singular causal statements, with special reference to their use by historians, which is substantially equivalent to the account I am suggesting. Many further references are made to this article, especially in n. 9 below.

[3] Cf. n. 8 on p. 227 of Marc-Wogau's article, where it is pointed out that in order to infer that the disjunction of all the minimal sufficient conditions will be a necessary condition, "it is necessary to presuppose that an arbitrary event C, if it occurs, must have sufficient reason to occur." This presupposition is equivalent to the presupposition that there is some (possibly complex) condition that is both necessary and sufficient for C.

It is of some interest that some common turns of speech embody this presupposition. To say "Nothing but X will do," or "Either X or Y will do, but nothing else will," is a natural way of saying that X, or the disjunction (X or Y), is a *necessary* condition for whatever result we have in mind. But taken literally these remarks say only that there is no sufficient condition for this result other than X, or other than (X or Y). That is, we use to mean "a necessary condition" phrases whose literal meanings would be "the only sufficient condition," or "the disjunction of all sufficient conditions." Similarly, to say that Z is "all that's needed" is a natural way of saying that Z is a sufficient condition, but taken literally this remark says that Z is the only necessary condition. But, once again, that the only necessary condition will also be a sufficient one follows only if we presuppose that some condition is both necessary and sufficient.

sufficient conditions — here "$D\bar{E}F$ or $\overline{GH}I$ or ..." — by the single term Y. Then an INUS condition is defined as follows:

A is an INUS condition of a result P if and only if, for some X and for some Y, $(AX$ or $Y)$ is a necessary and sufficient condition of P, but A is not a sufficient condition of P and X is not a sufficient condition of P.

We can indicate this type of relation more briefly if we take the provisos for granted and replace the existentially quantified variables X and Y by dots. That is, we can say that A is an INUS condition of P when $(A . . .$ or $. . .)$ is a necessary and sufficient condition of P.

(To forestall possible misunderstandings, I would fill out this definition as follows.[4] First, there could be a set of minimal sufficient conditions of P, but no necessary conditions, not even a complex one; in such a case, A might be what Marc-Wogau calls a moment in a minimal sufficient condition, but I shall not call it an INUS condition. I shall speak of an INUS condition only where the disjunction of all the minimal sufficient conditions is also a necessary condition. Second, the definition leaves it open that the INUS condition A might be a conjunct in each of the minimal sufficient conditions. If so, A would be itself a necessary condition of the result. I shall still call A an INUS condition in these circumstances: it is not part of the definition of an INUS condition that it should *not* be necessary, although in the standard cases, such as that sketched above, it is not in fact necessary.[5] Third, the requirement that X by itself should not be sufficient for P insures that A is a nonredundant part of the sufficient condition AX; but there is a sense in which it may not be strictly necessary or indispensable even as a part of *this* condition, for it may be replaceable: for example, KX might be another minimal sufficient condition of P.[6] Fourth, it *is* part of the definition that the minimal sufficient condition, AX, of which A is a nonredundant part, is not also a necessary condition, that there is another sufficient condition Y (which may itself be a disjunction of sufficient conditions). Fifth, and similarly, it *is* part of the definition that A is not by itself sufficient for P. The fourth and fifth of these

[4] I am indebted to the referees for the suggestion that these points should be clarified.

[5] Special cases where an INUS condition is also a necessary one are mentioned at the end of § 3.

[6] This point, and the term *nonredundant*, are taken from Michael Scriven's review of Nagel's *The Structure of Science*, in *Review of Metaphysics*, 1964. See especially the passage on p. 408 quoted below.

points amount to this: I shall call A an INUS condition only if there are terms which actually occupy the places occupied by X and Y in the formula for the necessary and sufficient condition. However, there may be cases where there is only one minimal sufficient condition, say AX. Again, there may be cases where A is itself a minimal sufficient condition, the disjunction of all minimal sufficient conditions being (A or Y); again, there may be cases where A itself is the only minimal sufficient condition and is itself both necessary and sufficient for P. In any of these cases, as well as in cases where A is an INUS condition, I shall say that A is *at least an* INUS *condition*. As we shall see, we often have evidence which supports the conclusion that something is *at least* an INUS condition; we may or may not have other evidence which shows that it is *no more than* an INUS condition.)

I suggest that a statement which asserts a singular causal sequence, of such a form as "A caused P," often makes, implicitly, the following claims:

(i) A is at least an INUS condition of P — that is, there is a necessary and sufficient condition of P which has one of these forms: (AX or Y), (A or Y), AX, A.

(ii) A was present on the occasion in question.

(iii) The factors represented by the X, if any, in the formula for the necessary and sufficient condition were present on the occasion in question.

(iv) Every disjunct in Y which does not contain A as a conjunct was absent on the occasion in question. (As a rule, this means that whatever Y represents was absent on this occasion. If Y represents a single conjunction of factors, then it was absent if at least one of its conjuncts was absent; if it represents a disjunction, then it was absent if each of its disjuncts was absent. But we do not wish to exclude the possibility that Y should be, or contain as a disjunct, a conjunction one of whose conjuncts is A, or to require that *this* conjunction should have been absent.)[7]

I do not suggest that this is the whole of what is meant by "A caused P" on any occasion, or even that it is a part of what is meant on every occasion: some additional and alternative parts of the meaning of such statements are indicated below.[8] But I am suggesting that this is an

---

[7] See example of the wicket-keeper discussed below.
[8] See §§ 7, 8.

important part of the concept of causation; the proof of this suggestion would be that in many cases the falsifying of any one of the above-mentioned claims would rebut the assertion that *A* caused *P*.

This account is in fairly close agreement, in substance if not in terminology, with at least two accounts recently offered of the cause of a single event.

Konrad Marc-Wogau sums up his account thus: "when historians in singular causal statements speak of a cause or the cause of a certain individual event β, then what they are referring to is another individual event α which is a moment in a minimal sufficient and at the same time necessary condition *post factum* β."[9]

He explained his phrase "necessary condition *post factum*" by saying that he will call an event a_1 a necessary condition *post factum* for *x* if the disjunction "a_1 or a_2 or a_3 . . . or a_n" represents a necessary condition for *x,* and of these disjuncts only a_1 was present on the particular occasion when *x* occurred.

Similarly, Michael Scriven has said:

Causes are *not* necessary, even contingently so, they are not sufficient — but they are, to talk that language, *contingently sufficient*. . . . They are part of *a* set of conditions that does guarantee the outcome, and they are non-redundant in that the rest of *this* set (which does not include all the other conditions present) is not alone sufficient for the outcome. It is not even true that they are relatively necessary, i.e., necessary with regard to that set of conditions rather than the total circumstances of their occurrence, for there may be several possible

---

[9] See pp. 226–227 of the article referred to in n. 2 above. Marc-Wogau's full formulation is as follows:

"Let 'msc' stand for minimal sufficient condition and 'nc' for necessary condition. Then suppose we have a class *K* of individual events $a_1, a_2, \ldots, a_n$. (It seems reasonable to assume that *K* is finite; however even if *K* were infinite the reasoning below would not be affected.) My analysis of the singular causal statement: α is the cause of β, where α and β stand for individuals events, can be summarily expressed in the following statements:

(1) (EK) $(K = \{a_1, a_2, \ldots, a_n\}$);
(2) (x) $(x \in K \equiv x$ msc β);
(3) $(a_1 \vee a_2 \vee \ldots a_n)$ nc β;
(4) (x) $((x \in K \ x \neq a_1) \supset x$ is not fulfilled when α occurs) ;
(5) α is a moment in a_1.

(3) and (4) say that a_1 is a necessary condition *post factum* for β. If a_1 is a necessary condition *post factum* for β, then every moment in a_1 is a necessary condition *post factum* for β, and therefore also α. As has been mentioned before (n. 6) there is assumed to be a temporal sequence between α and β; β is not itself an element in *K*."

replacements for them which happen not to be present. There remains a ghost of necessity; a cause is a factor from a set of possible factors the presence of one of which (*any* one) is necessary in order that a set of conditions actually present be sufficient for the effect.[10]

There are only slight differences between these two accounts, or between each of them and that offered above. Scriven seems to speak too strongly when he says that causes are not necessary: it is, indeed, not part of the definition of a cause of this sort that it should be necessary, but, as noted above, a cause, or an INUS condition, may be necessary, either because there is only one minimal sufficient condition or because the cause is a moment in each of the minimal sufficient conditions. On the other hand, Marc-Wogau's account of a minimal sufficient condition seems too strong. He says that a minimal sufficient condition contains "only those moments relevant to the effect" and that a moment is relevant to an effect if "it is a necessary condition for β: β would not have occurred if this moment had not been present." This is less accurate than Scriven's statement that the cause only needs to be nonredundant.[11] Also, Marc-Wogau's requirement, in his account of a necessary condition *post factum,* that only one minimal sufficient condition (the one containing a) should be present on the particular occasion, seems a little too strong. If two or more minimal sufficient conditions (say a_1 and a_2) were present, but a was a moment in each of them, then though neither a_1 nor a_2 was necessary *post factum,* a would be so. I shall use this phrase "necessary *post factum*" to include cases of this sort: that is, a is a necessary condition *post factum* if it is a moment in every minimal sufficient condition that was present. For example, in a cricket team the wicket-keeper is also a good batsman. He is injured during a match, and does not bat in the second innings, and the substitute wicket-keeper drops a vital catch that the original wicket-keeper would have taken. The team loses the match, but it would have won if the wicket-keeper had *both* batted *and* taken that catch. His injury was a moment in two minimal sufficient conditions for the loss of the match; either his not batting, or the catch's not being

[10] *Op. cit.,* p. 408.

[11] However, in n. 7 on pp. 222–233, Marc-Wogau draws attention to the difficulty of giving an accurate definition of "a moment in a sufficient condition." Further complications are involved in the account given in § 5 below of "clusters" of factors and the progressive localization of a cause. A condition which is minimally sufficient in relation to one degree of analysis of factors may not be so in relation to another degree of analysis.

taken, would on its own have insured the loss of the match. But we can certainly say that his injury caused the loss of the match, and that it was a necessary condition *post factum*.

This account may be summed up, briefly and approximately, by saying that the statement "*A* caused *P*" often claims that *A* was necessary and sufficient for *P* in the circumstances. This description applies in the standard cases, but we have already noted that a cause is non-redundant rather than necessary even in the circumstances, and we shall see that there are special cases in which it may be neither necessary nor nonredundant.

§ 2. Difficulties and Refinements[12]

Both Scriven and Marc-Wogau are concerned not only with this basic account, but with certain difficulties and with the refinements and complications that are needed to overcome them. Before dealing with these I shall introduce, as a refinement of my own account, the notion of a causal field.[13]

This notion is most easily explained if we leave, for a time, singular causal statements and consider general ones. The question "What causes influenza?" is incomplete and partially indeterminate. It may mean "What causes influenza in human beings in general?" If so, the (full) cause that is being sought is a difference that will mark off cases in which human beings contract influenza from cases in which they do not; the causal field is then the region that is to be thus divided, *human beings in general*. But the question may mean, "Given that influenza viruses are present, what makes some people contract the disease whereas others do not?" Here the causal field is *human beings in conditions where influenza viruses are present*. In all such cases, the cause is required to differentiate, within a wider region in which the effect sometimes occurs and sometimes does not, the subregion in which it occurs: this wider region is the causal field. This notion can now be applied to singular causal questions and statements. "What caused this

[12] This section is something of an aside: the main argument is resumed in § 3.

[13] This notion of a causal field was introduced by John Anderson. He used it, e.g., in "The Problem of Causality," first published in the *Australasian Journal of Psychology and Philosophy*, vol. 16 (1938), and reprinted in *Studies in Empirical Philosophy* (Sydney, 1962), pp. 126–136, to overcome certain difficulties and paradoxes in Mill's account of causation. I have also used this notion to deal with problems of legal and moral responsibility, in "Responsibility and Language," *Australasian Journal of Philosophy*, vol. 33 (1955), pp. 143–159.

man's skin cancer?"[14] may mean "Why did this man develop skin cancer now when he did not develop it before?" Here the causal field is the career of this man: it is within this that we are seeking a difference between the time when skin cancer developed and times when it did not. But the same question may mean "Why did this man develop skin cancer, whereas other men who were also exposed to radiation did not?" Here the causal field is the class of men thus exposed to radiation. And what is the cause in relation to one field may not be the cause in relation to another. Exposure to a certain dose of radiation may be the cause in relation to the former field: it cannot be the cause in relation to the latter field since it is part of the description of that field, and being present throughout that field it cannot differentiate one subregion of it from another. In relation to the latter field, the cause may be, in Scriven's terms, "Some as-yet-unidentified constitutional factor."

In our first example of the house which caught fire, the history of this house is the field in relation to which the experts were looking for the cause of the fire: their question was "Why did this house catch fire on this occasion, and not on others?" However, there may still be some indeterminacy in this choice of a causal field. Does this house, considered as the causal field, include all its features, or all its relatively permanent features, or only some of these? If we take all its features, or even all of its relatively permanent ones, as constituting the field, then some of the things that we have treated as conditions — for example, the presence of inflammable material near the place where the short-circuit occurred — would have to be regarded as parts of the field, and we could not then take them also as conditions which in relation to this field, as additions to it or intrusions into it, are necessary or sufficient for something else. We must therefore take the house, insofar as it constitutes the causal field, as determined only in a fairly general way, by only some of its relatively permanent features, and we shall then be free to treat its other features as conditions which do not constitute the field and are not parts of it, but which may occur within it or be added to it. It is in general an arbitrary matter whether a particular feature is regarded as a condition (that is, as a possible causal factor) or as part of the field, but it cannot be treated in both ways at

---

[14] These examples are borrowed from Scriven, *op. cit.*, pp. 409–410. Scriven discusses them with reference to what he calls a "contrast class," the class of cases where the effect did not occur with which the case where it did occur is being contrasted. What I call the causal field is the logical sum of the case (or cases) in which the effect is being said to be caused with what Scriven calls the contrast class.

once. If we are to say that something happened to this house because of, or partly because of, a certain feature, we are implying that it would still have been *this* house, the house in relation to which we are seeking the cause of this happening, even if it had not had this particular feature.

I now propose to modify the account given above of the claims often made by singular causal statements. A statement of such a form as "*A* caused *P*" is usually elliptical and is to be expanded into "*A* caused *P* in relation to the field *F*." And then in place of the claim stated in (i) above, we require this:

(ia) *A* is at least an INUS condition of *P* in the field *F* — that is, there is a condition which, given the presence of whatever features characterize *F* throughout, is necessary and sufficient for *P*, and which is of one of these forms: $(AX$ or $Y)$, $(A$ or $Y)$, AX, A.

In analyzing our ordinary causal statements, we must admit that the field is often taken for granted or only roughly indicated rather than specified precisely. Nevertheless, the field in relation to which we are looking for a cause of this effect, or saying that such-and-such is a cause, may be definite enough for us to be able to say that certain facts or possibilities are irrelevant to the particular causal problem under consideration, because they would constitute a shift from the intended field to a different one. Thus, if we are looking for the cause, or causes, of influenza, meaning its cause(s) in relation to the field *human beings,* we may dismiss, as not directly relevant, evidence which shows that some proposed cause fails to produce influenza in rats. If we are looking for the cause of the fire in *this house,* we may similarly dismiss as irrelevant the fact that a proposed cause would not have produced a fire if the house had been radically different or had been set in a radically different environment.

This modification enables us to deal with the well-known difficulty that it is impossible, without including in the cause the whole environment, the whole prior state of the universe (and so excluding any likelihood of repetition), to find a genuinely sufficient condition, one which is "by itself, adequate to secure the effect."[15] It may be hard to find

[15] Cf. Bertrand Russell, "On the Notion of Cause," *Mysticism and Logic* (London, 1917), p. 187. Cf. also Scriven's first difficulty, *op. cit.,* p. 409: "First, there are virtually no known sufficient conditions, literally speaking, since human or accidental interference is almost inexhaustibly possible, and hard to exclude by specific qualification without tautology." The introduction of the causal field also automatically covers Scriven's third difficulty and third refinement, that of the contrast class and the relativity of causal statements to contexts.

even a complex condition which was absolutely sufficient for this fire because we should have to include, as one of the negative conjuncts, such an item as the earth's not being destroyed by a nuclear explosion just after the occurrence of the suggested INUS condition; but it is easy and reasonable to say simply that such an explosion would, in more senses than one, take us outside the field in which we are considering this effect. That is to say, it may be not so difficult to find a condition which is sufficient in relation to the intended field. No doubt this means that causal statements may be vague, insofar as the specification of the field is vague, but this is not a serious obstacle to establishing or using them, either in science or in everyday contexts.[16]

It is a vital feature of the account I am suggesting that we can say that *A* caused *P*, in the sense described, without being able to specify exactly the terms represented by *X* and *Y* in our formula. In saying that *A* is at least an INUS condition for *P* in *F,* one is *not* saying what other factors, along with *A,* were both present and nonredundant, and one is *not* saying what other minimal sufficient conditions there may be for *P* in *F.* One is not even claiming to be able to say what they are. This is in no way a difficulty: it is a readily recognizable fact about our ordinary causal statements and one which this account explicitly and correctly reflects.[17] It will be shown (in § 5 below) that this elliptical or indeterminate character of our causal statements is closely connected with some of our characteristic ways of discovering and confirming causal relationships: it is precisely for statements that are thus "gappy" or indeterminate that we can obtain fairly direct evidence from quite modest ranges of observation. On this analysis, causal statements implicitly contain existential quantifications; one can assert an existentially

[16] J. R. Lucas, "Causation," *Analytical Philosophy,* ed. R. J. Butler (Oxford, 1962), pp. 57–59, resolves this kind of difficulty by an informal appeal to what amounts to this notion of a causal field: ". . . these circumstances [cosmic cataclysms, etc.] . . . destroy the whole causal situation in which we had been looking for *Z* to appear. . . . predictions are not expected to come true when quite unforeseen emergencies arise."

[17] This is related to Scriven's second difficulty, *op. cit.,* p. 409: "there still remains the problem of saying what the other factors are which, with the cause, make up the sufficient condition. If they can be stated, causal explanation is then simply a special case of subsumption under a law. If they cannot, the analysis is surely mythological." Scriven correctly replies that "a combination of the thesis of macrodeterminism . . . and observation-plus-theory frequently gives us the very best of reasons for saying that a certain factor combines with an unknown subset of the conditions present into a sufficient condition for a particular effect." He gives a statistical example of such evidence, but the whole of my account of typical sorts of evidence for causal relationships in §§ 5 and 7 below is an expanded defense of a reply of this sort.

quantified statement without asserting any instantiation of it, and one can also have good reason for asserting an existentially quantified statement without having the information needed to support any precise instantiation of it. I can know that there is someone at the door even if the question "Who is he?" would floor me.

Marc-Wogau is concerned especially with cases where "there are two events, each of which independently of the other is a sufficient condition for another event." There are, that is to say, two minimal sufficient conditions, both of which actually occurred. For example, lightning strikes a barn in which straw is stored, and a tramp throws a burning cigarette butt into the straw at the same place and at the same time. Likewise, for an historical event there may be more than one "cause," and each of them may, on its own, be sufficient.[18] Similarly, Scriven considers a case where "... conditions (perhaps unusual excitement plus constitutional inadequacies) [are] present at 4.0 P.M. that guarantee a stroke at 4.55 P.M. and consequent death at 5.0 P.M.; but an entirely unrelated heart attack at 4.50 P.M. is still correctly called the cause of death, which, as it happens, does occur at 5.0 P.M."[19] Before we try to resolve these difficulties, let us consider another of Marc-Wogau's problems: Smith and Jones commit a crime, but if they had not done so the head of the criminal organization would have sent other members to perform it in their stead, and so it would have been committed anyway.[20] Now in this case, if A stands for the actions of Smith and Jones, what we have is that AX is one minimal sufficient condition of the result (the crime), but $\overline{A}Z$ is another, and both X and Z are present. A combines with one set of the standing conditions to produce the result by one route, but the absence of A would have combined with another set of the standing conditions to produce the same result by another route. In this case we *can* say that A was a necessary condition *post factum*. This sample satisfies the requirements of Marc-Wogau's analysis, and of mine, of the statement that A caused this result; and this agrees with what we would ordinarily say in such a case. (We might indeed add that there was *also* a deeper cause — the existence of the criminal organization, perhaps — but this does not matter: our formal analyses do not insure that a particular result will have a unique cause, nor does our ordinary causal talk require this.) It is

[18] *Op. cit.*, pp. 228–233.

[19] *Op. cit.*, pp. 410–411; this is Scriven's fourth difficulty and refinement.

[20] *Op. cit.*, p. 232; the example is taken from P. Gardiner, *The Nature of Historical Explanation* (Oxford, 1952), p. 101.

true that in this case we cannot say what will usually serve as an informal substitute for the formal account, that the cause, here A, was necessary (as well as sufficient) in the circumstances, for $\overline{A}$ would have done just as well. We cannot even say that A was nonredundant. But this shows merely that a formal analysis may be superior to its less formal counterparts.

Now in Scriven's example we might take it that the heart attack prevented the stroke from occurring. If so, then the heart attack *is* a necessary condition *post factum;* it is a moment in the only minimal sufficient condition that was present in full, for the heart attack itself removed some factor that was a necessary part of the minimal sufficient condition which has the excitement as one of its moments. This is strictly parallel to the Smith and Jones case. Again it is odd to say that the heart attack was in any way necessary, since the absence of the heart attack would have done just as well: this absence would have been a moment in that other minimal sufficient condition, one of whose other moments was the excitement. Nevertheless, the heart attack was necessary *post factum,* and the excitement was not. Scriven draws the distinction, quite correctly, in terms of continuity and discontinuity of causal chains: "the heart attack was, and the excitement was not the cause of death because the 'causal chain' between the latter and death was interrupted, while the former's 'went to completion.' " But it is worth noting that a break in the causal chain corresponds to a failure to satisfy the logical requirements of a moment in a minimal sufficient condition that is also necessary *post factum.*

Alternatively, if the heart attack did not prevent the stroke, then we have a case parallel to that of the straw in the barn or of the man who is shot by a firing squad and two bullets go through his heart simultaneously. In such cases the requirements of my analysis or of Marc-Wogau's or of Scriven's are not met: each proposed cause *is* redundant and not even necessary *post factum,* though the disjunction of them is necessary *post factum* and nonredundant. But this agrees very well with the fact that we *would* ordinarily hesitate to say, of either bullet, that it caused the man's death, or of either the lightning or the cigarette butt that it caused the fire, or of either the excitement or the heart attack that it was the cause of death. As Marc-Wogau says, "in such a situation as this we are unsure also how to use the word *cause.*" Our ordinary concept of cause does not deal clearly with cases of this sort, and we are free to decide whether or not to add to our ordinary use, and to the various more or less formal descriptions of it, rules which allow us to say that where more than one at-least-inus-condition, and their conjunct conditions, are present, each of them caused the result.[21]

The account thus far developed of singular causal statements has been expressed in terms of statements about necessity and sufficiency; it is therefore incomplete until we have added an account of necessity and sufficiency themselves. This question is considered in § 4 below. But the present account is independent of any particular analysis of necessity and sufficiency. Whatever analysis of these we finally adopt, we shall use it to complete the account of what it is to be an inus condition, or to be at least an inus condition. But in whatever way this account is completed, we can retain the general principle that at least part of what is often done by a singular causal statement is to pick out, as the cause, something that is claimed to be at least an inus condition.

§ 3. General Causal Statements

Many general causal statements are to be understood in a corresponding way. Suppose, for example, that an economist says that the restriction of credit causes (or produces) unemployment. Again, he will no doubt be speaking with reference to some causal field; this is now not an individual object, but a class, presumably economies of a certain general kind; perhaps their specification will include the feature that each economy of the kind in question contains a large private enterprise sector with free wage-earning employees. The result, unemployment, is something which sometimes occurs and sometimes does not occur within this field, and the same is true of the alleged cause, the restriction of credit. But the economist is not saying that (even in relation to this field) credit restriction is either necessary or sufficient for unemployment, let alone both necessary and sufficient. There may well be other circumstances which must be present along with credit restriction, in an economy of the kind referred to, if unemployment is to result; these other circumstances will no doubt include various negative ones, the absence of various counteracting causal factors which, if they were present, would prevent this result. Also, the economist will probably be quite prepared to admit that in an economy of this kind

[21] Scriven's fifth difficulty and refinement are concerned with the direction of causation. This is considered briefly in § 8 below.

unemployment could be brought about by other combinations of circumstances in which the restriction of credit plays no part. So once again the claim that he is making is merely that the restriction of credit is, in economies of this kind, a nonredundant part of one sufficient condition for unemployment: that is, an INUS condition. The economist is probably assuming that there is some condition, no doubt a complex one, which is both necessary and sufficient for unemployment in this field. This being assumed, what he is asserting is that, for some X and for some Y, $(AX$ or $Y)$ is a necessary and sufficient condition for P in F, but neither A nor X is sufficient on its own, where A stands for the restriction of credit, P for unemployment, and F for the field, economies of such-and-such a sort. In a developed economic theory the field F may be specified quite exactly, and so may the relevant combinations of factors represented here by X and Y. (Indeed, the theory may go beyond statements in terms of necessity and sufficiency to ones of functional dependence, but this is a complication which I am leaving aside for the present.) In a preliminary or popular statement, on the other hand, the combinations of factors may either be only roughly indicated or be left quite undetermined. At one extreme we have the statement that $(AX$ or $Y)$ is a necessary and sufficient condition, where X and Y are given definite meanings; at the other extreme we have the merely existentially quantified statement that this holds for *some* pair X and Y. Our knowledge in such cases ordinarily falls somewhere between these two extremes. We can use the same convention as before, deliberately allowing it to be ambiguous between these different interpretations, and say that in any of these cases, where A is an INUS condition of P in F, $(A\ldots$ or $\ldots)$ is a necessary and sufficient condition of P in F.

A great deal of our ordinary causal knowledge is of this form. We know that the eating of sweets causes dental decay. Here the field is human beings who have some of their own teeth. We do not know, indeed it is not true, that the eating of sweets by any such person is a sufficient condition for dental decay: some people have peculiarly resistant teeth, and there are probably measures which, if taken along with the eating of sweets, would protect the eater's teeth from decay. All we know is that sweet-eating combined with a set of positive and negative factors which we can specify, if at all, only roughly and incompletely, constitutes a minimal sufficient condition for dental decay — but not a necessary one, for there are other combinations of factors, which do not include sweet-eating, which would also make teeth decay, but which we can specify, if at all, only roughly and incompletely. That is, if A now represents sweet-eating, P dental decay, and F the class of human beings with some of their own teeth, we can say that, for some X and Y, $(AX$ or $Y)$ is necessary and sufficient for P in F, and we *may* be able to go beyond this merely existentially quantified statement to at least a partial specification of the X and Y in question. That is, we can say that $(A \ldots$ or $\ldots)$ is a necessary and sufficient condition, but that A itself is only an INUS condition. And the same holds for many general causal statements of the form "A causes (or produces) P." It is in this sense that the application of a potential difference to the ends of a copper wire produces an electric current in the wire, that a rise in the temperature of a piece of metal makes it expand, that moisture rusts steel, that exposure to various kinds of radiation causes cancer, and so on.

However, it is true that not all ordinary general causal statements are of this sort. Some of them are implicit statements of functional dependence. Functional dependence is a more complicated relationship of which necessity and sufficiency can be regarded as special cases. (It is briefly discussed in § 7 below.) Here, too, what we commonly single out as causing some result is only one of a number of factors which jointly affect the result. Again, some causal statements pick out something that is not only an INUS condition, but also a necessary condition. Thus, we may say that the yellow fever virus is the cause of yellow fever. (This statement is not, as it might appear to be, tautologous, for the yellow fever virus and the disease itself can be independently specified.) In the field in question — human beings — the injection of this virus is not by itself a sufficient condition for this disease, for persons who have once recovered from yellow fever are thereafter immune to it, and other persons can be immunized against it. The injection of the virus, combined with the absence of immunity (natural or artificial), and perhaps combined with some other factors, constitutes a sufficient condition for the disease. Beside this, the injection of the virus is a necessary condition of the disease. If there is more than one complex sufficient condition for yellow fever, the injection of the virus into the patient's bloodstream (either by a mosquito or in some other way) is a factor included in every such sufficient condition. If A stands for this factor, the necessary and sufficient condition has the form $(A \ldots$ or $A \ldots$, etc.$)$, where A occurs in every disjunct. We sometimes note the difference between this and the standard case by using the phrase "the cause." We may say not merely that this virus *causes* yellow fever, but that it is *the cause* of yellow fever; but we would say only that sweet-eating *causes* dental decay, not that it is *the cause* of dental decay. But about an individual case we could say that sweet-eating was *the cause* of the decay of this person's teeth, meaning (as in § 1 above) that the only sufficient condition present here was the one of which sweet-eating is a nonredundant part. Nevertheless, there will not in general be any one item which has a unique claim to be regarded as *the cause* even of an individual event, and even after the causal field has been determined. Each of the moments in the minimal sufficient condition, or in each minimal sufficient condition, that was present can equally be regarded as the cause. They may be distinguished as predisposing causes, triggering causes, and so on, but it is quite arbitrary to pick out as "main" and "secondary" different moments which are equally nonredundant items in a minimal sufficient condition, or which are moments in two minimal sufficient conditions each of which makes the other redundant.[22]

§ 4. Necessity and Sufficiency

One possible account of general statements of the forms "*S* is a necessary condition of *T*" and "*S* is a sufficient condition of *T*" — where *S* and *T* are general terms — is that they are equivalent to simple universal propositions. That is, the former is equivalent to "All *T* are *S*" and the latter to "All *S* are *T*." Similarly, "*S* is necessary for *T* in the field *F*" would be equivalent to "All *FT* are *S*," and "*S* is sufficient for *T* in the field *F*" to "All *FS* are *T*." Whether an account of this sort is adequate is, of course, a matter of dispute, but it is not disputed that these statements about necessary and sufficient conditions at least *entail* the corresponding universals. I shall work on the assumption that this account is adequate, that general statements of necessity and sufficiency are equivalent to universals; it will be worth while to see how far this account will take us, how far we are able, in terms of it, to understand how we use, support, and criticize these statements of necessity and sufficiency.

A directly analogous account of the corresponding singular statements is not satisfactory. Thus, it will not do to say that "A short-

---

[22] Cf. Marc-Wogau's concluding remarks, *op. cit.*, pp. 232–233.

circuit here was a necessary condition of a fire in this house" is equivalent to "All cases of this house's catching fire are cases of a short-circuit occurring here," because the latter is automatically true if this house has caught fire only once and a short-circuit has occurred on that occasion, but this is not enough to establish the statement that the short-circuit was a necessary condition of the fire, and there would be an exactly parallel objection to a similar statement about a sufficient condition.

It is much more plausible to relate singular statements about necessity and sufficiency to certain kinds of nonmaterial conditionals. Thus "A short-circuit here was a necessary condition of a fire in this house" is closely related to the counterfactual conditional "If a short-circuit had not occurred here this house would not have caught fire," and "A short-circuit here was a sufficient condition of a fire in this house" is closely related to what Goodman has called the factual conditional, "Since a short-circuit occurred here, this house caught fire."

However, a further account would still have to be given of these nonmaterial conditionals themselves. I have argued elsewhere that they are best considered as condensed or telescoped *arguments*, but that the statements used as premises in these arguments are no more than simple factual universals.[23] To use the above-quoted counterfactual conditional is, in effect, to run through an incomplete argument: "Suppose that a short-circuit did not occur here, then the house did not catch fire." To use the factual conditional is, in effect, to run through a similar incomplete argument, "A short-circuit occurred here; therefore the house caught fire." In each case the argument might in principle be completed by the insertion of other premises which, together with the stated premise, would entail the stated conclusion. Such additional premises may be said to *sustain* the nonmaterial conditional. It is an important point that someone can use a nonmaterial conditional without completing or being able to complete the argument, without being prepared explicitly to assert premises that would sustain it, and similarly that we can understand such a conditional without knowing exactly how the argument would or could be completed. But to say that a short-circuit here was a necessary condition of a fire in this house is to say that there is some set of true propositions which would sustain the above-stated counterfactual, and to say that it was a sufficient condition

---

[23] "Counterfactuals and Causal Laws," *Analytical Philosophy*, ed. R. J. Butler (Oxford, 1962), pp. 66–80.

is to say that there is some set of true propositions which would sustain the above-stated factual conditional. If this is conceded, then the relating of singular statements about necessity and sufficiency to nonmaterial conditionals leads back to the view that they refer indirectly to certain simple universal propositions. Thus, if we said that a short-circuit here was a necessary condition for a fire in this house, we should be saying that there are true universal propositions from which, together with true statements about the characteristics of this house and together with the supposition that a short-circuit did not occur here, it would follow that the house did not catch fire. From this we could infer the universal proposition which is the more obvious, but unsatisfactory, candidate for the analysis of this statement of necessity, "All cases of this house's catching fire are cases of a short-circuit occurring here," or, in our symbols, "All *FP* are *A*." We can use this to represent approximately the statement of necessity on the understanding that it is to be a consequence of some set of wider universal propositions and is not to be automatically true merely because there is only this one case of an *FP*, of this house's catching fire.[24] A statement that *A* was a sufficient condition may be similarly represented by "All *FA* are *P*." Correspondingly, if all that we want to say is that (*A*. . . or . . .) was necessary and sufficient for *P* in *F*, this will be represented approximately by the pair of universals "All *FP* are (*A*. . . or . . .) and all *F* (*A*. . . or . . .) are *P*," and more accurately by the statement that there is some set of wider universal propositions from which, together with true statements about the features of *F*, this pair of universals follows. This, therefore, is the fuller analysis of the claim that in a particular case *A* is an INUS condition of *P* in *F*, and hence of the singular statement that *A* caused *P*. (The statement that *A* is *at least* an INUS condition includes other alternatives, corresponding to cases where the necessary and sufficient condition is (*A* or . . .), *A*. . ., or *A*.)

Let us go back now to general statements of necessity and sufficiency and take *F* as a class, not as an individual. On the view that I am adopting, at least provisionally, the statement that *Z* is a necessary and

[24] This restriction may be compared with one which Nagel imposes on laws of nature: "the vacuous truth of an unrestricted universal is not sufficient for counting it a law; it counts as a law only if there is a set of other assumed laws from which the universal is logically derivable" (*The Structure of Science* [New York, 1961], p. 60). It might have been better if he had added "or if there is some other way in which it is supported (ultimately) by empirical evidence." Cf. my remarks in "Counterfactuals and Causal Laws," *op. cit.*, pp. 72–74, 78–80.

sufficient condition for *P* in *F* is equivalent to "All *FP* are *Z* and all *FZ* are *P*." Similarly, if we cannot completely specify a necessary and sufficient condition for *P* in *F*, but can only say that the formula (*A* . . . or . . .) represents such a condition, this is equivalent to the pair of incomplete universals, "All *FP* are (*A* . . . or . . .) and all *F* (*A* . . . or . . .) are *P*." In saying that our general causal statements often do no more than specify an inus condition, I am therefore saying that much of our ordinary causal knowledge is knowledge of such pairs of incomplete universals, of what we may call elliptical or *gappy* causal laws.

§ 5. Evidence for Causal Connections

If we assume that the general causal statement that *A* causes *P,* or the singular causal statement that *A* caused *P,* often makes the claims set out in §§ 1, 2, 3, and 4, including the claim that *A* is at least an inus condition of *P,* then we can give an account of a combination of reasoning and observation which constitutes evidence for these causal statements.

This account is based on what von Wright calls a complex case of the Method of Difference.[25] Like any other method of eliminative induction, this can be formulated in terms of an assumption, an observation, and a conclusion which follows by a deductively valid argument from the assumption and the observation together. To get any positive conclusion by a process of elimination, we must assume that the result (the phenomenon a cause of which we are going to discover) has *some* cause in the sense that there is some condition the occurrence of which is both necessary and sufficient for the occurrence (as a rule, shortly afterwards) of the result. Also, if we are to get anywhere by elimination, we must assume that the range of possibly relevant causal factors, the items that might in some way constitute this necessary and sufficient condition, is restricted in some way. On the other hand, even if we had specified some such set of possibly relevant factors, it would in most cases be quite implausible to assume that the supposed necessary and sufficient condition is identical with just one of these factors on its own,

[25] *A Treatise on Induction and Probability* (New York, 1951), pp. 90 ff. The account that I am here giving of the Method of Difference, and that I would give of the eliminative methods of induction in general, differs, however, in several respects from that of von Wright. An article on "Eliminative Methods of Induction," which sets out my account, is to appear in the *Encyclopedia of Philosophy,* edited by Paul Edwards, to be published by the Free Press of Glencoe, Collier-Macmillan.

and fortunately we have no need to do so. If we represent each possibly relevant factor as a single term, the natural assumption to make is merely that the supposed necessary and sufficient condition will be represented by a formula which is constructed in some way out of some selection of these single terms, by means of negation, conjunction, and disjunction. However, any formula so constructed is equivalent to some formula in disjunctive normal form — that is, one in which negation, if it occurs, is applied only to single terms, and conjunction, if it occurs, only to single terms and/or negations of single terms. So we can assume without loss of generality that the formula of the supposed necessary and sufficient condition is in disjunctive normal form, that it is at most a disjunction of conjunctions in which each conjunct is a single term or the negation of one, that is, a formula such as (ABC or GH or J). Summing this up, the assumption that we require will have this form:

For some Z, Z is a necessary and sufficient condition for the phenomenon P in the field F; that is, all FP are Z and all FZ are P, and Z is a condition represented by some formula in disjunctive normal form all of whose constituents are taken from the range of possibly relevant factors A, B, C, D, E, etc.

Along with this assumption, we need an observation which has the form of the classical difference observation described by Mill. This we can formulate as follows:

There is an instance I_1 in which P occurs, and there is a negative case N_1 in which P does not occur, such that one of the possibly relevant factors (or the negation of one), say A, is present in I_1 and absent from N_1, but each of the other possibly relevant factors is either present in both I_1 and N_1 or absent both from I_1 and from N_1.

We can set out an example of such an observation as follows, using a and p to stand for "absent" and "present."

$$
\begin{array}{c c c c c c c}
 & P & A & B & C & D & E \\
I_1 & p & p & p & a & a & p \\
N_1 & a & a & p & a & a & p
\end{array} \Bigg\} \text{etc.}
$$

Given the above-stated assumption, we can reason in the following way about any such observation:

Since P is absent from N_1, every sufficient condition for P is absent from N_1, and therefore every disjunct in Z is absent from N_1. Every disjunct in Z which does not contain A is therefore also absent from I_1. But since P is present in I_1, and Z is a necessary condition for P, Z is present in I_1. Therefore, at least one disjunct in Z is present in I_1. Therefore, at least one disjunct in Z contains A.

What this shows is that Z, the supposed necessary and sufficient condition for P in F, is either A itself, or a conjunction containing A, or a disjunction containing as a disjunct either A itself or a conjunction containing A. That is, Z has one of these four forms: A, $A \ldots$, $(A$ or $\ldots)$, $(A \ldots$ or $\ldots)$. We can sum these up by saying that Z has the form $(A$ - - - or - - -), where the dashes indicate that these parts of the formula may or may not be filled in. This represents briefly the statement that A is at least an INUS condition. It follows also that if there are in the (unknown) formula which represents the complete necessary and sufficient condition any disjuncts not containing A, none of them was present as a whole in N_1 (but of course some of their component terms may have been present there), and also that in at least one of the disjuncts that contains A, the terms, if any, conjoined with A stand for factors (or negations of factors) that were present in I_1. This is all that follows from this single observation. But in general other observations will show that the dotted spaces do need to be filled in, and that A alone is neither sufficient nor necessary for P in F. We can then infer that the necessary and sufficient condition actually has the form $(A \ldots$ or $\ldots)$ and that A itself is only an INUS condition.

This analysis is so far merely formal, and we have still to consider whether such a method can be, or is, actually used, whether an assumption of the sort required can be justified, and whether an observation of the sort required can ever be made. Even at this stage, however, it is worth noting that the Method of Difference does not require the utterly unrealistic sort of assumption used in what von Wright calls the simple case — namely, that the supposed necessary and sufficient condition is some single factor on its own — but that the much less restrictive assumption used here will still yield information when it is combined with nothing more than the classical difference observation. It is worth noting also that the information thus obtained, though it falls far short of what von Wright calls absolutely perfect analogy, that is, of a full specification of a necessary and sufficient condition, is information of exactly the form that is implicit in our ordinary causal assertions, both singular and general.[26]

[26] What is established by the present method may be compared with the four claims listed in § 1 above, that A is at least an INUS condition, that A was present on the occasion in question, that the factors represented by X — that is, the other

But can observations of the kind required be made? A preliminary answer is that the typical controlled experiment is an attempt to approximate to an observation of this sort. The experimental case corresponds to our I_1, the control case to our N_1, and the experimenter tries to insure that there will be no possibly relevant difference between these two except the one whose effect he is trying to determine, our A. Any differential outcome, present in the experimental case but not in the control case, is what he takes to be this effect, corresponding to our P.

The before-and-after observation is a particularly important variety of this kind. Suppose, for example, that we take a piece of blue litmus paper and dip it in a certain liquid and it turns red. The situation before it is dipped provides the negative case N_1; the situation after it is dipped provides the instance I_1. As far as we can see, no other possibly relevant feature of the situation has changed, so I_1 and N_1 are alike with regard to all possibly relevant factors except A, the paper's being dipped in a liquid of this sort, but the result P, the paper's turning red, is present in I_1 but not in N_1. We can take this in either of two ways. First, we may take the field F to be pieces of blue litmus paper, and if we assume that in this field there is some necessary and sufficient condition for P, made up in some way from some selection from the factors we are considering as possibly relevant, we can conclude that $(A$ - - - or - - -$)$ is necessary and sufficient for P in F. Other observations may show that A alone is neither necessary nor sufficient and hence that the necessary and sufficient condition is $(A \ldots$ or $\ldots)$. Thus, we can establish the gappy causal law, "All FP are $(A \ldots$ or $\ldots)$ and all $F(A \ldots$ or $\ldots)$ are P." This amounts to the assertion that in some circumstances being dipped in a liquid of this sort turns blue litmus paper red. Second, we can take the field (which we shall here call F_1) to be this particular piece of paper, and what the experiment then establishes is the singular causal statement that on this particular occasion the dipping in this liquid turned this piece of paper red. This is established in accordance with the analysis of singular causal statements completed in § 4. For the experiment, together with the assumption, has established the wider universals indicated by the above-stated gappy causal law. It has shown that for some X and Y all FP are $(AX$ or $Y)$ and all $F(AX$ or $Y)$ are P, and from these, since F_1 is an F (that is, this

moments in at least one minimal sufficient condition in which A is a moment — were present, and that every disjunct in Y which does not contain A — that is, every minimal sufficient condition which does not contain A — was absent.

piece of paper is a piece of blue litmus paper), it follows that for some X and Y all F_1P are (AX or Y) and all $F_1(AX$ or Y) are P. Also, X represents circumstances which were present on this occasion, and Y circumstances which were not present in N_1, the "before" situation. That is to say, the observation, together with the appropriate assumption, entails that there are true propositions which sustain the counterfactual and factual conditionals, "If, in the circumstances, this paper had not been dipped in this liquid it would not have turned red, but since it was dipped it did turn red"; but it does not fully determine what these propositions are; it does not fill in the gaps in the causal laws which sustain these conditionals. The importance of this is that it shows how an observation can reveal not merely a sequence but a causal sequence: what we discover is not merely that the litmus paper was dipped *and then* turned red, but that the dipping *made* it turn red.

It is worth noting that despite the stress traditionally laid, in accounts of the Method of Difference, on the requirement that there should be only *one* point of difference between I_1 and N_1, very little really turns upon this. For suppose that two of our possibly relevant factors, say A and B, were both present in I_1 and both absent from N_1, but that each of the possibly relevant factors was either present in both or absent from both. Then reasoning parallel to that given above will show that at least one of the disjuncts in Z either contains A or contains B (and may contain both). That is, this observation still serves to show that the cluster of factors (A, B) *contains* something that is at least an INUS condition of P in F, whether this condition turns out in the end to be A alone or B alone or the conjunction AB or the disjunction (A or B). And similar considerations apply if there are more than two points of difference between I_1 and N_1. However many there are, an observation of this form, coupled with our assumption, shows that a cause in our sense (in general an INUS condition) lies somewhere within the cluster of terms, positive or negative, in respect of which I_1 differs from N_1. (Note that it does *not* show that the other terms, those common to I_1 and N_1, are causally irrelevant; our reasoning does not exclude factors as irrelevant, but positively locates some of the relevant factors within the differentiating cluster.)

This fact rebuts the criticism sometimes leveled against the eliminative methods that they presuppose and require a finally satisfactory analysis of causal factors into their simple components which we never actually achieve. On the contrary, any distinction of factors, however rough, enables us to start using such a method. We can proceed, and there is no doubt that discovery has often proceeded, by what we may call *the progressive localization of a cause.* Using the Method of Difference in a very rough way, we can discover first, say, that the drinking of wine causes intoxication; that is, the cluster of factors which is crudely summed up in the single term "the drinking of wine" contains somewhere within it an INUS condition of intoxication; and we can subsequently go on to distinguish various possibly relevant factors within this cluster, and by further observations of the same sort locate a cause of intoxication more precisely. In a context in which this cluster is either introduced or excluded as a whole, it is correct to say that the introduction of this cluster was nonredundant or necessary *post factum,* and experiments can establish this, even if, in a different context, in which distinct items in the cluster are introduced or excluded separately, it would be correct to say that only one item, the alcohol, was nonredundant or necessary *post factum,* and this could be established by more exact experimentation.

One merit of this formal analysis is that it shows in what sense a method of eliminative induction, such as the Method of Difference, rests upon a deterministic principle or presupposes the uniformity of nature. In fact, each application of this method requires an assumption which in one respect says much less than this, in another a little more. No sweeping general assumption is needed: we need not assume that every event has a cause, but merely that for events of the kind in question, P, in the field in question, F, there is some necessary and sufficient condition. But — and this is where we need something more than determinism or uniformity in general — we must also assume that this condition is constituted in some way by some selection from a restricted range of possibly relevant factors.

It is this further assumption that raises a doubt about the use of this method to make causal discoveries. As for the mere deterministic assumption that the phenomenon in question has some necessary and sufficient condition, we may be content to say that this is one which we simply do make in all inquiries of this kind, and leave its justification to be provided by whatever solution we can eventually find for the general problem of induction. But the choice of a range of possibly relevant factors cannot be brushed aside so easily. Also, the wider a range of possibly relevant factors we admit, the harder it will be to defend the claim that I_1 and N_1 are observed to be alike with respect to all the possibly relevant factors except the one, or the indicated cluster of factors, in which they are observed to differ. Alternatively, the more narrowly the range of possibly relevant factors is restricted, the easier it will be to defend the claim that we have made an observation of the required form, but at the same time the less plausible will our assumption be.

However, this difficulty becomes less formidable if we consider the assumption and the observation together. We want to be able to say that there is no possibly relevant difference, other than the one (or ones) noted, between I_1 and N_1. We need not draw up a complete list of possibly relevant factors before we make the observation. In practice we usually assume that a causally relevant factor will be in the spatial neighborhood of the instance of the field in or to which the effect occurs in I_1, or fails to occur in N_1, and it will either occur shortly before or persist throughout the time at which the effect occurs in I_1, or might have occurred, but did not, in N_1. No doubt in a more advanced application of the Method of Difference within an already-developed body of causal knowledge we can restrict the range of possibly relevant factors much more narrowly and can take deliberate steps to exclude interferences from our experiments; but I am suggesting that even our most elementary and primitive causal knowledge rests upon implicit applications of this method, and the spatiotemporal method of restricting possibly relevant factors is the only one initially available. And perhaps it is all we need. Certainly in terms of it the observer could say, about the litmus paper, for example, "I cannot see any difference, other than the dipping into this liquid, between the situation in which the paper turned red and that in which it did not that might be relevant to this change."

It may be instructive to compare the Method of Difference as a logical ideal with any actual application of it. If the assumption and the observation were known to be true, then the causal conclusion would be established. Consequently, anything that tells in favor of both the assumption and the observation tells equally in favor of the causal conclusion. No doubt we are never in a position to say that they are known to be true, and therefore that the conclusion is established; but we are often in a position to say that, given the deterministic part of the assumption, we cannot see any respect in which they are not true (since we cannot see any difference that might be relevant between I_1 and N_1), and consequently that we cannot see any escape from the causal conclusion. In this sense at least we can say that an application of this method confirms a causal conclusion: the observer has looked for but failed to find an escape from this conclusion.[27]

In practice we do not rely as much on single observations as this account might suggest. We assure ourselves that it was the dipping in this liquid that turned the litmus paper red by dipping other pieces of litmus paper and seeing them, too, turn red just after they are dipped.

---

[27] An account of how eliminative inductive reasoning supports causal conclusions is given by J. R. Lucas in the article cited in n. 16 above. His account differs from mine in many details but agrees with it in general outline. Contrast with this the remarks of von Wright, *op. cit.*, p. 135: "... in normal scientific practice we have to reckon with plurality rather than singularity, and with complexity rather than simplicity of conditions. This means that the weaker form of the Deterministic Postulate, or the form which may be viewed as a reasonable approximation to what is commonly known as the Law of Universal Causation, is practically useless as a supplementary premise or 'presupposition' of induction." I hope I have shown that this last remark is misleading.

It has been argued by A. Michotte (*La Perception de la causalité* [Louvain, 1946], translated by T. R. and E. Miles as *The Perception of Causality* [London, 1963]) that we have in certain cases an immediate perception or impression of causation. His two basic experimental cases are these. In one, an object *A* approaches another object *B*; on reaching *B*, *A* stops and *B* begins to move off in the same direction; here the observer gets the impression that *A* has "launched" *B*, has set *B* in motion. In the other case, *A* continues to move on reaching *B*, and *B* moves at the same speed and in the same direction; here the observer gets the impression that *A* is carrying *B* with it. In both cases observers typically report that *A* has caused the movement of *B*. Michotte argues that it is an essential feature of observations that give rise to this causal impression that there should be two distinguishable movements, that of the "agent" *A* and that of the "patient" *B*, but also that it is essential that the movement of the patient should in some degree copy or duplicate that of the agent.

This would appear to be a radically different account of the way in which we can detect causation by observing a single sequence, for on Michotte's view our awareness of causation can be direct, perceptual, and noninferential. It must be conceded that not only spatiotemporal continuity, but also qualitative continuity between cause and effect (*l'ampliation du mouvement*), are important ingredients in the primitive concept of causation; they may contribute to the notion of causal "necessity"; and both these continuities can sometimes be directly perceived. But it is equally clear that these continuities are not in general required either as observed or as postulated features of a causal sequence, and that a sequence which has these continuities may fail to be causal. What is perceived in Michotte's examples is neither necessary nor sufficient for causal relationship as we now understand it, though it may have played an important part in the genesis of the causal concept. It is worth noting that these examples also exhibit the features stressed in my account. They present the observer with an apparently simple and isolated causal field, within which there occurs a marked change, *B*'s beginning to move. The approach of *A* is the only observed possibly relevant difference between the times when *B* is stationary and when *B* begins to move. If *B*'s beginning to move has a cause, then *A*'s approach is a suitable candidate, and nothing else that the observer is allowed to see or encouraged to suspect is so. Thus, these examples could *also* give rise to an inferential awareness of causation, though it is true that other examples which would do this equally well would fail, and in Michotte's experiments do fail, to produce a direct impression of causation.

This repetition is effective because it serves as a check on the possibility that some other relevant change might have occurred, unnoticed, just at the moment when the first piece of litmus paper was dipped in the liquid. After a few trials it will be most unlikely that any other relevant change has kept on occurring just as each piece was dipped (or even that there has been a succession of different relevant changes at the right times). Of course, it may be that there is some other relevant change (or set of relevant changes) which keeps on occurring just as each paper is dipped because it is linked with the dipping by what Mill calls "some fact of causation."[28] If so, then this other relevant change may be regarded as part of a cluster of factors which can be grouped together under the title "the dipping of the paper in this liquid," taking this in a broad sense as possibly including items other than the actual entry of the paper into the liquid. But if this is not so, then it would be a sheer coincidence if this other relevant change kept on occurring just as each piece of paper was dipped, or if there was a succession of relevant changes at the right times. The hypothesis that such coincidences have continued will soon become implausible, even if it cannot be conclusively falsified.[29] It is an important point that it is not the repetition as such that supports the conclusion that the dipping causes the turning red, but the repetition of a sequence which, on each single occasion, is already *prima facie* a causal one. The repetition tends to disconfirm the set of hypotheses each of which explains a single sequence of a dipping followed by a turning red as a mere coincidence, and by contrast it confirms the hypothesis that in each such single sequence the dipping is causally connected with the change of color.

The analysis offered here of the Method of Difference has this curious consequence: in employing this method we are liable to use the word "cause" in different senses at different stages. In the assumption, it is said that the phenomenon *P* has some "cause," meaning some

[28] E.g., in the Fifth Canon, *A System of Logic,* Book III, Chapter VIII, § 6.

[29] Cf. J. R. Lucas, *op. cit.,* p. 53: "It might be that two quite independent processes were going on, and we were getting constant concomitance for no reason except the chance fact that the two processes happened to keep in step. If this be so, an arbitrary disturbance in one will reveal the independence of the other. If an arbitrary disturbance in the one is followed by a corresponding alteration in the other, it always could be that it was a genuine coincidence. . . . But to argue this persistently is to make the same illicit extension of 'coincidence' as some phenomenalists do of 'illusion.' . . . It is no longer a practical possibility that we are eliminating but a Cartesian doubt."

necessary and sufficient condition; but the "cause" actually found —
A in our formal example — may be only an INUS condition. But we
do need to assume that *something* is both necessary and sufficient for
P in F to be able to conclude that A is at least an INUS condition, that
it is a moment in a minimal sufficient condition that was present, and
that it was necessary *post factum*.

§ 6. FALSIFICATION OF INCOMPLETE STATEMENTS

A possible objection to this account is that the gappy laws and singular statements used here are so incomplete that they are internally
guaranteed against falsification and are therefore not genuine scientific
statements at all. However, it is not a satisfactory criterion of a scientific statement that it should be exposed to conclusive falsification:
what is important is that to treat a statement as a scientific hypothesis
involves handling it in such a way that evidence would be allowed to
tell against it. And there are ways in which evidence can be, and is,
allowed to tell against a statement which asserts that something is an
INUS condition.

Suppose, for example, that by using the I_1 and N_1 set out in § 5
above we have concluded that A is at least an INUS condition of P —
taking this both as a singular causal statement about an individual
field F_1 and as an incomplete law about the general field F. Now suppose that closer examination shows that some other factor, previously
unnoticed, say K, was present in I_1 and absent from N_1 and that we
also discover (or construct experimentally) further cases I_2 and N_2
such that the observational evidence is now of this form:

	P	A	B	C	D	E	...	K	...
I_1	p	p	p	a	a	p	...	p	...
N_1	a	a	p	a	a	p	...	a	...
I_2	p	a	p	a	a	p	...	p	...
N_2	a	p	p	a	a	p	...	a	...

Here N_2 shows that for any X which does not contain K, AX is not
sufficient: so X must contain K. But any X that contains K is present
in I_2 and *may* therefore be sufficient for P on its own, without A. This
evidence does not conclusively falsify the hypothesis that A is an INUS
condition as stated above, but it takes away all the reason that the
previous evidence gave us for this conclusion. Observations of this pattern would tell against this conclusion and would lead us to replace the

view that A causes P, and caused P in I_1, with the view that K causes P, and caused P both in I_2 and in I_1, with A not even forming an indispensable part of the sufficient condition which was present in I_1. (A fuller treatment of this kind of additional evidence would require accounts of the Method of Agreement and of the Joint Method parallel to that of the Method of Difference given in § 5.)

It remains true that some of the claims made by singular causal statements and by causal laws as here analyzed — that is, claims that some factor is at least an INUS condition of the effect — are not conclusively falsifiable. But ordinary causal laws and singular causal statements are not conclusively falsifiable, as direct consideration will show. It is a merit of the account offered here, not a difficulty for it, that it reproduces this feature of ordinary causal knowledge.[30]

§ 7. FUNCTIONAL DEPENDENCE AND CONCOMITANT VARIATION

As I mentioned in § 3, causal statements sometimes refer not to relations of necessity and sufficiency, nor to any more complex relations based on these, like that of being an INUS condition, but to relations of functional dependence. That is, the effect and the possible causal factors are things which can vary in magnitude, and the cause of some effect P is that on whose magnitude the magnitude of P functionally depends. But causal statements of this sort can be expanded and analyzed in an account parallel to that which we have given of causal statements of the previous kinds. Again we speak of a field, individual or general, in relation to which a certain functional dependence holds. Also, we can speak of the *total cause,* the complete set of factors on whose magnitude the magnitude of P, given the field F, wholly depends: that is, variations of P in F are completely covered by a formula which is a function of the magnitudes of all of the factors in this "complete set," and of these alone. This total cause is analogous to a necessary and sufficient condition. It can be distinguished from each of the factors that compose it, each of which is causally relevant to the effect, but it is not the whole cause of its variations: each of these *partial causes* is analogous to an INUS condition.

The problem of finding a cause in this new sense would require, for its full solution, the completion of two tasks. We should have both to identify all the factors in this total cause, and also to discover in what

---

[30] This was pointed out by D. C. Stove.

way the effect depends upon them — that is, to discover the law of functional dependence of the effect on the total cause, or the partial differential equations relating it to each of the partial causes. The first — but only the first — of these two tasks can be performed by what is really the Method of Concomitant Variation, developed in a style analogous to that in which the Method of Difference was developed in § 5. That is, we assume that there is something on which the magnitude of P in F functionally depends, and that there is a restricted set of possibly relevant factors; then if while all other possibly relevant factors are held constant, one factor, say A, varies, and P also varies, it follows that A is at least a partial cause, that it is one of the actually relevant factors. It is this relationship that is commonly asserted by statements of such forms as "A affects P" and "On this occasion A affected P." Some of our causal statements, singular or general, have just this force, and all that I am trying to show here is that these statements can be supported by reasoning along the lines of the Method of Concomitant Variation, developed analogously with the development in § 5 of the Method of Difference. Just as we there assumed that there was some necessary and sufficient condition, and by combining this assumption with our observations discovered something which is at least an INUS condition, so we here assume that there is some total cause and so discover something which is at least a partial cause. However, a complete account of the Method of Concomitant Variation would involve the examination of several other cases besides the one sketched here.[31] For our present purpose, we need note only that there is this functional dependence part of the concept of causation as well as the presence-or-absence part; indeed, that the latter can be considered as a special limiting case of the former,[32] but that the two parts are systematically analogous to one another, and that our knowledge of both singular and general causal relationships of these two kinds can be accounted for on corresponding principles.

§ 8. THE DIRECTION OF CAUSATION

This account of causation is still incomplete in that nothing has yet been said about the direction of causation, about what distinguishes A causing P from P causing A. This is a difficult question, and it is linked with the equally difficult question of the direction of time. I cannot

---

[31] I have given a fuller account of this method in the article cited in n. 25.
[32] Cf. J. R. Lucas, *op. cit.*, p. 65.

hope to resolve it completely here, but I shall state some of the relevant considerations.[33]

First, it seems that there is a relation which may be called *causal priority,* and that part of what is meant by "*A* caused *P*" is that this relation holds in one direction between *A* and *P,* not the other. Second, this relation is not identical with temporal priority; it is conceivable that there should be evidence for a case of backward causation, for *A* being causally prior to *P* whereas *P* was temporally prior to *A.* Most of us believe, and I think with good reason, that backward causation does not occur, so that we can and do normally use temporal order to limit the possibilities about causal order, but the connection between the two is synthetic. Third, it could be objected to the analysis of "necessary" and "sufficient" offered in § 4 above that it omits any reference to causal order, whereas our most common use of "necessary" and "sufficient" in causal contexts includes such a reference. Thus "*A* is (causally) sufficient for *B*" says "If *A,* then *B,* and *A* is causally prior to *B,*" but "*B* is (causally) necessary for *A*" is not equivalent to this: it says "If *A,* then *B,* and *B* is causally prior to *A.*" However, it is simpler to use "necessary" and "sufficient" in senses which exclude this causal priority, and to introduce the assertion of priority separately into our accounts of "*A* caused *P*" and "*A* causes *P.*" Fourth, although "*A* is (at least) an INUS condition of *P*" is not synonymous with "*P* is (at least) an INUS condition of *A,*" this difference of meaning cannot exhaust the relation of causal priority. If it did exhaust it, the direction of causation would be a trivial matter, for, given that there is some necessary and sufficient condition of *A* in the field, it can be proved that if *A* is (at least) an INUS condition of *P,* then *P* is also (at least) an INUS condition of *A:* we can construct a minimal sufficient condition of *A* in which *P* is a moment.[34]

Fifth, it is often suggested that the direction of causation is linked with controllability. If there is a causal relation between *A* and *B,* and we can control *A* without making use of *B* to do so, and the relation between *A* and *B* still holds, then we decide that *B* is not causally prior

---

[33] As was mentioned in n. 21, Scriven's fifth difficulty and refinement are concerned with this point (*op. cit.,* pp. 411–412), but his answer seems to me inadequate. Lucas touches on it (*op. cit.,* pp. 51–53). The problem of temporal asymmetry is discussed, e.g., by J. J. C. Smart, *Philosophy and Scientific Realism* (London, 1963), pp. 142–148, and by A. Grünbaum in the article cited in n. 36 below.

[34] I am indebted to one of the referees for correcting an inaccurate statement on this point in an earlier version.

to *A* and, in general, that *A* is causally prior to *B*. But this means only that if one case of causal priority is known, we can use it to determine others: our rejection of the possibility that *B* is causally prior to *A* rests on our knowledge that our action is causally prior to *A*, and the question how we know the latter, and even the question of what causal priority is, have still to be answered. Similarly, if one of the causally related kinds of event, say *A*, can be randomized, so that occurrences of *A* are either not caused at all or are caused by something which enters this causal field *only* in this way, by causing *A*, we can reject both the possibility that *B* is causally prior to *A* and the possibility that some common cause is prior both to *A* and separately to *B*, and we can again conclude that *A* is causally prior to *B*. But this still means only that we can infer causal priority in one place if we first know that it is absent from another place. It is true that our knowledge of the direction of causation in ordinary cases is thus based on what we find to be controllable, and on what we either find to be random or find that we can randomize; but this cannot without circularity be taken as providing a full account either of what we mean by causal priority or of how we know about it.

A suggestion put forward by Popper about the direction of time seems to be relevant here.[35] If a stone is dropped into a pool, the entry of the stone will explain the expanding circular waves. But the reverse process, with contracting circular waves, "would demand a vast number of distant coherent generators of waves the coherence of which, to be explicable, would have to be shown . . . as originating from one centre." That is, if *B* is an occurrence which involves a certain sort of "coherence" between a large number of separated items, whereas *A* is a single event, and *A* and *B* are causally connected, *A* will explain *B* in a way in which *B* will not explain *A* unless some other single event, say *C*, first explains the coherence in *B*. Such examples give us a *direction of explanation,* and it may be that this is the basis, or part of the basis, of the relation I have called causal priority.

§ 9. Conclusions

Even if Mill was wrong in thinking that science consists mainly of causal knowledge, it can hardly be denied that such knowledge is an

[35] "The Arrow of Time," *Nature,* vol. 177 (1956), p. 538; also vol. 178, p. 382, and vol. 179, p. 1297.

indispensable element in science and that it is worth while to investigate the meaning of causal statements and the ways in which we can arrive at causal knowledge. General causal relationships are among the items which a more advanced kind of scientific theory explains and is confirmed by its success in explaining. Singular causal assertions are involved in almost every report of an experiment: doing such and such *produced* such and such an effect. Materials are commonly identified by their causal properties: to recognize something as a piece of a certain material, therefore, we must establish singular causal assertions about it, that this object affected that other one, or was affected by it, in such and such a way. Causal assertions are embedded in both the results and the procedures of scientific investigation.

The account that I have offered of the force of various kinds of causal statements agrees both with our informal understanding of them and with accounts put forward by other writers: at the same time it is formal enough to show how such statements can be supported by observations and experiments, and thus to throw a new light on philosophical questions about the nature of causation and causal explanation and the status of causal knowledge.

One important point is that, leaving aside the question of the direction of causation, the analysis has been given entirely within the limits of what can still be called a regularity theory of causation, in that the causal laws involved in it are no more than straightforward universal propositions, although their terms may be complex and perhaps incompletely specified. Despite this limitation, I have been able to give an account of the meaning of statements about singular causal sequences, regardless of whether such a sequence is or is not of a kind that frequently recurs: repetition is not essential for causal relation, and regularity does not here disappear into the mere fact that this single sequence has occurred. It has, indeed, often been recognized that the regularity theory could cope with single sequences if, say, a unique sequence could be explained as the resultant of a number of laws each of which was exemplified in many other sequences; but my account shows how a singular causal statement can be interpreted, and how the corresponding sequence can be shown to be causal, even if the corresponding complete laws are not known. It shows how even a unique sequence can be directly recognized as causal.

One consequence of this is that it now becomes possible to reconcile what have appeared to be conflicting views about the nature of historical explanation. We are accustomed to contrast the "covering-law" theory adopted by Hempel, Popper, and others with the views of such critics as Dray and Scriven, who have argued that explanations and causal statements in history cannot be thus assimilated to the patterns accepted in the physical sciences.[36] But while my basic analysis of singular causal statements in §§ 1 and 2 agrees closely with Scriven's, I have argued in § 4 that this analysis can be developed in terms of complex and elliptical universal propositions, and this means that wherever we

[36] See, for example, C. G. Hempel, "The Function of General Laws in History," *Journal of Philosophy,* vol. 39 (1942), reprinted in *Readings in Philosophical Analysis,* ed. by H. Feigl and W. Sellars (New York, 1949), pp. 459–471; C. G. Hempel and P. Oppenheim, "Studies in the Logic of Explanation," *Philosophy of Science,* vol. 15 (1948), reprinted in *Readings in the Philosophy of Science,* ed. by H. Feigl and M. Brodbeck (New York, 1953), pp. 319–352; K. R. Popper, *Logik der Forschung* (Vienna, 1934), translation *The Logic of Scientific Discovery* (London, 1959), pp. 59–60, also *The Open Society* (London, 1952), vol. II, p. 262; W. Dray, *Laws and Explanation in History* (Oxford, 1957); N. Rescher, "On Prediction and Explanation," *British Journal for the Philosophy of Science,* vol. 9 (1958), pp. 281–290; various papers in *Minnesota Studies in the Philosophy of Science,* vol. III, ed. by H. Feigl and G. Maxwell (Minneapolis, 1962); A. Grünbaum, "Temporally-asymmetric Principles, Parity between Explanation and Prediction, and Mechanism versus Teleology," *Philosophy of Science,* vol. 29 (1962), pp. 146–170.
Dray's criticisms of the covering-law theory include the following: we cannot state the law used in a historical explanation without making it so vague as to be vacuous (*op. cit.,* especially p. 24–37) or so complex that it covers only a single case and is trivial on that account (p. 39); the historian does not come to the task of explaining an event with a sufficient stock of laws already formulated and empirically validated (pp. 42–43); historians do not need to replace judgment about particular cases with deduction from empirically validated laws (pp. 51–52). It will be clear that my account resolves each of these difficulties. Grünbaum draws an important distinction between (1) an asymmetry between explanation and prediction with regard to the grounds on which we claim to know that the explanandum is true, and (2) an asymmetry with respect to the logical relation between the explanans and the explanandum; he thinks that only the former sort of asymmetry obtains. I suggest that my account of the use of gappy laws will clarify both the sense in which Grünbaum is right (since an explanation and a tentative prediction can use similarly gappy laws which are similarly related to the known initial conditions and the result) and the sense in which, in such a case, we may contrast an entirely satisfactory explanation with a merely tentative prediction. Scriven (in his most recent statement, the review cited in n. 10 above) says that "we often pin down a factor as a cause by excluding other possible causes. Simple — but disastrous for the covering-law theory of explanation, because we can eliminate causes only for something *we know has occurred.* And if the grounds for our explanation of an event *have* to include knowledge of that event's occurrence, they cannot be used (without circularity) to predict the occurrence of that event" (p. 414). That is, the observation of this event in these circumstances may be a vital part of the evidence that justifies the particular causal explanation that we give of this event: it may itself go a long way toward establishing the elliptical law in relation to which we explain it (as I have shown in § 5), whereas a law used for prediction cannot thus rest on the observation of the event predicted. But as my account also shows, this does not introduce an asymmetry of Grünbaum's second sort and is therefore not disastrous for the covering-law theory.

have a singular causal statement we shall still have a covering law, albeit a complex and perhaps elliptical one. Also, I have shown in § 5, and indicated briefly, for the functional dependence variants, in § 7, that the evidence which supports singular causal statements also supports general causal statements or covering laws, though again only complex and elliptical ones. Hempel recognized long ago that historical accounts can be interpreted as giving incomplete "explanation sketches," rather than what he would regard as full explanations, which would require fully-stated covering laws, and that such sketches are also common outside history. But in these terms what I am saying is that explanation sketches and the related elliptical laws are often all that we can discover, that they play a part in all sciences, that they can be supported and even established without being completed, and that they do not serve merely as preliminaries to or summaries of complete deductive explanations. If we modify the notion of a covering law to admit laws which not only are complex but also are known only in an elliptical form, the covering-law theory can accommodate many of the points that have been made in criticism of it while preserving the structural similarity of explanation in history and in the physical sciences. In this controversy, one point at issue has been the symmetry of explanation and prediction, and my account may help to resolve this dispute. It shows, in agreement with what Scriven has argued, how the actual occurrence of an event in the observed circumstances — the I_1 of my formal account in § 5 — may be a vital part of the evidence which supports an explanation of that event, which shows that it was A that caused P on this occasion. A prediction, on the other hand, cannot rest on observation of the event predicted. Also, the gappy law which is sufficient for an explanation will not suffice for a prediction (or for a retrodiction): a statement of initial conditions together with a gappy law will not entail the assertion that a specific result will occur, though of course such a law may be, and often is, used to make tentative predictions the failure of which will not necessarily tell against the law. But the recognition of these differences between prediction and explanation does not affect the covering-law theory as modified by the recognition of elliptical laws.

Although what I have given is primarily an account of physical causation, it may be indirectly relevant to the understanding of human action and mental causation. It is sometimes suggested that our ability to recognize a single occurrence as an instance of mental causation is a feature which distinguishes mental causation from physical or "Humean" causation.[37] But this suggestion arises from the use of too simple a regularity account of physical causation. If we first see clearly what we mean by singular causal statements in general, and how we can support such a statement by observation of the single sequence itself, even in a physical case, we shall be better able to contrast with this our awareness of mental causes and to see whether the latter has any really distinctive features.

This account also throws light on both the form and the status of the "causal principle," the deterministic assumption which is used in any application of the methods of eliminative induction. These methods need not presuppose determinism in general, but only that each specific phenomenon investigated by such a method is deterministic. Moreover, they require not only that the phenomenon should have some cause, but that there should be some restriction of the range of possibly relevant factors (at least to spatiotemporally neighboring ones, as explained in § 5). Now the general causal principle, that every event has some cause, is so general that it is peculiarly difficult either to confirm or to disconfirm, and we might be tempted either to claim for it some *a priori* status, to turn it into a metaphysical absolute presupposition, or to dismiss it as vacuous. But the specific assumption that this phenomenon has some cause based somehow on factors drawn from this range, or even that this phenomenon has some neighboring cause, is much more open to empirical confirmation and disconfirmation; indeed, the former can be conclusively falsified by the observation of a positive instance I_1 of P and a negative case N_1 in which P does not occur, but where each of the factors in the given range is either present in both I_1 and N_1 or absent from both. This account, then, encourages us to regard the assumption as something to be empirically confirmed or disconfirmed. At the same time it shows that there must be some principle of the confirmation of hypotheses other than the eliminative methods themselves, since each such method rests on an empirical assumption.

[37] See, for example, G. E. M. Anscombe, *Intention* (Oxford, 1957), especially p. 16; J. Teichmann, "Mental Cause and Effect," *Mind,* vol. 70 (1961), pp. 36–52. Teichmann speaks (p. 36) of "the difference between them and ordinary (or 'Humean') sequences of cause and effect" and says (p. 37) "it is sometimes in order for the person who blinks to say absolutely dogmatically that the cause is such-and-such, and to say this independently of his knowledge of any previously established correlations," and again "if the noise is a cause it seems to be one which is known to be such in a special way. It seems that while it is necessary for an observer to have knowledge of a previously established correlation between noises and Smith's jumpings, before he can assert that one causes the other, it is not necessary for Smith himself to have such knowledge."

On the Analysis of Causation

Myles Brand and Marshall Swain

Reprinted with permission of the editor and D. Reidel Publishing Co. from *Synthese*, 21 (1970), 222–227.

ON THE ANALYSIS OF CAUSATION

According to the regularity theory of causation, one set of conditions (or factors or events or states of affairs) causes another to occur only if a set of conditions similar to the latter occurs whenever a set of conditions similar to the former occurs. A well-known difficulty for the regularity theory is its failure to distinguish between cases of accidental correlation and causation. Thomas Reid's example of the coming of day regularly following the coming of night and Russell's example of the workmen leaving the Manchester factory regularly following the sounding of the hooter at the London factory illustrate this difficulty. The regularity theory, further, cannot be salvaged by the following sort of reply. 'Similar', in the regularity formula, means 'relevantly similar': the hooting at the London factory does not cause the workmen's leaving in Manchester because these sets of conditions lack a relevant similarity, for example, that they occur in the same general area. This attempted defense of the regularity theory fails because the resulting analysis is viciously circular. In this context 'relevantly similar' can only mean 'similar in the *causally* relevant respects'.

Problems of this kind have led some philosophers to suggest analyses of causation in terms of natural laws. Accordingly, one set of conditions causes another to occur only if there are natural laws from which it can be deduced that the latter set of conditions occurs given that the former set occurs. Since 'whenever the hooter sounds at the London factory, the workmen leave the Manchester factory' is an accidental universal and not a law of nature, Russell's case does not constitute a counterexample to the laws-of-nature theory. However, there are difficulties for this theory that closely resemble those of the regularity theory. There are several kinds of natural laws. Consider the developmental law which states that whenever the formation of the circulatory system of an human embryo occurs, the formation of the lungs in the embryo occurs. On the laws-of-nature theory, then, the formation of the circulatory system in *this* particular embryo caused the formation of its lungs. This consequence, however, is false; the formation of the circulatory system and the formation of the lungs may both have been caused by some other event, but they do not cause each other. A developmental law, and some other sorts of natural laws, state a correlation and *not* a causal connection. The attempt to defend the laws-of-nature view by specifying that only causal laws can be used to deduce the effect given the cause, moreover, results in vicious circularity: to distinguish between causal and noncausal laws presupposes an analysis of causation.

Though there may be ways to resurrect the regularity theory or the laws-of-nature theory, many philosophers have given up these approaches and turned instead to an analysis of causation in terms of necessary and sufficient conditions. One of the most vigorous proponents of this view is Richard Taylor. He says, "A true interpreted statement of the form '*A* was the cause of *B*' means [in part], that both *A* and *B* are conditions or sets of conditions that occurred; that each was, given all the other conditions that occurred, but only those, both necessary and sufficient for the occurrence of the other...."[1] (Presumably 'necessary' and 'sufficient' here do not mean 'logically necessary' and 'logically sufficient'; in the sense intended, *A* can be necessary and sufficient for *B* even though *A* and *B* are logically independent.) Consider, for example, a case in which the throwing of a ball causes a window to break. *A* consists of the ball's moving with a certain velocity and momentum, the ball's having a certain irregular external shape, and so on; *B* consists of the glass breaking, pieces of glass moving with certain velocities, and so on. Given the other conditions that occurred, if any of the conditions in *A* had not occurred, then the conditions in *B* would not have occurred; that is to say, given all the other conditions that occurred, the occurrence of the conditions in *A* was necessary for the occurrence of the conditions in *B*. Moreover, given the other conditions that occurred, the occurrence of the conditions in *A* was sufficient for the occurrence of the conditions in *B*. It is important to realize, however, that this formula can at best provide a partial analysis of causation. Since the relation 'necessary and sufficient' is symmetrical, the asymmetry between cause and effect cannot be preserved without specifying further conditions in the analysis.

In the remainder of this paper we shall argue that if the partial analysis of causation in terms of necessary and sufficient conditions is stated in a way that avoids the circularity inherent in the regularity and laws-of-nature theories, then a contradiction results. In addition, we shall argue that one plausible way of revising this analysis to avoid the contradiction is subject to the charge of circularity. While these arguments do not prove that no form of this theory is acceptable, they do, in our opinion, provide good reasons for thinking that this is so.

II

The following partial analysis of causation in terms of necessary and sufficient conditions is noncircular:

(D1)   For every A and every B, A caused B only if (i) A and B are sets of conditions that occurred and (ii) A is that set of conditions individually necessary and jointly sufficient for the occurrence of the set of conditions B.

However, in conjunction with several acceptable principles governing the relations of causation, necessity and sufficiency, (D1) entails a contradiction. The first principle says that A causes B only if A and B are distinct. That is,

(P1)   For every A and every B, if A caused B, then there is some condition in B that is not identical with any condition in A and there is some condition in A that is not identical with any condition in B.

To deny (P1) leads to a paradox. From the denial of (P1) it follows that there is some case in which A is the cause of B, and either every condition in B is also a condition in A or every condition in A is also a condition in B. And it follows from this that either A is the cause of A or B is the effect of B. This result is paradoxical because the causal relation is normally taken to obtain between *two* sets of conditions (or events). (It might be claimed that we sometimes significantly say that something causes itself. But we can significantly say this only if the sense of 'cause' is different from the ordinary sense considered here.)

ON THE ANALYSIS OF CAUSATION   225

The relation 'is necessary and sufficient for the occurrence of' is symmetrical and transitive. That is:

(P2)   For every A and every B, if A is the set of conditions individually necessary and jointly sufficient for the occurrence of B, then B is the set of conditions individually necessary and jointly sufficient for the occurrence of A.

(P3)   For every A, every B, and every C, if A is the set of conditions individually necessary and jointly sufficient for the occurrence of B and B is the set of conditions individually necessary and jointly sufficient for the occurrence of C, then A is the set of conditions individually necessary and jointly sufficient for the occurrence of C;

A further principle about necessary and sufficient conditions is also needed.

(P4)   For every A, every B, and every C, if A is the set of conditions individually necessary and jointly sufficient for the occurrence of B, then if C is a set of conditions individually necessary for the occurrence of B, every member of C is a member of A.

Principle (P4) is tautological.

On the assumption that there is at least one set of conditions A and one set of conditions B such that A caused B, these principles and the partial analysis (D1) yield a contradiction. The proof is as follows.

(1) A caused B, where A consists of a set of conditions and B consists of a set of conditions.   (assumption)

(2) A is the set of conditions individually necessary and jointly sufficient for the occurrence of B.   (from (1) and (D1))

(3) B is the set of conditions individually necessary and jointly sufficient for the occurrence of A.   (from (2) and (P2))

(4) B is the set of conditions individually necessary and jointly sufficient for the occurrence of B.   (from (2), (3), and (P3))

(5)   Every condition of B is a condition of A (from (2), (4), and (P4))

(6)   Some condition of B is not a condition of A.   (from (1) and (P1))

226   MYLES BRAND AND MARSHALL SWAIN

Statements (5) and (6) are contradictories. And since (D1) taken in conjunction with the acceptable principles (P1)–(P4) and the trivial assumption that there is at least one case of causation yields a contradiction, (D1) must be rejected.

There is a plausible way of revising (D1) that is not subject to the above argument. Namely,

(D2)   For every A and every B, A caused B only if (i) A and B are sets of conditions that occurred and (ii) A is a proper subset of the set of conditions individually necessary and jointly sufficient for the occurrence of B.

The partial analysis (D2), unlike (D1), says that there are some conditions necessary for the occurrence of B that are not included in A. Principle (P4) is true only if A is the *total set* of conditions necessary and sufficient for the occurrence of B. According to (D2), however, the cause A is merely a subset of this total set. Hence, the argument against (D1) will not work against (D2), since principle (P4) plays an essential role in the argument. That is, (D2) is consistent with (P1)–(P4).

Although the revised analysis (D2) avoids the difficulties that arose for (D1), it is subject to other difficulties. In particular, (D2) does not indicate *which* subset of the set of conditions necessary and sufficient for B is the cause, A. It is, of course, that set of conditions that are *causally* relevant to the occurrence of B. The problem of vicious circularity that confronted the regularity and laws-of-nature theories also confronts the revised necessary-and-sufficient-condition theory of causation, as formulated in (D2).

Statements (D1) and (D2) are two straightforward and plausible attempts at formulating a partial analysis of causation in terms of necessary and sufficient conditions. There are undoubtedly other ways of formulating such an analysis. The arguments we have given do not prove that every such analysis is either contradictory or circular. However, it is difficult to see how such an analysis can differ significantly from those we have considered; for one thing, it seems that any such analysis must either identify the cause with the total set of conditions necessary and sufficient for the occurrence of the effect, or with some subset of that total set of conditions, and this will lead to an analysis either similar to (D1) or similar to (D2). Consequently, we believe our arguments render

ON THE ANALYSIS OF CAUSATION 227

it likely that an attempt to define causation in terms of necessary and sufficient conditions will prove defective.

University of Pittsburgh,
University of Pennsylvania

REFERENCE

[1] Richard Taylor, *Action and Purpose*, 1966, p. 39. Taylor also affirms this position in 'Causation', *The Monist* **47** (1962–63), 287–313, and in 'Causation' in *The Encyclopedia of Philosophy*, New York 1967, vol. II, pp. 56–66. Some others who hold this view are A. J. Ayer, *The Problem of Knowledge*, Edinburgh 1961 (first published 1956), especially p. 171, and H. L. A. Hart and A. M. Honore, *Causation in the Law*, Oxford 1959, especially p. 104. Also see J. L. Mackie, 'Causes and Conditions', *American Philosophical Quarterly* **2** (1965), especially pp. 245–48.

V. Supplementary Issues

Causal Relations

Donald Davidson

Reprinted with permission of the editor and the author from *The Journal of Philosophy*, 64, no. 21 (Nov. 9, 1967), 691–703.

CAUSAL RELATIONS*

WHAT is the logical form of singular causal statements like: 'The flood caused the famine', 'The stabbing caused Caesar's death', 'The burning of the house caused the roasting of the pig'? This question is more modest than the question how we know such statements are true, and the question whether they can be analyzed in terms of, say, constant conjunction. The request for the logical form is modest because it is answered when we have identified the logical or grammatical roles of the words (or other significant stretches) in the sentences under scrutiny. It goes beyond this to define, analyze, or set down axioms governing, particular words or expressions.

I

According to Hume, "we may define a cause to be an object, followed by another, and where all the objects similar to the first are followed by objects similar to the second." This definition pretty clearly suggests that causes and effects are entities that can be named or described by singular terms; probably events, since one can follow another. But in the *Treatise*, under "rules by which to judge of causes and effects," Hume says that "where several different objects produce the same effect, it must be by means of some quality, which we discover to be common amongst them. For as like effects imply like causes, we must always ascribe the causation to the circumstances, wherein we discover the resemblance." Here it seems to be the "quality" or "circumstances" of an event that is the cause rather than the event itself, for the event itself is the same as others in some respects

* To be presented in APA symposium of the same title, December 28, 1967.

I am indebted to Harry Lewis and David Nivison, as well as to other members of seminars at Stanford University to whom I presented the ideas in this paper during 1966/67, for many helpful comments. I have profited greatly from discussion with John Wallace of the questions raised here; he may or may not agree with my answers. My research was supported in part by the National Science Foundation.

and different in other respects. The suspicion that it is not events, but something more closely tied to the descriptions of events, that Hume holds to be causes, is fortified by Hume's claim that causal statements are never necessary. For if events were causes, then a true description of some event would be 'the cause of b', and, given that such an event exists, it follows logically that the cause of b caused b.

Mill said that the cause "is the sum total of the conditions positive and negative taken together . . . which being realized, the consequent invariably follows." Many discussions of causality have concentrated on the question whether Mill was right in insisting that the "real Cause" must include all the antecedent conditions that jointly were sufficient for the effect, and much ingenuity has been spent on discovering factors, pragmatic or otherwise, that guide and justify our choice of some "part" of the conditions as the cause. There has been general agreement that the notion of cause may be at least partly characterized in terms of sufficient and (or) necessary conditions.[1] Yet it seems to me we do not understand how such characterizations are to be applied to particular causes.

Take one of Mill's examples: some man, say Smith, dies, and the cause of his death is said to be that his foot slipped in climbing a ladder. Mill would say we have not given the whole cause, since having a foot slip in climbing a ladder is not always followed by death. What we were after, however, was not the cause of death in general but the cause of Smith's death: does it make sense to ask under what conditions Smith's death invariably follows? Mill suggests that part of the cause of Smith's death is "the circumstance of his weight," perhaps because if Smith had been light as a feather his slip might not have injured him. Mill's explanation of why we don't bother to mention this circumstance is that it is too obvious to bear mention, but it seems to me that if it was Smith's fall that killed him, and Smith weighed twelve stone, then Smith's fall was the fall of a man who weighed twelve stone, whether or not we know it or mention it. How could Smith's actual fall, with Smith weighing, as he did, twelve stone, be any more efficacious in killing him than Smith's actual fall?

The difficulty has nothing to do with Mill's sweeping view of the cause, but attends any attempt of this kind to treat particular causes as necessary or sufficient conditions. Thus Mackie asks, "What is the exact force of [the statement of some experts] that this short-circuit caused this fire?" And he answers, "Clearly the experts are not saying that the short-circuit was a necessary condition for this house's catch-

[1] For a recent example, with reference to many others, see J. L. Mackie, "Causes and Conditions," *American Philosophical Quarterly*, II, 4 (October 1965): 245–264.

ing fire at this time; they know perfectly well that a short-circuit somewhere else, or the overturning of a lighted oil stove . . . might, if it
had occurred, have set the house on fire" (*ibid.*, 245). Suppose the
experts know what they are said to; how does this bear on the question whether the short circuit was a necessary condition of this
particular fire? For a short circuit elsewhere could not have caused
this fire, nor could the overturning of a lighted oil stove.

To talk of particular events as conditions is bewildering, but perhaps causes aren't events (like the short circuit, or Smith's fall from
the ladder), but correspond rather to sentences (perhaps like the fact
that this short circuit occurred, or the fact that Smith fell from the
ladder). Sentences can express conditions of truth for others—hence
the word 'conditional'.

If causes correspond to sentences rather than singular terms, the
logical form of a sentence like:

(1)   The short circuit caused the fire.

would be given more accurately by:

(2)   *The fact that* there was a short circuit *caused it to be the case that*
there was a fire.

In (2) the italicized words constitute a sentential connective like
'and' or 'if . . . then . . .'. This approach no doubt receives support
from the idea that causal laws are universal conditionals, and singular
causal statements ought to be instances of them. Yet the idea is not
easily implemented. Suppose, first that a causal law is (as it is usually
said Hume taught) nothing but a universally quantified material
conditional. If (2) is an instance of such, the italicized words have
just the meaning of the material conditional, 'If there was a short
circuit, then there was a fire'. No doubt (2) entails this, but not conversely, since (2) entails something stronger, namely the conjunction
'There was a short circuit *and* there was a fire'. We might try treating (2) as the conjunction of the appropriate law and 'There was
a short circuit and there was a fire'—indeed this seems a possible interpretation of Hume's definition of cause quoted above—but then (2)
would no longer be an instance of the law. And aside from the inherent implausibility of this suggestion as giving the logical form of (2) (in
contrast, say, to giving the grounds on which it might be asserted)
there is also the oddity that an inference from the fact that there was a
short circuit and there was a fire, and the law, to (2) would turn out
to be no more than a conjoining of the premises.

Suppose, then, that there is a non-truth-functional causal connective, as has been proposed by many.[2] In line with the concept of a cause as a condition, the causal connective is conceived as a conditional, though stronger than the truth-functional conditional. Thus Arthur Pap writes, "The distinctive property of causal implication as compared with material implication is just that the falsity of the antecedent is no ground for inferring the truth of the causal implication" (212). If the connective Pap had in mind were that of (2), this remark would be strange, for it is a property of the connective in (2) that the falsity of either the "antecedent" or the "consequent" is a ground for inferring the falsity of (2). That treating the causal connective as a kind of conditional unsuits it for the work of (1) or (2) is perhaps even more evident from Burks' remark that "p is causally sufficient for q is logically equivalent to $\sim q$ is causally sufficient for $\sim p$" (369). Indeed, this shows not only that Burks' connective is not that of (2), but also that it is not the subjunctive causal connective 'would cause'. My tickling Jones would cause him to laugh, but his not laughing would not cause it to be the case that I didn't tickle him.

These considerations show that the connective of (2), and hence by hypothesis of (1), cannot, as is often assumed, be a conditional of any sort, but they do not show that (2) does not give the logical form of singular causal statements. To show this needs a stronger argument, and I think there is one, as follows.

It is obvious that the connective in (2) is not truth-functional, since (2) may change from true to false if the contained sentences are switched. Nevertheless, substitution of singular terms for others with the same extension in sentences like (1) and (2) does not touch their truth value. If Smith's death was caused by the fall from the ladder and Smith was the first man to land on the moon, then the fall from the ladder was the cause of the death of the first man to land on the moon. And if the fact that there was a fire in Jones's house caused it to be the case that the pig was roasted, and Jones's house is the oldest building on Elm street, then the fact that there was a fire in the oldest building on Elm street caused it to be the case that the pig was roasted. We must accept the principle of extensional substitution, then. Surely also we cannot change the truth value of the likes of (2) by substituting logically equivalent sentences for sentences in it. Thus (2) retains its truth if for 'there was a fire' we substitute the logically equivalent '$\hat{x} (x = x$ & there was a fire$) = \hat{x} (x = x)$'; retains it still

[2] For example by: Mackie, *op. cit.*, p. 254; Arthur Burks, "The Logic of Causal Propositions," *Mind*, LX, 239 (July 1951): 363–382; and Arthur Pap, "Disposition Concepts and Extensional Logic," in *Minnesota Studies in the Philosophy of Science*, II, ed. by H. Feigl, M. Scriven, and G. Maxwell (Minneapolis: Univ. of Minnesota Press, 1958), pp. 196–224.

if for the left side of this identity we write the coextensive singular term '$\hat{x}$ ($x = x$ & Nero fiddled)'; and still retains it if we replace '$\hat{x}$ ($x = x$ & Nero fiddled) $= \hat{x}$ ($x = x$)' by the logically equivalent 'Nero fiddled'. Since the only aspect of 'there was a fire' and 'Nero fiddled' that matters to this chain of reasoning is the fact of their material equivalence, it appears that our assumed principles have led to the conclusion that the main connective of (2) is, contrary to what we supposed, truth-functional.[3]

Having already seen that the connective of (2) cannot be truth-functional, it is tempting to try to escape the dilemma by tampering with the principles of substitution that led to it. But there is another, and, I think, wholly preferable way out: we may reject the hypothesis that (2) gives the logical form of (1), and with it the ideas that the 'caused' of (1) is a more or less concealed sentential connective, and that causes are fully expressed only by sentences.

II

Consider these six sentences:

(3) *It is a fact that* Jack fell down.
(4) Jack fell down *and* Jack broke his crown.
(5) Jack fell down *before* Jack broke his crown.
(6) Jack fell down, *which caused it to be the case that* Jack broke his crown.
(7) *Jones forgot the fact that* Jack fell down.
(8) *That* Jack fell down *explains the fact that* Jack broke his crown.

Substitution of equivalent sentences for, or substitution of coextensive singular terms or predicates in, the contained sentences, will not alter the truth value of (3) or (4): here extensionality reigns. In (7) and (8), intensionality reigns, in that similar substitution in or for the contained sentences is not guaranteed to save truth. (5) and (6) seem to fall in between; for in them substitution of coextensive singular terms preserves truth, whereas substitution of equivalent sentences does not. However this last is, as we just saw with respect to (2), and hence also (6), untenable middle ground.

Our recent argument would apply equally against taking the 'before' of (5) as the sentential connective it appears to be. And of course we don't interpret 'before' as a sentential connective, but

---

[3] This argument is closely related to one spelled out by Dagfinn Føllesdal [in "Quantification into Causal Contexts" in *Boston Studies in the Philosophy of Science*, II, ed. R. S. Cohen and M. W. Wartofsky (New York: Humanities, 1966), pp. 263–274] to show that unrestricted quantification into causal contexts leads to difficulties. His argument is in turn a direct adaptation of Quine's [*Word and Object* (Cambridge, Mass.: MIT Press, 1960), pp. 197–198] to show that (logical) modal distinctions collapse under certain natural assumptions. My argument derives directly from Frege.

696　　　　　THE JOURNAL OF PHILOSOPHY

rather as an ordinary two-place relation true of ordered pairs of times; this is made to work by introducing an extra place into the predicates ('x fell down' becoming 'x fell down at t') and an ontology of times to suit. The logical form of (5) is made perspicuous, then, by:

(5′)　There exist times t and t′ such that Jack fell down at t, Jack broke his crown at t′, and t preceded t′.

This standard way of dealing with (5) seems to me essentially correct, and I propose to apply the same strategy to (6), which then comes out:

(6′)　There exist events e and e′ such that e is a falling down of Jack, e′ is a breaking of his crown by Jack, and e caused e′.

Once events are on hand, an obvious economy suggests itself: (5) may as well be construed as about events rather than times. With this, the canonical version of (5) becomes just (6′), with 'preceded' replacing 'caused'. Indeed, it would be difficult to make sense of the claim that causes precede, or at least do not follow, their effects if (5) and (6) did not thus have parallel structures. We will still want to be able to say when an event occurred, but with events this requires an ontology of pure numbers only. So 'Jack fell down at 3 P.M.' says that there is an event e that is a falling down of Jack, and the time of e, measured in hours after noon, is three; more briefly, $(\exists e)\,(F\,(\text{Jack}, e)\,\&\,t\,(e) = 3)$.

On the present plan, (6) means some fall of Jack's caused some breaking of Jack's crown; so (6) is not false if Jack fell more than once, broke his crown more than once, or had a crown-breaking fall more than once. Nor, if such repetitions turned out to be the case, would we have grounds for saying that (6) referred to one rather than another of the fracturings. The same does not go for 'The short circuit caused the fire' or 'The flood caused the famine' or 'Jack's fall caused the breaking of Jack's crown'; here singularity is imputed. ('Jack's fall', like 'the day after tomorrow', is no less a singular term because it may refer to different entities on different occasions.) To do justice to 'Jack's fall caused the breaking of Jack's crown' what we need is something like 'The one and only falling down of Jack caused the one and only breaking of his crown by Jack'; in some symbols of the trade, '$(\imath e)\,F\,(\text{Jack}, e)$ caused $(\imath e)\,B\,(\text{Jack's crown}, e)$'.

Evidently (1) and (2) do not have the same logical form. If we think in terms of standard notations for first-order languages, it is (1) that more or less wears its form on its face; (2), like many existentially quantified sentences, does not (witness 'Somebody loves somebody').

The relation between (1) and (2) remains obvious and close: (1) entails (2), but not conversely.[4]

III

The salient point that emerges so far is that we must distinguish firmly between causes and the features we hit on for describing them, and hence between the question whether a statement says truly that one event caused another and the further question whether the events are characterized in such a way that we can deduce, or otherwise infer, from laws or other causal lore, that the relation was causal. "The cause of this match's lighting is that it was struck.—Yes, but that was only *part* of the cause; it had to be a dry match, there had to be adequate oxygen in the atmosphere, it had to be struck hard enough, etc." We ought now to appreciate that the "Yes, but" comment does not have the force we thought. It cannot be that the striking of this match was only part of the cause, for this match was in fact dry, in adequate oxygen, and the striking was hard enough. What is partial in the sentence "The cause of this match's lighting is that it was struck" is the *description* of the cause; as we add to the description of the cause, we may approach the point where we can deduce, from this description and laws, that an effect of the kind described would follow.

If Flora dried herself with a coarse towel, she dried herself with a towel. This is an inference we know how to articulate, and the articulation depends in an obvious way on reflecting in language an ontology that includes such things as towels: if there is a towel that is coarse and was used by Flora in her drying, there is a towel that was used by Flora in her drying. The usual way of doing things does not, however, give similar expression to the similar inference from 'Flora dried herself with a towel on the beach at noon' to 'Flora dried herself with a towel', or for that matter, from the last to 'Flora dried herself'. But if, as I suggest, we render 'Flora dried herself' as about an event, as well as about Flora, these inferences turn out to be quite parallel to the more familiar ones. Thus if there was an event that was a drying by Flora of herself and that was done with a towel, on the beach, at noon, then clearly there was an event that was a drying by Flora of herself—and so on.

---

[4] A familiar device I use for testing hypotheses about logical grammar is translation into standard quantificational form; since the semantics of such languages is transparent, translation into them is a way of providing a semantic theory (a theory of the logical form) for what is translated. In this employment, canonical notation is not to be conceived as an improvement on the vernacular, but as a comment on it.

For elaboration and defense of the view of events sketched in this section, see my "The Logical Form of Action Sentences" in *The Logic of Action and Preference*, ed. Nicholas Rescher (Pittsburgh: University Press, 1967).

The mode of inference carries over directly to causal statements. If it was a drying she gave herself with a coarse towel on the beach at noon that caused those awful splotches to appear on Flora's skin, then it was a drying she gave herself that did it; we may also conclude that it was something that happened on the beach, something that took place at noon, and something that was done with a towel, that caused the tragedy. These little pieces of reasoning seem all to be endorsed by intuition, and it speaks well for the analysis of causal statements in terms of events that on that analysis the arguments are transparently valid.

Mill, we are now in better position to see, was wrong in thinking we have not specified the whole cause of an event when we have not wholly specified it. And there is not, as Mill and others have maintained, anything elliptical in the claim that a certain man's death was caused by his eating a particular dish, even though death resulted only because the man had a particular bodily constitution, a particular state of present health, and so on. On the other hand Mill was, I think, quite right in saying that "there certainly is, among the circumstances that took place, some combination or other on which death is invariably consequent . . . the whole of which circumstances perhaps constituted in this particular case the conditions of the phenomenon . . ." (*A System of Logic,* book III, chap. v, § 3.) Mill's critics are no doubt justified in contending that we may correctly give the cause without saying enough about it to demonstrate that it was sufficient; but they share Mill's confusion if they think every deletion from the description of an event represents something deleted from the event described.

The relation between a singular causal statement like 'The short circuit caused the fire' and necessary and sufficient conditions seems, in brief, to be this. The fuller we make the description of the cause, the better our chances of demonstrating that it was sufficient (as described) to produce the effect, and the worse our chances of demonstrating that it was necessary; the fuller we make the description of the effect, the better our chances of demonstrating that the cause (as described) was necessary, and the worse our chances of demonstrating that it was sufficient. The symmetry of these remarks strongly suggests that in whatever sense causes are correctly said to be (described as) sufficient, they are as correctly said to be necessary. Here is an example. We may suppose there is some predicate '$P(x,y,e)$' true of Brutus, Caesar, and Brutus's stabbing of Caesar and such that any stab (by anyone of anyone) that is P is followed by the death of the stabbed. And let us suppose further that this law meets Mill's requirements of being *unconditional*—it supports counterfactuals of the form 'If Cleopatra had received a stab that was *P,* she would have died'. Now we can prove (assuming a man dies only once) that Brutus's stab was sufficient for Caesar's death. Yet it was not the cause of Caesar's death, for Caesar's death was the death of a man with more wounds than Brutus inflicted, and such a death could not have been caused by an event that was *P* ('*P*' was chosen to apply only to stabbings administered by a single hand). The trouble here is not that the description of the cause is partial, but that the event described was literally (spatio-temporally) only part of the cause.

Can we then analyze '*a* caused *b*' as meaning that *a* and *b* may be described in such a way that the existence of each could be demonstrated, in the light of causal laws, to be a necessary and sufficient condition of the existence of the other? One objection, foreshadowed in previous discussion, is that the analysandum does, but the analysans does not, entail the existence of *a* and *b*. Suppose we add, in remedy, the condition that either *a* or *b,* as described, exists. Then on the proposed analysis one can show that the causal relation holds between any two events. To apply the point in the direction of sufficiency, imagine some description '$(\imath x)\, Fx$' under which the existence of an event *a* may be shown sufficient for the existence of *b*. Then the existence of an arbitrary event *c* may equally be shown sufficient for the existence of *b*: just take as the description of *c* the following: '$(\imath y)\, (y = c\ \&\ (\exists! x)\, Fx)$'.[5] It seems unlikely that any simple and natural restrictions on the form of allowable descriptions would meet this difficulty, but since I have abjured the analysis of the causal relation, I shall not pursue the matter here.

There remains a legitimate question concerning the relation between causal laws and singular causal statements that may be raised independently. Setting aside the abbreviations successful analysis might authorize, what form are causal laws apt to have if from them, and a premise to the effect that an event of a certain (acceptable) description exists, we are to infer a singular causal statement saying that the event caused, or was caused by, another? A possibility I find attractive is that a full-fledged causal law has the form of a conjunction:

$$
\text{(L)} \left\{
\begin{array}{ll}
\text{(S)} & (e)\,(n)\,((Fe\ \&\ t(e) = n) \to \\
& \qquad (\exists! f)\,(Gf\ \&\ t(f) = n + \epsilon\ \&\ C(e,f)))\ \textit{and} \\
\text{(N)} & (e)\,(n)\,((Ge\ \&\ t(e) = n + \epsilon) \to \\
& \qquad (\exists! f)\,(Ff\ \&\ t(f) = n\ \&\ C(f,e)))
\end{array}
\right.
$$

[5] Here I am indebted to Professor Carl Hempel, and in the next sentence to John Wallace.

Here the variables '*e*' and '*f*' range over events, '*n*' ranges over numbers, *F* and *G* are properties of events, '*C*(*e*, *f*)' is read '*e* causes *f*', and '*t*' is a function that assigns a number to an event to mark the time the event occurs. Now, given the premise:

(P) $(\exists !e)(Fe \,\&\, t(e) = 3)$

(C) $(\imath e)(Fe \,\&\, t(e) = 3)$ caused $(\imath e)(Ge \,\&\, t(e) = 3 + \epsilon)$

It is worth remarking that part (N) of (L) is as necessary to the proof of (C) from (P) as it is to the proof of (C) from the premise '$(\exists !e)(Ge \,\&\, t(e) = 3 + \epsilon))$'. This is perhaps more reason for holding that causes are, in the sense discussed above, necessary as well as sufficient conditions.

Explaining "why an event occurred," on this account of laws, may take an instructively large number of forms, even if we limit explanation to the resources of deduction. Suppose, for example, we want to explain the fact that there was a fire in the house at 3:01 P.M. Armed with appropriate premises in the form of (P) and (L), we may deduce: that there was a fire in the house at 3:01 P.M.; that it was caused by a short circuit at 3:00 P.M.; that there was only one fire in the house at 3:01 P.M.; that this fire was caused by the one and only short circuit that occurred at 3:00 P.M. Some of these explanations fall short of using all that is given by the premises; and this is lucky, since we often know less. Given only (S) and (P), for example, we cannot prove there was only one fire in the house at 3:01 P.M., though we can prove there was exactly one fire in the house at 3:01 P.M. that was caused by the short circuit. An interesting case is where we know a law in the form of (N), but not the corresponding (S). Then we may show that, given that an event of a particular sort occurred, there must have been a cause answering to a certain description, but, given the same description of the cause, we could not have predicted the effect. An example might be where the effect is getting pregnant.

If we explain why it is that a particular event occurred by deducing a statement that there is such an event (under a particular description) from a premise known to be true, then a simple way of explaining an event, for example the fire in the house at 3:01 P.M., consists in producing a statement of the form of (C); and this explanation makes no use of laws. The explanation will be greatly enhanced by whatever we can say in favor of the truth of (C); needless to say, producing the likes of (L) and (P), if they are known true, clinches the matter. In most cases, however, the request for explanation will describe the event in terms that fall under no full-fledged law. The device to which we will then resort, if we can, is apt to be redescription of the event. For we can explain the occurrence of any event a if we know (L), (P), and the further fact that $a = (\imath e) (Ge \ \& \ t(e) = 3 + \epsilon)$. Analogous remarks apply to the redescription of the cause, and to cases where all we want, or can, explain is the fact that there was *an* event of a certain sort.

The great majority of singular causal statements are not backed, we may be sure, by laws in the way (C) is backed by (L). The relation in general is rather this: if 'a caused b' is true, then there are descriptions of a and b such that the result of substituting them for 'a' and 'b' in 'a caused b' is entailed by true premises of the form of (L) and (P); and the converse holds if suitable restrictions are put on the descriptions.[6] If this is correct, it does not follow that we must be able to dredge up a law if we know a singular causal statement to be true; all that follows is that we know there must be a covering law. And very often, I think, our justification for accepting a singular causal statement is that we have reason to believe an appropriate causal law exists, though we do not know what it is. Generalizations like 'If you strike a well-made match hard enough against a properly prepared surface, then, other conditions being favorable, it will light' owe their importance not to the fact that we can hope eventually to render them untendentious and exceptionless, but rather to the fact that they summarize much of our evidence for believing that full-fledged causal laws exist covering events we wish to explain.[7]

If the story I have told is true, it is possible to reconcile, within limits, two accounts thought by their champions to be opposed. One account agrees with Hume and Mill to this extent: it says that a singular causal statement 'a caused b' entails that there is a law to the effect that "all the objects similar to a are followed by objects similar to b" and that we have reason to believe the singular statement only in so far as we have reason to believe there is such a law. The second

---

[6] Clearly this account cannot be taken as a definition of the causal relation. Not only is there the inherently vague quantification over expressions (of what language?), but there is also the problem of spelling out the "suitable restrictions."

[7] The thought in these paragraphs, like much more that appears here, was first adumbrated in my "Actions, Reasons, and Causes," this JOURNAL, LX, 23 (Nov. 7, 1963): 685–700, especially pp. 696–699; reprinted in *Free Will and Determinism*, ed. Bernard Berofsky (New York: Harper & Row, 1966). This conception of causality was subsequently discussed and, with various modifications, employed by Samuel Gorovitz, "Causal Judgments and Causal Explanations," this JOURNAL, LXII, 23 (Dec. 2, 1965): 695–711, and by Bernard Berofsky, "Causality and General Laws," this JOURNAL, LXIII, 6 (Mar. 17, 1966): 148–157.

account (persuasively argued by C. J. Ducasse [8]) maintains that singular causal statements entail no law and that we can know them to be true without knowing any relevant law. Both of these accounts are entailed, I think, by the account I have given, and they are consistent (I therefore hope) with each other. The reconciliation depends, of course, on the distinction between knowing there is a law "covering" two events and knowing what the law is: in my view, Ducasse is right that singular causal statements entail no law; Hume is right that they entail there is a law.

IV

Much of what philosophers have said of causes and causal relations is intelligible only on the assumption (often enough explicit) that causes are individual events, and causal relations hold between events. Yet, through failure to connect this basic *aperçu* with the grammar of singular causal judgments, these same philosophers have found themselves pressed, especially when trying to put causal statements into quantificational form, into trying to express the relation of cause to effect by a sentential connective. Hence the popularity of the utterly misleading question: can causal relations be expressed by the purely extensional material conditional, or is some stronger (non-Humean) connection involved? The question is misleading because it confuses two separate matters: the logical form of causal statements and the analysis of causality. So far as form is concerned, the issue of nonextensionality does not arise, since the relation of causality between events can be expressed (no matter how "strong" or "weak" it is) by an ordinary two-place predicate in an ordinary, extensional first-order language. These plain resources will perhaps be outrun by an adequate account of the form of causal laws, subjunctives, and counterfactual conditionals, to which most attempts to analyze the causal relation turn. But this is, I have urged, another question.

   This is not to say there are no causal idioms that directly raise the issue of apparently non-truth-functional connectives. On the contrary, a host of statement forms, many of them strikingly similar, at least at first view, to those we have considered, challenge the account just given. Here are samples: 'The failure of the sprinkling system caused the fire', 'The slowness with which controls were applied caused the rapidity with which the inflation developed', 'The col-

---

[8] See his "Critique of Hume's Conception of Causality," this JOURNAL, LXIII, 6 (Mar. 17, 1966): 141–148; *Causation and the Types of Necessity* (Seattle: University of Washington Press, 1924); *Nature, Mind, and Death* (La Salle, Ill.: Open Court, 1951), part II. I have omitted from my "second account" much that Ducasse says that is not consistent with Hume.

lapse was caused, not by the fact that the bolt gave way, but by the fact that it gave way so suddenly and unexpectedly', 'The fact that the dam did not hold caused the flood'. Some of these sentences may yield to the methods I have prescribed, especially if failures are counted among events, but others remain recalcitrant. What we must say in such cases is that in addition to, or in place of, giving what Mill calls the "producing cause," such sentences tell, or suggest, a causal story. They are, in other words, rudimentary causal explanations. Explanations typically relate statements, not events. I suggest therefore that the 'caused' of the sample sentences in this paragraph is not the 'caused' of straightforward singular causal statements, but is best expressed by the words 'causally explains'.[9]

A final remark. It is often said that events can be explained and predicted only in so far as they have repeatable characteristics, but not in so far as they are particulars. No doubt there is a clear and trivial sense in which this is true, but we ought not to lose sight of the less obvious point that there is an important difference between explaining the fact that there was *an* explosion in the broom closet and explaining the occurrence of *the* explosion in the broom closet. Explanation of the second sort touches the particular event as closely as language can ever touch any particular. Of course this claim is persuasive only if there are such things as events to which singular terms, especially definite descriptions, may refer. But the assumption, ontological and metaphysical, that there are events, is one without which we cannot make sense of much of our most common talk; or so, at any rate, I have been arguing. I do not know any better, or further, way of showing what there is.

DONALD DAVIDSON

Princeton University

[9] Zeno Vendler has ingeniously marshalled the linguistic evidence for a deep distinction, in our use of 'cause', 'effect', and related words, between occurrences of verb-nominalizations that are fact-like or propositional, and occurrences that are event-like. [See Zeno Vendler, "Effects, Results and Consequences," in *Analytic Philosophy*, ed. R. J. Butler (New York: Barnes & Noble, 1962), pp. 1–15.] Vendler concludes that the 'caused' of 'John's action caused the disturbance' is always flanked by expressions used in the propositional or fact-like sense, whereas 'was an effect of' or 'was due to' in 'The shaking of the earth was an effect of (was due to) the explosion' is flanked by expressions in the event-like sense. My distinction between essentially sentential expressions and the expressions that refer to events is much the same as Vendler's and owes much to him, though I have used more traditional semantic tools and have interpreted the evidence differently.

My suggestion that 'caused' is sometimes a relation, sometimes a connective, with corresponding changes in the interpretation of the expressions flanking it, has much in common with the thesis of J. M. Shorter's "Causality, and a Method of Analysis," in *Analytic Philosophy*, II, 1965, pp. 145–157.

Annotated Bibliography on Causation

I. Historical Material

Though for the most part only his discussion of efficient causation is relevant to the contemporary debate, Aristotle's treatment of causation is vital background reading. See his *Metaphysics* A.3.Δ.2; *Physics* II.3.7; and *Posterior Analytics* II.11. Among modern authors writing on causation, Hume is the most important. In addition to the selection from *An Inquiry Concerning Human Understanding* reprinted in the text, also see sections 4–6 of that work and his *Treatise of Human Nature*, book I, part 3. See section III of this bibliography for recent discussion of Hume's views. Other modern authors to consult for background material are John Stuart Mill, *A System of Logic*, book 3, chap. 4–6, 10, 15; Thomas Reid, *Essays on the Active Powers of the Human Mind*, esp. essays 1 and 4; Immanuel Kant, *Critique of Pure Reason*, B232–256, B560–576, and *Prolegemena to Any Future Metaphysics*, pp. 14–20, 28.

II. Contemporary Material

(Prepared by Doug Johnston)

This section includes major and representative works on laws and counterfactuals and an extensive listing of contemporary material specifically on causation. There is some selectivity, and it favors recent work and analytic methodology (though an effort was made to represent all perspectives) and tends to exclude material on historical figures, abstracts of papers, non-English language contributions, book reviews, nonphilosophical literature, and discussions of causation which are peripheral, secondary, or redundant. Pieces reprinted in the text are not included in this bibliography. The following abbreviations for journals are used:

A	*Analysis*
AJP	*Australasian Journal of Philosophy*
APQ	*American Philosophical Quarterly*
BJPS	*British Journal for the Philosophy of Science*
M	*Mind*
N	*Nous*
JP	*Journal of Philosophy*
P	*Philosophy*
PAS	*Proceedings of the Aristotelian Society*
PASS	*Proceedings of the Aristotelian Society, Supplementary Volume*
PPR	*Philosophy and Phenomenological Research*
PQ	*Philosophical Quarterly*
PR	*Philosophical Review*
PS	*Philosophical Studies*
RM	*Review of Metaphysics*
S	*Synthese*
T	*Theoria*

Abrahams, Gerald. "The verb 'to cause.'" *P* 24 (1949) 248–252. Causal propositions not hypotheticals.

Achinstein, Peter. *Law and Explanation.* Oxford: Clarendon Press, 1971, chap. 3. Brief critique of Goodman and Reichenbach and development of five "features" of laws.

Alexander, H. Gavin. "General statements as rules of inference?" In H. Feigl, M. Scriven, and G. Maxwell (eds.), *Minnesota Studies in the Philosophy of Science,* vol. 1. Minneapolis: University of Minnesota Press, 1958, pp. 309–329. Includes critique of Toulmin, 1953, and Sellars, 1953, on laws.

Alexander, Peter. "Are causal laws purely general?" *PASS* 44 (1970) 15–36. The notion of causation originates from our own experience of acting. Anti-regularity theory.

Anderson, John. "The problem of causality." *AJP* 16 (1938) 127–142. On plurality of causes. The notion of a "causal field" is introduced. Reprinted in his *Studies in Empirical Philosophy.*

Angell, R. B. "A propositional logic with subjunctive conditionals." *Journal of Symbolic Logic* 27 (1962) 327–343. "→" is primitive.

Anscombe, G. E. M. "Causality and extensionality." *JP* 66 (1969) 152–159. On causal contexts. See Travis, 1973, for discussion.

———. *Causality and Determination.* London: Cambridge University Press, 1971. The concept of causation is one of neither necessity nor universality.

Aronson, Jerrold. "Explanations without laws." *JP* 66 (1969) 541–557. "Transitive verb model" of explanation by causal statements. Against regularity view.

———. "On the grammar of 'cause.'" *S* 22 (1971) 414–430. A discussion of Gasking's "Causation and recipes" and causation in science. Transitive verbs. In causation a "quantity" is transferred and relevant objects are contiguous.

———. "The legacy of Hume's analysis of causation." *Studies in History and Philosophy of Science* 2 (1971–72) 135–156. Hume's analysis rests on the denial of the numerical identity of quantities (for example, energy, momentum) throughout various physical processes. Such identity is required by principles of conservation in mechanics and provides the basis for an analysis of causation. There is no reason to accept the Humean ontology of time-slices.

Ayer, A. J. *The Problem of Knowledge.* Baltimore: Penguin Books, 1956, pp. 170–175. An explanation of the convention that an effect cannot precede its cause.

———. "What is a law of nature?" *Revue Internationale de Philosophie* 10 (1956) 144–165. A defense of the regularity view of laws in terms of belief.

Barker, John. "Brand and Swain on causation." *S* 26 (1974) 396–400. A critique of Brand and Swain's "On the analysis of causation" (in text).

Beardsley, Elizabeth Lane. "Non-accidental and counterfactual sentences." *JP* 46 (1949) 573–591. An analysis of counterfactuals in terms of "restricted" sentences.

Beardsley, Monroe C. "A dilemma for Hume." *PR* 52 (1943) 28–46. As a relation between events, causation is logical connection.

Beauchamp, Tom L. "Hume on causal contiguity and causal succession." *Dialogue* 13 (1974) 271–282.

Bennett, Jonathan. "Counterfactuals and possible worlds." *Canadian Journal of Philosophy* 4 (1974–75) 381–402. A discussion of Lewis, 1973.

Berofsky, Bernard. "Causality and general laws." *JP* 63 (1966) 148–157. Pro-

regularity theory includes necessary conditions for "*c* is the cause of *e*" in terms of laws. Includes critique of Ducasse, a reply to which is Ducasse, 1966b.

———. "The regularity theory." *N* 2 (1968) 315–340. A defense as it applies to laws.

———. *Determinism.* Princeton: Princeton University Press, 1971, chaps. 4–7. An extended discussion and defense of the regularity view.

Black, Max. "Why cannot an effect precede its cause?" *A* 16 (1956) 49–58. Critique of Flew, 1954. Flew replies at 104–110.

———. "Making something happen." In Sidney Hook (ed.), *Determinism and Freedom.* New York: New York University Press, 1958, pp. 15–30. Anti-regularity theory and apparently antireductive.

Blanshard, Brand. *The Nature of Thought.* 2 vols. London: G. Allen & Unwin, Ltd., 1939, vol. 2, chap. 32. An earlier development of his entailment view. For a critique, see Nagel, 1947, and for a reply, see Knox, 1966–67.

———. "Internal relations and their importance in philosophy." *RM* 21 (1967–68) 227–236. His most recent defense of the entailment view with a critique of the regularity view. A critique by B. Aune is at 237–243, followed by a reply at 262–272.

Braithwaite, R. B. "The idea of necessary connexion." *M* 36 (1927) 467–477; 37 (1928) 62–72. An extended development and defense of the regularity view.

———. *Scientific Explanation.* Cambridge: Cambridge University Press, 1953, chap. 9. A major formulation and defense of the regularity view of laws; in terms of deduction from a theoretical system.

Brand, Myles. "On Philosophical Definitions." *PPR* forthcoming. Further explication of the systemic-extrasystemic distinction, and a defense of "causes" as being purely systemically definable.

Braybrooke, David. "Vincula vindicata." *M* 66 (1957) 222–227. A critique of Hanson, 1955. Hanson replies in his *Patterns of Discovery.* For Braybrooke's rejoinder, see below.

———, and Rosenberg, Alexander. "Vincula Revindicata." In Tom L. Beauchamp (ed.), *Philosophical Problems of Causation.* Belmont, Calif.: Dickenson Publishing Co., 1974, pp. 217–222. A rejoinder to Hanson's reply in his *Patterns of Discovery.*

Broad, C. D. "The principles of demonstrative induction." *M* 39 (1930) 302–317, 426–439. A working out of a conditions analysis.

———. *Examination of McTaggart's Philosophy.* 2 vols. Cambridge: Cambridge University Press, 1933, vol. 1, pp. 212–221, 228, 245. Antiregularity theory.

———. "Mechanical and teleological causation." *PASS* 14 (1935) 83–112. An extended and careful discussion of both the regularity view and the entailment view.

Brown, Robert, and Watling, John. "Counterfactual conditionals." *M* 61 (1952) 222–233. An antireductive view.

Bunge, Mario. *Causality.* Cambridge, Mass.: Harvard University Press, 1959, chaps. 2–7, 9, 12. An important and wide-ranging work, generally critical of the regularity view and the entailment view, holding causation as "necessary production." For his defense against criticisms, see *Philosophy of Science,* 29 (1962) 306–317.

————. "Causality, chance, and law." *American Scientist* 49 (1961) 432–448. Includes discussion of causal laws.

Burkill, Alec. "Modes of causality." *P* 16 (1941) 185–197. Critique of the ontological atomism of Hume and defense of cause and effect as distinguishable but not distinct phases in a continuum.

Burks, Arthur W. *Cause, Chance, Reason: An Inquiry into the Nature of Scientific Evidence.* Chicago: University of Chicago Press, 1975, chaps. 6, 7. Based upon his "The logic of causal propositions" (text), these chapters include a development of a logic of causal statements which is then used as a formal model of causal laws, causal subjunctive conditionals, and singular causal statements.

Capek, Milic. "The doctrine of necessity re-examined." *RM* 5 (1951–52) 11–54. Causal connection not necessary, that is, deductive, but contingent and temporal.

————. "Toward a widening of the notion of causality." *Diogenes,* no. 28 (1959) 63–90. Rejects necessity for temporal succession.

Chisholm, Roderick M. "The contrary-to-fact conditional." *M* 55 (1946) 289–307. An important reductive view.

————. "Query on substitutivity." In Robert S. Cohen and Marx W. Wartofsky (eds.), *Boston Studies in the Philosophy of Science,* vol. 2. N.Y.: Humanities Press, 1965, pp. 275–278. Causal contexts are referentially opaque. See Davis, 1974, for critique.

————, and Taylor, Richard. "Making things to have happened." *A* 20 (1960) 73–78. Causation as sufficiency is compatible with backward causation. See Dray, 1959–60, for critique.

Clark, Romane. "On what is naturally necessary." *JP* 62 (1965) 613–625. Not explicable by inference rules or modal logic but by "relative necessity." See von Wright, 1957. Defense of the modal approach by R. C. Buck at 625–629.

Clarke, W. Norris. "Causality and time." In Irwin C. Lieb (ed.), *Experience, Existence, and the Good.* Carbondale: Southern Illinois University Press, 1961, pp. 143–157. Temporal sequence incompatible with causal efficacy. Cause and effect simultaneous.

Cohen, Barry, and Humber, James. "Sterling Lamprecht's critique of causality." *Transactions of the Charles S. Pierce Society* 9 (1973) 41–54. Explication and defense of Lamprecht's systemic account; against Hume by advocating a view similar to those of Harré, 1970, and Madden, 1969.

Cohen, Morris R. "Causation and its application to history." *Journal of the History of Ideas* 3 (1942) 12–29. As a kind of necessary and sufficient conditions.

Collier, Kenneth W. "Physical modalities and the system E." *Notre Dame Journal of Formal Logic* 14 (1973) 185–194.

Collingwood, R. G. "On the so-called idea of causation." *PAS* 38 (1937–38) 85–112. Similar to his treatment in *An Essay on Metaphysics.*

Collins, Arthur. "Explanation and causality." *M* 75 (1966) 482–500, esp. 491–500. Knowing a singular causal statement does not require knowing a law.

Cummins, Robert, and Gottlieb, Dale. "On an argument for truth-functionality." *APQ* 9 (1972) 265–269. On causal contexts.

Davis, Lawrence. "Extensionality and singular causal sentences." *PS* 25 (1974) 69–72. A criticism of an argument of Chisholm's (1965).

Demos, Raphael. "Nature, mind, and death." *RM* 6 (1952–53) 563–582. Critique of Ducasse's view. Reply by Ducasse in *RM* 7 (1953–54) 290–298.

Dennes, W. R. "Causation as continuity and production." In J. Loewenberg, *et al.* (eds.), *University of California Publications in Philosophy* 15 (1932) 147–176. An extended discussion of the regularity view.

Dewey, John. *Logic*. New York: Henry Holt & Co., 1938, chap. 22. Cause to effect as means to end. The activity theory defended.

Dietl, Paul J. "Abnormalism." *T* 36 (1970) 93–99. Critique of Hart and Honore, 1959, and White, 1965, and their "abnormalism" account of "the cause"; a positive analysis is proffered.

Diggs, B. J. "Counterfactual conditionals." *M* 61 (1952) 513–527. Analysis in terms of laws.

Domotor, Zoltan. "Causal models and space-time geometries." *S* 24 (1972) 5–57. On the possibility of a set-theoretical model.

Downing, P. B. "Subjunctive conditionals, time order, and causation." *PAS* 59 (1958–59) 125–140. Subjunctive conditionals can provide temporal ordering of cause and effect.

————. "Are causal laws purely general?" *PASS* 44 (1970) 37–49. On the uniformity of causation.

Dray, William. *Laws and Explanation in History*. London: Oxford University Press, 1957, chap. 4. Causation as manipulability, and discussion of "the cause."

————. "Taylor and Chisholm on making things to have happened." *A* 20 (1959–60) 79–82.

————. "Some causal accounts of the American Civil War." *Daedalus* 91 (1962) 578–592. On the relativity of "the cause" by the use of historical accounts.

————. *Philosophy of History*. Englewood Cliffs, N.J.: Prentice-Hall, Inc., 1964, chap. 4. *The* cause and related topics.

————. "On importance in history." In H. E. Kiefer and M. K. Munitz (eds.), *Mind, Science and History*. Albany: State University of New York Press, 1970, pp. 251–269. Involves, secondarily, the idea of a causal series and causal consequences. For critique, see Vollrath, 1973.

Dretske, Frederick I., and Snyder, Aaron. "Causal irregularity." *Philosophy of Science* 39 (1972) 69–71. An argument against uniformity. A critique by T. Beauchamp at 40 (1973) 285–287 and a reply at 288–291.

Ducasse, C. J. *Causation and the Types of Necessity*. University of Washington Publications in the Social Sciences. Vol. 1, 1924, pp. 70–200. An important and extended work, containing a unique analysis of causation involving temporal and spatial relations, which view Ducasse has consistently defended. Also a critique of the regularity view and a Kantian view and argument against temporal priority of a cause. See Santoni, 1966, and Madden and Humber, 1971.

————. "On the nature and the observability of the causal relation." *JP* 23 (1926) 57–68. Similar to parts of Ducasse, 1924. See Mackie, 1974.

————. *Nature, Mind, and Death*. La Salle, Ill.: Open Court Publishing Co., 1951, chaps. 7–10. A substantial critique of the regularity view. See Demos, 1952–53; Gale, 1961–62; Pap, 1958; and Humber, 1971. (Partially reprinted in text.)

———. "Causation: perceivable? or only inferred?" *PPR* 26 (1965–66) 173–179. Perceivable. A critique by N. L. Rankin in *PPR* 28 (1967–68) and a reply by Ducasse at 271–273.

———. " 'Cause' and 'condition.' " *JP* 63 (1966) 238–241. Defense against Gorovitz, 1965.

———. "Concerning Berofsky's 'Causality and general laws.' " *JP* 63 (1966) 524–527. Defense against Berofsky, 1966.

———. "Critique of Hume's conception of causality." *JP* 63 (1966) 141–148.

Dummett, A. E. "Can an effect precede its cause?" *PASS* 28 (1954) 27–44. Backward causation allowed by certain kinds and accounts of causation. An article responsible for much of the contemporary discussion of the issue. See Flew, 1954; Black, 1956; and Pears, 1956–57.

Dummett, Michael. "Bringing about the past." *PR* 73 (1964) 338–359. The direction of causation has a basis in the world. For critique, see Swinburne, 1966, and Gorovitz, 1964.

Eames, Elizabeth R. "Cause: necessary and sufficient?" *Proceedings of the 14th International Congress of Philosophy,* 1968, vol. 3, pp. 177–183. A critique.

Ewing, A. C. "A defense of causality." *PAS* 33 (1932–33) 95–128. Causal connection is something "like" a logical relation.

———. "Mechanical and teleological causation." *PASS* 14 (1935) 66–82. Entailment but not *a priori.*

———. "Cause and reason." *IXe Congres International de Philosophie,* 1937, vol. 7, pp. 78–83. Defense of causal necessity as synthetic logical necessity.

———. *The Fundamental Questions of Philosophy.* New York: The Macmillan Co., 1951, chap. 8. Antiregularity and antiactivity theories and developed defense of causal necessity as "analogous" to entailment.

———. *Idealism,* 3d ed. London: Methuen & Co., Ltd., 1933, 1961, chap. 4. Includes a substantial critique of the regularity view.

Fain, Haskell. "Some problems of causal explanation." *M* 72 (1963) 519–532. A modification of the regularity view.

———. "Hart and Honore on causation in the law." *Inquiry* 9 (1966) 322–328. A critique.

Fales, Walter. "Causes and effects." *Philosophy of Science* 20 (1953) 67–74. Distinction between transeunt and immanent causation.

Feigl, Herbert. "Notes on causality." In Herbert Feigl and May Brodbeck (eds.), *Readings in the Philosophy of Science.* New York: Appleton-Century-Crofts, Inc., 1953, pp. 408–418. Wide-ranging (though often brief) characterization of the view of causation as "predictability according to a law."

Finch, Henry Albert. "An explication of counterfactuals by probability theory." *PPR* 18 (1957–58) 368–378.

Fisk, Milton. "Causation and action." *RM* 19 (1965–66) 235–247. Some instances of causation are not sequences but involve objects and agents.

———. "Are there necessary connections in nature?" *Philosophy of Science* 37 (1970) 385–404.

———. *Nature and Necessity.* Bloomington: Indiana University Press, 1973. Generally a defense of the "objective basis of physical necessity" but also includes a definition of causation in terms of "action."

Flew, Antony. "Can an effect precede its cause?" *PASS* 28 (1954) 45–62. No, since causes are "levers." Critique of Dummett, 1954. Critique by Black, 1956, which is followed by Flew's reply. Also critique by Pears, 1956–57.

———. "Causal disorder again." *A* 17 (1956–57) 81–86. Comment on Scriven, 1956, and defense of original view against Pears, 1956–57.

Føllesdal, Dagfinn. "Quantification into causal contexts." In Robert S. Cohen and Marx W. Wartofsky (eds.), *Boston Studies in the Philosophy of Science,* vol. 2. New York: Humanities Press, 1965, pp. 263–274. Critique of Burk's "The logic of causal propositions" (in text).

Foot, Philippa. "Hart and Honore: causation in the law." *PR* 72 (1963) 505–515. A defense of their abnormality view.

Foster, J. A. "Psychophysical causal relations." *APQ* 5 (1968) 64–70. Includes a working out of the relation of singular causal statements to laws.

Frey, R. G. "On causal consequences." *Canadian Journal of Philosophy* 4 (1974–75) 365–379. In *The Forms and Limits of Utilitarianism* David Lyons holds a view he calls "linearity": that the effects of a series are identical with the sum of the effects of each member of the series. Frey critiques this view by maintaining that if *c* is a consequence of *A,* then *A* is a necessary condition of *c.*

Gale, Richard M. "Professor Ducasse on determinism." *PPR* 22 (1961–62) 92–96. Critique of Ducasse's 1951 claim that his view entails uniformity. Ducasse's reply at 97–101.

———. "Why a cause cannot be later than its effect." *RM* 19 (1965–66) 209–234. Partly because causation involves manipulability.

Gallie, W. B. "An interpretation of causal law." *M* 48 (1939) 409–426. A critique and modification of Ramsey's 1931 view of laws.

Gardiner, Patrick. *The Nature of Historical Explanation.* London: Oxford University Press, 1952, pp. 99–112. A relativistic view of "the cause."

Good, I. J. "A theory of causality." *BJPS* 9 (1959) 307–310. Definition in terms of probability.

———. "A causal calculus." *BJPS* 11 (1961) 305–318; 12 (1961) 43–51. The primitive notion seems to be "physical probability."

Goodman, Nelson. *Fact, Fiction, and Forecast,* 2d ed. Indianapolis: Bobbs-Merrill Co., Inc., 1965. Analysis of laws in terms of confirmation. An important and influential work. (Chap. 1, "The problem of counterfactual conditionals," reprinted in text.) For an "important improvement" in the theory of projectability, see *JP* 67 (1970) 605–608.

Gorovitz, Samuel. "Leaving the past alone." *PR* 73 (1964) 360–371. Critique of Dummett, 1964.

———. "Causal judgments and causal explanations." *JP* 62 (1965) 695–711. A careful definition of "the cause." See Ducasse, 1966a.

———. "Aspects of the pragmatics of explanation." *N* 3 (1969) 61–72. Includes a development of Gorovitz, 1965.

Götlind, Erik. *Bertrand Russell's Theories of Causation.* Uppsala: Almquist and Wiksells, 1952. A work-by-work exposition.

Gottlieb, Dale. See Cummins and Gottlieb, 1972.

Greenberg, Leonard. "Necessity in Hume's causal theory." *RM* 8 (1954–55) 612–613. On uniformity and necessity.

Grene, Marjorie. "Causes." *P* 38 (1963) 149–159. Antireductive.

Gruner, Rolf. "Plurality of causes." *P* 42 (1967) 367–374.

Haack, R. J. "Recipes and causes." *M* 76 (1967) 98–102. Critique of Gasking's "Causation and recipes" (in text).

Hanson, N. R. "Causal chains." *M* 64 (1955) 479–487. Causes are "theory-laden." For critique, see Braybrooke, 1957. Hanson replies in his *Patterns of Discovery,* to which Braybrooke rejoins (1974).

Hare, P. H., and Madden, Edward H. "The powers that be." *Dialogue* 10 (1971) 12–31. Cf. Madden, 1969. A critique by E. J. Furlong at 768–769, to which there is a reply by R. Harré and G. J. Moran at 12 (1973) 319–321.

———, and ———. *Causing, Perceiving and Believing: An Examination of the Philosophy of C. J. Ducasse.* Boston: D. Reidel, 1975. (Unseen by the compiler.)

Harré, R. "Concepts and criteria." *M* 73 (1964) 353–363. Includes a novel view of causal necessity and a critique of both the regularity view and necessary and sufficient conditions.

———. *Principles of Scientific Thinking.* Chicago: University of Chicago Press, 1970, esp. pp. 102–114, 228–230. Critical of Humean regularity; Harré introduces the notions of causal powers and generative or productive mechanisms.

———, and Madden, Edward H. "In defence of natural agents." *PQ* 23 (1973) 117–132. A defense and explication of causation as the operation of natural agents with causal powers against Humean objections. Arguments against Hume's atomistic ontology of causes.

———, and ———. *Causal Powers.* Totowa, N.J.: Rowman and Littlefield, 1975. (Unseen by the compiler.)

Hart, H. L. A., and Honore, A. M. *Causation in the Law.* Oxford: Clarendon Press, 1959. A substantial and important work dealing largely with the notions of *the* cause and related legal concepts such as "proximate cause" and "contributory cause." See Dietl, 1970; Foot, 1963; Fain, 1966; and Mackie, 1974.

Hartnack, Justus. "Some remarks on causality." *JP* 50 (1953) 466–471. On the unity of cause and effect; the entailment theory.

Hartshorne, Charles. "Causal necessities: an alternative to Hume." *PR* 63 (1954) 479–499. Includes the claim that an effect "must be able to integrate within its unity reference to (the cause) as its predecessor." See his later development below.

———. "Creativity and the deductive logic of causality." *RM* 27 (1973–74) 62–74.

Hedman, Carl G. "On when there must be a time-difference between cause and effect." *Philosophy of Science* 39 (1972) 507–511. It depends on a criterion of event individuation.

Hempel, Carl G., and Oppenheim, Paul. "Studies in the logic of explanation." *Philosophy of Science* 15 (1948) 135–175. Includes a statement of a major view of laws, the deductive-nomological model.

Henderson, G. P. "Causal implication." *M* 63 (1954) 504–518. A critique of Burks's "The logic of causal prepositions," but critical sympathy for modal systems generally.

Hilpinen, Risto. "On the conditions of causation." *PS* 24 (1973) 386–389. Critique of Brand and Swain's "On the analysis of causation." See Brand and Swain's reply, *PS* 25 (1974) 357–364. A rejoinder by Hilpinen in *PS* 26 (1974) 447–448.

Hobart, R. E. (apparently pseudonym of D. S. Miller). "Hume without skepticism." *M* 39 (1930) 273–301, 409–425. An extended defense of the regularity view as preserving necessity in causation.

Hofstadter, Albert. "Universality, explanation, and scientific law." *JP* 50 (1953)

101–115. Critique of Ushenko, 1953. Causal connection satisfied by universality or generality.

Honore, A. M. See Hart and Honore, 1959.

Hospers, John. *An Introduction to Philosophical Analysis,* 2d ed. Englewood Cliffs, N.J.: Prentice-Hall, Inc., 1967, pp. 279–305. Introductory survey, but good summaries and criticisms.

Houlgate, Laurence. "Causation, recipes and theory." *T* 29 (1963) 265–276. An attempt to leave a place for causation as both law and manipulability.

Humber, James M. "A note on Ducasse's notions of cause and etiological necessity." *Transactions of the Charles S. Pierce Society* 7 (1971) 237–242. Most references to 1951.

———. See Cohen and Humber, 1973.

———, and Madden, Edward. "Natural necessity." *New Scholasticism* 47 (1973) 214–227. How Locke anticipated their view of causation in terms of powers of natural agents.

Jack, Henry. "Robinson on partial entailment and causality." *M* 75 (1966) 135–137. Critique of Robinson, 1961.

Johnston, P. L. H. "A hypothesis concerning singular causal laws." *Philosophical Linguistics,* no. 4 (1972) 60–69. Analysis of laws in terms of counterpart theory.

Jonas, Hans. "Causality and perception." *JP* 47 (1950) 319–324. Idea of causality derived from the experience of bodily exertion. Kantian.

Karlin, Eli. "The nature of causation." *RM* 2 (1948–49) 53–98. "A causal act is the expression of an effort by an actuality, prompted by other actualities which it needs and which are abstractly future to it, to satisfy its needs."

Kelsen, Hans. "Causality and retribution." *Philosophy of Science* 8 (1941) 533–556. The original notion of causation, with its asymmetry and necessity, derives from the notion of divine or cosmic retribution but has now been replaced by the notion of probability.

Kim, Jaegwon. "Causes and events: Mackie on causation." *JP* 68 (1971) 426–441. Includes a discussion of the ontology of necessary and sufficient conditions. For reply see Mackie, 1974.

———. "Causation, nomic subsumption, and the concept of event." *JP* 70 (1973) 217–236. A working out of the ontology required by the regularity theory and contiguity. See Rosenberg, 1974, for critique.

Kneale, William. *Probability and Induction.* Oxford: Clarendon Press, 1949, esp. pp. 70–89. Laws as "principles of necessitation." Against the regularity view. For discussion, see Popper, 1959.

———. "Universality and Necessity." *BJPS* 12 (1961) 89–102. Formal logic is pure theory of necessitation. For discussion, see 1968 edition of Popper, 1959. For defense see Molnar, 1974.

Knox, John, Jr. "Blanshard on causation and necessity." *RM* 20 (1966–67) 518–532. A defense of Blanshard against Nagel, 1947.

Lamprecht, Sterling P. "Causality." In *Essays in Honor of John Dewey.* New York: Holt, Rinehart & Winston, Inc., 1929, pp. 191–205. Explicitly anti-reductive. Causation as action of a natural agent and critique of the regularity view. These two themes are emphasized in two essays printed along with this essay in his *Metaphysics of Naturalism.* (New York: Appleton-Century-Crofts, 1967). See also Cohen and Humber, 1973.

Lenzen, Victor F. "Physical causality." In J. Loewenberg, *et al.* (eds.), *Univer-*

sity of California Publications in Philosophy 15 (1932) 3–37. Explication of the notion of cause as function.

Lewis, David. "Completeness and decidability of three logics of counterfactual conditionals." *T* 37 (1971) 74–85.

———. *Counterfactuals.* Cambridge: Harvard University Press, 1973. An analysis of counterfactuals in terms of possible world semantics. Interesting and important. For discussion, see Bennett, 1974–75.

———. "Causation." *JP* 70 (1973) 556–567. An analysis in terms of counterfactuals. Followed by abstracts of critiques by B. Berofsky and J. Kim. Scriven, 1975, also has a criticism.

Loeb, Louis E. "Causal theories and causal overdetermination." *JP* 71 (1974) 525–544. On the need to distinguish between a cause and an "overdeterminant" and how three theories of causation — in terms of (i) conditions, (ii) laws, and (iii) counterfactuals — can draw this distinction.

Lucas, J. R. "Causation." In R. J. Butler (ed.), *Analytical Philosophy.* New York: Barnes & Noble, 1962, pp. 32–65. Includes discussion of the claim that causal relations between events hold by virtue of their being of a particular type. Regularity required. Also a discussion of "the cause" and spurious causes.

Lyon, Ardon. "Causality." *BJPS* 18 (1967) 1–20. Antireductive. In terms of kinds of conditions.

MacIver, R. M. *Social Causation.* Boston: Ginn & Co., 1942, esp. chaps. 1, 2, 6–8. Includes a developed discussion of "the cause." Cf. review by Myles Brand, *Theory and Decision* 2 (1972) 295–298.

Mackie, J. L. "Counterfactuals and causal laws." In R. J. Butler (ed.), *Analytical Philosophy.* New York: Barnes & Noble, 1962, pp. 66–80. Counterfactuals as condensed arguments.

———. "The direction of causation." *PR* 75 (1966) 441–466. Account of the asymmetry of causation with a critique of positions holding that either temporal order, counterfactuals, or manipulability provide it. For critique, see Miller, 1973, and Suchting, *PPR* 29 (1968–69) 289–291.

———. *Truth, Probability and Paradox.* Oxford: Clarendon Press, 1973, chap. 3. An assessment of various accounts of counterfactuals and a defense of the "supposition" view.

———. *The Cement of the Universe — A Study of Causation.* Oxford: Clarendon Press, 1974. Fuller and later views than those expressed in Mackie's "Causes and conditions" (see text) and Mackie, 1966. The volume is wideranging and includes discussion of Hart and Honore, 1959; Russell, 1905; Ducasse, 1926; and causal contexts. It contains a defense of a modified regularity view and a reply to Kim, 1971.

Madden, Edward H. "Causality and the notion of necessity." In Robert S. Cohen and Marx W. Wartofsky (eds.), *Boston Studies in the Philosophy of Science,* vol. 4. New York: Humanities Press, 1969, pp. 419–441. Causation involves "definitional necessity." Causal necessity is consistent with a change in the course of nature, *contra* Hume *et al.*

———. "A third view of causality." *RM* 23 (1969) 67–84. Causal necessity derives from causal powers part of essential nature of objects. See also Harré and Madden, 1973.

———. "Nonlogical necessity." *Idealistic Studies* 5 (1975) 7–19. In reply to Cakes, 1975, Madden distinguishes his own view of causation from the entailment view.

———. See also Hare and Madden, 1969, 1975; Harré and Madden, 1973, 1975; and Humber and Madden, 1971, 1973.

Marc-Wogau, K. "On historical explanation." *T* 28 (1962) 213–233. Causally necessary and sufficient condition analysis. For discussion, see Tranøy, 1962.

———. "Remarks on Nilson's paper 'On the logic of historical explanation.' " *T* 37 (1971) 15–20. Discussion of Nilson, 1970. Response by Nilson, *T* 40 (1974) 1–8.

Martin, Raymond. "Conditionally necessary causes." *A* 30 (1970) 147–150. On how a cause is not necessary for its effect.

———. "Causes and alternate causes." *T* 36 (1970) 82–92. *The* cause and related topics.

———. "Marc-Wogau and Mackie on singular causal statements." *Philosophical Forum* 3 (1971–72) 145–151. A critique of the conditions analysis of Marc-Wogau, 1962, and Mackie (text).

———. "Singular causal explanations." *Theory and Decision* 2 (1972) 221–237. *The* cause.

———. "On Weighting Causing." *APQ* 9 (1972) 291–299. *The* cause and related topics.

———. "The sufficiency thesis." *PS* 23 (1972) 205–211. Against a cause as a member of a set of conditions which are sufficient for the effect.

Maxwell, Nicholas. "Can there be necessary connections between successive events?" *BJPS* 19 (1968) 1–25. Entailment theory.

McCall, Storrs. "Time and physical modalities." *Monist* 53 (1969) 426–446.

McCloskey, H. J. "Some concepts of cause." *RM* 17 (1963–64) 586–607. Several kinds of causation distinguished in this careful systemic analysis.

McLaughlin, James A. "Proximate cause." *Harvard Law Review* 39 (1925–26) 149–199. Proximate causation is causation of events for which the agent is to be held legally responsible. McLaughlin explicates this apparently contextual notion. See Raphael, 1956, for some discussion.

McTaggart, J. E. "The meaning of causality." *M* 24 (1915) 326–344. Causation is a relation of determination like logical implication. A cause exerts an "activity" on the effect.

McWilliams, James A. " 'Cause' in science and philosophy." *Modern Schoolman* 25 (1947–48) 11–18. Causation as production. Strictly speaking, cause and effect are simultaneous.

Mercier, Charles A. *On Causation*. London: Longmans, Green & Co., 1916. An extended treatment, including discussion of contiguity and antecedence, plurality of causes, and a critique of the regularity view and the identity of cause and effect. Mercier himself seems to view causation as natural agency.

Michotte, A. *The Perception of Causality*, 1st English ed. New York: Basic Books, Inc., 1963. A work primarily on experimental psychology, but some portions may be relevant to spatiotemporal relations of cause and effect and the regularity view. There is appended a commentary by translator T. R. Miles which includes some discussion of the philosophical implications of the work.

Miller, Barry. "Causation and necessary connection." *New Scholasticism* 47 (1973) 76–83. Empiricist accounts of causation; cannot distinguish cause from effect. Including J. L. Mackie's attempt (1966).

Miller, Dickinson S. "An event in modern philosophy." *PR* 54 (1945) 593–606. In defense of the regularity theory.

———. See also Hobart, 1930.

Molnar, George. "Kneale's argument revisited." PR 78 (1969) 79–89. A defense of a reconstruction of an argument of Kneale, 1961, against the regularity view of laws.

Montague, William Pepperell. "A defence of causality." *Proceedings of the Seventh International Congress of Philosophy*, 1930, pp. 198–202. Against the regularity view as implying randomness. Reprinted in his *The Way of Things*.

Morrison, Paul G. "Partial identity of cause and effect." *BJPS* 11 (1960–61) 42–49.

Moyal, J. E. "Causality, determinism and probability." *P* 24 (1949) 310–317. The notion of causality may be extended to include probabilistic as well as deterministic relations between events.

Mullatti, L. C. "On the status of causal propositions." *Philosophical Quarterly* (India) 37 (1964–65) 93–101, 151–163, 233–243. Developed discussion and criticism of both the regularity view and the entailment view.

Nagel, Ernest. "Sovereign reason." In Sidney Hook and Milton R. Konvitz (eds.), *Freedom and Experience*. Ithaca, N.Y.: Cornell University Press, 1947, pp. 260–288, esp. pp. 280–288. Critique of Blanshard's arguments for his entailment view. Reprinted in Nagel's *Sovereign Reason*. For related discussion, see W. Sellars, "Actions and events." *N* (1973) 179–202.

———."Some issues in the logic of historical analysis." *Scientific Monthly* 74 (1952) 162–169. On "the cause" and conditions. Reprinted in P. Gardiner, *Theories of History*.

———. "Types of causal explanation in science." In Daniel Lerner (ed.), *Cause and Effect*. New York: The Free Press, 1965, pp. 11–32. Includes discussion of "the cause" and causal laws.

Nerlich, G. C., and Suchting, W. A. "Popper on law and natural necessity." *BJPS* 18 (1967) 233–235. A critique of Popper, 1959. For a reply, see Popper, 1968.

Nilson, Sten Sparre. "On the logic of historical explanation." *T* 36 (1970) 65–81. For discussion, see Marc-Wogau, 1971.

Nuchelmans, Gabriel. " 'Counterfactual conditionals' and singular causal statements." *Proceedings of the 11th International Congress of Philosophy*, 1953, vol. 8, pp. 16–19. The latter in terms of the former.

Oakes, Robert. "Professor Blanshard, causality, and internal relations: some perspectives." *Idealistic Studies* 1 (1971) 172–178. A defense.

———. "The fiery furnace: 'Natural Necessity' or entailment?" *Idealistic Studies* 5 (1975) 1–6. Oakes agrees with Madden's 1969 view of causation but argues that it does not differ from Blanshard's entailment view. For a reply, see Madden, 1975.

O'Conner, D. J. "The analysis of conditional sentences." *M* 60 (1951) 351–362.

———. "Causal statements." *PQ* 6 (1956) 17–26. Causality is not a purely descriptive concept, but also classificatory.

Pap, Arthur. *Elements of Analytic Philosophy*. New York: The Macmillan Co., 1949, chap. 10. A critique of the entailment view.

———. "Philosophical analysis, translation schemas and the regularity theory of causation." *JP* 49 (1952) 657–666. Defense of the theory against the claim that the antecedent class is not specified.

———. "A note on causation and the meaning of 'event.'" *JP* 54 (1957) 155–159. Critique of Ducasse, 1951. Reply by Ducasse at 422–426.

———. "Disposition concepts and extensional logic." In H. Feigel, M. Scriven, and G. Maxwell (eds.), *Minnesota Studies in the Philosophy of Science*, vol. 2. Minneapolis: University of Minnesota Press, 1958, pp. 196–224. Burks's causal implication (in "The logic of causal propositions") must be primitive, and extensional analyses of causal necessity are unsatisfactory, though both of these claims are compatible with Hume and empiricism.

Pears, D. F. "The priority of causes." *A* 17 (1956–57) 54–63. Temporal relations between cause and effect. Critique of Dummett, 1954; discussion of Flew, 1954, and Black, 1956. Discussed by Flew, 1956–57.

Piaget, Jean. *The Child's Conception of Physical Causality*, 1st English ed. London: Routledge and Kegan Paul, Ltd., 1930. A well-known psychological work which generally relies largely on the beliefs and verbal responses with respect to specific causal relations. For critique of Piaget's concept of causation, see Allen Pearson's essay in *Educational Theory* 22 (1972) 434–442.

Popper, Karl R. "A note on natural laws and so-called 'contrary-to-fact conditionals.'" *M* 58 (1949) 62–66. Against the use of the counterfactual to analyze the notion of law.

———. *The Logic of Scientific Discovery*. London: Hutchinson & Co., Ltd., 1959, app. 10. Popper defends his regularity view against Kneale, 1949, and adds the notion of possible worlds. This definition is criticized by Kneale, 1961, and Nerlich and Suchting, 1967–68. The 1968 edition contains a reply to Kneale. Popper, 1968, contains a reply to Nerlich and Suchting.

———. "A revised definition of natural necessity." *BJPS* 18 (1968) 316–324. Suchting rejoins in *BJPS* 20 (1969).

Ramsey, Frank P. "General propositions and causality." In *The Foundations of Mathematics and Other Logical Essays*. London: Routledge & Kegan Paul, Ltd., 1931, pp. 237–255. Laws as "rules," "formulas," or "guides." Historically important. For discussion, see Gallie, 1939.

Raphael, D. D. "The consequences of actions." *PASS* 30 (1956) 100–119. Like the concept of a cause, the concept of a consequence is a practical or contextual one. Includes some discussion of McLaughlin, 1925–26.

Reichenbach, Hans. *Elements of Symbolic Logic*. New York: The Macmillan Co., 1947, chap. 8. A definition of physical necessity.

———. *Nomological Statements and Admissible Operations*. Amsterdam: North-Holland Publishing Co., 1954. A definition of laws. Substantial.

Rescher, Nicholas. "Some remarks on an analysis of the causal relation." *JP* 51 (1954) 239–241. Critique of Simon, 1952.

———. "Belief-contravening suppositions." *PR* 70 (1961) 176–196. On counterfactuals.

———. *Hypothetical Reasoning*. Amsterdam: North-Holland Publishing Co., 1964. A substantial and original work on counterfactuals.

———. "Lawfulness as mind-dependent." In Nicholas Rescher (ed.), *Essays in Honor of Carl G. Hempel*. Dordrecht: D. Reidel, 1969.

———. See also Simon and Rescher, 1966.

Riker, William H. "Causes of events." *JP* 55 (1958) 281–291. A view much like Ducasse's.

Robinson, R. G. "Partial entailment and the causal relation." *M* 70 (1961) 526–533. A defense of the entailment view. For critique, see Jack, 1966.

Rosenberg, Alexander. "Causation and recipes: the mixture as before?" *PS* 24 (1973) 378–385. Critique of Gasking (text).

———. "Mill and some contemporary critics on 'cause.'" *Personalist* 54 (1973) 123–129. Mill's notion of cause as a sufficient condition is compatible with a distinction between cause and condition.

———. "On Kim's account of events and event-identity." *JP* 71 (1974) 327–336. Kim's 1973 account as it stands is incompatible with the regularity view he holds, though it can be patched up and also be made to complement Davidson (text) and Mackie (text).

———. See also Braybrooke and Rosenberg, 1975.

Ruddick, William. "Causal connection." *S* 18 (1968) 46–67. A semantic relation between cause and effect in some instances of causation, for example, explanatory causes.

———. "Causal connection." In Robert S. Cohen and Marx W. Wartofsky (eds.), *Boston Studies in the Philosophy of Science*, vol. 4. New York: Humanities Press, 1969, pp. 419–441. Followed by a critique by M. M. Schuster at 442–447. See Ruddick, 1968.

Russell, Bertrand. "On the notion of cause." *PAS* 13 (1912–13) 1–26. An important and influential article which criticizes several features of the idea of causation and suggests its replacement by the notion of a function. Reprinted in Russell's *Mysticism and Logic*. Garden City, N.Y.: Doubleday, Anchor Books, 1957. For additional discussion, see Götlind, 1952, and Mackie, 1974.

Sanford, David H. "Causal necessity and logical necessity." *PS* 28 (1975), 103–112. A critique of Brand and Swain (text). Their reply will also be published in *PS*.

Santoni, Ronald E. "Ducasse on 'cause' — another look." In Frederick C. Dommeyer (ed.), *Current Philosophical Issues*. Springfield, Ill.: Charles C. Thomas, Publisher, 1966, pp. 151–162. A critique.

Saw, R. L. "An aspect of causal connexion." *PAS* 35 (1934–35) 95–112. Causal connection is a relation of succession between particulars. Causal explanation is a nontemporal relation which is a function of the properties of the particulars.

Schlick, Moritz. "Causality in everyday life and in recent science." In J. Loewenbert *et al.* (eds.), *University of California Publications in Philosophy* 15 (1932) 99–125. An extended defense of the regularity view. Reprinted in Feigl and Sellars, *Readings in Philosophical Analysis*.

———. "Causality in contemporary physics." *BJPS* 12 (1961–62) 177–193, 281–298. (Translation of an article first published in *Die Naturwissenschaften* 19 [1931].) Causation as predictability. Brief critique of the notion of cause as function. In defense of the regularity theory.

Schneider, Erna F. "Recent discussion of subjunctive conditionals." *RM* 6 (1952–53) 623–647. A survey.

Schock, Rolf. "Some definitions of subjunctive implication, of counterfactual implication, and of related concepts." *Notre Dame Journal of Formal Logic* 2 (1961) 206–221. By a formal system.

Scriven, Michael. "Randomness and the causal order." *A* 17 (1956) 5–9. There can be at least backward "determination." See discussion by Flew, 1956–57.

———. "Truisms as the grounds for historical explanations." In Patrick Gardiner (ed.), *Theories of History*. New York: The Free Press, 1959, pp. 443–475, esp. app. pp. 471–475. On the uniformity of causation.

———. "The Structure of Science." *RM* 17 (1963–64) 403–424. This review of Nagel's *Structure of Science* is an important contribution to discussion of "the cause" and conditions.

————. "Causes, connections and conditions in history." In William Dray (ed.), *Philosophical Analysis and History.* New York: Harper and Row, 1966, pp. 238–264.

————. "The logic of cause." *Theory and Decision* 2 (1971) 49–66. Interesting and wide-ranging, but compact. Includes criticism of causation as requiring uniformity, temporal order, contiguity, necessary or sufficient conditions, restriction of relata. Causation is a contextually dependent notion. Antireductive.

————. "Causation as explanation." *N* 9 (1975) 3–16. Being a basic concept, causation cannot be reduced, and a cause is best understood as an "explanatory factor." A difficulty for the regularity view and one for the counterfactual analysis are cited.

Sellars, Wilfrid. "Concepts as involving laws and inconceivable without them." *Philosophy of Science* 15 (1948) 287–315. Causal modality as logical necessity.

————. "Inference and meaning." *M* 62 (1953) 313–338. Physical modalities as "material rules of inference." For critique, see Alexander, 1958.

————. "Counterfactuals, dispositions, and the causal modalities." In H. Feigl, M. Scriven, and G. Maxwell (eds.), *Minnesota Studies in the Philosophy of Science,* vol. 2. Minneapolis: University of Minnesota Press, 1958, pp. 225–308. Interesting, careful, and extended discussion of both the regularity and entailment views, with a defense of the latter. Includes interesting critique of Goodman's "The problem of counterfactual conditionals" (in text).

Sharpe, R. A. "Laws, coincidences, counterfactuals and counter-identicals." *M* 80 (1971) 572–582. On the relation between laws and counterfactuals.

Shimony, Abner. "An ontological examination of causation." *RM* 1 (1947) 52–68. Part of the cause is "ontologically continuous" with the effect.

Shrope, Robert K. "Explanation in terms of 'the cause.'" *JP* 64 (1967) 312–320. A critique and modification of Gorovitz, 1965.

Shorter, J. M. "Causality, and a method of analysis." In R. J. Butler (ed.), *Analytical Philosophy.* Oxford: Basil Blackwell, 1965, pp. 144–157. A discussion of Vendler, 1962.

Simon, Herbert A. "On the definition of the causal relation." *JP* 49 (1952) 517–528. Causation defined in a system of functional relations where the experimental manipulability of the independent variable provides the asymmetry. Simon's views have had some influence in contemporary sociology and econometrics. A reply to Rescher, 1954, at *JP* 52 (1955) 20–21.

————. "Causal ordering and identifiability." In W. C. Hood and T. C. Koopmans (eds.), *Studies in Econometric Method.* New York: John Wiley and Sons, Inc., 1953, pp. 49–74. See Simon, 1952.

————, and Rescher, Nicholas. "Cause and counterfactual." *Philosophy of Science* 33 (1966) 323–340. A causal relation is a function — a mapping of one variable (the cause) onto another (the effect).

Snyder, Aaron. See Dretske and Snyder, 1972.

Sommers, F. T. "Truth-functional counterfactuals." *A* 24 (1964) 120–126.

Sosa, Ernest. "Introduction." In Ernest Sosa (ed.), *Causation and Conditionals.* London: Oxford University Press, 1975, pp. 1–14. Brief and largely descriptive but a critical discussion of the conditional analysis.

Stalnaker, Robert C., and Thomason, Richmond H. "A semantic analysis of conditional logic." *T* 36 (1970) 23–42. Possible world semantics. Complements Stalnaker's "A theory of conditionals" (in text).

Stout, F. G. *Mind and Matter*. Cambridge: Cambridge University Press, 1931, pp. 15–36. Defense, against Hume, of the view that we have insight into the causal process in our experience of willing and striving.

———. "Mechanical and teleological causation." *PASS* 14 (1935) 46–65. Causation as "rational" and "active tendency."

Suchting, W. A. See Nerlich and Suchting, 1967.

Suppes, Patrick. *A Probabilistic Theory of Causality*. *Acta Philosophica Fennica*, fasc. 24 (1970). An extended treatment of various issues, including conditions and spatial and temporal contiguity. It also includes an "abstract algebra" of causal relations. A Humean approach. Suggestive.

Swinburne, R. G. "Affecting the past." *PQ* 16 (1966) 341–347. Includes a critique of Dummett, 1964.

Taylor, Richard. "Can a cause precede its effect?" *Monist* 48 (1964) 136–142. An interesting discussion.

———. *Action and Purpose*. Englewood Cliffs, N.J.: Prentice-Hall, Inc., 1966, esp. chaps. 2, 3. An important systemic and antireductive contribution.

———. "Causation." In Paul Edwards (ed.), *The Encyclopedia of Philosophy*. New York: The Macmillan Co. and The Free Press, 1967, vol. 2, pp. 56–66. A useful and wide-ranging survey.

———. See also Chisholm and Taylor, 1960.

Todd, William. "Causal laws and accidents." *T* 31 (1965) 110–124. Defense of the regularity view of laws by (a) arguing for a cause-accident continuum and (b) properly specifying the relevant properties.

Toulmin, Stephen. *The Philosophy of Science*. London: Hutchinson, 1953, chap. 3. Laws are like "inference-tickets," and it is misleading to call them true or false, necessary or contingent. For critique, see Alexander, 1958.

Tranøy, Knut Erik. "Historical explanation: causes and conditions." *T* 28 (1962) 234–249. Discussion of Marc-Wogau, 1962.

Travis, Charles. "Causes, events and ontology." *Philosophia* 3 (1973) 201–245. On the ontology of causation and also substitutivity into causal (actually "because") contexts. Criticism of Davidson (text) and Anscombe, 1969.

Ushenko, A. P. "The principles of causality." *JP* 50 (1953) 85–101. Causation as a tendency. For critique, see Hofstadter, 1953.

———. "The counterfactual." *JP* 51 (1954) 369–383. The counterfactual is irreducible beyond the notion of "power."

Van Quickenborne, Marc. "An analysis of causality in everyday language." *Logique et Analyse* 12 (1969) 311–328. A developed treatment of a conditions analysis, *the* cause, and plurality of causes.

Vendler, Zeno. "Effects, results, and consequences." In R. J. Butler (ed.), *Analytical Philosophy*. New York: Barnes & Noble, 1962, pp. 1–15. Causes are not events but "fact-like entities." Followed by criticisms by W. Dray and S. Bromberger and Vendler's reply. See also Shorter, 1965.

———. *Linguistics in Philosophy*. Ithaca, N.Y.: Cornell University Press, 1967, chap. 6. Similar to Vendler, 1962.

Vogel, Arthur A. "Efficient causation and the categories." *Modern Schoolman* 32 (1954–55) 243-256. A defense of the Aristotelian view that beyond making a potential actual, efficient causation cannot be defined.

Vollrath, John F. "Counting the consequences." *Canadian Journal of Philosophy* 3 (1973) 225–233. A critique of Dray's 1970 argument that consequences of an event do not accrue endlessly.

von Wright, G. H. "On conditionals." In his *Logical Studies*. London: Routledge and Kegan Paul, Ltd., 1957, pp. 127–165. Conditionals as "modes of asserting."

———. *Explanation and Understanding*. Ithaca, N.Y.: Cornell University Press, 1971, chap. 2. A recent development of the manipulability view.

———. "On the logic and epistemology of the causal relation." In P. Suppes (ed.), *Logic, Methodology and Philosophy of Science,* vol. 4. Amsterdam: North-Holland Publishing Co., 1973. Within the context of a formal system von Wright maintains his manipulative view.

———. *Causality and Determinism*. New York: Columbia University Press, 1974.

Wallace, William. *Causality and Scientific Explanation*. 2 vols. Ann Arbor: University of Michigan Press, 1972, 1973. A historical work.

Walsh, W. H. "Historical causation." *PAS* 63 (1962–63) 217–236.

Walters, R. S. "The problem of counterfactuals." *AJP* 39 (1961) 30–46. A deduction theory and critique of the claim that counterfactuals can be used to distinguish laws from nonlaws.

Wand, Bernard. "The origin of causal necessity." *JP* 56 (1959) 493–500. Animistic explanation of events is not the origin of the idea of causal necessity. In fact, they are incompatible.

Waterlow, S. "Backwards causation and continuing." *M* 83 (1974) 372–387. An argument against backward causation by an argument that the temporal direction of causation is determined by the temporal direction of the continuing of events.

Watling, John. "Propositions asserting causal connection." *A* 14 (1953–54) 31–37. Argument against uniformity and regularity accounts. Causation in terms of counterfactuals of certain sorts.

———. "Are causes events or facts?" PAS 74 (1973–74) 161–170. Beginning with a discussion of the issue as it is raised in Davidson's "Mental events," Watling answers: "neither."

———. See also Brown and Watling, 1952.

Weinberg, Julius. "The idea of causal efficacy." *JP* 47 (1950) 397–407. Against the view that knowledge of causes indicates something of the character of their effects.

———. "Contrary-to-fact conditions." *JP* 48 (1951) 17–22. Analysis in terms of belief upon evidence.

White, Morton. *Foundations of Historical Knowledge*. New York: Harper & Row, 1965, esp. chaps. 3, 4. Critique of the cause as necessary condition or manipulability. A defense of a kind of uniformity. For discussion, see Dietl, 1970.

Whitehead, Alfred North. *Symbolism: Its Meaning and Effect*. New York: The Macmillan Co., 1927, chap. 2. Causal efficacy is perceived in the world as primitive.

Wild, John. "A realistic defense of causal efficacy." *RM* 2, no. 8 (1948–49) 1–14. "Causal efficacy is the diffusion of being from one entity to another already potentially determined to receive it." Humean atomism of causes cannot accommodate this notion. Defends an entailment view.

Wilkie, J. S. "The problem of the temporal relation of cause and effect." *BJPS* 1 (1950) 211–229. Cause and effect are simultaneous.

Winn, Ralph B. "The nature of causation." *Philosophy of Science* 7 (1940) 192–204. Continuity is not compatible with temporal priority.

Wisdom, J. O. "Criteria for causal determination and functional relationship." *M* 54 (1945) 323–341. Modification and elaboration of Mill's methods for determining, *inter alia*, plurality of causes and probably causal connection.

Wold, Herman O. "Mergers of economics and philosophy of science." *S* 20 (1969) 427–482, esp. 448–460. An attempt to set up a schema of causal relations in the spirit of Simon, 1952.

III. Recent Literature on Hume's View

Aschenbrenner, Karl. "Psychologism in Hume." *PQ* 11 (1961) 28–38. Two analyses of causation — one logical and one psychological.

Beauchamp, Tom L. "Hume's two theories of causation." *Archiv für Geschichte der Philosophie* 55 (1973) 281–300. Includes some discussion of Robinson, 1962.

Bennett, Jonathan. *Locke, Berkeley, Hume.* Oxford: Clarendon Press, 1971, chaps. 11–12. Explication and modification of Hume's regularity view.

Flew, Antony. *Hume's Philosophy of Belief.* London: Routledge and Kegan Paul, Ltd., 1961, chap. 6. Includes defense against Passmore, 1968.

Gotterbarn, Donald. "Hume's two lights on cause." *PQ* 21 (1971) 168–171. The two definitions are two aspects of the same relation. They are intensionally distinct but extensionally equivalent.

Hausman, Alan. "Hume's theory of relations." *N* 1 (1967) 255–282. A distinction between an analysis of the relation and an explanation of people's belief that there is necessary connection in the relation.

Lesher, James H. "Hume's analysis of 'cause' and the 'two definitions' dispute." *Journal of the History of Philosophy* 11 (1973) 387–392.

MacNabb, D. G. C. *David Hume.* London: Hutchinson, 1951, chaps. 4, 7. Includes defense against criticisms of Whitehead.

Munsat, Stanley. "Hume's argument that causes must preceded their effects." *PS* 22 (1971) 24–26.

O'Donnell, Matthew. "Hume's approach to causation." *Philosophical Studies* (Ireland) 10 (1960) 64–99.

Passmore, John. *Hume's Intentions,* rev. ed. New York: Basic Books, 1968, pp. 76–78. Brief, but discussed in the literature. Critical review by J. L. Mackie, *AJP* 32 (1954) 56–70.

Richards, Thomas J. "Hume's two definitions of 'cause.' " *PQ* 15 (1965) 247–253. Both definitions, *contra* Robinson, 1962, were intended by Hume.

Robinson, J. A. "Hume's two definitions of 'cause.' " *PQ* 12 (1962) 162–171. Hume defined causation as an objective relation. Critique by Richards, 1965.

———. "Hume's two definitions of 'cause' reconsidered." In V. C. Chappell (ed.), *Hume.* New York: Doubleday, 1966, pp. 162–168. Reply to Richards, 1965.

Smith, James Ward. "Concerning Hume's intentions." *PR* 69 (1960) 63–77.

Smith, Norman Kemp. *The Philosophy of David Hume.* London: Macmillan and Co., Ltd., 1964, chaps, 16, 17. Emphasis on necessity and custom.

Warnock, G. J. "Hume on causation." In D. F. Pears (ed.), *David Hume*. London: Macmillan and Co., Ltd., 1963, pp. 55–66. Explication along the lines of a view like that of Braithwaite, 1953.

Wolff, Robert Paul. "Hume on mental activity." *PR* 69 (1960) 289–310. Hume not just an associationist, but the concept of cause depends on mental propensities.